Francine Williamson 4/22/90
Personal

W9-CBJ-298

WordPerfect®
QuickStart

Developed by Que® Corporation

Text and graphics pages developed by
Kathie-Jo Arnoff and Shelley O'Hara

Que Corporation
Carmel, Indiana

WordPerfect® QuickStart.

Copyright© 1988 by Que® Corporation.

All rights reserved. Printed in the United States of America. No part of this book may be used or reproduced in any form or by any means, or stored in a database or retrieval system, without prior written permission of the publisher except in the case of brief quotations embodied in critical articles and reviews. Making copies of any part of this book for any purpose other than your own personal use is a violation of United States copyright laws. For information, address Que Corporation, 11711 N. College Ave., Carmel, IN 46032.

Library of Congress Catalog No.: LC 88-61789

ISBN 0-88022-387-1

This book is sold *as is*, without warranty of any kind, express or implied, respecting the contents of this book, including but not limited to implied warranties for the book's quality, performance, merchantability, or fitness for any particular purpose. Neither Que Corporation nor its dealers or distributors shall be liable to the purchaser or any other person or entity with respect to any liability, loss, or damage caused or alleged to be caused directly or indirectly by this book.

92 91 90   10 9 8 7 6

Interpretation of the printing code: the rightmost double-digit number is the year of the book's printing; the rightmost single-digit number, the number of the book's printing. For example, a printing code of 88-4 shows that the fourth printing of the book occurred in 1988.

Screen reproductions in this book were created by means of the INSET program from Inset Systems, Inc., Danbury, CT.

WordPerfect® QuickStart is based on version 5 of WordPerfect.

Trademark Acknowledgments

Que Corporation has made every effort to supply trademark information about company names, products, and services mentioned in this book. Trademarks indicated below were derived from various sources. Que Corporation cannot attest to the accuracy of this information.

1-2-3 is a registered trademark of Lotus Development Corporation.

Hercules Graphics Card and Hercules InColor card are trademarks of Hercules Computer Technology.

IBM, IBM PC, IBM PC AT, and Personal System/2 are registered trademarks and IBM PC XT is a trademark of International Business Machines Corporation.

MS-DOS is a registered trademark of Microsoft Corporation.

WordPerfect is a registered trademark of WordPerfect Corporation.

Publishing Director

David P. Ewing

Product Director

Charles O. Stewart III

Acquisitions Editor

Terrie Lynn Solomon

Editors

Kathie-Jo Arnoff
Shelley O'Hara

Technical Editor

Joel Shore

Production

William Hartman
Dennis Sheehan
Cheryl English
Annette Knox

Proofreaders

Lori Lyons
Peter Tocco
Carolyn Spitler

Indexer

Sherry Massey

Composed in Garamond by

H<small>ARTMA</small>N
Publishing

Page Design by

William Hartman, Hartman Publishing

Acknowledgments

Que Corporation thanks the following individuals for their contributions to this book:

Kathie-Jo Arnoff, for her excellent work developing and editing this book, including organizing the chapters and topics within each chapter, developing concepts for the graphics, and supervising all stages of this book project.

Shelley O'Hara, for her exceptional contributions to developing the graphics, her skillful editing, and her development of the WordPerfect screens shown in the book.

Bill Hartman, of Hartman Publishing, for the excellent design of the pages and graphics in this book, his willingness to make modifications and additions to the book, and the extra hours spent completing this project.

Joel Shore, for his expert technical review of the text and graphics in this book and his dedication to ensuring the book's technical accuracy.

Tim Stanley, for his assistance in producing the screens for the graphics pages.

Joanetta Hendel and Stacey Beheler, for their invaluable support to the developmental and editing staff working on this book.

Dennis Sheehan and Cheryl English, for their skillful paste-up and photographic work and their efforts during the final production stages of this book.

Contents

To the Reader

WordPerfect® QuickStart uses an exciting new approach to introduce the fundamental concepts of WordPerfect 5 to beginning users. Throughout the book, each WordPerfect topic generally is presented in two pages of easy-to-follow text, followed by two pages of graphics. The graphics illustrate the topic discussed on the text pages.

This innovative book shows you how to create, edit, format, and print documents, use the built-in speller and thesaurus, and manipulate blocks of text. You also learn to use WordPerfect's more advanced features. The book helps you produce text columns, create and import graphics, and automate procedures with simple macros.

After you become familiar with WordPerfect's commands and features, you can use the graphics in *WordPerfect QuickStart* for reference when you need to be reminded of the steps and sequence of commands. Become productive with WordPerfect quickly with *WordPerfect QuickStart!*

Introduction

WordPerfect QuickStart is a step forward in the evolution of how a book can be organized and structured. The entire book is built around the concept of two-page *spreads* or topics. Each spread, of either text or graphics, presents an overview of a topic. The graphics spreads illustrate the relationships among the elements.

Spreads are connected to form chapters, which in turn make up the complete book. Titles of all the chapters in the book are listed down the right side of each spread. Topics in the current chapter are listed across the top of the page. Highlighted rectangles pick out the current chapter and topic. The rectangles work like a set of crosshairs, zeroing in on the major subject and the specific topic covered in that spread.

How Does *WordPerfect QuickStart* Do Its Job?

Using this book is a lot like using a map. First, to grasp all the main elements, you look at the aerial view. Then you look closer to find street names and the place where you are heading. The visual structure of this book, like a map, offers you quick access to information.

The key to using this book is to use the text and graphics for what each does best. The graphics convey overviews, relationships, and connections. Text supplies essential information that the graphics can't, provides comments on what you see, and describes abstract ideas.

Every two-page spread in this book (after this Introduction) contains highlighted rectangles that show your exact location. The side rectangle shows which chapter you are in. The top rectangle shows which topic of the chapter you are in. To see everything that is covered in a chapter, scan across the topics at the top of the page.

Each rectangle moves as you move through the text. If you flip through the pages quickly, you can see the side rectangle moving up and down and the top rectangle moving left and right. By watching the rectangles, you always can see where you are in this book.

What Is WordPerfect?

WordPerfect is one of the most popular word processing software programs.

Why is WordPerfect so popular? Because it has all the "basic" features you would expect in a word processing package, plus a full complement of advanced features. The program is suited to your needs, whether they entail short memos or complex documents.

"What makes WordPerfect attractive is that it gets out of your way," explains W. E. "Pete" Peterson, executive vice president of WordPerfect Corporation. "It's like a well-mannered house guest who is kind enough not to disrupt your life or the way you do things."

An editing screen uncluttered by menus or cryptic codes, an abundance of features, support for a wide range of printers, and unparalleled customer assistance are just a few of the reasons why WordPerfect enjoys the prominence it so rightly deserves.

Introduction

WordPerfect QuickStart takes you through WordPerfect step by step, describing all the essentials you need to know about the software.

The graphics convey overviews, relationships, and connections. Text supplies information that the graphics can't, provides comments on what you see, and explains abstract ideas.

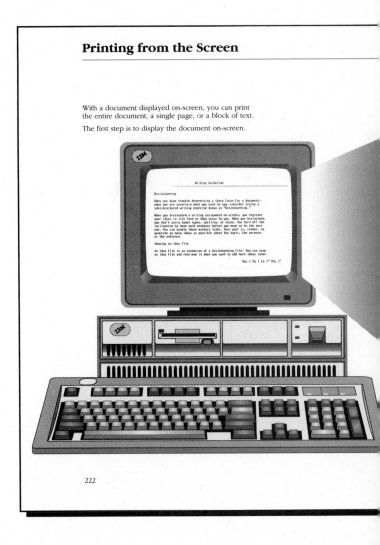

4

Topics

Each chapter contains a group of topics, listed across the top of the right-hand page.

As you flip through the chapter, the highlighted rectangle moves from left to right, showing your location within the chapter.

In this example, the rectangle shows that you are in the topic called "Printing from the Screen."

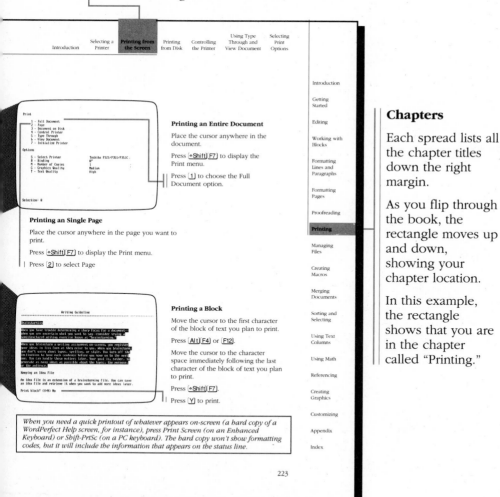

Chapters

Each spread lists all the chapter titles down the right margin.

As you flip through the book, the rectangle moves up and down, showing your chapter location.

In this example, the rectangle shows that you are in the chapter called "Printing."

5

Introduction

What Does This Book Contain?

Each chapter in *WordPerfect QuickStart* focuses on a particular
WordPerfect operation or set of operations. Overall, the book's
movement reflects the steps typical to the creation of any document,
from entering text to spell-checking and printing. Later chapters
concentrate on more specialized topics, such as macros, columns, and
graphics.

Chapter 1, "Getting Started," shows you how to start WordPerfect and
introduces you to the editing screen, keyboard, and help system. You
also learn the basics of using the program: typing text, moving the
cursor, making a menu selection, printing and saving a document,
clearing the screen, and exiting.

In Chapter 2, "Editing," you learn to retrieve a file and modify it by
inserting and deleting text. You also investigate WordPerfect's hidden
codes and two document windows. Chapter 3, "Working with Blocks,
shows you how to highlight a block and manipulate it in numerous
ways; for instance, you learn to move, copy, delete, print, and save a
block of text.

Chapters 4 and 5 cover formatting. First you work with formatting lines
and paragraphs: change the left and right margins, insert boldface and
italic codes, set tab stops, indent text, align text in various ways, use
hyphenation, and more. Then you move to formatting pages: choose
the paper size, change the top and bottom margins, design headers
and footers, number pages, control page breaks, use redline and
strikeout, use special characters and type equations, and create styles
for special formats.

After you create a document, you will want to proofread it. Chapter 6,
"Proofreading," not only introduces you to WordPerfect's built-in
Speller and Thesaurus, but also demonstrates how to use Search and
Replace features to find particular words or codes in your document.

You learn to print your document in Chapter 7. After you see how to select a printer, you learn to print from the screen or disk. Other specialized printing features also are covered.

Chapter 8, "Managing Files," explains how to use WordPerfect's List Files screen to manage your files—copy a file or change directories, for example. You also learn how to use the program's document summary feature to help you keep track of the content of your documents.

The rest of the book deals with more specialized features of the program. You learn the basics of creating macros in Chapter 9. Chapter 10 covers merging documents. Chapter 11 introduces sorting and selecting. In Chapter 12, you practice setting up text columns; in Chapter 13, you find out how to set up math columns and perform math operations.

Chapter 14, "Referencing," explains how to create footnotes and endnotes, insert the current date into your documents, create an outline, number the lines of your text, and insert comments into your documents. The chapter also presents an overview of WordPerfect's other referencing tools.

Suppose that you want to illustrate your document with graphics. Chapter 15, "Creating Graphics," shows you how to create, import, and edit graphics. You also experiment with creating graphic lines.

The book's final chapter—Chapter 16, "Customizing"—gives you an idea of how you can customize the program to meet your everyday needs. You learn to set automatic backups, adjust the screen display, change the default formatting settings, choose an alternative keyboard layout, and more.

The appendix provides step-by-step instructions to install WordPerfect on both a hard disk system and a dual floppy disk system. A detailed index helps you quickly find the specific information you need.

Introduction

Getting
Started

Editing

Working with
Blocks

Formatting
Lines and
Paragraphs

Formatting
Pages

Proofreading

Printing

Managing
Files

Creating
Macros

Merging
Documents

Sorting and
Selecting

Using Text
Columns

Using Math

Referencing

Creating
Graphics

Customizing

Appendix

Index

Introduction

Who Should Use This Book?

WordPerfect QuickStart is an easy guide for anyone just starting with WordPerfect 5. The book is intended for new users or for people who have not yet been able to understand WordPerfect. Basic information is presented to help a first-time user get started quickly. And enough essential information is provided so that a more experienced user can use the book as a reference tool.

Where To Find More Help

After you learn the fundamentals presented in this book, you may want to go on to learn more advanced applications of WordPerfect. Que Corporation has a full line of WordPerfect books you can use: *Using WordPerfect 5*; *WordPerfect Tips, Tricks, and Traps,* 2nd Edition; *WordPerfect Quick Reference*; and *WordPerfect Macro Library.*

If you find yourself stymied at a particular point, WordPerfect's Help (F3) feature may be able to answer your questions. Using Help is explained and illustrated in Chapter 1, "Getting Started."

Should all else fail, WordPerfect Corporation provides toll-free telephone support: 1-800-321-5906. The phone staff is helpful and knowledgeable. The line is open 7 a.m. to 6 p.m., Mountain Standard Time, Monday through Friday.

What Hardware Do You Need To Run WordPerfect?

You can run WordPerfect on an IBM® PC or compatible computer with a hard disk drive or dual floppy disk drives. WordPerfect requires DOS 2.0 or later and at least 384K of memory. At least 512K of random-access memory (RAM) is recommended.

Because WordPerfect comes on twelve 5 1/4-inch floppy disks or seven 3 1/2-inch microfloppy disks, you frequently must swap disks in and out of your drives if you have a dual floppy system. To run

WordPerfect with fewer interruptions, you probably should invest in a hard disk. Although WordPerfect is already a speedy program, it runs faster and performs better on a hard disk system.

WordPerfect runs on a wide variety of printers, from dot-matrix to laser. To take full advantage of WordPerfect's graphics capabilities, you need a graphics card, such as a Hercules Graphics Card™ or an InColor™ card.

Conventions Used in This Book

Certain conventions are used throughout the text and graphics of *WordPerfect QuickStart* to help you better understand the book.

In the Text

Function key commands are identified by both their name and keystroke—for example, Spell (Ctrl-F2). To choose this command, you press and hold down the Ctrl key while you next press the F2 key. Menu options are referred to first by the name of the option, followed by the number of the option in parentheses—for example Line (1). You press 1 to select the Line option.

When you press a series of keys, the names of the keys are separated in the text by commas, and you press and release each key in turn. For example, to move to the top of a document, you press and release Home, then Home, then the up-arrow key.

Text you should type is displayed in **boldface**. Screen messages and hidden codes appear in a `special typeface`.

In the Graphics

Keys are shown as they appear on the keyboard. Red lines emphasize the most important areas of the graphic illustrations.

1 ⟍ *Getting Started*

This chapter begins with the basics of WordPerfect: starting the program, looking at the editing screen, learning the keyboard, and using the Help feature. You learn some fundamental skills for using a word processor, including how to move around the editing screen, save a document, and exit WordPerfect. After you master these basic skills, you can begin to explore the program and its many features.

▼

Key Terms

This chapter introduces the following key terms:

Defaults	Standard WordPerfect settings that are automatically put into effect each time you start the program.
Status line	The bottom line on the WordPerfect editing screen. The status line indicates the disk drive and file name, and the position of the cursor on the screen. From time to time, the WordPerfect status line displays system messages and prompts.
Cursor	An on-screen marker that indicates where a character would appear if typed. The cursor also marks the location where hidden codes will be entered.
Word wrap	A WordPerfect feature that eliminates the need to press the Enter (Return) key each time you reach the right margin. With word wrap, you need to press Enter only when you come to the end of a paragraph, a short line, or a command.

Introduction

Getting Started

Editing

Working with Blocks

Formatting Lines and Paragraphs

Formatting Pages

Proofreading

Printing

Managing Files

Creating Macros

Merging Documents

Sorting and Selecting

Using Text Columns

Using Math

Referencing

Creating Graphics

Customizing

Appendix

Index

Soft return   The code inserted at the end of each line when the text reaches the right margin and is automatically wrapped to the next line.

Hard return   The code inserted when you press the Enter key to insert a carriage return at the end of a line.

File name   A properly expressed descriptive title assigned to a file before storing it in system memory.

▲

Tasks Covered in This Chapter

This chapter covers the basics for getting started using WordPerfect. You learn the following techniques:

- Starting WordPerfect on a dual floppy system and on a hard disk system
- Understanding the parts of the editing screen
- Using the keyboard
- Using the Help system
- Understanding WordPerfect's built-in settings
- Entering text
- Inserting blank lines
- Moving the cursor
- Making menu selections
- Using the Cancel key
- Printing an unsaved document
- Saving and naming a document
- Clearing the screen
- Exiting WordPerfect

Starting WordPerfect

This section tells you how to start WordPerfect on a hard disk system and on a dual floppy disk system. Before you start the program, you must install it. If you have a hard disk, you also need to make directories and copy the WordPerfect program files. If you have a floppy disk system, you need to format floppy disks and make working copies of the original WordPerfect disks. Instructions for installing the program and copying files are provided in the Appendix.

Starting WordPerfect on a Hard Disk System

Follow these steps to start WordPerfect on a hard disk system:

1. Check to be sure that the drive door is open for the floppy drive(s).
2. Turn on your computer.
3. If necessary, respond to the prompts for date and time.
4. When the C> prompt appears, type **cd \wp50** and press Enter.
5. Type **wp** and press Enter.

You should see the opening screen for just a moment, and then the editing screen is displayed.

If you start WordPerfect and the power fails, the following message appears at the bottom of your screen when you restart the program:

```
Are other copies of WordPerfect currently running? Y/N
```

Press N in response to this prompt.

Starting WordPerfect on a Dual Floppy System

Follow these steps to start WordPerfect on a dual floppy disk system:

1. Insert the working copy of your WordPerfect 1 disk into drive A.

   Note: If you are using an IBM Personal System/2® machine, the main program files are combined on one 3 1/2-inch microfloppy disk labeled WordPerfect 1/WordPerfect 2.

2. Insert a formatted data disk into drive B.

3. Turn on your computer.

4. If necessary, respond to the prompts for date and time.

5. When the A> prompt appears, type **b:** and press Enter.

   Drive B is now the *default* drive, which means that any data you save to disk is saved to the disk in drive B.

6. Type **a:wp** and press Enter.

   Unless you have an IBM PS/2 computer, WordPerfect's opening screen appears. This screen contains WordPerfect copyright information, the version number of your copy, and an indication of the default directory that the system will use.

7. Remove the WordPerfect 1 disk from drive A and insert the WordPerfect 2 disk into drive A.

8. Press any key.

Using the Editing Screen and Keyboard

Before you begin to use WordPerfect, you should take a few minutes to become familiar with WordPerfect's screen display and keyboard.

Editing Screen

WordPerfect displays your document almost exactly as it will appear when it is printed. What you see on-screen is approximately one-half of a standard typed page. The main portion of the screen displays the document.

The Status Line

The line of information that appears at the bottom of the screen is called the *status line*, because that information describes the cursor's status. The left side of the status line shows the current document's name. From time to time, the document name is replaced temporarily by system messages and prompts.

The second item in the status line (Doc) indicates which of two available documents is currently displayed on-screen. WordPerfect is capable of holding two documents in memory simultaneously. The documents are identified as Doc 1 and Doc 2.

Pg identifies the number of the page on which the cursor currently rests.

Ln indicates the number of the line, in inches, centimeters, points, or lines (on your document page), on which the cursor rests. You can change the units used for the status line display by selecting that option on the Setup menu (see Chapter 4, "Formatting Lines and Paragraphs").

The Position Indicator

Pos tells you where on your document's page the cursor lies. The Pos indicator serves the following functions as well:

- The Pos indicator appears in uppercase letters (POS) if the Caps Lock key is activated for typing in uppercase letters.
- When the Pos indicator blinks, the Num Lock key is activated so that you can use the numeric keypad to type numbers.
- When you create or move through boldface letters, the position indicator number changes from regular type to boldface type.
- When the cursor moves into underlined or double-underlined text, the position indicator number reflects the enhancement of the text.

Status line information appears only on-screen; it does not appear in your printed document.

Keyboard

WordPerfect uses the following three main areas of the keyboard:

- The function keys, labeled F1 to F12 at the top of the IBM Enhanced Keyboard (or F1 to F10 at the left of the PC keyboard)
- The alphanumeric or "typing" keys, located in the center of the keyboard. (These keys are most familiar to you from your experience with typewriter keyboards.)
- The numeric and cursor keys, found at the right end of the keyboard

15

Using the Editing Screen and Keyboard

Function Keys

As the WordPerfect function key template illustrates, each function key can carry out four tasks when used by itself or in combination with another key. You routinely use the function keys to give your computer instructions called *commands.*

The commands on the WordPerfect templates are color coded for easy use:

- Black means the key is used by itself. Simply press the function key.
- Green means that you must hold down the Shift key while you next press the function key.
- Blue means that you must hold down the Alt key while you next press the function key.
- Red means that you must hold down the Ctrl key while you next press the function key.

Some function keys are used as toggle switches to turn on and off a feature. For example, to create boldface type, you first press function key F6 (to turn on Bold); then you type the text that will be printed in boldface type and press F6 again to turn off Bold.

Some function keys permit you to select from a menu. When you press Ctrl-F7, for example, your system displays the Footnote/Endnote menu.

Some function keys start a feature that is ended by pressing the Enter key. For instance, you activate the Center feature by pressing Shift-F6 and end centering by pressing Enter (or the down-arrow key).

Alphanumeric Keys

The alphanumeric keys work similar to those on a typewriter. Keep in mind one critical but easily overlooked difference between composing with a typewriter and composing with WordPerfect: When you type normal text, you do not need to end lines at the right margin by pressing the Enter key. When you type text in WordPerfect and reach the end of a line, the text "wraps" automatically to the next line.

The Enter, or Return, key can be used as a carriage return. You also press Enter to insert blank lines in your text, such as the lines that separate paragraphs.

The Shift, Alt, and Control (Ctrl) keys are part of the alphanumeric keyboard. The Shift key creates uppercase letters and other special characters, just as it does on a typewriter keyboard. Shift is used also with the function keys to carry out certain operations in WordPerfect.

The Alt and Ctrl keys are used in combination with other keys to provide WordPerfect capabilities that a single key can't provide. The Alt and Ctrl keys don't do anything by themselves, but work with the function keys, number keys, or letter keys to operate various commands in WordPerfect.

Cursor-Movement Keys

The *cursor* is the blinking underline character that marks the location on the screen where the next character you type will appear. The cursor also marks the location in your text where codes (such as those used to create new margin settings) will be entered.

You use the keys marked with arrows at the far right of the keyboard to control cursor movement. When you press an arrow key, the cursor moves in the direction indicated by the arrow on that key.

If you try to move the cursor with a cursor-arrow key on a blank screen, nothing happens. WordPerfect doesn't permit the cursor to move where nothing exists. The cursor moves only through text, spaces, or codes.

When the Num Lock key is activated, the cursor-movement keys become the numeric keys used to perform math functions.

17

Using the Editing Screen and Keyboard

The Editing Screen

What you see on-screen is almost exactly what appears when your document is printed.

```
Mr. Franklin Abbot
Director
Michigan Department of Commerce
P.O. Box 36226
Lansing, Michigan  48909

Dear Mr. Abbot:

Thank you for your willingness to help with our public relations
efforts for the River Park in Indianapolis.  I have enclosed the
preliminary market research.  Also, I have added your name to our
WaterNotes mailing list.

Please send us a list of TV and radio stations in Michigan along
with any other information you think would be helpful.

I look forward to your valuable input.

Sincerely,


Charles Gosnell
```

```
Mr. Franklin Abbot
Director
Michigan Department of Commerce
P.O. Box 36226
Lansing, Michigan  48909

Dear Mr. Abbot:

Thank you for your willingness to help with our public relations
efforts for the River Park in Indianapolis.  I have enclosed the
preliminary market research.  Also, I have added your name to our
WaterNotes mailing list.

Please send us a list of TV and radio stations in Michigan along
with any other information you think would be helpful.

I look forward to your valuable input.

Sincerely,


Charles Gosnell

                                        Doc 1 Pg 1 Ln 1" Pos 1"
```

Status Line

The status line describes the cursor's position with four elements:

Doc 1

The document displayed on-screen. WordPerfect also can hold a second document in memory: Doc 2.

Pg 1

The number of the page on which the cursor rests.

Ln 1"

The cursor's vertical position in inches (the default). You can change this measurement to centimeters, points, or lines on the page.

Pos 1"

The cursor's horizontal position in inches (the default). You can change this measurement to centimeters, points, or columns on the page.

18

Function Keys

To issue a WordPerfect command, you press a function key alone or in combination with the Ctrl, ⇧Shift, or Alt keys.

	Shell	Spell	Screen	Move	Ctrl	Text In/Out	Tab Align	Footnote	Font	Ctrl	Merge/Sort	Macro Define		
	Thesaurus	Replace	Reveal Codes	Block	Alt	Mark Text	Flush Right	Math/Columns	Style	Alt	Graphics	Macro		
	Setup	◀ Search	Switch	◀ Indent ◀	Shift	Date/Outline	Center	Print	Format	Shift	Merge Codes	Retrieve		
	Cancel	▶ Search	Help	▶ Indent		List Files	Bold	Exit	Underline		Merge R	Save	Reveal Codes	Block
	F1	F2	F3	F4		F5	F6	F7	F8		F9	F10	F11	F12

[F1] [F2] [F3] [F4] [F5] [F6] [F7] [F8] [F9] [F10] [F11] [F12]

[Ctrl] [F2]

[Alt] [F2]

[⇧ Shift] [F2]

[F2]

Press and hold the Ctrl key while you press F2 to issue the Spell command.

Press and hold the Alt key while you press F2 to issue the Replace command.

Press and hold the ⇧Shift key while you press F2 to issue the Backward Search command.

Press F2 alone to issue the Forward Search command.

The IBM Enhanced Keyboard has 12 functions keys. If your keyboard has only 10 keys, you still can use all WordPerfect's commands.

Using Help

WordPerfect has an on-line Help feature you can access while working on WordPerfect documents. The screens in the Help system can help you learn more about WordPerfect commands and keys.

Also included in the Help system are two valuable tools: an alphabetical listing of all WordPerfect features and an on-screen function key template. Use these tools as reference aids for finding the WordPerfect command you need.

Accessing the Help Screens

If you have a question about a WordPerfect command or key, you can press Help (F3) to access the Help system. Then press the key about which you want to know more. WordPerfect displays information about that key. The Help screens explain the function key commands and menu options as well as the Esc, Del, Ins, Backspace, Tab, Home, and cursor-arrow keys. For example, if you press Shift-F7, the Print Help menu is displayed. From within the Print Help screen, you can learn more about Printer Control by pressing 4 or C.

Using the Help Files

WordPerfect's two Help files, WPHELP.FIL and WPHELP2.FIL, are located on the WordPerfect 1 disk. If you get an error message indicating that WordPerfect cannot find the Help files, insert the WordPerfect 1 disk in a floppy drive, close the drive door, type the drive letter and a colon (**a:**, for example), and press Enter. Help should now be displayed properly.

Displaying the Alphabetical Feature List

The alphabetical list provides the name of each feature along with the key name and keystrokes required to access that feature. After accessing Help, you type any letter of the alphabet to view a list of the features that begin with that letter. For example, to display a list of features that begin with the letter A, you press Help (F3) and then press A.

Displaying the On-Screen Template

The on-screen template shows you the command assignments for all the function keys and function key combinations. To display this template, you press Help (F3) twice. If you lose your template, display the on-screen template, press Print Screen on the Enhanced Keyboard (or Shift-PrtSc on the PC keyboard) to print the screen, and then use red, green, and blue highlighters to create your own function key template.

Exiting Help

After you have reviewed the Help information, you can return to your file by using either of two methods. Press Enter or press the space bar.

Using Help

Accessing the Help Screens

To get information about any WordPerfect command or key, use WordPerfect's Help system.

```
Help                                    WP 5.0   05/05/88


     Press any letter to get an alphabetical list of features.

          The list will include the features that start with that letter,
          along with the name of the key where the feature is found.  You
          can then press that key to get a description of how the feature
          works.

     Press any function key to get information about the use of the key.

          Some keys may let you choose from a menu to get more information
          about various options.  Press HELP again to display the template.

     Press Enter or Space bar to exit Help.
```

Press F3 to display the opening Help screen.

Press the key about which you want to know more.

For example, press ⇧Shift F7 to display the Print Help menu. From within the Print Help screen, press 4 to learn more about Printer Control.

```
Control Printer

     Provides options which help you manage your print jobs.

     Cancel Job(s):  Cancels one or all print jobs listed on the Printer
          Control menu.

     Rush Job:  Changes the priority of a document waiting in the print job
          list.

     Display Jobs:  Displays the print jobs which are not listed in the job
          list.

     Go (start printer):  Restarts the printer after it has been stopped for a
          form or cartridge change, or after using the Stop option.

     Stop:  Stops the printer without canceling the print jobs. Type g to
          restart the print job.  The job restarts at the page you select.
```

Exiting Help

After you have reviewed the Help information, return to your file by using either of two methods:

Press ↵Enter.

Or

Press the space bar.

Displaying the Alphabetical Feature List

Display an alphabetical list of WordPerfect features along with the key names and keystrokes required to access those features.

Key	Feature	Key Name
Ctrl-F5	Add Password	Text In/Out,2
Shft-F7	Additional Printers	Print,S
Shft-F8	Advance Up, Down or Line	Format,4
Ctrl-PgUp	Advanced Macros	Macro Commands
Ctrl-F10	Advanced Macros, Help on	Macro Definition
Shft-F8	Align/Decimal Character	Format,4
Ctrl-F6	Align on Tabs	Tab Align
Ctrl-F8	Appearance of Printed Text	Font
Ctrl-F1	Append to Shell	Shell
Ctrl-F4	Append text to a file (Block On)	Move
Ctrl-F8	Attributes, Printed	Font
Shft-F1	Attributes, On-Screen	Setup,3
Shift-F5	Automatic Paragraph Numbering	Date/Outline
Alt-F5	Automatic Reference	Mark Text
Shft-F1	Automatically Format and Rewrite	Setup,3
Shft-F1	Auxiliary Files Location	Setup

Press F3.

Press any letter key to display a list of features that begin with that letter. For example, press A to display a list of features that begin with the letter A.

Displaying the On-Screen Template

The on-screen template shows you the command assignments for all the function keys and function key combinations.

Press F3 twice.

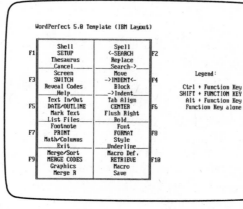

Typing Text

With a word processor, you can get words on-screen as fast as you can type them. In a short time, you will realize that putting words on-screen can be far easier than putting them on paper. WordPerfect doesn't think or plan for you, of course, but it certainly simplifies self-expression.

At any stage of the writing process, you easily can revise your words on-screen. With a word processor, you can alter what you write with great freedom; you easily can insert new words, delete ones you don't want, or move up and down through a document to see what you've written. Because altering text can be accomplished so effortlessly, you can focus on first getting words on-screen. Then, you can wait until later to edit, revise, and spell-check the text. If you're a poor typist, you can leave spelling errors for WordPerfect's Speller to catch.

With WordPerfect's many formatting features, you can change the look of the text on the page, as you see in subsequent chapters. You can change margins, indent text, vary line spacing, control word spacing, put text in columns, create headers and footers, right-justify text, and so on. In this section, though, you focus on those built-in settings that WordPerfect assumes most users use (at least initially). Later you learn how to modify these defaults to meet your needs.

WordPerfect's Built-In Settings

Before you even put fingers to keys and begin typing, WordPerfect has been at work for you. You'll recall from your experience with a typewriter that you must set margins, line spacing, and tabs, for example, before you begin composing. With WordPerfect, you don't need to make any formatting decisions before you begin unless the preset values do not suit you. WordPerfect comes with a number of default settings—for margins, page numbers, tab settings, base font (basic character style), line spacing, and other features. You should be familiar with the basic default settings before you begin writing. Subsequent chapters, especially those devoted to formatting and printing, explore the many ways you can alter the look of a document.

Here are just a few of WordPerfect's many built-in settings:

- Margins—1-inch from the top, bottom, left, and right
- Tabs—every half inch
- Line spacing—single-spaced
- Page numbering—none
- Right-justification—on
- Hyphenation—off
- Form size—letter-size paper (8 1/2 by 11 inches)
- Date format—Month (word), day, year (all four digits). Example—July 4, 1990

Entering Text

As you type in WordPerfect, characters appear at the position of the cursor, just as they do when you use a typewriter. After you type a few words, look at the Pos indicator on the status line. This value increases as you type and as the cursor moves horizontally across the line to the right. Unlike a typewriter, WordPerfect doesn't require you to press Enter to end a line. Word wrap inserts what is known as a *soft return* at the end of each line and "wraps" the text to the beginning of the next line.

Inserting Blank Lines

To end a paragraph or insert blank lines in the text, you use the Enter key. When you come to the end of the last sentence in a paragraph, you press Enter twice.

When you press Enter the first time, WordPerfect inserts a *hard return.* When you press Enter a second time, WordPerfect inserts another hard return, creating a blank line in the text.

Typing Text

Built-In Settings

WordPerfect provides some built-in settings for your document even before you begin to type.

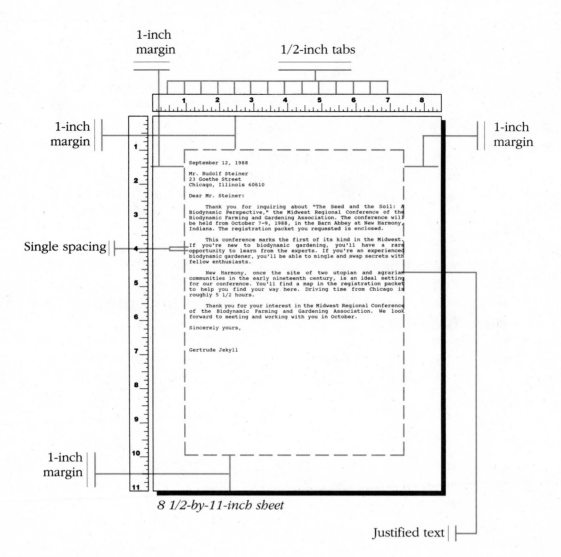

1-inch margin

1/2-inch tabs

1-inch margin

1-inch margin

Single spacing

1-inch margin

8 1/2-by-11-inch sheet

Justified text

September 12, 1988

Mr. Rudolf Steiner
23 Goethe Street
Chicago, Illinois 60610

Dear Mr. Steiner:

Thank you for inquiring about "The Seed and the Soil: A Biodynamic Perspective," the Midwest Regional Conference of the Biodynamic Farming and Gardening Association. The conference will be held from October 7-9, 1988, in the Barn Abbey at New Harmony, Indiana. The registration packet you requested is enclosed.

This conference marks the first of its kind in the Midwest. If you're new to biodynamic gardening, you'll have a rare opportunity to learn from the experts. If you're an experienced biodynamic gardener, you'll be able to mingle and swap secrets with fellow enthusiasts.

New Harmony, once the site of two utopian and agrarian communities in the early nineteenth century, is an ideal setting for our conference. You'll find a map in the registration packet to help you find your way here. Driving time from Chicago is roughly 5 1/2 hours.

Thank you for your interest in the Midwest Regional Conference of the Biodynamic Farming and Gardening Association. We look forward to meeting and working with you in October.

Sincerely yours,

Gertrude Jekyll

Introduction

Starting
WordPerfect

Using the
Editing Screen
and Keyboard

Using
Help

**Typing
Text**

Moving the
Cursor

Making a Menu
Selection, Using
the Cancel Key

Printing, Saving,
Clearing, Exiting

Entering Text

When you type, text "wraps" from the end of the line to the beginning of the next line. You don't have to press the ⏎Enter key (or Return) when you reach the end of the line. WordPerfect inserts a soft return at the end of each line.

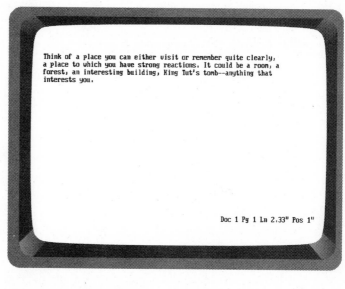

```
Think of a place you can either visit or remember quite clearly,
a place to which you have strong reactions. It could be a room, a
forest, an interesting building, King Tut's tomb--anything that
interests you.




                                              Doc 1 Pg 1 Ln 2.33" Pos 1"
```

```
Think of a place you can either visit or remember quite clearly,
a place to which you have strong reactions. It could be a room, a
forest, an interesting building, King Tut's tomb--anything that
interests you.

Write a personal description of it, attempting to re-create for
your reader the experience of seeing or entering the place you've
chosen to write about. Details are essential in picturing whatever
you describe.




                                              Doc 1 Pg 1 Ln 2.83" Pos 2.3"
```

Inserting Blank Lines

Press ⏎Enter to end a paragraph. WordPerfect inserts a hard return at the end of the line. To insert a blank line, press ⏎Enter again.

Moving the Cursor

You move the cursor through text in WordPerfect by using the following methods:

- Pressing the cursor-arrow keys
- Pressing Ctrl or Home in combination with the right- or left-arrow key
- Pressing End
- Pressing PgUp, PgDn, Screen Up (–), or Screen Down (+)
- Using GoTo (Ctrl-Home)
- Using the repeat value (Esc)

Using PgUp, PgDn, and GoTo

Use the PgUp or PgDn keys to move the cursor a page at a time. When you press one of these keys, the prompt Repositioning appears on the status line.

Use GoTo (Ctrl-Home) in combination with other keys to move to a specific page or character in your document. You also can use this command to move to the top or bottom of the page.

After pressing certain keys, you press GoTo (Ctrl-Home) alone to move the cursor to its starting position. The cursor will return to its starting position only after you have used one of these features: Escape, GoTo, Home and arrow keys, PgUp or PgDn, Replace, Screen Up or Screen Down, or Search.

Using the Repeat Value

Use Esc (the Repeat key) to repeat an operation *n* number of times. You can use Esc to move the cursor *n* number of characters (right or left), *n* number of words (right or left), *n* number of lines (up or down), or *n* number of pages forward or backward.

Normally, the value of *n* is 8; that is, WordPerfect repeats 8 times. But you can change this repeat value. You press Esc, enter the number of repetitions, and then enter the key you want to repeat. For example, to move the cursor down 15 lines, you would press Esc, type **15**, and press the down-arrow key.

Some of the keys on your keyboard automatically repeat when you hold down the key. Many other WordPerfect functions can be repeated only with the aid of the Esc key.

You can use the following features with the repeat value:

- Cursor-movement keys
- Delete, Delete to EOL, Delete to EOP, Delete Word
- Macro
- PgUp, PgDn
- Screen Up, Screen Down
- Word Left, Word Right

Moving the Cursor

Move the cursor with the cursor-arrow keys, PgUp, PgDn, Screen Up, Screen Down, GoTo, or the Repeat key (Esc).

Cursor-Arrow Keys

You can use the keys marked with arrows to control cursor movement. When you press an arrow key, the cursor moves in the direction indicated by the arrow on that key.

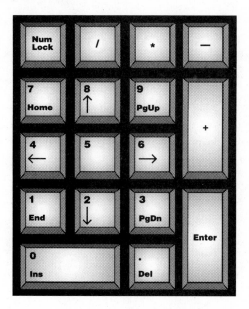

 Moves the cursor up one line

 Moves the cursor down one line

 Moves the cursor one position to the left

 Moves the cursor one position to the right

 Moves the cursor one word to the right

 Moves the cursor one word to the left

 or Moves the cursor to the right end of the line

 Moves the cursor to the left edge of the screen

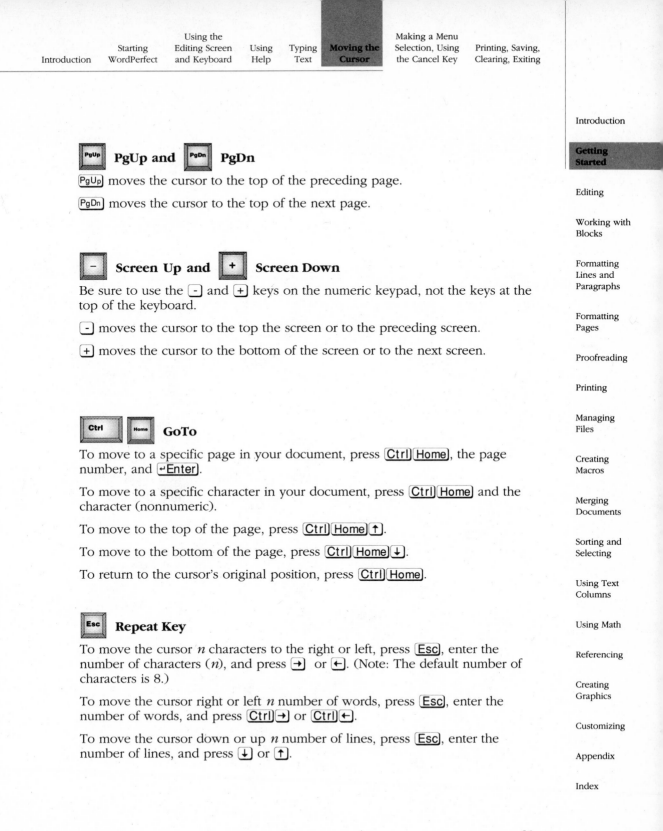

PgUp and PgDn

PgUp moves the cursor to the top of the preceding page.

PgDn moves the cursor to the top of the next page.

Screen Up and + Screen Down

Be sure to use the - and + keys on the numeric keypad, not the keys at the top of the keyboard.

- moves the cursor to the top the screen or to the preceding screen.

+ moves the cursor to the bottom of the screen or to the next screen.

GoTo

To move to a specific page in your document, press Ctrl Home, the page number, and Enter.

To move to a specific character in your document, press Ctrl Home and the character (nonnumeric).

To move to the top of the page, press Ctrl Home ↑.

To move to the bottom of the page, press Ctrl Home ↓.

To return to the cursor's original position, press Ctrl Home.

Repeat Key

To move the cursor n characters to the right or left, press Esc, enter the number of characters (n), and press → or ←. (Note: The default number of characters is 8.)

To move the cursor right or left n number of words, press Esc, enter the number of words, and press Ctrl → or Ctrl ←.

To move the cursor down or up n number of lines, press Esc, enter the number of lines, and press ↓ or ↑.

31

Making a Menu Selection, Using the Cancel Key

Making a Menu Selection

WordPerfect uses two types of menus. Many times when you press a function key combination, a one-line menu appears at the bottom of the screen. Other commands in WordPerfect display full-screen menus.

You can make a selection from both types of menus in either of two ways:

- Press the number next to the menu selection.
- Press the highlighted letter in the name of the menu option.

When you press the Math/Columns key (Alt-F7), for instance, a one-line menu appears at the bottom of the screen. To turn on Math, you can press 1 or M for Math On.

When you press the Format key (Shift-F8), the Format menu appears on-screen. If you want to change the margins, for example, you press 1 or L for Line to choose that option. Another menu is then displayed, from which you can choose other options to adjust the margin settings.

Using the Cancel Key

The Cancel key (the F1 "oops" key) allows you to do the following:

- Back out of a menu without making a selection
- Restore text you have deleted

Introduction

Getting Started

Editing

Working with Blocks

Formatting Lines and Paragraphs

Formatting Pages

Proofreading

Printing

Managing Files

Creating Macros

Merging Documents

Sorting and Selecting

Using Text Columns

Using Math

Referencing

Creating Graphics

Customizing

Appendix

Index

When used to back out of a menu, Cancel (F1) cancels the most recent command and returns you either to the preceding menu or to your document. When used to restore text, Cancel (F1) retrieves one of the last three items you've deleted. An *item* in this case means the characters (numbers, letters, or punctuation) deleted before moving the cursor. Cancel (F1) always acts as an "undelete" key when a menu is not visible.

Backing Out of a Menu

Some menus disregard your selections if you leave the menu by pressing the Cancel key (F1). These menus display a message that instructs you to leave the menu by pressing the Exit key (F7) if you want to save your selections in memory.

You press Cancel (F1) to return to a preceding menu without making a choice from the current menu. When there is no preceding menu to which to return, you are returned to the current document.

Restoring Deleted Text

Press Cancel (F1) to restore deleted text either to its original location or to another location. Remember, however, that WordPerfect stores only the last three deletions. When you make a fourth deletion, the oldest of the three preceding deletions is erased from memory.

Cancel (F1) is not used to remove the hidden format and character codes that control formatting and character display. See Chapter 2, "Editing," to learn how to remove hidden codes.

Selecting a Menu Option

WordPerfect displays two types of menus: one-line menus and full-screen menus.

For example, press [Alt][F7] to display the one-line Math/Columns menu.

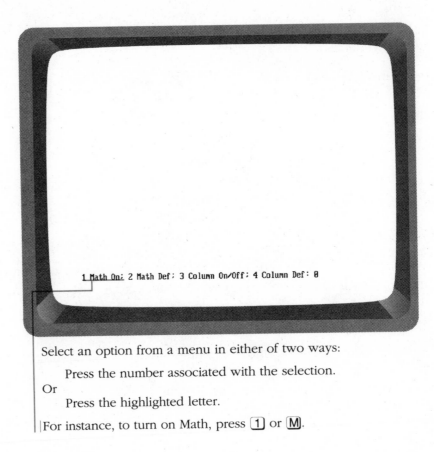

1 Math On: 2 Math Def; 3 Column On/Off; 4 Column Def: 0

Select an option from a menu in either of two ways:

Press the number associated with the selection.

Or

Press the highlighted letter.

For instance, to turn on Math, press [1] or [M].

Some menus are full screens and lead to other menus. For example, press ⟨⇧Shift⟩ ⟨F8⟩ to display the Format menu.

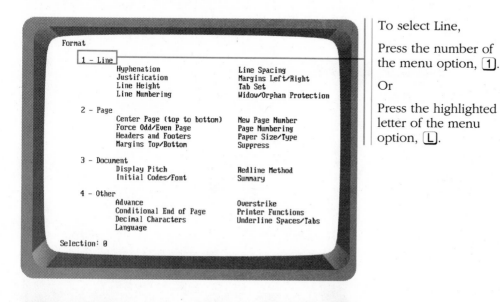

```
Format
  1 - Line
        Hyphenation              Line Spacing
        Justification            Margins Left/Right
        Line Height              Tab Set
        Line Numbering           Widow/Orphan Protection

  2 - Page
        Center Page (top to bottom)   New Page Number
        Force Odd/Even Page           Page Numbering
        Headers and Footers           Paper Size/Type
        Margins Top/Bottom            Suppress

  3 - Document
        Display Pitch            Redline Method
        Initial Codes/Font       Summary

  4 - Other
        Advance                  Overstrike
        Conditional End of Page  Printer Functions
        Decimal Characters       Underline Spaces/Tabs
        Language

Selection: 0
```

To select Line,

Press the number of the menu option, ⟨1⟩.

Or

Press the highlighted letter of the menu option, ⟨L⟩.

```
Format: Line
  1 - Hyphenation                 Auto
  2 - Hyphenation Zone - Left     10%
                        Right     4%
  3 - Justification               Yes
  4 - Line Height                 Auto
  5 - Line Numbering              No
  6 - Line Spacing                1
  7 - Margins - Left              1"
              Right               1"
  8 - Tab Set                     0", every 0.5"
  9 - Widow/Orphan Protection     No

Selection: 0
```

Another menu appears. You can make your selections—change left and right margins, for example—from this menu.

Making a Menu Selection, Using the Cancel Key

Using the Cancel Key

Use the Cancel key ([F1]) for two purposes.

To Back Out of a Menu

Press [F1] to return to the preceding menu without making a selection.

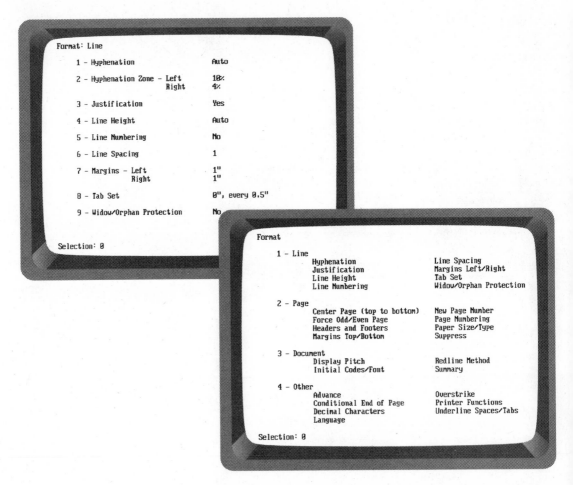

```
Format: Line

     1 - Hyphenation                      Auto

     2 - Hyphenation Zone - Left          10%
                            Right         4%

     3 - Justification                    Yes

     4 - Line Height                      Auto

     5 - Line Numbering                   No

     6 - Line Spacing                     1

     7 - Margins - Left                   1"
                   Right                  1"

     8 - Tab Set                          0", every 0.5"

     9 - Widow/Orphan Protection          No


  Selection: 0
```

```
Format

     1 - Line
              Hyphenation                 Line Spacing
              Justification               Margins Left/Right
              Line Height                 Tab Set
              Line Numbering              Widow/Orphan Protection

     2 - Page
              Center Page (top to bottom) New Page Number
              Force Odd/Even Page         Page Numbering
              Headers and Footers         Paper Size/Type
              Margins Top/Bottom          Suppress

     3 - Document
              Display Pitch               Redline Method
              Initial Codes/Font          Summary

     4 - Other
              Advance                     Overstrike
              Conditional End of Page     Printer Functions
              Decimal Characters          Underline Spaces/Tabs
              Language

  Selection: 0
```

To Restore Deleted Text

Press F1 to restore deleted text either to its original location or to another location.

Original Text

Second sentence deleted

Text restored in a new location

Printing, Saving, Clearing, Exiting

After you have worked on a document, you may want to print it. You also will need to save it to disk before you work on another document, leave WordPerfect, or turn off your computer. This section tells you how to save a document, give it a file name, clear the screen, and exit WordPerfect.

Printing an Unsaved Document

With WordPerfect, you can be flexible about printing. You may not want or need to save every document to disk. If you do not want to save a document, WordPerfect still lets you print it without requiring you to save it to disk first. Printing in this manner is called making a screen print, because you print what has been created and stored in temporary memory (also known as random-access memory or RAM).

Before you print, you must be sure that your printer is installed properly. If you haven't installed your printer, see Chapter 7, "Printing."

To print the document on-screen, you press Print (Shift-F7). The Print menu is displayed. If the text you want to print is more than one page, you select Full Document (1). Or, if the text you want to print is a page or less, you select Page (2).

WordPerfect displays a * Please Wait * prompt on the status line as the program prepares to print your text. If your printer is properly configured and hooked up, printing should begin almost immediately.

Your document doesn't, however, have to be on-screen for you to print it. With WordPerfect you can print any number of documents stored on disk (floppy or hard). You can even have documents in both windows and print a document stored on disk. The various ways of printing and managing print jobs are treated in-depth in Chapter 7. But you know enough now to make a quick print of the text on-screen.

Saving a Document

Usually you keep copies on disk of the documents you create. WordPerfect gives you two methods of saving a file:

- With Save (F10), you save a copy of the on-screen document to disk. When you use Save, the document remains on-screen for additional work.
- With Exit (F7), you save a copy of the document to disk, but the document does not remain on-screen. You can keep the document on-screen by pressing Cancel (F1) when you get the Exit WP? prompt.

Using Save (F10)

The first time you save a document, WordPerfect prompts you for a file name. Suppose that you've created a document, and you now want to save the file. With your document on-screen, you press Save (F10). The prompt Document to be saved: appears on the status line. Next, you type a file name for the document and press Enter.

Be sure to give each file a unique name. A file name consists of two parts: a *root name* and an *extension*. The root name can have one to eight characters. You can use the root name to describe the file's contents. The optional extension can have one to three characters. If you use an extension, you must separate it from the root name by a period (.). You may omit the optional extension if you like. When you name a file, you must observe your operating system's (MS-DOS® or PC DOS) guidelines for naming files.

Printing, Saving, Clearing, Exiting

A prompt on the status line indicates that WordPerfect is saving the file to the current directory unless you indicate otherwise. To save the file to a directory other than the current drive/directory, you must precede the file name with the drive/directory information. After you name and save a file, the file name is displayed on the status line in the left corner of the screen.

WordPerfect responds a bit differently when you want to save a file you've saved before. When you press Save (F10), WordPerfect asks whether you want to replace the file on disk. You can press Y to replace the previous version of the file with the new version. Or, you can press N, rename the file, and save it under a different name. If you want to save the document on-screen under a different file name, use the right-arrow key to move the cursor to the previous file name and change it accordingly. You can change any of the information following the `Document to be saved:` prompt.

Using Exit (F7)

The other method for saving a document to disk is to use Exit (F7). After you press Exit (F7), the current document is cleared from the screen and the prompt `Save document? (Y/N) Yes` is displayed. To begin the Save process, you press Y. When WordPerfect prompts you to enter the name of the document to be saved, you type the file name and press Enter.

If the document already exists, WordPerfect prompts:

```
Replace (file name)? (Y/N) No
```

You can press Y to save the document with the old name; or you can press N, type the file name, and press Enter. Your document is stored under the name you select. For easy retrieval, use descriptive file names.

Clearing the Screen and Exiting WordPerfect

You must clear the current document from the screen before you start work on a new document—or before you retrieve a document. You can use Exit (F7) to clear the screen without saving the document. This method is handy when you decide to discard what you've written. If you do not clear the current document before starting a new document, or before retrieving a document from memory, the old and the new documents will merge with one another to form a continuous (and confusing) document!

If you don't want to save the document you've created, or if you've saved the document previously but you want to clear your screen, you press Exit (F7). In response to the Save Document? (Y/N) Yes prompt, you press N.

The following prompt appears on-screen:

```
Exit WP? (Y/N) No
```

In response to the prompt, you can either press Y to exit WordPerfect and return to DOS, or you can press N or Enter to clear the screen. If you press Cancel (F1), you will return to the document displayed on-screen.

Never turn off your computer or remove your working copy of the 5 1/4-inch WordPerfect 2 disk or the 3 1/2-inch WordPerfect 1/WordPerfect 2 disk from the disk drive before you have cleared the current document from the screen and exited to DOS. You will know that you've returned to DOS when you see the DOS prompt (A>, B>, or C>) on-screen.

Printing, Saving, Clearing, Exiting

Printing an Unsaved Document

To make a quick print of a document on-screen, display the document you want to print.

Press ⟨⇧Shift⟩⟨F7⟩ to display the Print menu.

```
Print
    ┌1 - Full Document
     2 - Page
     3 - Document on Disk
     4 - Control Printer
     5 - Type Through
     6 - View Document
     7 - Initialize Printer

Options

     S - Select Printer          Toshiba P321/P351/P351C
     B - Binding                 0"
     N - Number of Copies        1
     G - Graphics Quality        Medium
     T - Text Quality            High




Selection: 0
```

To print a document that is more than one page, press ⟨1⟩ for Full Document.

To print a single page, position the cursor on that page, and press ⟨2⟩ for Page.

Naming a File

When you save a document, WordPerfect prompts you for a file name. Each file name must be unique and follow these guidelines:

- A file name has two parts: a *root name* and an *extension*, separated by a ⎡.⎤ (period).
- The root name can have one to eight characters; the extension can have one to three characters.
- Including an extension is optional. You can omit it if you want.
- Choose names that are descriptive of the files' contents.

Valid	Unacceptable	
FILENAME	FILENAMES	(The name has too many characters.)
A	"A"	(Quotation marks cannot be used in file names.)
1-23-89	1/23/89	(/ is not an admissible character.)
december.90	december,90	(A comma cannot be used in a file name.)
ASSETS.DOC	ASSETS.FILE	(The extension is too long, but WordPerfect will shorten it to ASSETS.FIL.)
REPORT.NEW	REPORTNEW	(The period before the extension is missing.)

43

Printing, Saving, Clearing, Exiting

Use either of two methods to save a document to disk. Save the document with Save ([F10]) and remain in WordPerfect, or save the document with Exit ([F7]) and exit WordPerfect.

Saving a Document and Remaining in WordPerfect

To save a copy of an on-screen document for the first time, press [F10], the Save key.

```
Think of a place you can either visit or remember quite clearly,
a place to which you have strong reactions. It could be a room, a
forest, an interesting building, King Tut's tomb--anything that
interests you.

Write a personal description of it, attempting to re-create for
your reader the experience of seeing or entering the place you've
chosen to write about. Details are essential in picturing whatever
you describe.




Document to be saved:
```

Type a file name, and then press [↵Enter]. The document remains on-screen.

```
Document to be saved: C:\WP50\REPORT.TXT
```

To save a file you've saved before, press [F10]. WordPerfect supplies the file name.

Press [↵Enter] to keep the same file name.

```
Replace C:\WP50\REPORT.TXT? (Y/N) No
```

If you want to replace the file, press [Y].

Or

If you want to save this version, but also retain the previous version, press [N], and then rename the file to save it under a different name.

The document remains on-screen.

Saving a Document and Exiting WordPerfect

To save a copy of an on-screen document and exit WordPerfect, press F7, the Exit key.

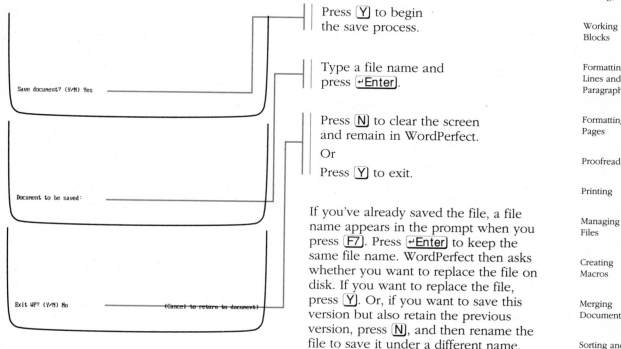

Save document? (Y/N) Yes

Document to be saved:

Exit WP? (Y/N) No   (Cancel to return to document)

Press Y to begin the save process.

Type a file name and press ↵Enter.

Press N to clear the screen and remain in WordPerfect.

Or

Press Y to exit.

If you've already saved the file, a file name appears in the prompt when you press F7. Press ↵Enter to keep the same file name. WordPerfect then asks whether you want to replace the file on disk. If you want to replace the file, press Y. Or, if you want to save this version but also retain the previous version, press N, and then rename the file to save it under a different name.

Clearing the Screen and Exiting WordPerfect

Before you work on a new document or before you retrieve a document, you must clear the current document from the screen.

Press F7 (Exit).

WordPerfect asks whether you want to save the document.

Press N for No.

Or

Press Y to save the document. Type a file name and press ↵Enter.

WordPerfect asks whether you want to exit the program.

If you want to exit the program and return to DOS, press Y.

Or

If you want only to clear the screen, press N.

Or

If you want to return to the document displayed on-screen, press F1, the Cancel key.

Editing

Revising a draft is an important part of creating any polished document. Revision can consist of changing, adding to, or deleting material; correcting grammar and punctuation; and making any other changes to your document. WordPerfect lets you revise text easily by using a number of built-in editing tools. This chapter focuses on the basic editing changes you can make with WordPerfect.

▼

Key Terms

This chapter introduces the following key terms:

Insert mode	The alternative to WordPerfect's Typeover mode. When you type in Insert mode (WordPerfect's default), new characters are inserted and existing text moves forward.
Typeover mode	The alternative to WordPerfect's Insert mode. When you type in Typeover mode, the characters you type replace the original text.

Reveal Codes   The hidden codes inserted in the text when you press certain keys. Hidden codes tell WordPerfect when to execute tabs, margin settings, hard returns, and so on.

Document window An area in which to work. In WordPerfect, you can open two document windows, Doc 1 and Doc 2.

▲

Tasks Covered in This Chapter

In this chapter, you learn to perform the following tasks:

- Retrieve files
- Insert text
- Delete text: characters, words, lines, and pages
- Display and delete Reveal Codes
- Use both document windows

Retrieving Files

You can retrieve documents stored on disk in two ways: press Retrieve (Shift-F10) or press List Files (F5) to use the List Files screen.

Before you retrieve a file using either method, be sure to clear the screen using Exit (F7). If you do not clear your screen before retrieving a document, WordPerfect inserts the retrieved file into the document displayed on-screen.

Using the Retrieve Command

To retrieve a file using the Retrieve command, you press Retrieve (Shift-F10). At the prompt for a file name, you type the name of the document and press Enter.

If the message ERROR: File Not Found is displayed, either you have typed the name incorrectly or the file doesn't exist in the directory. Type the name again. If you cannot remember the name of the document you want to retrieve, use the List Files screen.

Suppose that after you press Retrieve (Shift-F10), you decide not to retrieve a file. You can press Cancel (F1) to cancel the command.

Using the List Files Screen

To retrieve a document with List Files, you press List Files (F5). WordPerfect displays a file specification similar to the following in the lower left corner of the screen:

```
Dir C:\WP50\*.*
```

To view the documents stored on the named drive, you press Enter. Or, to view files on a drive other than the one designated, you type the letter of the disk drive, a colon, and the path name (**c:\letters**, for example). Then you press Enter.

The List Files screen and menu appear. The List Files screen displays a two-column alphabetized list of your files, including the file size and the date and time each file was last saved. The menu at the bottom of the screen shows the options you can choose.

WordPerfect provides two ways to specify file names from the List Files screen. The first method is to use the arrow keys to move the highlight bar to the file you want to retrieve. The second method is to press N for Name Search and type the file name. As you type the file name, the cursor moves the highlight bar to the name of the file you want to retrieve. Press Enter or an arrow key to end the name search.

If the document you want to retrieve is stored on another disk or in another subdirectory, you select Other Directory (7) from the List Files menu and type a new subdirectory. The subdirectory you enter automatically becomes the new default. Until you change the default again, documents are saved in this subdirectory; pressing List Files (F5) automatically displays the new default directory.

After you specify a file name, you select the Retrieve (1) option from the menu displayed at the bottom of the screen. The file is then retrieved to the screen.

After you display the List Files screen, you might decide not to retrieve a file. You can press Cancel (F1) to cancel the command.

Retrieving Files

Retrieve files using either of two methods: the Retrieve command or the List Files screen.

Using the Retrieve Command

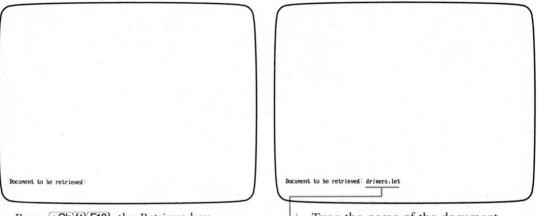

Document to be retrieved:

Press ⇧Shift F10, the Retrieve key.

Document to be retrieved: drivers.let

Type the name of the document and press ↵Enter.

If the message ERROR: File Not Found is displayed, either you have typed the name incorrectly or the file doesn't exist in the directory. Type the name again.

If you cannot remember the name of the document you want to retrieve, use the List Files screen.

August 18, 1988

Dear Dane,

There's been a change in the location for this year's drivers school for the Windy City Chapter, and I know you'll love this one! Instead of going to Blackhawk Farms, we'll be going up to Road America in beautiful Elkhart Lake, Wisconsin.

The dates will remain the same, September 12 and 13. Lodging, as always, will be available at Siebkens and Barefoot Bay in Elkhart Lake, or at motels in Sheboygan or Fond du Lac. Remember, you must make your own reservations.

Driving directions to Elkhart Lake will be included with your registration package, along with a map of the area.

See you soon,

Tom Malone

Doc 1 Pg 1 Ln 1.33" Pos 1.6"

Using the List Files Screen

The List Files screen displays a two-column alphabetized list of your files, including the file size and the date and time each file was last saved. From this screen, you can retrieve a file.

```
08/05/88 13:56              Directory C:\WP50\*.*
Document size:      0  Free: 2400256  Used: 2090051     Files: 96

.  <CURRENT>  <DIR>                  .. <PARENT>  <DIR>
LEARN    ,       <DIR>  05/16/88 11:32   22F      .WPM      57  05/24/88 15:34
8514A    .WPD    3466  04/27/88 14:24   AIRPLANE.WPG    8404  04/27/88 14:24
ALTC     .WPM      78  04/29/88 09:00   ALTF     .WPM      65  06/01/88 16:43
ALTL     .WPM      98  05/24/88 15:32   ALTN     .WPM      72  04/29/88 09:00
ALTO     .WPM      95  06/01/88 16:40   ALTRMAT .WPK     919  04/27/88 11:00
ALTS     .WPM     158  06/01/88 13:34   ALTV     .WPM      72  06/01/88 13:30
AMD      .WPG    1970  04/27/88 14:24   ANNOUNCE.WPG    5300  04/27/88 14:24
APPLAUSE.WPG    1522  04/27/88 14:24   ARROW1   .WPG     366  04/27/88 14:24
ARROW2   .WPG     738  04/27/88 14:24   AWARD    .WPG    1746  04/27/88 14:24
BADNEWS .WPG    3750  04/27/88 14:24   BOOK     .WPG    1000  04/27/88 14:24
BORDER   .WPG   13510  04/27/88 14:24   CALENDAR.WPM      85  05/23/88 11:28
CHAP1    ,       1096  08/04/88 09:11   CHECK    .WPG    1074  04/27/88 14:24
CLOCK    .WPG    6234  04/27/88 14:24   COMPARE  ,       1494  06/21/88 10:23
COMPOSE  ,        810  05/27/88 08:15   CONFIDEN.WPG    3226  04/27/88 14:24
DOTEXPRI.PRS    1813  06/09/88 15:40   DRIVERS  .LET    1407  08/05/88 13:53
EGA512   .FRS    3504  04/27/88 14:24   EGAITAL .FRS    3504  04/27/88 14:24
EGASMC   .FRS    3504  04/27/88 14:24   EGAUMD  .FRS    3504  04/27/88 14:24
ENHANCED.WPK    3375  04/27/88 11:00 ▼ FIGURES  .TXT    1715  06/10/88 08:00

1 Retrieve; 2 Delete; 3 Move/Rename; 4 Print; 5 Text In;
6 Look; 7 Other Directory; 8 Copy; 9 Word Search; N Name Search: 6
```

Press **F5**, the List Files key.

To view the documents stored on the named drive, press **⏎Enter**.

Or

To view files on a drive other than the one designated, type the letter of the disk drive, a colon, and the path name. Then press **⏎Enter**.

```
08/05/88 13:56              Directory C:\WP50\*.*
Document size:      0  Free: 2400256  Used: 2090051     Files: 96

.  <CURRENT>  <DIR>                  .. <PARENT>  <DIR>
LEARN    ,       <DIR>  05/16/88 11:32   22F      .WPM      57  05/24/88 15:34
8514A    .WPD    3466  04/27/88 14:24   AIRPLANE.WPG    8404  04/27/88 14:24
ALTC     .WPM      78  04/29/88 09:00   ALTF     .WPM      65  06/01/88 16:43
ALTL     .WPM      98  05/24/88 15:32   ALTN     .WPM      72  04/29/88 09:00
ALTO     .WPM      95  06/01/88 16:40   ALTRMAT .WPK     919  04/27/88 11:00
ALTS     .WPM     158  06/01/88 13:34   ALTV     .WPM      72  06/01/88 13:30
AMD      .WPG    1970  04/27/88 14:24   ANNOUNCE.WPG    5300  04/27/88 14:24
APPLAUSE.WPG    1522  04/27/88 14:24   ARROW1   .WPG     366  04/27/88 14:24
ARROW2   .WPG     738  04/27/88 14:24   AWARD    .WPG    1746  04/27/88 14:24
BADNEWS .WPG    3750  04/27/88 14:24   BOOK     .WPG    1000  04/27/88 14:24
BORDER   .WPG   13510  04/27/88 14:24   CALENDAR.WPM      85  05/23/88 11:28
CHAP1    ,       1090  08/04/88 09:11   CHECK    .WPG    1074  04/27/88 14:24
CLOCK    .WPG    6234  04/27/88 14:24   COMPARE  ,       1494  06/21/88 10:23
COMPOSE  ,        810  05/27/88 08:15   CONFIDEN.WPG    3226  04/27/88 14:24
DOTEXPRI.PRS    1813  06/09/88 15:40   DRIVERS  .LET    1407  08/05/88 13:53
EGA512   .FRS    3504  04/27/88 14:24   EGAITAL .FRS    3504  04/27/88 14:24
EGASMC   .FRS    3504  04/27/88 14:24   EGAUMD  .FRS    3504  04/27/88 14:24
ENHANCED.WPK    3375  04/27/88 11:00 ▼ FIGURES  .TXT    1715  06/10/88 08:00

ch
                        (Name Search: Enter or arrows to Exit)
```

```
08/05/88 13:56              Directory C:\WP50\*.*
Document size:      0  Free: 2400256  Used: 2090051     Files: 96

.  <CURRENT>  <DIR>                  .. <PARENT>  <DIR>
LEARN    ,       <DIR>  05/16/88 11:32   22F      .WPM      57  05/24/88 15:34
8514A    .WPD    3466  04/27/88 14:24   AIRPLANE.WPG    8404  04/27/88 14:24
ALTC     .WPM      78  04/29/88 09:00   ALTF     .WPM      65  06/01/88 16:43
ALTL     .WPM      98  05/24/88 15:32   ALTN     .WPM      72  04/29/88 09:00
ALTO     .WPM      95  06/01/88 16:40   ALTRMAT .WPK     919  04/27/88 11:00
ALTS     .WPM     158  06/01/88 13:34   ALTV     .WPM      72  06/01/88 13:30
AMD      .WPG    1970  04/27/88 14:24   ANNOUNCE.WPG    5300  04/27/88 14:24
APPLAUSE.WPG    1522  04/27/88 14:24   ARROW1   .WPG     366  04/27/88 14:24
ARROW2   .WPG     738  04/27/88 14:24   AWARD    .WPG    1746  04/27/88 14:24
BADNEWS .WPG    3750  04/27/88 14:24   BOOK     .WPG    1000  04/27/88 14:24
BORDER   .WPG   13510  04/27/88 14:24   CALENDAR.WPM      85  05/23/88 11:28
CHAP1    ,       1090  08/04/88 09:11   CHECK    .WPG    1074  04/27/88 14:24
CLOCK    .WPG    6234  04/27/88 14:24   COMPARE  ,       1494  06/21/88 10:23
COMPOSE  ,        810  05/27/88 08:15   CONFIDEN.WPG    3226  04/27/88 14:24
DOTEXPRI.PRS    1813  06/09/88 15:40   DRIVERS  .LET    1407  08/05/88 13:53
EGA512   .FRS    3504  04/27/88 14:24   EGAITAL .FRS    3504  04/27/88 14:24
EGASMC   .FRS    3504  04/27/88 14:24   EGAUMD  .FRS    3504  04/27/88 14:24
ENHANCED.WPK    3375  04/27/88 11:00 ▼ FIGURES  .TXT    1715  06/10/88 08:00

1 Retrieve; 2 Delete; 3 Move/Rename; 4 Print; 5 Text In;
6 Look; 7 Other Directory; 8 Copy; 9 Word Search; N Name Search: 6
```

WordPerfect provides two ways to specify file names.

Press **N** for Name Search and type the file name. As you type the file name, the cursor moves the highlight bar to the name of the file you want to retrieve. Press **⏎Enter** or an arrow key to end Name Search.

Or

Use the arrow keys to move the highlight bar to the file you want to retrieve.

Press **1** to select the Retrieve option.

51

Inserting Text

Inserting text is a basic part of the editing process. This section shows how easily you can improve what you have written by *inserting* additional text using Insert mode or by *typing over* and replacing the existing text with new text using Typeover mode. The basic difference between Typeover mode and Insert mode is that Typeover mode *replaces* your original text; Insert mode *adds* new text to existing text.

Adding Text with Insert Mode

WordPerfect normally operates in Insert mode. Insert mode means that as you type, the new characters are inserted, and existing text moves forward and is automatically formatted. As you type, sentences may push beyond the right margin and may not immediately wrap to the next line. Don't worry. The lines adjust as you continue to type. Or, you can press the down-arrow key to reformat the text.

To add text by using Insert mode, you place the cursor where you want to insert new text. Then you type the new text.

Typing Over Existing Text

You generally use Typeover mode if you have typed text incorrectly. For example, you probably would select Typeover mode to replace text if you mistakenly had typed the name Jane instead of Dane.

To add text by typing over existing text, you place the cursor where you want the new text to begin. Then you press Ins to turn off Insert mode and turn on Typeover mode. The Typeover mode indicator appears at the lower left of your screen. Next, you type the new text, and then you press Ins again to return to Insert mode.

Inserting Spaces

In Insert or Typeover mode, you can add blank character spaces by pressing the space bar.

Inserting Blank Lines

You can insert blank lines by pressing the Enter key once for each blank line you want to insert. Inserting blank lines causes existing lines of text to move down on the page.

Inserting Text

Use WordPerfect's Insert mode to *add* new text to existing text. Use Typeover mode to *replace* your original text.

August 18, 1988

Dear Dane,

There's been a change in the location for this year's drivers school for the Windy City Chapter, and I know you'll love this one! Instead of going to Blackhawk Farms, we'll be going up to Road America in beautiful Elkhart Lake, Wisconsin.

The dates will remain the same, September 12 and 13. Lodging, as always, will be available at Siebkens and Barefoot Bay in Elkhart Lake, or at motels in Sheboygan. Remember, you must make your own reservations.

Driving directions to Elkhart Lake will be included with your registration package, along with a map of the area.

See you soon,

Tom Malone

Doc 1 Pg 1 Ln 2.83" Pos 4.1"

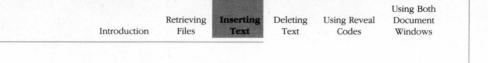
Adding Text Using Insert Mode

```
August 18, 1988

Dear Dane,

There's been a change in the location for this year's drivers
school for the Windy City Chapter, and I know you'll love this one!
Instead of going to Blackhawk Farms, we'll be going up to Road
America in beautiful Elkhart Lake, Wisconsin.

The dates will remain the same, September 12 and 13. Lodging, as
always, will be available at Siebkens and Barefoot Bay in Elkhart
Lake, or at motels in Sheboygan. Remember, you must make your own
reservations.

Driving directions to Elkhart Lake will be included with your
registration package, along with a map of the area.

See you soon,


Tom Malone

                                          Doc 1 Pg 1 Ln 2.83" Pos 4.1"
```

Place the cursor where you want to insert new text.

```
August 18, 1988

Dear Dane,

There's been a change in the location for this year's drivers
school for the Windy City Chapter, and I know you'll love this one!
Instead of going to Blackhawk Farms, we'll be going up to Road
America in beautiful Elkhart Lake, Wisconsin.

The dates will remain the same, September 12 and 13. Lodging, as
always, will be available at Siebkens and Barefoot Bay in Elkhart
Lake, or at motels in Sheboygan or Fond du Lac. Remember, you must make your ow
reservations.

Driving directions to Elkhart Lake will be included with your
registration package, along with a map of the area.

See you soon,


Tom Malone

                                          Doc 1 Pg 1 Ln 2.83" Pos 5.6"
```

Type the new text. Note how adding text (or Fond du Lac, in the example) pushes existing text to the right.

Press ⬇ to reformat the text.

Adding Text by Typing Over Existing Text

```
August 18, 1988

Dear Jane,

There's been a change in the location for this year's drivers
school for the Windy City Chapter, and I know you'll love this one!
Instead of going to Blackhawk Farms, we'll be going up to Road
America in beautiful Elkhart Lake, Wisconsin.

The dates will remain the same, September 12 and 13. Lodging, as
always, will be available at Siebkens and Barefoot Bay in Elkhart
Lake, or at motels in Sheboygan or Fond du Lac. Remember, you must
make your own reservations.

Driving directions to Elkhart Lake will be included with your
registration package, along with a map of the area.

See you soon,


Tom Malone

                                          Doc 1 Pg 1 Ln 1.33" Pos 1.6"
```

Place the cursor where you want the new text to begin.

```
August 18, 1988

Dear Dane,

There's been a change in the location for this year's drivers
school for the Windy City Chapter, and I know you'll love this one!
Instead of going to Blackhawk Farms, we'll be going up to Road
America in beautiful Elkhart Lake, Wisconsin.

The dates will remain the same, September 12 and 13. Lodging, as
always, will be available at Siebkens and Barefoot Bay in Elkhart
Lake, or at motels in Sheboygan or Fond du Lac. Remember, you must
make your own reservations.

Driving directions to Elkhart Lake will be included with your
registration package, along with a map of the area.

See you soon,


Tom Malone

Typeover                                  Doc 1 Pg 1 Ln 1.33" Pos 1.5"
```

Press [Ins] to turn on Typeover mode.

Type the new text. For instance, you can type over the J in Jane to make the word Dane. Note that existing text is replaced with the new text.

Press [Ins] again to return to Insert mode.

55

Deleting Text

With WordPerfect, you can delete unwanted text of various lengths. For example, you can delete single characters, a word, a line, several lines, or an entire page. You also can delete blank lines.

Deleting Single Characters

To delete a character at the cursor position, you use the arrow keys to position the cursor under the character to be deleted. Then you press the Del key. The text that lies to the right of the deleted characters moves in to fill the gap.

To delete a character to the left of the cursor, you move the cursor so that it lies one character to the right of the character you want to delete. Then you press the Backspace key to erase the character to the left of the cursor. (On some keyboards, the Backspace key is marked with a single left arrow at the top of the keyboard.) When you use the Backspace key, any text to the right moves one character position to the left.

Keep in mind that both the Del and Backspace keys are repeat keys. If you hold down either key (rather than press it once), multiple characters are deleted.

Deleting Words

To delete a word at the cursor position, you position the cursor anywhere in the word to be deleted. Then you press Delete Word (Ctrl-Backspace).

To delete a word to the left of the cursor, you place the cursor in the blank space to the right of the word to be deleted. Then you can press Delete Word (Ctrl-Backspace); or you can press Home, and then press Backspace.

To delete a word to the right of the cursor, you place the cursor on the first character of the word to be deleted. Next, you press Home, and then you press the Del key.

Deleting Lines

To delete a single line of text or a portion of a line, you position the cursor under the character from where you want to start the deletion. Then you press Delete to End of Line (Ctrl-End).

To delete several lines at a time, you position the cursor under the character from where you want to start the deletion. Then you count the number of lines (following the cursor) you want to erase, and you press Esc (the Repeat key). The message n=8 appears on the status line. The default repeat value number is 8, but you can change that number to reflect the number of lines to be deleted. If the number of lines is more or less than 8, you type that number. Finally, you press Ctrl-End.

To delete a blank line, you move the cursor to the left margin at the beginning of the blank line. Then you press Del.

Deleting Pages

To delete an entire page of text or a portion of a page, you position the cursor under the character from where you want to start the deletion. Then you press Delete to End of Page (Ctrl-PgDn). WordPerfect prompts you to confirm that you want to delete the rest of the page. You can press Y to delete the text or N if you've changed your mind.

To delete several pages at once, you press Esc and enter the number of pages you want to delete. Then you press Ctrl-PgDn.

Deleting Text

Use a variety of methods to delete unwanted text.

Deleting Characters

```
August 18, 1988

Dear Dane,

There's been a change in the location for this year's drivers
school for the Windy City Chapter, and I know you'll love this one!
Instead of going to Blackhawk Farms, we'll be going up to Road
America in beautifull Elkhart Lake, Wisconsin.

The dates will remain the same, September 12 and 13. Lodging, as
always, will be available at Siebkens and Barefoot Bay in Elkhart
Lake, or at motels in Sheboygan or Fond du Lac. Remember, you must
make your own reservations.

Driving directions to Elkhart Lake will be included with your
registration package, along with a map of the area.

See you soon,


Tom Malone

                                        Doc 1 Pg 1 Ln 2.16" Pos 3.1"
```

To delete a character at the cursor position (the extra l in beautiful), use the arrow keys to position the cursor under the character to be deleted. Press the Del key.

To delete a character to the left of the cursor, move the cursor so that it lies one character to the right of the character you want to delete. Press the +Backspace key.

Deleting Words

To delete a word at the cursor position (the word beautiful), position the cursor anywhere in the word to be deleted.

Hold down Ctrl while you press +Backspace.

To delete a word to the right of the cursor, place the cursor on the first character of the word to be deleted.

Press Home, and then press Del.

```
August 18, 1988

Dear Dane,

There's been a change in the location for this year's drivers
school for the Windy City Chapter, and I know you'll love this one!
Instead of going to Blackhawk Farms, we'll be going up to Road
America in beautiful Elkhart Lake, Wisconsin.

The dates will remain the same, September 12 and 13. Lodging, as
always, will be available at Siebkens and Barefoot Bay in Elkhart
Lake, or at motels in Sheboygan or Fond du Lac. Remember, you must
make your own reservations.

Driving directions to Elkhart Lake will be included with your
registration package, along with a map of the area.

See you soon,


Tom Malone

                                        Doc 1 Pg 1 Ln 2.16" Pos 3"
```

To delete a word to the left of the cursor, place the cursor in the blank space to the right of the word to be deleted.

Hold down Ctrl while you press +Backspace.

Or

Press Home, and then press +Backspace.

Deleting Lines

```
August 18, 1988

Dear Dane,

There's been a change in the location for this year's drivers
school for the Windy City Chapter, and I know you'll love this one!
Instead of going to Blackhawk Farms, we'll be going up to Road
America in beautiful Elkhart Lake, Wisconsin.

The dates will remain the same, September 12 and 13. Lodging, as
always, will be available at Siebkens and Barefoot Bay in Elkhart
Lake, or at motels in Sheboygan or Fond du Lac. Remember, you must
make your own reservations.

Driving directions to Elkhart Lake will be included with your
registration package, along with a map of the area.

See you soon,


Tom Malone


                                           Doc 1 Pg 1 Ln 2.16" Pos 3"
```

Position the cursor where you want to begin deleting text.

To delete a single line, press Ctrl End.

To delete several lines at a time, position the cursor where you want to begin deleting text. Count the number of lines (following the cursor) you want to erase. Then press Esc. Enter the number of lines you want to delete. Press Ctrl End.

To delete blank lines, move the cursor to the left margin at the beginning of the blank line. Press Del.

Deleting Pages

```
August 18, 1988

Dear Dane,

There's been a change in the location for this year's drivers
school for the Windy City Chapter, and I know you'll love this one!
Instead of going to Blackhawk Farms, we'll be going up to Road
America in beautiful Elkhart Lake, Wisconsin.

The dates will remain the same, September 12 and 13. Lodging, as
always, will be available at Siebkens and Barefoot Bay in Elkhart
Lake, or at motels in Sheboygan or Fond du Lac. Remember, you must
make your own reservations.

Driving directions to Elkhart Lake will be included with your
registration package, along with a map of the area.

See you soon,


Tom Malone

Delete Remainder of page? (Y/N) No
```

To delete a page, position the cursor so that it lies under the character from where you want to begin deleting text. Press Ctrl PgDn.

Press Y to delete the text.

Or

Press N if you've changed your mind.

Using Reveal Codes

Many times when you press a key in WordPerfect, a *hidden code* is inserted into the text. The term hidden is used because you cannot see the code on-screen. By hiding the codes, WordPerfect keeps the document editing screen uncluttered.

These hidden codes, called *Reveal Codes*, tell WordPerfect when to execute tabs, margin settings, hard returns, indents, and so on. Some codes—such as the codes for math and columns—turn those features on and off. Other codes—such as the codes for bold, underline, and italic—work as a pair. The first code in a pair acts as a toggle switch to turn on the feature; the second code serves to turn off the feature. You can view the hidden codes in your document.

Displaying Hidden Codes

To see the hidden codes, you press Reveal Codes (Alt-F3, or F11 on the Enhanced Keyboard). The screen splits in half. The same text is displayed in both windows, but the text in the bottom half includes the hidden codes. The bar between screens displays the tab and margin settings for the line on which the cursor rests. Codes are highlighted and appear in brackets. You press Reveal Codes (Alt-F3, or F11) again to restore the normal screen.

Editing in Reveal Codes

Editing in Reveal Codes is a little different than editing in the document editing screen. The cursor in the upper window looks the same, but the cursor in the lower window is displayed as a highlight bar. When the cursor comes upon a hidden code (in the lower window), the cursor expands to cover the entire code.

Deleting Hidden Codes

You can delete hidden codes in the normal typing screen or in the Reveal Codes screen. Because you can see the codes in the Reveal Codes screen, deleting them with Reveal Codes is easier.

As you delete codes from the Reveal Codes screen, notice that the effect of your changes is reflected in the upper portion of the screen. In Reveal Codes mode, you can enter commands and text and immediately observe the position of any new hidden codes.

To delete codes, you first move the cursor to the place in your document where the code is likely to be located. Then you press Reveal Codes (Alt-F3, or F11). You use the arrow keys to position the cursor on the hidden code. Then you press Del to delete the hidden code. To return to the normal typing screen, you press Reveal Codes (Alt-F3, or F11) again.

Using Reveal Codes

Many times when you press a key in WordPerfect, a *hidden code* is inserted into the text. Hidden codes tell WordPerfect when to execute tabs, margin settings, hard returns, indents, and so on.

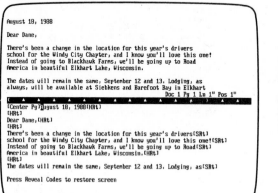

Displaying Hidden Codes

Press Alt F3 or F11 to display Reveal Codes.

The bar between the screens displays the tab and margin settings for the line on which the cursor rests. Note that the same text is displayed in both screens.

The cursor in the upper window looks the same, but in the lower window, the cursor is displayed as a highlight bar. When the cursor comes upon a code in the lower window, the cursor expands to cover the entire code.

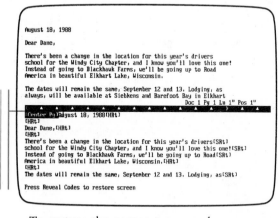

To restore the screen to normal, press Alt F3 or F11 again.

Deleting Hidden Codes

Delete hidden codes in the normal typing screen or in the Reveal Codes screen. Because you can see the codes in the Reveal Codes screen, deleting them with Reveal Codes is easier.

Move the cursor to the place in your document where the code is likely to be located.

Press Alt F3 or F11.

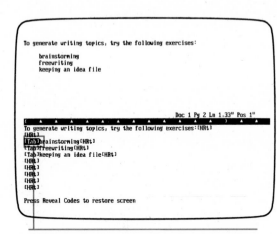

Use the arrow keys to position the cursor on the hidden code you want to delete. For instance, place the cursor on the [TAB] code.

Press Del to delete the hidden code.

Your text reflects any editing changes you make in Reveal Codes. Because you deleted the [TAB] code, the text in the example moves back to the left margin.

Using Both Document Windows

WordPerfect gives you two "sheets of paper" to work on at once if you choose to do so. The two document *windows* you can open are called Doc 1 and Doc 2. The status line tells you which window is the "active" work space. The cursor's position determines whether the window is active.

You can type in both windows and switch back and forth between them with ease. Initially, each window is the entire size of the screen. You can split the screen to look at two documents or at different parts of the same document at once.

Switching between Windows

To switch between document windows, you press Switch (Shift-F3). The status line displays Doc 2, and the second document window is displayed in a full screen. Although any text in the first window is not visible now, the text is not lost. To display the Doc 1 window, you press Switch (Shift-F3) again.

Splitting the Screen

You can split the screen so that WordPerfect's 24-line display is split between 2 windows. When you display 2 documents at once, WordPerfect reserves 2 lines for its own use. These lines are used by an additional status line and a ruler line. For example, if you display 12 lines in Doc 1, only 10 lines are displayed in Doc 2; the other 2 lines are taken up by the additional status line and the ruler line. When 2 windows are displayed on-screen, the triangles in the ruler line point to the active window.

Before you split the screen, decide how many lines you want to display in the current document. The other document will take what is left, less two lines. For example, sometimes you may want to split the screen in half. Other times, you may prefer to allow two-thirds of the screen for the primary document, such as a letter or report, and the rest of the screen for supporting material, such as notes.

To split the screen, you press Screen (Ctrl-F3). From the displayed menu, you select Window (1). In response to the prompt for the number of lines in the window, you type the number of lines you want in the first window and press Enter. For example, to split the screen in half, you type **11**. The screen is split in half, with WordPerfect's tab ruler line displayed across the middle.

Caution: If the same document is open in two windows, make all your changes in only one of the windows. Then be sure to save only the document in the window in which you've made changes. Otherwise, you may lose edits.

Resizing the Window to a Full-Screen Display

When you want to resize the window to a full-screen display, you press Screen (Ctrl-F3). From the menu, you then select Window. At the prompt asking for the number of lines in the window, you type **24** and press Enter. The window is returned to a full-screen display.

Using Both Document Windows

Use both of WordPerfect's document windows: Doc 1 and
Doc 2. Switch between full-screen displays of each
window, or divide the screen to display two different
documents or different parts of the same document.

Switching between Windows

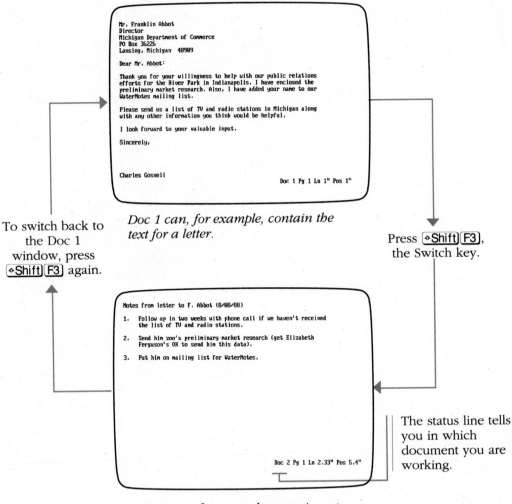

Doc 1 can, for example, contain the text for a letter.

Press ⚿Shift F3,
the Switch key.

To switch back to
the Doc 1
window, press
⚿Shift F3 again.

The status line tells
you in which
document you are
working.

*Doc 2 can, for example, contain notes
for the letter.*

Splitting the Screen

Press Ctrl F3, the Screen key.

Press 1 to choose the Window option.

Type the number of lines you want in the first window, and then press Enter.

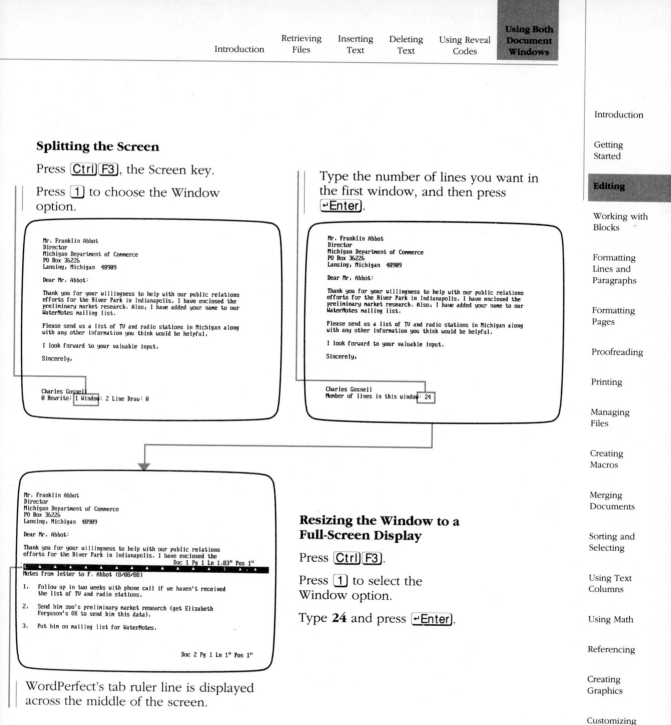

WordPerfect's tab ruler line is displayed across the middle of the screen.

Resizing the Window to a Full-Screen Display

Press Ctrl F3.

Press 1 to select the Window option.

Type **24** and press Enter.

3 *Working with Blocks*

The most powerful and flexible command in WordPerfect is the Block command (Alt-F4, or F12 on the Enhanced Keyboard). You use this command with other WordPerfect features to block (identify) specific segments of text so that only the blocked text is affected by the selected feature.

Key Terms

This chapter introduces the following key terms:

Block   A segment of text marked (identified) as a unit so that only that segment is affected by a selected WordPerfect function. A block can be a single character, a single word, a phrase, a sentence, a paragraph, a page, a column, a rectangle of text of any size, or an entire document.

Move   An operation that moves a block of text from one location to a new location. The text appears only in the new location.

Copy   An operation that duplicates a block of text. The text appears in the original location and in the location to which you copy it.

Tasks Covered in This Chapter

In this chapter, you learn to perform the following tasks:

- Define a block of text
- Move or copy a block of text to any location within your document
- Delete any size block of text
- Save a block of text
- Print a block of text from within your document
- Append a block of text
- Change the text in a block from uppercase to lowercase (or vice versa)
- Center a block of text
- Underline and boldface a block of text
- Work with rectangles of text

Highlighting Text

Before you do anything to a block of text, you must tell WordPerfect exactly what portion of the text you want affected. To do so, you first use the Block (Alt-F4, or F12) command to define the block of text. Then you can perform any number of operations on the defined block.

Defining a Block

To define a block of text, you first move the cursor to the character that begins the block of text you want to define. Then you press Block (Alt-F4, or F12). The Block on message flashes in the lower left corner of your screen. You move the cursor until the last character in the block of text is highlighted.

Keys for Defining a Block

As you define text, you can use the cursor-arrow, PgDn, PgUp, and GoTo (Ctrl-Home) keys to move the cursor. To highlight an entire line, for example, you can press the End key; to highlight from the cursor to the bottom of the current screen, you can press Screen Down (+); and to highlight multiple pages, you can press Ctrl-Home (GoTo). You can move the cursor either forward or backward to define text. The highlighting moves with the cursor.

Shortcuts for Defining a Block

You can use shortcuts to define text. For example, to define a sentence, you can turn on Block at the beginning of the sentence, and then type a period (.). The highlighting extends to the period at the end of the sentence. To define a paragraph, you turn on Block and press Enter. The highlighting extends to the next hard return in your text.

Performing a Block Operation

After a block is highlighted, you press the key that invokes the feature you plan to use on the highlighted block of text. The feature you select executes only on the highlighted block of text. If the feature you've selected will not work with the Block command, WordPerfect signals you with a beep. (Although the Block function is flexible, it can't be used with all WordPerfect features.)

Some commands, such as Block Print or Block Delete, require confirmation. If a Y/N prompt appears at the lower left of the screen, you can press Y for Yes or N for No.

Rehighlighting a Block

Block highlighting disappears automatically as soon as the task (such as move, copy, or bold) is completed. To rehighlight the block for use with another feature, or to restore highlighting if you accidentally turn off the Block feature, you press Block (Alt-F4, or F12). Next, you press GoTo (Ctrl-Home) to activate the GoTo command. Finally, you press GoTo (Ctrl-Home) again to return to the beginning of the block.

Backing Out of a Block Operation

To back out of the feature while the block is highlighted, you either press Cancel (F1) or press Block (Alt-F4, or F12) to turn off the Block command. The Block on message disappears, and the text no longer appears highlighted. The cursor remains at the end of the block (where it was when you finished highlighting).

Highlighting Text

Highlighting text is the first step in any block operation. After you define a block, you can go on to perform any number of operations on the highlighted block.

Defining a Block

When you have trouble determining a sharp focus for a document--
when you are uncertain what you want to say--consider trying a
semistructured writing exercise known as "brainstorming."

When you brainstorm a writing assignment on-screen, you record your
ideas in list form as they occur to you. When you brainstorm, you
don't worry about typos, spelling errors, or style. You turn off
the inclination to hone each sentence before you move on to the
next one. You can handle those matters later. Your goal is, rather,
to generate as many ideas as possible about the topic, the purpose,
or the audience.

Block on   Doc 1 Pg 1 Ln 1" Pos 1"

When you have trouble determining a sharp focus for a document--
when you are uncertain what you want to say--consider trying a
semistructured writing exercise known as "brainstorming."

When you brainstorm a writing assignment on-screen, you record your
ideas in list form as they occur to you. When you brainstorm, you
don't worry about typos, spelling errors, or style. You turn off
the inclination to hone each sentence before you move on to the
next one. You can handle those matters later. Your goal is, rather,
to generate as many ideas as possible about the topic, the purpose,
or the audience.

Block on   Doc 1 Pg 1 Ln 1.33" Pos 3.7"

Move the cursor to the character that begins the block of text you want to define.

Press Alt F4 or F12 to begin the Block command.

Move the cursor to the right until the last character in the block of text is highlighted.

Use the cursor-arrow, PgDn, PgUp, and Ctrl Home keys to move the cursor. You can move the cursor either forward or backward to define the block. The highlighting moves with the cursor.

Performing a Block Operation

After a block is highlighted, you can perform an operation on the defined block.

Press the key that invokes the feature you plan to use on the highlighted block of text.

If the feature you've selected will not work with the Block command, WordPerfect signals you with a beep.

Rehighlighting a Block

Block highlighting disappears automatically as soon as you complete the task (such as move, copy, or bold). You can rehighlight the block for use with another feature or restore highlighting if you accidentally turn off the Block feature.

Press Alt F4 or F12.

Press Ctrl Home, the GoTo command.

Press Ctrl Home again to return to the beginning of the block.

Backing Out of a Block Operation

Press F1, the Cancel key.

Or

Press Alt F4 or F12 to turn off Block.

The Block on message disappears, and the text no longer appears highlighted. The cursor remains at the end of the block (where it was when you finished highlighting).

Moving, Copying, Deleting, and Restoring

Moving and Copying

Moving a block of text is a "cut-and-paste" operation—except that you don't fuss with scissors, paper, paste, and tape. Using WordPerfect, you simply define the block, cut it from its current location, and paste it to a new location in your document. The block is erased from its previous location and appears in the new location. The new location can even be in another document.

When you copy a block of text, WordPerfect places into memory a duplicate of the block you've defined. You then can retrieve this block from memory and insert the block at another location in your document or in another document.

If the block you want to move or copy is a sentence, paragraph, or page, WordPerfect highlights the block for you. Instead of using the Block command, you press Move (Ctrl-F4); select Sentence (1), Paragraph (2), or Page (3); select Move (1) or Copy (2); move the cursor to the new position; and press Enter.

Moving a Block

To move a block of text, you first use Block (Alt-F4, or F12) to define the block of text you want to move. Then you press Move (Ctrl-F4) to display the Move menu. From this menu, you select Block (1). From the next menu, you select Move (1). WordPerfect cuts the defined block, and it disappears from the screen. Don't worry; the block is stored in temporary memory. Next, you move the cursor to the location in your document where you want the cut block to appear. Then you press Enter to insert the block at the new location.

Copying a Block

To copy a block of text, you use the Block command (Alt-F4, or F12) with the Move command (Ctrl-F4). First you use Block (Alt-F4, or F12) to define the block to be copied. Then you press Move (Ctrl-F4) to display the Move menu. From this menu, you select Block (1). Then you select Copy (2). Next, you move the cursor to the location in your document where you want the duplicate text to appear. Then you press Enter.

You can retrieve the copied block as many times as you want. Usually, the Copy feature is used to repeat (without typing) standard blocks of text in lengthy documents, such as legal, technical, or sales documents.

To duplicate the same block of text and retrieve it again, you place the cursor in your document where you want the text to appear. Then you press Move (Ctrl-F4), select Retrieve (4), and then select Block (1).

Deleting a Block

In a few keystrokes, you can delete a sentence or three full pages of text. To delete a block of text, you first use Block (Alt-F4, or F12) to define the block to be deleted. Then you press the Del key or the Backspace key. When you are prompted to confirm the deletion, you press Y. (If you press N, you are returned to the highlighted text.) The block is deleted from your document.

Restoring Deleted Text

You can delete as many as three blocks and restore all of them using the Cancel (F1) feature.

To restore deleted text, you press Cancel (F1) to display the most recently deleted text. The Undelete menu appears. To restore the text you deleted most recently, you select Restore (1). To restore a previous deletion, you choose Previous Deletion (2). Then you can select Restore (1) to restore this text. Or, you can select Previous Deletion (2) to see the third deletion. You select Restore (1) to restore this third deletion.

Moving, Copying, Deleting, and Restoring

Moving and Copying a Block

```
When you have trouble determining a sharp focus for a document--
when you are uncertain what you want to say--consider trying a
semistructured writing exercise known as "brainstorming."

When you brainstorm a writing assignment on-screen, you record your
ideas in list form as they occur to you. When you brainstorm, you
don't worry about typos, spelling, or style. You turn off the
inclination to hone each sentence before you move on to the next
one. You can handle those matters later. Your goal is, rather, to
generate as many ideas as possible about the topic, the purpose,
or the audience.




Block on                               Doc 1 Pg 1 Ln 1.33" Pos 3.7"
```

Press [Alt][F4] or [F12] and highlight the block of text you want to move.

Press [Ctrl][F4] to display the Move menu.

```
When you have trouble determining a sharp focus for a document--
when you are uncertain what you want to say--consider trying a
semistructured writing exercise known as "brainstorming."

When you brainstorm a writing assignment on-screen, you record your
ideas in list form as they occur to you. When you brainstorm, you
don't worry about typos, spelling, or style. You turn off the
inclination to hone each sentence before you move on to the next
one. You can handle those matters later. Your goal is, rather, to
generate as many ideas as possible about the topic, the purpose,
or the audience.




Move: 1 Block; 2 Tabular Column; 3 Rectangle: 0
```

Press [1] to select Block.

```
When you have trouble determining a sharp focus for a document--
when you are uncertain what you want to say--consider trying a
semistructured writing exercise known as "brainstorming."

When you brainstorm a writing assignment on-screen, you record your
ideas in list form as they occur to you. When you brainstorm, you
don't worry about typos, spelling, or style. You turn off the
inclination to hone each sentence before you move on to the next
one. You can handle those matters later. Your goal is, rather, to
generate as many ideas as possible about the topic, the purpose,
or the audience.




1 Move: 2 Copy: 3 Delete; 4 Append: 0
```

Press [1] to select Move.

Or

Press [2] to select Copy.

Introduction   Highlighting
Text   **Moving, Copying,
Deleting, and
Restoring**   Saving, Printing,
and Appending   Enhancing   Working with
Rectangles

```
When you have trouble determining a sharp focus for a document--
when you are uncertain what you want to say--consider trying a
semistructured writing exercise known as "brainstorming."

When you brainstorm a writing assignment on-screen, you record your
ideas in list form as they occur to you. When you brainstorm, you
don't worry about typos, spelling, or style. You turn off the
inclination to hone each sentence before you move on to the next
one. You can handle those matters later. Your goal is, rather, to
generate as many ideas as possible about the topic, the purpose,
or the audience.
```
```
Move cursor; press Enter to retrieve.        Doc 1 Pg 1 Ln 1.33" Pos 6.7"
```

Move the cursor to the location in your document where you want the block to appear.

Press ⏎Enter to insert the block at the new location.

Moving a Block

```
When you brainstorm a writing assignment on-screen, you record your
ideas in list form as they occur to you. When you brainstorm, you
don't worry about typos, spelling, or style. You turn off the
inclination to hone each sentence before you move on to the next
one. You can handle those matters later. Your goal is, rather, to
generate as many ideas as possible about the topic, the purpose,
or the audience.

When you have trouble determining a sharp focus for a document--
when you are uncertain what you want to say--consider trying a
semistructured writing exercise known as "brainstorming."
```
```
                                   Doc 1 Pg 1 Ln 2.66" Pos 1"
```

When you move a block, the text is deleted from the original location and appears at the new location you specify.

Copying a Block

```
When you have trouble determining a sharp focus for a document--
when you are uncertain what you want to say--consider trying a
semistructured writing exercise known as "brainstorming."

When you brainstorm a writing assignment on-screen, you record your
ideas in list form as they occur to you. When you brainstorm, you
don't worry about typos, spelling, or style. You turn off the
inclination to hone each sentence before you move on to the next
one. You can handle those matters later. Your goal is, rather, to
generate as many ideas as possible about the topic, the purpose,
or the audience.

When you have trouble determining a sharp focus for a document--
when you are uncertain what you want to say--consider trying a
semistructured writing exercise known as "brainstorming."
```
```
                                   Doc 1 Pg 1 Ln 3" Pos 1"
```

When you copy a block, the text appears both in the original location and in the new location you specify.

To duplicate the same block of text and retrieve it again, place the cursor in your document where you want the text to appear. Press Ctrl F4, press 4 for Retrieve, and press 1 for Block.

Moving, Copying, Deleting, and Restoring

Deleting a Block

When you have trouble determining a sharp focus for a document—
when you are uncertain what you want to say—consider trying a
semistructured writing exercise known as "brainstorming."

When you brainstorm a writing assignment on-screen, you record your
ideas in list form as they occur to you. When you brainstorm, you
don't worry about typos, spelling, or style. You turn off the
inclination to hone each sentence before you move on to the next
one. You can handle those matters later. Your goal is, rather, to
generate as many ideas as possible about the topic, the purpose,
or the audience.

Block on   Doc 1 Pg 1 Ln 1.33" Pos

Press Alt F4 or F12 and highlight the block you want to delete.

Press Del.

Or

Press +Backspace.

When you have trouble determining a sharp focus for a document—
when you are uncertain what you want to say—consider trying a
semistructured writing exercise known as "brainstorming."

When you brainstorm a writing assignment on-screen, you record your
ideas in list form as they occur to you. When you brainstorm, you
don't worry about typos, spelling, or style. You turn off the
inclination to hone each sentence before you move on to the next
one. You can handle those matters later. Your goal is, rather, to
generate as many ideas as possible about the topic, the purpose,
or the audience.

Delete Block? (Y/N) No

Press Y.

When you brainstorm a writing assignment on-screen, you record your
ideas in list form as they occur to you. When you brainstorm, you
don't worry about typos, spelling, or style. You turn off the
inclination to hone each sentence before you move on to the next
one. You can handle those matters later. Your goal is, rather, to
generate as many ideas as possible about the topic, the purpose,
or the audience.

Doc 1 Pg 1 Ln 1" Pos 1"

The block is deleted from your document.

78

Restoring Deleted Text

Delete as many as three blocks and restore them
all using the Cancel key (F1).

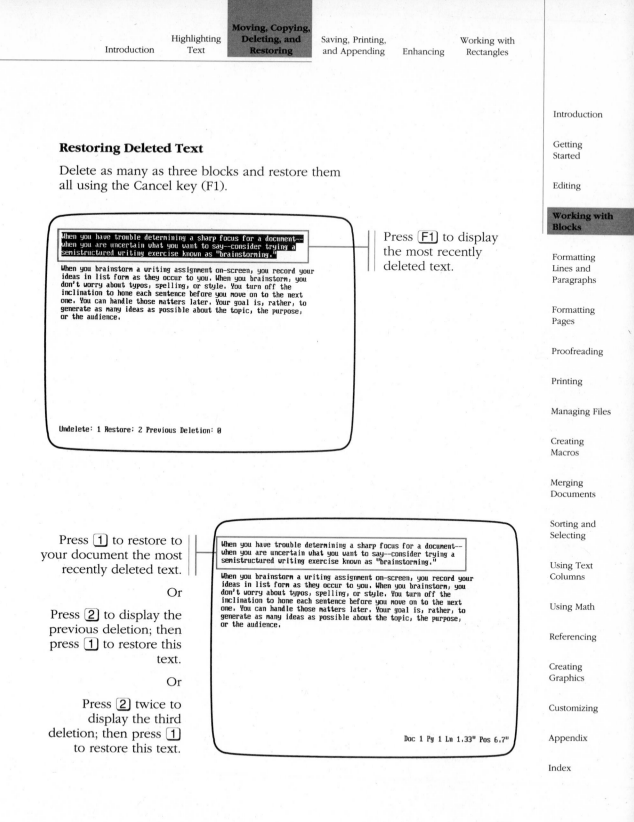

Press F1 to display
the most recently
deleted text.

Press 1 to restore to
your document the most
recently deleted text.

Or

Press 2 to display the
previous deletion; then
press 1 to restore this
text.

Or

Press 2 twice to
display the third
deletion; then press 1
to restore this text.

Saving, Printing, and Appending

Three useful functions for manipulating blocks of text in WordPerfect are Block Save, Block Print, and Block Append.

Block Save

When you must type the same block of text in one document several times, WordPerfect's Block Save function helps reduce the amount of work. With Block Save, you define the block of text you plan to use frequently, and then you save the block to a separate file. Block Save enables you to build a timesaving library of frequently used blocks of text. You can even build an entire document from these files.

To save a block of text, you first must define the block you want to save. Use Block (Alt-F4, or F12) to define the block. Then you press Save (F10). When WordPerfect prompts you to enter a block name, you type the name of the file in which you want to save the block and press Enter.

Select a file name that clearly identifies the block you are saving. Be sure to include a drive letter and path name before the file name if you want to save the block to a directory other than the current directory.

Block Print

Sometimes you may want to print only a single block of text from a document—perhaps a page that lists sales quotas or a list of new personnel. Use the Block Print command to print part of your document.

Introduction

Highlighting
Text

Moving, Copying,
Deleting, and
Restoring

**Saving, Printing,
and Appending**

Enhancing

Working with
Rectangles

To print a block of text, you first must define the block you want to print. Use Block (Alt-F4, or F12) to define the block. Then you press Print (Shift-F7). In response to the prompt to confirm printing, you press Y for Yes.

Block Append

WordPerfect provides a simple way to add text to one document while you are working on another. With the Block Append feature, you can add a paragraph from your on-screen document to the end of another file.

To append a block of text, you first must define the block you want to append. Use Block (Alt-F4, or F12) to define the block. Then you press Move (Ctrl-F4). From the Move menu, you select Block (1). Finally, from the next menu, you select Append (4).

When WordPerfect displays the message Append to:, you enter the file name of the document to which you want to append the block. The block remains in your current document and is appended to the end of your other document.

Saving, Printing, and Appending

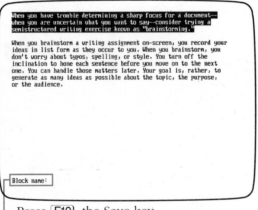

Saving or Printing a Block

To save or print a block, highlight it with $\boxed{\text{Alt}}$ $\boxed{\text{F4}}$ or $\boxed{\text{F12}}$.

Saving a Block

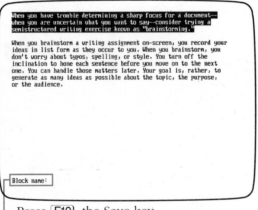

Press $\boxed{\text{F10}}$, the Save key.

Type the name of the file in which you want to save the block.

Select a file name that clearly identifies the block you are saving. Be sure to include a drive letter and path name before the file name if you want to save the block to a directory other than the current directory.

Press $\boxed{\text{←Enter}}$.

Printing a Block

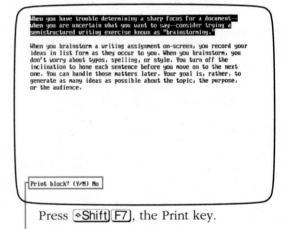

Press $\boxed{\text{⇧Shift}}$ $\boxed{\text{F7}}$, the Print key.

Press $\boxed{\text{Y}}$.

Appending a Block

Press [Alt][F4] or [F12] and highlight the text you want to append.

Press [Ctrl][F4], the Move key.

Press [1] to select Block.

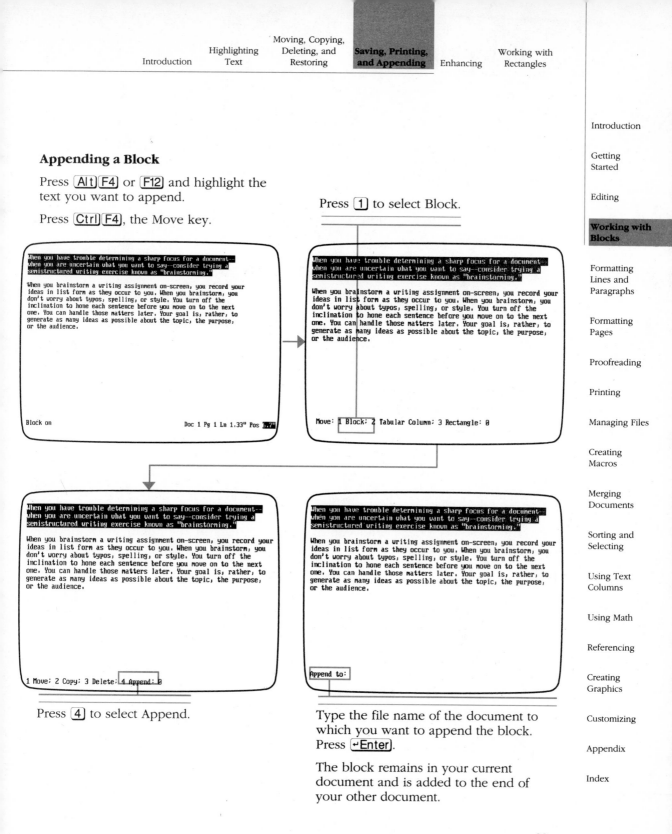

Press [4] to select Append.

Type the file name of the document to which you want to append the block. Press [↵Enter].

The block remains in your current document and is added to the end of your other document.

83

Enhancing

WordPerfect offers a number of ways to add visual impact to your text. One way you can create a dramatic special effect is to print a block of text in all uppercase letters (or all lowercase letters). Other ways you can call attention to a section of text are centering, boldfacing, and underlining.

Changing Upper- and Lowercase

WordPerfect can change whole words, sentences, paragraphs, or documents to upper- or lowercase automatically. This feature is useful when, for example, you discover that you've typed a section of text with Caps Lock turned on.

To change a section of text to upper- or lowercase letters, you first need to define the block. You position the cursor at the beginning of the section of text to be changed; then you press Block (Alt-F4, or F12). The Block on indicator appears on-screen. You move the cursor to the end of the text you want to change. The block is now defined.

To change the case of the letters in the block, you press Switch (Shift-F3). From the Switch menu, you can choose either Uppercase (1) or Lowercase (2) letters. After you make your selection, the highlighted text changes case, and the Switch menu disappears.

WordPerfect recognizes the first word of a sentence and the pronoun "I." These letters, therefore, remain capitalized when you change a block of text to lowercase. To ensure that WordPerfect recognizes that the block is a sentence, include the previous sentence's ending punctuation when you define your block of text.

Centering a Block between the Left and Right Margins

To center a block of text between the left and right margins, you first define the block of text you want to center. Use Block (Alt-F4, or F12)

Introduction

Highlighting
Text

Moving, Copying,
Deleting, and
Restoring

Saving, Printing,
and Appending

Enhancing

Working with
Rectangles

to define the block. Next, you press Center (Shift-F6). At the prompt asking you to confirm centering, press Y for Yes. The block is centered between the left and right margins.

If you think that you might want to restore the block to left-justified text, save a copy before centering. This process eliminates the need to delete the centering codes manually from each line.

If the block contains full lines in paragraph form, not much blank space is left between the margins for centering. As a result, the effect of centering may not be readily apparent. To correct this problem, shorten the individual lines by ending them with a hard return (press the Enter key); then center the text.

Boldfacing or Underlining a Block

To boldface or underline a block of text you have already typed, you first define the block of text you want to boldface or underline. Use Block (Alt-F4, or F12) to define the block. Next, you press Bold (F6) to turn on the Bold feature, or you press Underline (F8) to turn on the Underline feature.

If you want the block to be both boldfaced and underlined, you highlight the block again by pressing Block (Alt-F4, or F12). Then you press GoTo (Ctrl-Home) twice. Finally, you press Bold (F6) or Underline (F8), depending on which feature you used the first time.

Boldfaced text generally appears in a brighter intensity on-screen. Underlined text may appear with a fainter intensity, with an actual underline, or in reverse video. The display depends on the type of monitor you are using. A color monitor may show boldfaced and underlined text in colors different from the regular text. (For instructions on changing the way WordPerfect displays these features on your monitor, see Chapter 16, "Customizing.")

Enhancing

Changing Upper- and Lowercase

Press [Alt][F4] or [F12] and highlight the text you want to change.

Press [⇧Shift][F3], the Switch key.

Press [1] to change to uppercase letters.

Or

Press [2] to change to lowercase letters.

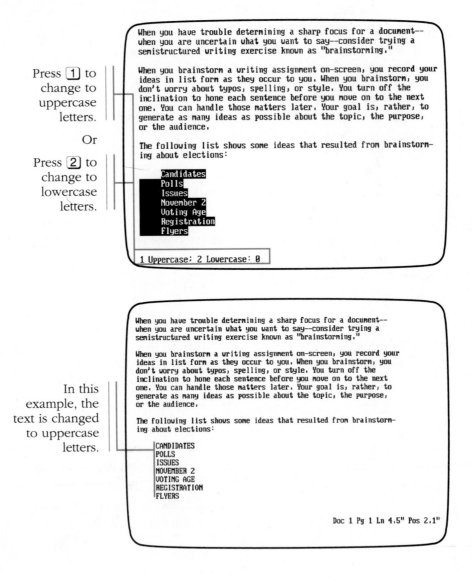

In this example, the text is changed to uppercase letters.

Centering a Block

Press Alt F4 or F12 and highlight the block of text you want to center.

Press ⬆Shift F6, the Center key.

```
When you have trouble determining a sharp focus for a document--
when you are uncertain what you want to say--consider trying a
semistructured writing exercise known as "brainstorming."

When you brainstorm a writing assignment on-screen, you record your
ideas in list form as they occur to you. When you brainstorm, you
don't worry about typos, spelling, or style. You turn off the
inclination to hone each sentence before you move on to the next
one. You can handle those matters later. Your goal is, rather, to
generate as many ideas as possible about the topic, the purpose,
or the audience.

The following list shows some ideas that resulted from brainstorm-
ing about elections:

     CANDIDATES
     POLLS
     ISSUES
     NOVEMBER 2
     VOTING AGE
     REGISTRATION
     FLYERS

[Cntr]? (Y/N) No
```

Press Y to center the block.

```
When you have trouble determining a sharp focus for a document--
when you are uncertain what you want to say--consider trying a
semistructured writing exercise known as "brainstorming."

When you brainstorm a writing assignment on-screen, you record your
ideas in list form as they occur to you. When you brainstorm, you
don't worry about typos, spelling, or style. You turn off the
inclination to hone each sentence before you move on to the next
one. You can handle those matters later. Your goal is, rather, to
generate as many ideas as possible about the topic, the purpose,
or the audience.

The following list shows some ideas that resulted from brainstorm-
ing about elections:

          CANDIDATES
            POLLS
            ISSUES
          NOVEMBER 2
          VOTING AGE
         REGISTRATION
            FLYERS

                              Doc 1 Pg 1 Ln 4.66" Pos 1"
```

The block is centered between the left and right margins.

Boldfacing or Underlining a Block

Press Alt F4 or F12 and highlight the block of text you want to boldface or underline.

Press F6 to turn on Bold.

Or

Press F8 to turn on Underline.

If you want the block to be both boldfaced and underlined, highlight the block again by pressing Alt F4 or F12, and then press Ctrl Home twice. Press F6 or F8, depending on which feature you used the first time.

87

Working with Rectangles

In WordPerfect, you can move either a grammatical block of text, such as a sentence or paragraph, or you can move any text that falls within a defined rectangular block. Being able to move or copy lines, sentences, paragraphs, and other grammatical blocks of text is a practical and useful function for editing text. But being able to move a block of text defined not as contiguous words, but simply as a rectangle of text, opens up a whole new chapter of creative possibilities. For example, you can move or copy a single column of text or numbers from a table with WordPerfect's Move Rectangle command.

To move or copy a rectangular block, you first use the Block (Alt-F4, or F12) command to highlight the text. Then you use the Move Rectangle command to move or copy the block. You can retrieve the block within the current document or use Switch (Shift-F3) to retrieve the text into a different document.

When you retrieve a rectangle, be aware of how it will be integrated into the current page. If the page is empty, WordPerfect places the rectangle on the page with a hard return at the end of each line. If text is currently in the position where you retrieve the rectangle, the retrieved text is woven into the existing text, producing unexpected results.

Moving or Copying a Rectangle

When you move a column, you can move tab stops along with the text or numbers. If you do, the tab stops are included in the new location and are deleted from the previous location. Unexpected results may occur. To see whether you are including tab stops in the block, use Reveal Codes (Alt-F3, or F11) during the Block operation.

To move or copy a rectangle, you first define the block you want to move or copy. You position the cursor at the top left corner of the text you want to move as a rectangle, press Block (Alt-F4, or F12), and then move the cursor to the bottom right corner of the rectangle. The text is highlighted all the way across the page, as usual.

Next, you need to define the rectangle as the area between where the cursor was when you pressed Block (Alt-F4, or F12) and where it is now. Text to the right will be excluded. You press Move (Ctrl-F4) and select Rectangle (3). Only the rectangle is highlighted.

After you have highlighted the rectangle, you can choose either Move (1) to move the rectangle or Copy (2) to copy the rectangle. Then you move the cursor to where you want to retrieve the rectangle and press Enter.

Deleting a Rectangle

You also can delete a rectangle of text. You may, for example, want to delete a whole column of numbers from a table.

To delete a rectangle, you first define the block by positioning the cursor at the top left corner of the text you want to delete as a rectangle, pressing Block (Alt-F4, or F12), and moving the cursor to the bottom right corner of the rectangle.

To define the rectangle as the area between where the cursor was when you pressed Block (Alt-F4, or F12) and where it is now, you press Move (Ctrl-F4) and select Rectangle (3).

After the rectangle is highlighted, you select Delete (3) to delete the rectangle.

Working with Rectangles

Use WordPerfect's Move Rectangle command to move, copy, or delete a rectangular section of text—a single column of text or numbers from a table, for example.

```
                    Election Poll

Block      % Decided    % Undecided   Not Home   Voting Site

Rosslyn       33            42           25       High School
Primrose      29            31           40       Field House
Kingsley      49            36           15       High School
Haverford     37            23           40       High School




Block on                              Doc 1 Pg 1 Ln 7.5" Pos 7.6"
```

Moving, Copying, or Deleting a Rectangle

Position the cursor at the top left corner of the text you want to move as a rectangle.

Press Alt F4 or F12.

Move the cursor to the bottom right corner of the rectangle.

Press Ctrl F4, the Move key.

```
                    Election Poll

Block      % Decided    % Undecided   Not Home   Voting Site

Rosslyn       33            42           25       High School
Primrose      29            31           40       Field House
Kingsley      49            36           15       High School
Haverford     37            23           40       High School




Move: 1 Block; 2 Tabular Column; 3 Rectangle: 0
```

Press 3 for Rectangle.

```
                    Election Poll

Block      % Decided    % Undecided   Not Home   Voting Site

Rosslyn       33            42           25       High School
Primrose      29            31           40       Field House
Kingsley      49            36           15       High School
Haverford     37            23           40       High School




1 Move; 2 Copy; 3 Delete; 4 Append: 0
```

Only the rectangle is highlighted; text to the right is now excluded.

Introduction

Highlighting
Text

Moving, Copying,
Deleting, and
Restoring

Saving, Printing,
and Appending

Enhancing

**Working with
Rectangles**

Move or Copy

Press ⬚1 to move the rectangle.

Or

Press ⬚2 to copy the rectangle.

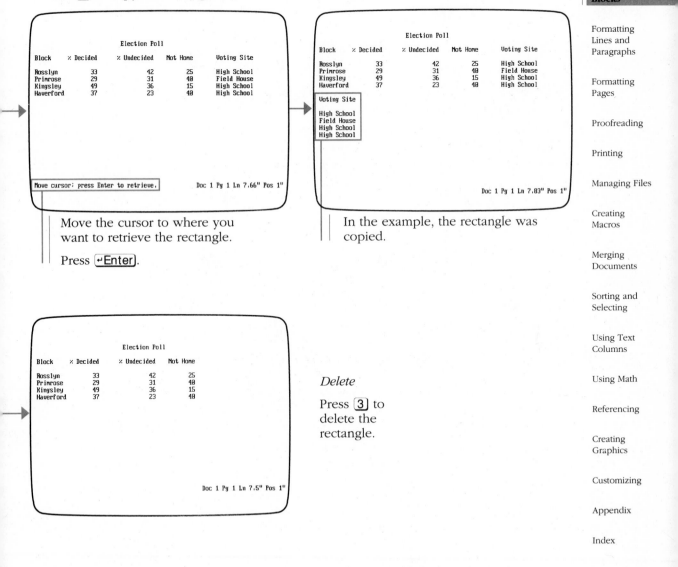

Move the cursor to where you want to retrieve the rectangle.

Press ⬚Enter.

In the example, the rectangle was copied.

Delete

Press ⬚3 to delete the rectangle.

4 Formatting Lines and Paragraphs

WordPerfect presets all initial or default settings for margins, tabs, and other basic features. If these settings do not fit your needs, you either can change the settings temporarily for the document on which you are working, or you can change the settings permanently with the Setup menu (Shift-F1). This chapter tells you how to change the settings temporarily for the current document only. For information on changing the settings permanently, see Chapter 16, "Customizing."

▼

Key Terms

This chapter introduces the following key terms:

Initial font	The font in which text is normally printed, also called default base font or current font. Other font sizes and appearances are usually variations of the initial font.
Alignment character	The character on which you align numbers or text. In WordPerfect, you can choose any alignment character you want. The decimal point, comma, percent sign, dollar sign, and equal sign are commonly used alignment characters.

Hyphenation zone   A preset zone that determines whether a word should be hyphenated or wrapped to the next line. The two parts of the hyphenation zone, the left and right zones, are separated by the right margin.

Line height   The vertical distance between the base of a line of text and the base of the line of text above or below. Printers call this distance leading.

▲

Tasks Covered in This Chapter

This chapter discusses the formatting techniques that apply to lines and paragraphs. The next chapter discusses formatting of pages. In this chapter, you learn to perform the following formatting tasks:

- Change left and right margins
- Change units of measurement
- Enhance text by boldfacing it, underlining it, or changing the font attributes
- Set tab stops
- Indent text
- Use Tab Align
- Make text flush right
- Center text
- Justify text
- Use hyphenation
- Change line height and line spacing

Changing Left and Right Margins

WordPerfect's default margins are one inch for the left and one inch for the right—appropriate margins for 8 1/2-by-11-inch paper. WordPerfect 5 measures margins from the right and left edges of the paper or from the perforation on pin-feed paper. You can change the margins temporarily (for the current document only) or permanently (for all future documents). You also can change the units that WordPerfect uses to measure settings such as margins.

If you want to change the margins, simply measure your stationery or paper and decide how many inches of white space you want as margins. Because measuring in rows and columns can be confusing, set margins in inches.

Changing Left and Right Margins Temporarily

To change the margin settings temporarily, you first place the cursor at the left margin of the line where you want the new margin setting to begin. If you want to change the margins for an entire document, go to the beginning of the document before setting the margins (press Home, Home, up arrow). After you place your cursor, you press Format (Shift-F8) to display the Format menu. You next select Line (1) to display the Format: Line menu. From this menu, you select Margins (7). You type a value for the right margin and press Enter. Then you type a value for the left margin and press Enter. Finally, you press Exit (F7) to return to your document. New margin settings override previous settings.

If you change your mind about the new margin settings, pressing Cancel (F1) won't cancel the new settings. You can use Reveal Codes (Alt-F3, or F11) to display the [L/R Mar:] code and then delete it.

Changing Left and Right Margins Permanently

If you only occasionally produce a document with different margins (or other format options), you can change the settings for individual documents. You may, however, always use different settings—3/4-inch margins, for example. In this case, you can change the margins permanently with Setup (Shift-F1). You can change many initial settings permanently with Setup (Shift-F1). See Chapter 16, "Customizing," for a complete list.

To change your margins permanently for all future documents, you press Setup (Shift-F1) to display the Setup menu. From this menu, you choose Initial Settings (5). Then you select Initial Codes (4) and press Format (Shift-F8). From this point, you follow the same steps you followed to change the margins temporarily: you select Line (1), select Margins (7), and type new left and right margins. You press Exit (F7) three times to return to your document.

Changing Units of Measurement

The default unit of measurement in WordPerfect is inches. If you prefer, you can change this measurement to centimeters, points, or units (lines and columns). You can change the unit of measurement for the settings you enter for menu selections such as left and right margins, tabs, and so on, and you can change the unit of measurement that appears in the status line.

To change the default unit of measurement, you press Setup (Shift-F1). From the Setup menu, you choose Units of Measure (8). You choose Display and Entry of Numbers for Margins, Tabs, etc. (1) and select a new unit to use for menu selections. You choose Status Line Display (2) and select a new unit to use in the status line. Finally, you press Exit (F7) to return to your document.

Changing Left and Right Margins

Changing Left and Right Margins

You can change the settings for left and right margins either temporarily for the current document or permanently for all future documents.

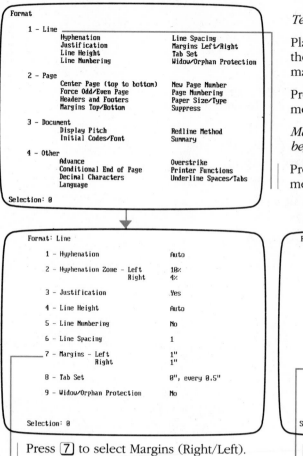

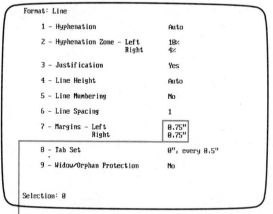

Temporarily

Place the cursor at the left margin of the line where you want the new margin setting to begin.

Press ⬆Shift F8 to display the Format menu.

Many of WordPerfect's formatting tasks begin at this Format menu.

Press 1 to display the Format: Line menu.

Press 7 to select Margins (Right/Left).

Type a value for the right margin and press ⏎Enter.

Type a value for the left margin and press ⏎Enter.

The margins have been changed to 3/4-inch (0.75").

Press F7 to return to your document.

Permanently

Press ⬆Shift F1, the Setup key.

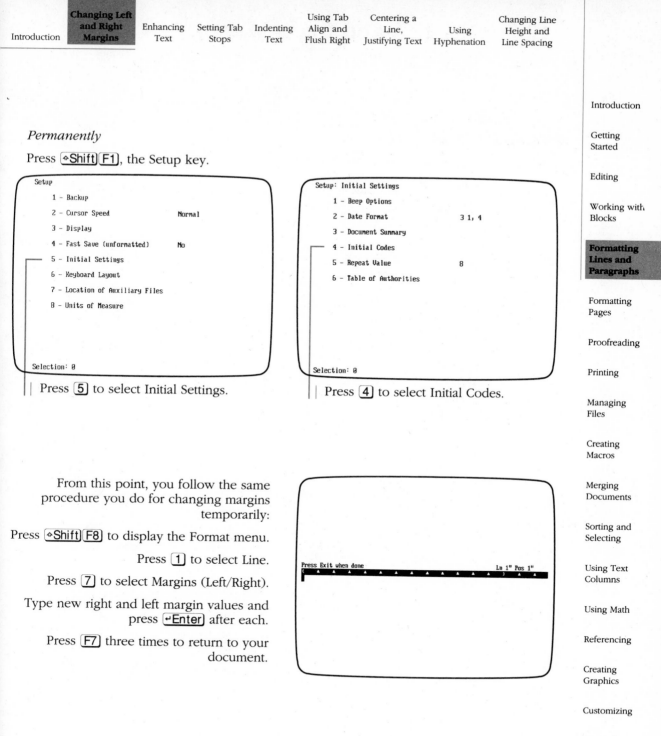

Press 5 to select Initial Settings.

Press 4 to select Initial Codes.

From this point, you follow the same procedure you do for changing margins temporarily:

Press ⬆Shift F8 to display the Format menu.

Press 1 to select Line.

Press 7 to select Margins (Left/Right).

Type new right and left margin values and press ↵Enter after each.

Press F7 three times to return to your document.

Changing Left and Right Margins

Changing Units of Measurement

The default unit of measurement in WordPerfect is inches. You can change this measurement to centimeters, points, or units (rows and columns). You can change the units you enter for settings, such as margins, and you can change the units that appear in the status line.

Press ⇧Shift F1 to display the Setup menu.

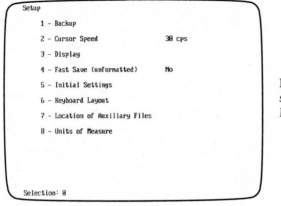

Press 8 to select Units of Measurement.

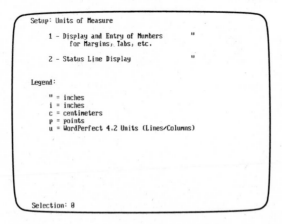

Press 1 to select Display and Entry of Numbers for Margins, Tabs, etc.

From the legend at the bottom of the menu, select a new measurement.

Press 2 to select Status Line Display.

Select a new measurement.

Press F7 to return to your document.

Inches

Doc 1 Pg 1 Ln 1" Pos 1"

The status line when inches is selected as the unit of measurement.

Centimeters

Doc 1 Pg 1 Ln 2.54c Pos 2.54c

The status line when centimeters is selected as the unit of measurement.

Points

Doc 1 Pg 1 Ln 1 Pos 10

The status line when points is selected as the unit of measurement.

Columns

Doc 1 Pg 1 Ln 72p Pos 72p

The status line when WordPerfect 4.2 units (lines/columns) is selected as the unit of measurement.

99

Enhancing Text

You can enhance your document by changing the size and appearance of your text. You accomplish some formatting tasks as you enter text simply by pressing the appropriate key, typing the text, and pressing the key again. For instance, from anywhere within your document, you can make text bold or underlined as you type. You apply other text enhancements by selecting them from the Font menu. For example, to make text italic, you choose the type style from the menu.

Enhancing Text from within the Document

A common text enhancement you make from within the document is to boldface or underline a portion of text. To enhance text you are about to type, use the procedures described here. To enhance text you've already typed, use the Block command as described in Chapter 3, "Working with Blocks."

To boldface a portion of text, you first press Bold (F6). Then you type the text. The text you type after pressing Bold (F6) appears brighter (or a different color) on-screen. The Pos number in the status line also changes in brightness or color. You press Bold (F6) again to turn off the Bold feature.

To underline text, you first press Underline (F8). Then you type the text. Press Underline (F8) again to turn off the Underline feature.

Both the Bold and Underline keys work as on/off toggle switches. You press the key once to turn on the feature; you press the key again to turn off the feature. If you press either Bold or Underline twice without entering text, the text you enter will not reflect either bold or underline.

Enhancing Text from the Font Menu

WordPerfect's Font feature lets you choose among the fonts (typefaces) available for use with your printer. The feature also controls size, color, and certain other variations of printed text, such as outline and shadow printing, subscripts, and superscripts.

When you installed your printer, you selected an *initial* font, also called the default base font or the current font. The *base* font is the font in which text is normally printed. Other font sizes and appearance options are usually variations of the base font. If 10-point Helvetica is the base font, boldface text will be printed in 10-point Helvetica Bold; italic text will be printed in 10-point Helvetica Italic; and so on.

Changing Font Attributes

Font *attributes* refer to the variations in a font's appearance that are available with your printer for a given base font: size, italic, boldface, shadow printing, outline, small caps, and so on. Remember that how the variations appear depends on your printer.

To change font attributes, you first press Font (Ctrl-F8). From the Font menu, you can choose either Size or Appearance. Then from the next menu, you select the attribute you want. The Size menu offers these selections: superscript, subscript, fine, small, large, very large, and extra large. From the Appearance menu, you can choose these attributes: bold, underline, double underline, italic, outline, shadow, small capitals, redline, and strikeout.

Enhancing Text

When you select options such as Fine, Large, Vry Large, and Ext Large on the Size menu, WordPerfect automatically chooses the correct line spacing (so that a large font won't overprint the preceding line, and fine print doesn't print with too much line spacing). If you later decide to print the same document with another printer or set of fonts, WordPerfect performs any required adjustments and sets the correct font, pitch, and line height automatically.

You can change an attribute of existing text by first blocking the text with Block (Alt-F4, or F12) and then selecting the new attribute using the procedure just described for changing font attributes.

Turning Off Attributes

To turn off attributes after typing your text, you can press Reveal Codes (Alt-F3, or F11) and find the attribute codes—for instance, [italc]. The attribute codes appear as paired codes. You press the right-arrow key to move the cursor past the attribute-off code.

When you have made a combination of attribute changes, you can turn off those attributes by pressing Font (Ctrl-F8) and selecting Normal (3). This selection cancels all size and appearance attributes.

Changing the Base Font

In addition to changing font attributes, you can change the base font the printer uses. You can change the base font permanently or temporarily. To change the base font permanently, you must use the Print menu (see Chapter 7, "Printing"). To change the base font temporarily for the current document only, you use the Font menu.

To change the base font temporarily, you first move the cursor to the point in your document where you want to change the base font. If you want to change the base font for the entire document, you position the cursor at the beginning of the document. Next, you press Font (Ctrl-F8) to display the Font menu.

From the Font menu, you select Base Font (4). WordPerfect displays a list of the fonts available for use with your printer. The fonts listed are the printer's built-in fonts, plus any fonts you've selected with the Cartridges and Fonts feature. You use the cursor keys to highlight the font you want. Then you choose Select (1) or press Enter to return to your document.

The screen display adjusts to reflect the number of characters that can be printed in a line with the new base font in the current margin settings. If you select a 6-pitch font, for example, the on-screen lines will be shorter than if you select a 10-pitch font. (Pitch indicates the number of characters per inch.)

Enhancing Text

Enhance your document by changing the size and appearance of your text. Accomplish some formatting tasks as you enter text simply by pressing the appropriate key, typing the text, and pressing the key again. Apply other text enhancements by selecting them from the Font menu.

Enhancing Text from within the Document

From within the document, you can boldface or underline a portion of text you are about to type.

To create boldface text, press **F6**, the Bold key. Then type the text, and press **F6** again to turn off Bold.

To create underlined text, press **F8**, the Underline key. Then type the text, and press **F8** again to turn off Underline.

Changing Font Attributes

Change the appearance of a base font by changing the font attributes.

Press **Ctrl****F8**, the Font key.

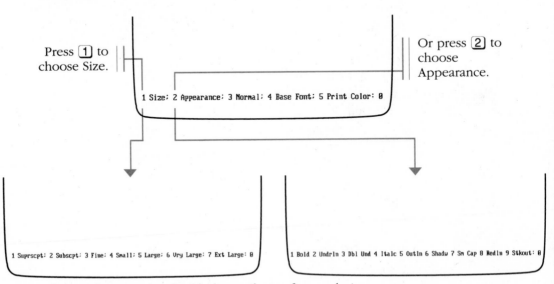

Press **1** to choose Size.

Or press **2** to choose Appearance.

1 Size; 2 Appearance; 3 Normal; 4 Base Font; 5 Print Color: 0

1 Suprscpt; 2 Subscpt; 3 Fine; 4 Small; 5 Large; 6 Vry Large; 7 Ext Large: 0

1 Bold 2 Undrln 3 Dbl Und 4 Italc 5 Outln 6 Shadw 7 Sm Cap 8 Redln 9 Stkout: 0

Press the number associated with the attribute of your choice.

Turning Off Attributes

After you have typed your text, you can turn off attributes using either of two methods.

Method 1

Press Alt F3 or F11. Find the attribute codes (they appear as paired codes). Press → to move the cursor past the attribute-off code.

```
Keeping an Idea File




                                        Doc 1 Pg 1 Ln 1" Pos 3"
▲▲▲▲▲▲▲▲▲▲▲▲▲▲▲▲▲▲▲▲▲▲
[ITALC]Keeping an Idea File[italc]


Press Reveal Codes to restore screen
```

Method 2

When you have made a combination of attribute changes, turn off those attributes by pressing Ctrl F8 and pressing 3 for Normal. This selection cancels all size and appearance attributes.

```
1 Size; 2 Appearance; 3 Normal; 4 Base Font; 5 Print Color; 0
```

Changing the Base Font

Use the following procedure to change the base font for the current document only.

Move the cursor to the point in your document where you want to change the base font.

Press Ctrl F8.

Press 4 to select Base Font.

Use the cursor keys to highlight the desired font.

```
Base Font

  Condensed
■ Courier
  Courier Double Wide
  Courier Double Wide Italic
  Courier Italic
  Courier PS
  Prestige Elite
  Prestige Elite Double Wide
  Prestige Elite Double Wide Italic
  Prestige Elite Italic




1 Select; N Name search; 1
```

Press 1 or ↵Enter to select the font and return to your document.

105

Setting Tab Stops

WordPerfect comes with tab stops predefined at one-half-inch intervals. Four basic kinds of tabs are available: left, center, right, and decimal. In addition, each type of tab can have a *dot leader* (a series of dots before the tab).

The following table explains the various types of tabs.

Tab Type	Operation
Left (L)	Indent to tab stop; text continues right. Left tab, the default, is the most commonly used tab stop.
Center (C)	Text is centered at tab stop. Center tab works much the same as Center (Shift-F6) except the center tab can force centering anywhere on the line, not just the center between margins. Use center tabs to create column headings.
Right (R)	After a right tab stop, text continues to the left. Right tab stop is similar to Flush Right (Alt-F6), except right tab stops can be placed anywhere on the line, not just at the right margin. Use right tabs to create headings over columns of numbers and dates.
Decimal (D)	After a decimal tab stop, text continues to the left until the alignment character is typed; then text continues to the right. Decimal tab stops are similar to Tab Align (Ctrl-F6), except you preset the alignment character as a tab stop. The default alignment character is a period (.), but you can change it to any character (: or $, for example). Use decimal tabs to line up columns of numbers.
Dot Leaders (.)	Any of the four tab types can be preceded by dots (periods) as leaders. Use dot leaders for long lists that require scanning from left to right (phone lists, for instance).

Displaying the Tab Ruler

To view current tab stop settings, you use the Window feature to display the tab ruler at the bottom of the screen. To display the tab ruler, you press Screen (Ctrl-F3). Then you select Window (1). WordPerfect displays a prompt that tells you the number of lines in the window. You type a number that is one less than the one displayed in the prompt. For example, if the prompt displays 24, you type **23** and press Enter.

The tab ruler at the bottom of the screen indicates the left and right margins with curly braces, { and }. Instead of braces, the tab ruler may display brackets, [and]. Braces indicate margins and tabs at the same position; brackets indicate margins alone. Tab stops are marked with triangles.

Erasing the Tab Ruler

To erase the tab ruler, you use the same procedure as you use to display the tab ruler, except you type a number one greater than the value displayed in the prompt.

Setting Tab Stops

Changing Tab Stops

You can change tab settings for all documents or for only the document on which you're currently working. When you change the settings for your current document only, the settings affect only the text from the point at which you make the change forward.

You can set tab stops one at a time, or you can specify the increment and set several tab stops at once. Similarly, you can delete one tab stop, all tab stops, or only the tab stops to the right of the cursor. You can set multiple tab stops across 8 1/2 inches of your page. If you print on wider paper, you can extend tab stops from 8 1/2 inches to 54 1/2 inches, but you must set those stops individually. You can set a maximum of 40 tab stops.

To change tab stops, you first display the tab ruler. You press Format (Shift-F8). Then you select Line (1) to display the Format: Line menu. Next, you select Tab Set (8) to display the tab ruler. After the tab ruler is displayed, you can delete or add single or multiple tab stops. After you have changed the tab stops, you press Exit (F7) twice to return to your document.

Deleting Tab Stops

To delete a single tab stop, you use the cursor keys to move to the tab you want to delete and press Del or Backspace to delete the tab. To delete all tab stops, you move the cursor to the left margin by pressing Home, Home, left-arrow; then you press Ctrl-End. To delete tab stops to the right of the cursor, you type the number (in inches) of the first tab stop you want to delete, press Enter, and then press Ctrl-End.

Adding Tab Stops

To add a single tab stop, you use the cursor keys to move to the position where you want a tab stop and press the appropriate tab type: L to add a left tab, C to add a center tab, R to add a right tab, or D to add a decimal tab. To add a dot leader, you press . (period). Or, type the position you want to place the tab and press Enter. For instance, type **3.125** and press Enter to place a tab at 3 1/8 inch.

To add multiple left tab stops, you type the number of inches that marks the location where tabs will begin, a comma, and the spacing increment; then you press Enter. For example, to space tabs one-half inch apart beginning at one inch, you type **1,.5** and press Enter.

To add multiple center, right, or decimal tab stops and dot leaders, you use the cursor keys to move the cursor to the position where you want tab stops to begin. Or, type the position for the first tab and press Enter. Then you press C (Center), R (Right), or D (Decimal). If you want a dot leader, you press . (period). Then you type the number of inches that marks the location where the tab stops are to begin, a comma, and the spacing increment; finally, you press Enter. For example, to space right-aligned tab stops one-half inch apart beginning at one inch, you position the cursor at one inch, press R, type **1,.5**, and then press Enter.

When adding multiple tab stops that start at a position less than one inch, enter the starting position as a decimal with a leading zero. For instance, if the tab stops start at one-half inch and are spaced one-half inch apart, you type **0.5,.5**.

Setting Tab Stops

Displaying the Tab Ruler

To view current tab stop settings, use the Window feature to
display the tab ruler at the bottom of the screen.

Press Ctrl F3, the Screen key.

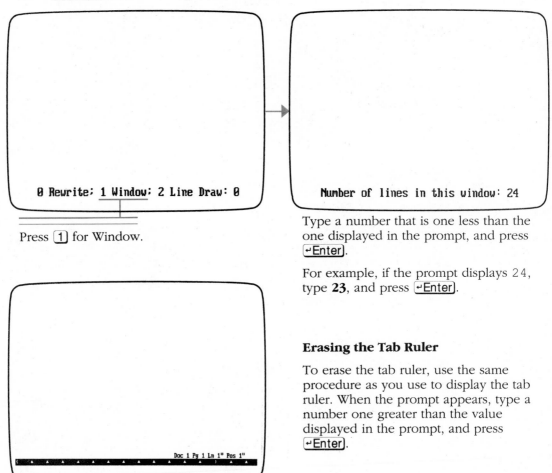

0 Rewrite; 1 Window; 2 Line Draw: 0

Press 1 for Window.

Number of lines in this window: 24

Type a number that is one less than the
one displayed in the prompt, and press
Enter.

For example, if the prompt displays 24,
type **23**, and press Enter.

Erasing the Tab Ruler

To erase the tab ruler, use the same
procedure as you use to display the tab
ruler. When the prompt appears, type a
number one greater than the value
displayed in the prompt, and press
Enter.

Doc 1 Pg 1 Ln 1" Pos 1"

The curly braces, { and }, mark the left
and right margins. Instead of braces, you
may see brackets, [and]. The braces
indicate margins and tabs at the same
position; the brackets indicate margins
alone. The triangles mark the tab stops.

Changing Tab Stops

You can set tab stops one at a time, or you can specify the increment and set several tab stops at once. Similarly, you can delete one tab stop, all tab stops, or only the tab stops to the right of the cursor.

Press ⬆Shift F8 to display the Format menu.

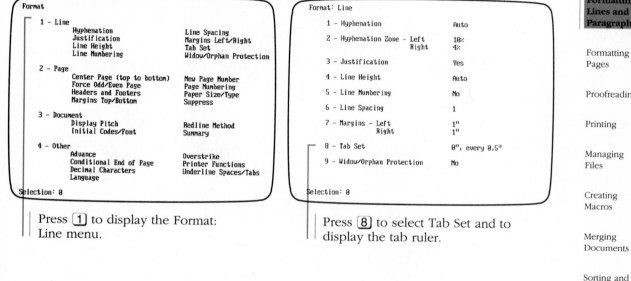

```
Format

  1 - Line
      Hyphenation              Line Spacing
      Justification            Margins Left/Right
      Line Height              Tab Set
      Line Numbering           Widow/Orphan Protection

  2 - Page
      Center Page (top to bottom)   New Page Number
      Force Odd/Even Page           Page Numbering
      Headers and Footers           Paper Size/Type
      Margins Top/Bottom            Suppress

  3 - Document
      Display Pitch            Redline Method
      Initial Codes/Font       Summary

  4 - Other
      Advance                  Overstrike
      Conditional End of Page  Printer Functions
      Decimal Characters       Underline Spaces/Tabs
      Language

Selection: 0
```

```
Format: Line

  1 - Hyphenation                        Auto

  2 - Hyphenation Zone - Left            10%
                         Right           4%

  3 - Justification                      Yes

  4 - Line Height                        Auto

  5 - Line Numbering                     No

  6 - Line Spacing                       1

  7 - Margins - Left                     1"
                Right                    1"

  8 - Tab Set                            0", every 0.5"

  9 - Widow/Orphan Protection            No

Selection: 0
```

Press 1 to display the Format:
Line menu.

Press 8 to select Tab Set and to
display the tab ruler.

At this point, you have many
options for deleting or adding
single or multiple tab stops. See
the preceding text pages to
learn how to make changes.

```
L....|....L....|....L....|....L....|....L....|....L....|....L....|....L....|....L..
|     ^     |     ^     |     ^     |     ^     |     ^     |     ^     |     ^     |
1"         2"          3"          4"          5"          6"          7"          8"
Delete EOL (clear tabs); Enter Number (set tab); Del (clear tab);
Left; Center; Right; Decimal; .= Dot Leader
```

Indenting Text

Although WordPerfect's Tab and Indent features are similar, they each have specific uses.

- **Tab** indents only the first line of the paragraph from the left margin.
- **Indent (F4)** indents the entire paragraph from the left margin.
- **Left-Right Indent (Shift-F4)** indents the entire paragraph from both the left and right margins.

Never use the space bar for indenting or tabbing. If your printer supports proportional spacing, text will not align properly at the left indent or tab stop. Instead, use the Tab or Indent keys.

The Tab Key

Use the Tab key to indent only the first line of a paragraph from the left margin. The Tab key, represented by left and right arrows at the left side of the keyboard, works like the Tab key on a typewriter. Each time you press Tab in WordPerfect, the cursor moves across the screen to the next tab stop.

Indent (F4)

Use Indent (F4) to indent an entire paragraph from the left margin. When you press Indent (F4), the cursor moves one tab stop to the right, and the left margin is reset temporarily. Everything you type, until you press Enter, is indented one tab stop. To indent more than one tab stop, you press Indent (F4) until the cursor rests at the point where you want to begin.

Left-Right Indent (Shift-F4)

Use Left-Right Indent (Shift-F4) to indent a paragraph from both the right and left margins. When you press Left-Right Indent (Shift-F4), the cursor moves to the right one tab stop and temporarily resets both the left and right margins. Everything you type, until you press Enter, is indented one tab stop from the left margin and the same distance from the right margin. To indent more than one tab stop from both margins, you press Left-Right Indent (Shift-F4) more than once.

Indenting an Existing Paragraph

You also can use Indent (F4) or Left-Right Indent (Shift-F4) to indent an existing paragraph. You first move the cursor to the first character of the text you want to indent (or to the left of a tab indent at the beginning of a paragraph). Then you press Indent (F4) or Left-Right Indent (Shift-F4). Finally, you press the down-arrow key to redraw the screen so that the entire paragraph is indented.

Creating a Hanging Paragraph

A *hanging paragraph* is formed so that the first line is flush with the left margin and the rest of the paragraph is indented to the first tab stop. Hanging paragraphs are useful in report formats such as bibliographies.

To create a hanging paragraph, you start with the cursor at the left margin. Then you press Indent (F4) to move the cursor to the next tab stop. You next press Margin Release (Shift-Tab) to move the cursor back to its original position, at the left margin. Then you type your text. To end the hanging paragraph, you press Enter.

113

Indenting Text

```
Keeping an Idea File

     An idea file is an extension of a brainstorming file. You can
save an idea file and retrieve it when you want to add more ideas
later.




                                          Doc 1 Pg 1 Ln 1.83" Pos 1"
```

The Tab Key

Use the Tab key to indent only the first line of a paragraph from the left margin. Each time you press Tab in WordPerfect, the cursor moves across the screen to the next tab stop.

```
Keeping an Idea File

     An idea file is an extension of a brainstorming file. You can
save an idea file and retrieve it when you want to add more
ideas later.




                                          Doc 1 Pg 1 Ln 1.66" Pos 2.7"
```

Indent

Use F4 (Indent) to indent an entire paragraph from the left margin.

Move the cursor to the left margin.

Press F4, the Indent key.

The cursor moves to the next tab setting.

Type your text.

Press ⏎Enter to end indenting and return to the original margin settings.

```
Keeping an Idea File

     An idea file is an extension of a brainstorming file. You
can save an idea file and retrieve it when you want to
add more ideas later.




                                          Doc 1 Pg 1 Ln 1.5" Pos 1.5"
```

Left-Right Indent

Use Shift-F4 (Left-Right Indent) to indent an entire paragraph from both margins.

Press ⇧Shift F4, the Left-Right Indent key.

Type your text.

Press ⏎Enter to end indenting and return to the original margin settings.

Indenting an Existing Paragraph

Use Indent or Left-Right Indent to indent an existing paragraph.

Move the cursor to the first character of the text you want to indent (or to the left of a tab indent at the beginning of a paragraph).

```
Keeping an Idea File

An idea file is an extension of a brainstorming file. You can save
an idea file and retrieve it when you want to add more ideas later.




                                              Doc 1 Pg 1 Ln 1,33" Pos 1"
```

Press F4 or ⇧Shift F4.

Press ↓ to redraw the screen so that the entire paragraph is indented.

```
Keeping an Idea File

    An idea file is an extension of a brainstorming file. You can
    save an idea file and retrieve it when you want to add more
    ideas later.




                                              Doc 1 Pg 1 Ln 1,5" Pos 1,5"
```

Creating a Hanging Paragraph

Create a hanging paragraph for report formats such as bibliographies.

Move the cursor to the left margin.

Press F4 to move the cursor to the next tab stop.

Press ⇧Shift Tab⇄, the Margin Release key.

The cursor moves back to its original position, at the left margin.

Type your text.

Press ↵Enter to end the hanging paragraph.

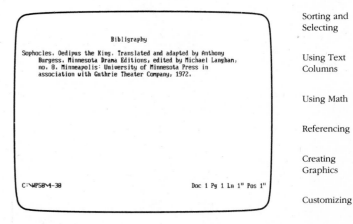

```
                       Bibliography

Sophocles. Oedipus the King. Translated and adapted by Anthony
    Burgess. Minnesota Drama Editions, edited by Michael Langhan,
    no. 8. Minneapolis: University of Minnesota Press in
    association with Guthrie Theater Company, 1972.




C:\WP50\4-30                                   Doc 1 Pg 1 Ln 1" Pos 1"
```

115

Using Tab Align and Flush Right

Using Tab Align

Use Tab Align (Ctrl-F6) to align text at the right on a specific character. For example, you might want to use this feature to align names and addresses, or numbers within columns.

When you press Tab Align (Ctrl-F6), the cursor jumps to the right one tab stop. All text you type moves to the left of the tab stop until you type the alignment character (the default is a period). After you type the alignment character, the text begins moving to the right of the tab stop.

If you want to align text at the right without displaying the alignment character, you can press Tab Align (Ctrl-F6), type the text, and press Enter before pressing the alignment character. The typed text is right-justified at the tab stop.

Changing the Alignment Character

The alignment character can be any character you want. The default is a period or decimal point (.). The default works well with numbers. To align names and addresses, use a colon (:). To align numbers in an equation, an equal sign (=) is best. To align monetary amounts, use a dollar sign ($).

You can change the alignment character permanently for all future documents or temporarily for the current document only. For instruction on changing the alignment character permanently, see

Chapter 16, "Customizing." To change the alignment character temporarily, you first press Format (Shift-F8). From the Format menu, you select Other (4). From the Format: Other menu, you select Decimal/Align Character (3). The cursor moves to the right of the Decimal/Align Character menu item. You type a new alignment character and press Enter twice. Finally, you press Exit (F7) to return to your document.

Using Flush Right

Use Flush Right (Alt-F6) to align text with the right margin. This code aligns the right edge of all headings, columns, and lines of text even (flush) with the right margin. You can make text align flush right either before or after you type the text.

To create flush right text as you type, you first press Flush Right (Alt-F6) to move the cursor to the right margin. Then you type your text. As you type, the cursor stays at the right margin, and the text moves to the left. You press Enter to stop aligning text at the right margin.

To align existing text with the right margin, you first place the cursor at the left margin. Then you press Flush Right (Alt-F6) to move the cursor and text to the right margin. Finally, you press the down-arrow key to redraw the screen. You can use Block (Alt-F4, or F12) to right-align several lines.

When you use Flush Right, some of the text may disappear past the right edge of the screen. Pressing the down-arrow key adjusts the screen display.

Using Tab Align and Flush Right

Using Tab Align

Use [Ctrl][F6] (Tab Align) to align text at the right on a specific character.

Press [Ctrl][F6], the Tab Align key.

Type your text.

Type the alignment character (in this case, a period).

Type any additional text, if necessary.

Press [Ctrl][F6] to tab to the next column.

Or

Press [↵Enter] to end the line.

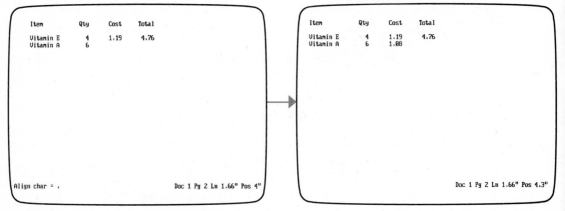

Changing the Alignment Character

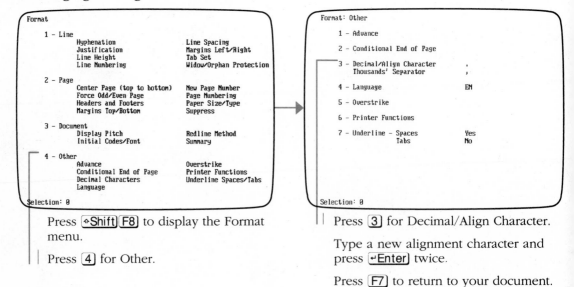

Press [⬧Shift][F8] to display the Format menu.

Press [4] for Other.

Press [3] for Decimal/Align Character.

Type a new alignment character and press [↵Enter] twice.

Press [F7] to return to your document.

Using Flush Right

Use [Alt][F6] (Flush Right) to align text with the right margin. You can make text align flush right either before or after you type the text.

```
The right margin is located a position 7.5".
1        2        3        4        5        6        7
                                                     012345

This is a line of existing text.




C:\WP50\4-36                          Doc 1 Pg 1 Ln 1" Pos 1"
```

To create flush right text as you type, press [Alt][F6] (Flush Right) to move the cursor to the right margin.

Type your text.

As you type, the cursor stays at the right margin, and the text moves to the left.

Press [⏎Enter] to end Flush Right.

```
The right margin is located a position 7.5".
1        2        3        4        5        6        7
                                                     012345
                               This is typed Flush Right.
                               <=== Direction of type travel




C:\WP50\4-35                          Doc 1 Pg 1 Ln 1" Pos 1"
```

To align existing text with the right margin, place the cursor at the left margin.

Press [Alt]-[F6] to move the cursor and text to the right margin.

```
The right margin is located a position 7.5".
1        2        3        4        5        6        7
                                                     012345
The following line shifted past the right margin when the Flush
Right key was first pressed.

                                              This is a line

After pressing the down arrow, the text past the right margin is
adjusted.

                               This is a line of existing text.

C:\WP50\4-37                      Doc 1 Pg 1 Ln 2.83" Pos 7.5"
```

Press [↓].

119

Centering a Line, Justifying Text

Centering a Line

WordPerfect lets you center text instantly, without laboriously counting characters. You can center a line of text between the right and left margins as you type it or after you type it. You also can center text around a specific point.

Centering between Margins

To center text you are about to type, you first move the cursor to the left margin of the line you want to center. Then you press Center (Shift-F6). The cursor centers between the margins. You type your text. As you type, the text adjusts to the left and to the right to stay centered. You press Enter to end centering.

The Center command is easy to use but can cause strange results on-screen if applied incorrectly. For example, if you press Center (Shift-F6) while the cursor is in the middle of a line, some of the text may disappear. Use Reveal Codes to remove the Center code ([Cntr]).

If you type more characters than will fit between the margins, the rest of the text moves to the next line. Only the first line is centered. To center several lines, use the Block Center function (see Chapter 3, "Working with Blocks").

To center an existing line of text, you first press Reveal Codes (Alt-F3, or F11) and check to be sure that the line ends with a Hard Return code ([HRt]). To return to the normal editing screen, you press Reveal Codes (Alt-F3, or F11) again. Then you place the cursor at the left margin of the line of text you want to center. You press Center (Shift-F6) to move the text to the center of the screen. Finally, you press the down-arrow key to redraw the screen.

Centering around a Specific Point

To center text around a specific point, you first position the cursor in the line to be centered and press Reveal Codes (Alt-F3, or F11) to make sure that no hidden codes, characters, or spaces are on the line. You press Reveal Codes (Alt-F3, or F11) again to leave the Reveal Codes screen. Then you move the cursor to the position on which you want to center the text. Next, you press Center (Shift-F6) and type your text. Finally, you press Enter. The text is centered on the character position. You cannot center previously typed text around a specific point.

Using Right-Justification

WordPerfect's right-justification feature inserts space between words and letters so that the text aligns flush with the right margin. Text that is not justified has a ragged right margin. You cannot see right-justification on the regular editing screen. When you print your document, the text prints even with the right margin. The default for right-justification is on.

To turn off justification temporarily for the current document only, you first move the cursor to the beginning of the document, and then you press Format (Shift-F8) to display the Format menu. From this menu, you select Line (1) to display the Format: Line menu. From this menu, you select Justification (3). Then you press N to turn off justification. Finally, you press Exit (F7) to return to your document.

Centering a Line, Justifying Text

Centering a Line

You can center text on a line between the right and left margins or around a specific point.

Centering between Margins

You can center a line of text between the right and left margins as you type it or after you type it.

To center text you are about to type, move the cursor to the left margin of the line.

Press ⬆Shift F6, the Center key.

Type your text.

Press ↵Enter.

To center an existing line of text, press Alt F3 or F11 and check to be sure that the line of text you want to center ends with a Hard Return code ([HRt]).

```
Planning Documents




                                        Doc 1 Pg 2 Ln 2.83" Pos 1"
[                  ▲   ▲   ▲   ▲   ▲   ▲   ▲   ▲   ▲   ▲   ▲   ]   ▲   ▲
Planning Documents[HRt]
[HRt]
█

Press Reveal Codes to restore screen
```

```
          Planning Documents










                                Doc 1 Pg 2 Ln 2.66" Pos 1"
```

Press Alt F3 or F11 to turn off Reveal Codes.

Place the cursor at the left margin of the line of text you want to center.

Press ⬆Shift F6.

Press ↓.

Centering around a Specific Point

In addition to centering text between the margins, you can center text around a specific point in your document.

Press Alt F3 or F11 to make sure that the line contains no hidden codes, characters, or spaces.

Press Alt F3 or F11 again to leave the Reveal Codes screen.

Move the cursor to the position on which you want to center the text.

Press ⬆Shift-F6.

Type your text.

Press ↵Enter.

Using Right-Justification

WordPerfect's right-justification feature inserts space between words and letters so that the text aligns flush with the right margin. Text that is not justified has a ragged right margin.

Right-justified text

Ragged text

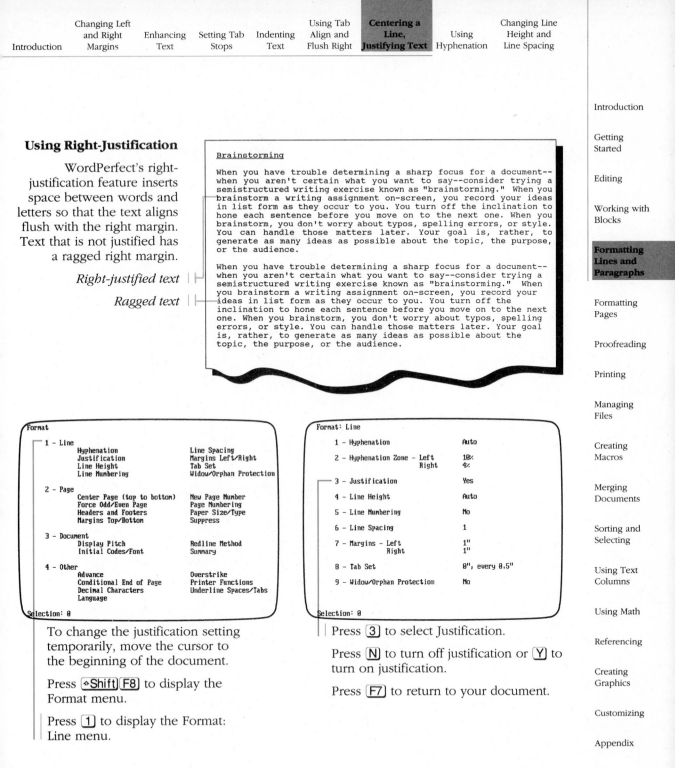

```
Brainstorming

When you have trouble determining a sharp focus for a document--
when you aren't certain what you want to say--consider trying a
semistructured writing exercise known as "brainstorming." When you
brainstorm a writing assignment on-screen, you record your ideas
in list form as they occur to you. You turn off the inclination to
hone each sentence before you move on to the next one. When you
brainstorm, you don't worry about typos, spelling errors, or style.
You can handle those matters later. Your goal is, rather, to
generate as many ideas as possible about the topic, the purpose,
or the audience.

When you have trouble determining a sharp focus for a document--
when you aren't certain what you want to say--consider trying a
semistructured writing exercise known as "brainstorming."  When
you brainstorm a writing assignment on-screen, you record your
ideas in list form as they occur to you. You turn off the
inclination to hone each sentence before you move on to the next
one. When you brainstorm, you don't worry about typos, spelling
errors, or style. You can handle those matters later. Your goal
is, rather, to generate as many ideas as possible about the
topic, the purpose, or the audience.
```

```
Format

  1 - Line
        Hyphenation              Line Spacing
        Justification            Margins Left/Right
        Line Height              Tab Set
        Line Numbering           Widow/Orphan Protection

  2 - Page
        Center Page (top to bottom)  New Page Number
        Force Odd/Even Page          Page Numbering
        Headers and Footers          Paper Size/Type
        Margins Top/Bottom           Suppress

  3 - Document
        Display Pitch            Redline Method
        Initial Codes/Font       Summary

  4 - Other
        Advance                  Overstrike
        Conditional End of Page  Printer Functions
        Decimal Characters       Underline Spaces/Tabs
        Language

Selection: 0
```

To change the justification setting temporarily, move the cursor to the beginning of the document.

Press ⬆Shift F8 to display the Format menu.

Press 1 to display the Format: Line menu.

```
Format: Line

  1 - Hyphenation                   Auto

  2 - Hyphenation Zone - Left       10%
                          Right     4%

  3 - Justification                 Yes

  4 - Line Height                   Auto

  5 - Line Numbering                No

  6 - Line Spacing                  1

  7 - Margins - Left                1"
                Right               1"

  8 - Tab Set                       0", every 0.5"

  9 - Widow/Orphan Protection       No

Selection: 0
```

Press 3 to select Justification.

Press N to turn off justification or Y to turn on justification.

Press F7 to return to your document.

Using Hyphenation

When a line of text becomes too long to fit within the margins, the last word wraps to the next line. With short words, wrapping doesn't present much of a problem. With long words, the following problems can occur:

- If justification is off, large gaps can appear at the right margin, producing a document with very ragged text.
- If justification is on, large spaces between words become visually distracting.

Hyphenating the word at the end of the line solves these formatting problems. When you use WordPerfect's hyphenation feature, the program fits as much of the word as possible on the line, hyphenates the word, and wraps the rest of the word to the next line.

Using Hyphenation Settings

To control hyphenation, use one of three possible settings: off, manual, or automatic.

When you use Manual hyphenation, WordPerfect prompts you to position the hyphen in a word that needs to be broken.

If you set hyphenation to Auto, WordPerfect uses an internal set of rules to hyphenate common words. Because many words are not covered by these rules, WordPerfect prompts you for the proper hyphenation of these words just as if you had selected Manual hyphenation.

To turn on hyphenation, you press Format (Shift-F8) to display the Format menu. Then you select Line (1) to display the Format: Line menu. From this menu, you select Hyphenation (1) to display the Hyphenation menu. Next, you select the type of hyphenation you want: Manual (2) or Auto (3). Finally, you press Exit (F7) to return to your document.

A [Hyph on] code is inserted in the text. Hyphenation remains on until you turn it off. To turn off hyphenation, you repeat the procedure described in the preceding paragraph, except you select Off (1) from the Hyphenation menu.

As you type or scroll through your document, WordPerfect automatically hyphenates words if you select Auto. If you select Manual or if WordPerfect can't find a rule to hyphenate the word, the program calls your attention to words that should be hyphenated. When WordPerfect reaches a word, such as *justification*, the program beeps and displays a message similar to the following:

```
Position hyphen; Press ESC justifi-cation
```

At this point, you have three options:

- You can press Esc to hyphenate the word as it is displayed.
- You can use the cursor keys to move the hyphen to another hyphenation point, and then press Esc to hyphenate the word.
- You can press Cancel (F1) to avoid hyphenating the word and wrap it to the next line. If you choose this option, a Cancel Hyphenation code [/] is inserted before the word; you must delete this code manually if you later decide to hyphenate the word.

If you want to turn off hyphenation temporarily (for example, while scrolling through a document or checking spelling), press Exit (F7). When WordPerfect finishes scrolling or checking spelling, hyphenation is automatically turned on again.

Using Hyphenation

Using Hyphenation Settings

To control hyphenation, use one of three possible settings: off, manual, or automatic.

Press ⇧Shift F8 to display the Format menu.

Press 1 to display the Format: Line menu.

Press 1 for Hyphenation.

Press 2 for Manual.

Or

Press 3 for Auto.

Press F7 (Exit).

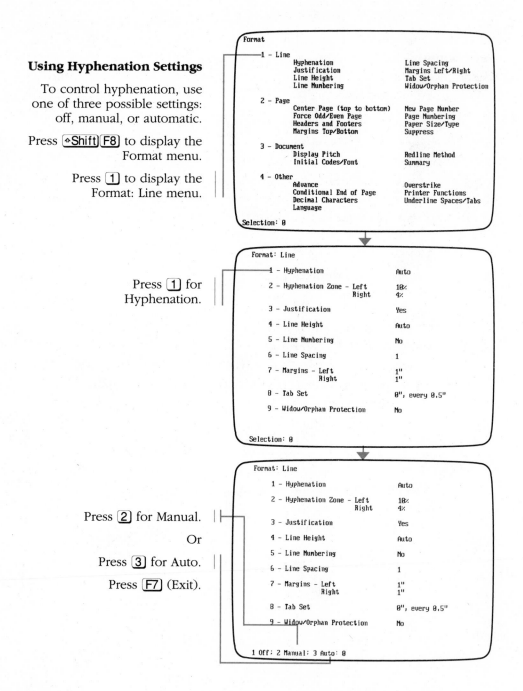

Manual

If you select Manual, the program beeps and prompts you to position the hyphen in a word that needs to be broken.

Auto

As you type or scroll through your document, WordPerfect automatically hyphenates words if you selected Auto. If WordPerfect can't find a rule to hyphenate a word, the program beeps and prompts you for hyphenation.

```
   When you are planning your printed document, consider the
appearance you want to present. With ragged text, you have an
uneven right margin and a less formal look. With right-justification




















Position hyphen; Press ESC justifica-tion
```

At this point, you have three options:

- Press (Esc) to hyphenate the word as it is displayed.

- Use the cursor keys to move the hyphen to another hyphenation point, and then press (Esc) to hyphenate the word.

- Press (F1) to avoid hyphenating the word and wrap it to the next line.

Using Hyphenation

Controlling Hyphenation

WordPerfect has a variety of features that let you control how the text is hyphenated at the right margin. Among these features are a variety of hyphens, returns, and hard spaces.

Understanding the Types of Hyphens

At first glance, a hyphen looks simply like a hyphen, but WordPerfect uses, and permits you to use, several kinds of hyphens: hard hyphens, hyphen characters, and soft hyphens.

A *hard hyphen* is part of the spelling of a word, as in *father-in-law* and *jack-of-all-trades*. A hard hyphen is displayed and printed at all times. The hard hyphen code appears on the Reveal Codes screen as [-]. If a hard hyphen appears in a word that needs to be hyphenated, WordPerfect uses the hard hyphen as the breaking point instead of prompting you for a hyphenation decision. To enter a hard hyphen, you press the Hyphen key (located on the same key as the underline character).

The *hyphen character* appears the same on-screen as a hard hyphen, but WordPerfect treats the hyphen character as if it were a character. A word containing a hyphen character is not necessarily split at the hyphen when it falls within the hyphenation zone. You may be prompted for hyphenation. In Reveal Codes, the hyphen appears as an unhighlighted –. To enter a hyphen character, you press Home and then Hyphen. Be sure to use the Hyphen key in the numeric key row, not the minus sign on the numeric keypad. (The minus sign is used in formulas.)

A *soft hyphen* is inserted between syllables during hyphenation. Soft hyphens are visible and print only when they appear as the last character in a line; otherwise, they remain hidden. A soft hyphen appears in Reveal Codes as a highlighted –. You can insert soft hyphens at points where you want hyphenation to occur by pressing Ctrl-Hyphen.

To insert a dash in your text, use a combination of two kinds of hyphens. For the first hyphen, you press Home and then Hyphen for the hyphen character. For the second hyphen, you press Hyphen for a hard hyphen. WordPerfect will not separate the two hyphens at the end of a line.

Understanding Line Breaks

Another way you can control the text at the right margin is by specifying what kind of line break you want. In WordPerfect, a line can end with a soft return, a hard return, or an invisible soft return.

WordPerfect inserts a *soft return* code ([SRt]) at the end of each line when the text reaches the right margin and is automatically wrapped to the next line.

The program inserts a *hard return* code ([HRt]) when you press Enter to end a line. You can insert a hard return whenever you don't want a line to wrap automatically to the next line or when you want to insert a blank line.

WordPerfect inserts an *invisible soft return* code ([ISRt]) when you press Home and then Enter. This feature is handy for dividing words without inserting a hyphen—for example, dividing words such as and/or or either/or after the slash or dividing words connected with an ellipsis.

WordPerfect inserts a *deletable soft return* code [DSRt] if hyphenation is off and a line doesn't fit between margins.

Using Hyphenation

Keeping Words Together

If you want to keep particular words together on a line, you can insert hard spaces between them by pressing Home, space bar. For instance, you can keep the words *San Francisco* on one line by pressing Home and then the space bar after you type *San.* Hard spaces signal WordPerfect to treat the words as a character string. WordPerfect will not divide the string when it falls at the end of a line but will move the entire word group to the following line. A hard space appears as [ ] in Reveal Codes.

Setting Hyphenation Zones

WordPerfect decides which words to hyphenate by using a hyphenation zone. When hyphenation is on, the zone determines whether a word should be hyphenated or wrapped to the next line. The left side of the zone is called the left hyphenation zone (H-zone), and the right side is called the right H-zone.

When hyphenation is turned on, three things can happen to words that fall near the right margin:

- Words that start on or after the left hyphenation zone but do not reach the right margin remain in position.
- Words that begin on or after the left hyphenation zone and pass the right margin wrap to the next line.
- Words that start before the left hyphenation zone and pass over the right hyphenation zone require hyphenation.

WordPerfect's hyphenation zone is preset to accommodate a variety of line lengths. The zone is determined by percentages of the line length: the left H-zone is preset at 10 percent; the right H-zone is set at 4 percent.

The distance between the left and right hyphenation zones determines the size of words selected for hyphenation. The shorter the distance between the two zones, the more hyphenation is needed. If you compare two hyphenation zones that have the same distance between the left and right hyphenation zones, the one with the larger left hyphenation zone wraps fewer words to the next line. If your documents require hyphenation, you should experiment with different hyphenation zone settings on a sample page of text to find the best setting.

To change the hyphenation zone for the current document only, you first move the cursor to the top of the document. Then you press Format (Shift-F8) to display the Format menu. Next, you select Line (1) to display the Format: Line menu. Then you choose Hyphenation Zone (2). You type a new value for the left H-zone setting and press Enter. You type a new value for the right H-zone setting and press Enter. Finally, you press Exit (F7) to return to the document.

Using Hyphenation

The hyphenation zone determines whether a word
should be hyphenated or wrapped to the next line.
When hyphenation is on, three things can happen to
words that fall near the right margin.

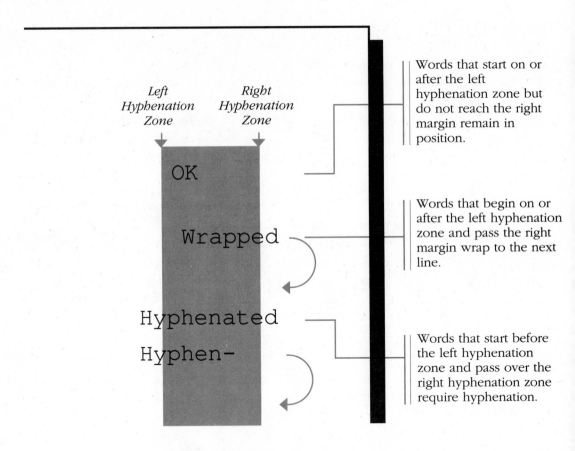

Left
Hyphenation
Zone

Right
Hyphenation
Zone

OK

Wrapped

Hyphenated

Hyphen-

Words that start on or
after the left
hyphenation zone but
do not reach the right
margin remain in
position.

Words that begin on or
after the left hyphenation
zone and pass the right
margin wrap to the next
line.

Words that start before
the left hyphenation
zone and pass over the
right hyphenation zone
require hyphenation.

Changing the Hyphenation Zone

You can change the hyphenation zone to control hyphenation. The shorter the distance between the left and right hyphenation zones, the more hyphenation is needed.

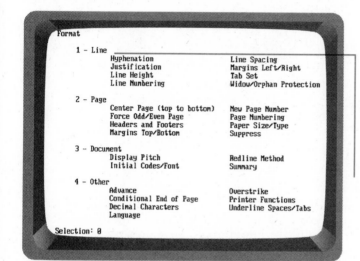

Move the cursor to the top of the document.

Press ⌖Shift F8 to display the Format menu.

Press 1 to display the Format: Line menu.

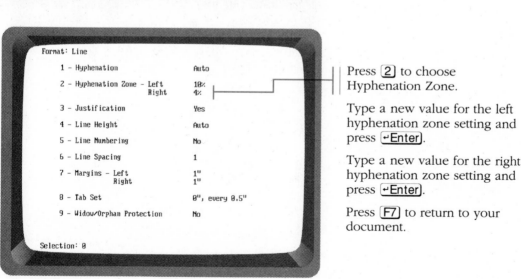

Press 2 to choose Hyphenation Zone.

Type a new value for the left hyphenation zone setting and press ↵Enter.

Type a new value for the right hyphenation zone setting and press ↵Enter.

Press F7 to return to your document.

Changing Line Height and Line Spacing

To format your text, you can change both the line height and the line spacing.

Line Height

The vertical distance between the base of a line of text and the base of the line of text above or below is called *line height*. Printers call the distance *leading*. WordPerfect automatically controls line height. If the line height was not adjusted and you changed to a larger type size, the vertical spacing would appear cramped on the printed page.

Because WordPerfect handles changes in line height automatically, you usually don't need to adjust it manually, except for special circumstances. If, for example, your document is one page plus two lines and you want the text to fit on one page, you could change the line height to accommodate the extra lines.

Like many WordPerfect formatting features, line height can be changed temporarily or permanently. Note, however, that this feature will not work if your printer can print only six lines per inch.

To change line height temporarily, you first move the cursor to the location in your document where you want to change line height. To change the line height for the entire document, you move the cursor to the beginning of the document. Next, you press Format (Shift-F8) to display the Format menu. From this menu, you select Line (1). From the Format: Line menu, you select Line Height (4). Then you select Fixed (2), type the line measurement you want (with up to two decimal places), and press Enter. Finally, you press Exit (F7) to return to your document.

To switch back to WordPerfect's automatic line height settings, you repeat this procedure, but you select Auto (1) instead of Fixed (2) from the menu.

Line Spacing

WordPerfect's line spacing default is single-spacing. To double-space or triple-space a document, you can change the line spacing default rather than enter hard returns as you type. You can make line spacing changes permanently or temporarily. You won't see changes in line spacing on-screen except when you select single (1), double (2), or triple (3) line spacing.

To change line spacing temporarily, you first press Format (Shift-F8) to display the Format menu. Then you select Line (2) to display the Format: Line menu. Next, you select Line Spacing (6). You type the amount of line spacing you want (with up to two decimal places) and press Enter. For instance, to double-space, you type **2**. For one and one-half spacing, you type **1.5**. Note that if you reduce the space between the lines too much, words may print on top of one another. Finally, you press Exit (F7) to return to your document.

Changing Line Height and Line Spacing

Changing Line Height

WordPerfect automatically controls line height—the vertical distance between the base of a line of text and the base of the line of text above or below. Sometimes you may want to adjust the line height, for example, to fit an extra line or two on a page.

Move the cursor to the location in your document where you want to change line height. To change the line height for the entire document, move the cursor to the beginning of the document.

Press ⬧Shift F8 to display the Format menu.

Press 1 to display the Format: Line menu.

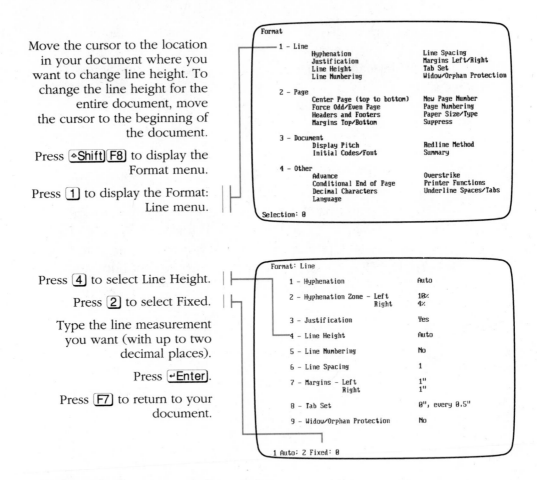

Press 4 to select Line Height.

Press 2 to select Fixed.

Type the line measurement you want (with up to two decimal places).

Press ↵Enter.

Press F7 to return to your document.

To change back to automatic line spacing, follow the preceding process. When the Line Height menu appears, press 1 to select Auto.

Changing Line Spacing

WordPerfect's line spacing default is single-spacing. To double-space or triple-space a document, you can change the line spacing default rather than enter hard returns as you type.

Press ⬆Shift F8 to display the Format menu.

Press 1 to display the Format: Line menu.

Press 6 to select Line Spacing.

Type the amount of line spacing you want (with up to two decimal places) and press ↵Enter.

```
Format: Line

    1 - Hyphenation                      Auto

    2 - Hyphenation Zone - Left          10%
                          Right          4%

    3 - Justification                    Yes

    4 - Line Height                      Auto

    5 - Line Numbering                   No

    6 - Line Spacing                     2

    7 - Margins - Left                   1"
                  Right                  1"

    8 - Tab Set                          0", every 0.5"

    9 - Widow/Orphan Protection          No


Selection: 6
```

For instance, to double-space, type **2**. For one and one-half spaces, type **1.5**. Note: If you reduce the space between lines too much, words may print on top of one another.

Press F7 to return to your document.

```
When you have trouble determining a sharp focus for a document--
when you are uncertain what you want to say--consider trying a
semistructured writing exercise known as "brainstorming."

When you brainstorm a writing assignment on-screen, you record your
ideas in list form as they occur to you. When you brainstorm, you
don't worry about typos, spelling, or style. You turn off the
inclination to hone each sentence before you move on to the next
one. You can handle those matters later. Your goal is, rather, to
generate as many ideas as possible about the topic, the purpose,
or the audience.

                                        Doc 1 Pg 1 Ln 1" Pos 1"
```

5 *Formatting Pages*

Designing a document means making formatting choices at several levels. In the preceding chapter, you learned to format lines and paragraphs. In this chapter, you will learn to make formatting choices for the entire document. You also will learn to make formatting choices for pages or groups of pages.

▼

Key Terms

This chapter introduces the following key terms:

Header	Information that prints automatically at the top margin of the page.
Footer	Information that prints automatically at the bottom margin of the page.
Soft page break	A page break that occurs automatically. Soft page breaks appear on-screen as a dashed line.
Hard page break	A page break you insert to force a break at a certain spot. On-screen a hard page break appears as a line of equal signs.
Widow	In WordPerfect, the first line of a paragraph left at the bottom of a page.

Changing Paper Size, Top and Bottom Margins   Centering Pages, Using Advance   Designing Headers and Footers   Numbering Pages   Controlling Page Breaks   Using Redline and Strikeout   Using Special Characters and Typing Equations   Creating and Using Styles

troduction

Orphan	In WordPerfect, the last line of a paragraph left at the top of a page.
Superscript	A number or letter written immediately above, or above and to the right or left of, another character.
Subscript	A distinguishing symbol written immediately below, or below and to the right or left of, another character.

▲

Tasks Covered in This Chapter

In this chapter, you learn to perform the following formatting tasks:

- Change paper size
- Change top and bottom margins
- Center pages
- Use the Advance feature
- Design headers and footers
- Number pages
- Control page breaks
- Use redline and strikeout as editing tools
- Use special characters and type equations
- Create formatting styles and style libraries

Changing Paper Size, Top and Bottom Margins

Changing Paper and Form Sizes

WordPerfect is preset for 8 1/2-by-11-inch paper. If you use 8 1/2-by-11-inch paper, you don't need to change the default settings. If you want to use a different size paper, you can change the settings. You can choose any of 9 predefined paper sizes, or you can define your own size.

Specifying paper size is a two-part process: you must define the *form* size and type for the printer, and you must specify the *paper* size and type in the document. You define the form size and type for the printer through the Printer menu. You identify the paper size and type through the Format: Page menu.

The paper and form always must match. If you specify in the document that the paper is an envelope, for example, a corresponding envelope form must be listed in the Printer menu.

Defining a Form for the Printer

WordPerfect documents are formatted for a particular size and type of paper. This formatting information is saved with the document in the form of a default Paper Size/Type specification or a special Paper Size/Type code you enter in the document.

When you choose a form using the Paper Size/Type menu, WordPerfect displays the forms you've designed, as well as the default form types supplied with the program. WordPerfect matches the forms from this Paper Type menu with the forms you define in the Form Type menu. If the program can't find a corresponding definition, WordPerfect chooses the form it considers to be the closest match.

WordPerfect comes with a list of default form sizes and types. You also can add customized form definitions to meet your special needs.

To define a form for your printer, you first press Print (Shift-F7). Then you choose Select Printer (S) and use the cursor keys to highlight the name of the printer you want to edit. (The current printer is already highlighted.) Next, you choose Edit (3). From the Select Printer: Edit screen, you select Forms (4) to display a list of form definitions in the Select Printer: Forms menu. From this menu, you can select Add (1) to add a form or Edit (2) to edit a form.

WordPerfect displays the Select Printer: Form Type menu. You choose a form type, and then WordPerfect displays the Select Printer: Forms menu. From this menu, you choose an option and enter the new information. You press Exit (F7) five times to return to your document.

Changing Paper Size, Top and Bottom Margins

When you define or edit a form type, you can choose from the following options:

Form Size: When you choose Form Size, the program displays a list of common paper sizes. You can press a number corresponding to a paper size; or choose Other (9), and then enter dimensions for height and width.

Orientation: This option toggles between Portrait (vertical) and Landscape (sideways) paper orientations.

Initially Present: If you press N for this option, WordPerfect stops and prompts you to insert the form when the program encounters the Paper Size/Type code. If you press Y, WordPerfect assumes that the form is immediately available and doesn't pause before beginning to print.

Location: You use this option to specify how the paper is inserted: Continuous (forms tractor feed), Bin Number (sheet feeder), or Manual (hand-fed). If you select Bin Number, you are prompted to enter the number of the bin where the forms are located.

Page Offsets: You can select this option and choose top and side offset measurements; the printing will be moved from the top and left margins by the amounts you specify.

Specifying Paper Size and Type in a Document

After you define the form, you must specify the paper size and type in the document, if you are using a size and type other than the default. To change the paper size and type from the default paper, you first press Format (Shift-F8) to display the Format menu. From this menu, you select Page (2). From the Format: Page menu, you select Paper

Size/Type (8). From this menu, you select the paper size you want—for example, legal, label, or letterhead.

After you choose a paper size, WordPerfect displays the Format: Paper Type menu. You select a paper type from the predefined types listed. Then you press Exit (F7) to return to your document.

If you select Other (0) at the Paper Size menu, WordPerfect prompts for width and length measurements. Use this option to define your own paper size and type so that you can print on nonstandard-size paper.

Changing Top and Bottom Margins

WordPerfect is preset to leave 1-inch margins at the top and bottom of the page. Page numbers, headers, footers, and footnotes must fit within the allotted text area.

WordPerfect's default measurement is inches; therefore, margins are measured in inches. The top margin is the distance between the top edge of the paper and the first line of text. The bottom margin is calculated from the bottom edge of the paper to the last line of text. A margin setting governs the placement of all text that follows the margin code—until a different setting changes the margins.

To change the top and bottom margins, you first move the cursor to the position in your document where you want to set margins—usually at the beginning of the document. Then you press Format (Shift-F8) to display the Format menu. Next, you select Page (2) to display the Format: Page menu. From this menu, you select Margins (Top/Bottom) (5). You type a new top margin and press Enter; then you type a new bottom margin and press Enter. Type the margin specifications in decimal inches. Finally, you press Exit (F7) to return to your document.

Changing Paper Size, Top and Bottom Margins

Changing Paper and Form Sizes

Specifying paper size is a two-part process: you must define the *form* size and type for the printer, and you must specify the *paper* size and type in the document. The paper and form always must match.

Defining a Form for the Printer

You define the form size and type for the printer through the Printer menu.

Press ⬆Shift F7, the Print key.

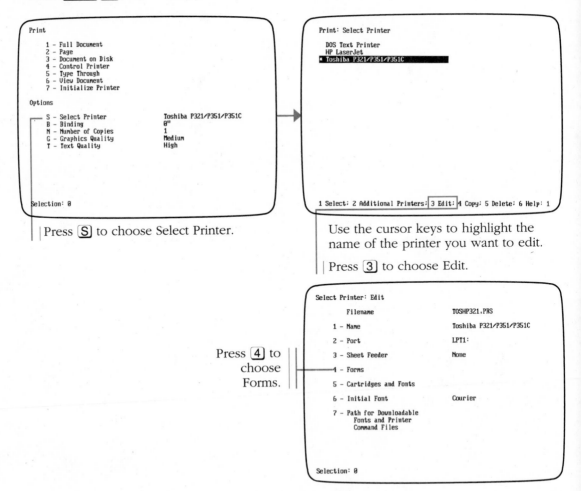

Press S to choose Select Printer.

Use the cursor keys to highlight the name of the printer you want to edit.

Press 3 to choose Edit.

Press 4 to choose Forms.

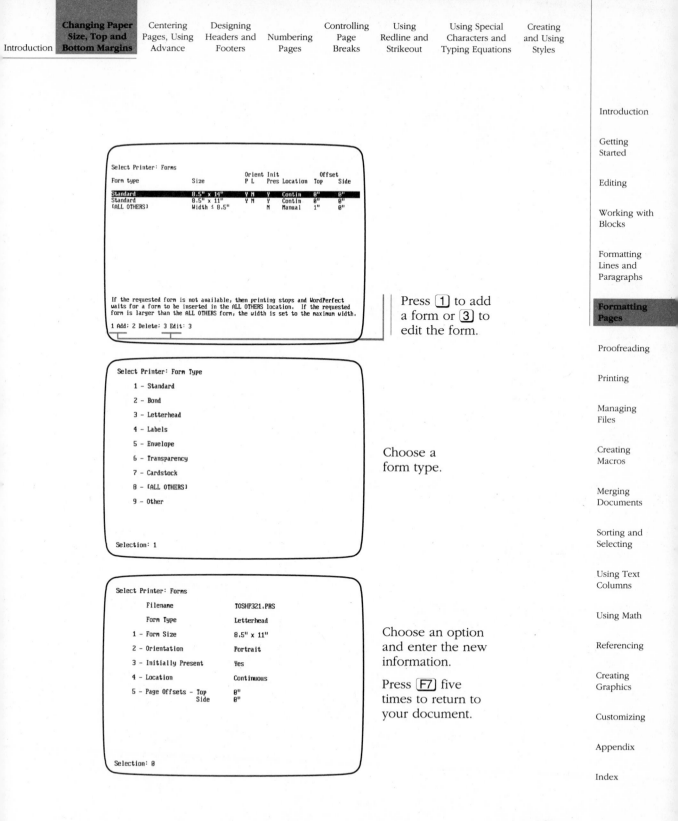

Press **1** to add a form or **3** to edit the form.

Choose a form type.

Choose an option and enter the new information.

Press **F7** five times to return to your document.

Changing Paper Size, Top and Bottom Margins

Specifying Paper Size and Type in a Document

You identify the paper size and type through the Format: Page menu.

Press ⬆Shift F8 to display the Format menu.

Press 2 to select Page.

Press 8 to select Paper Size/Type.

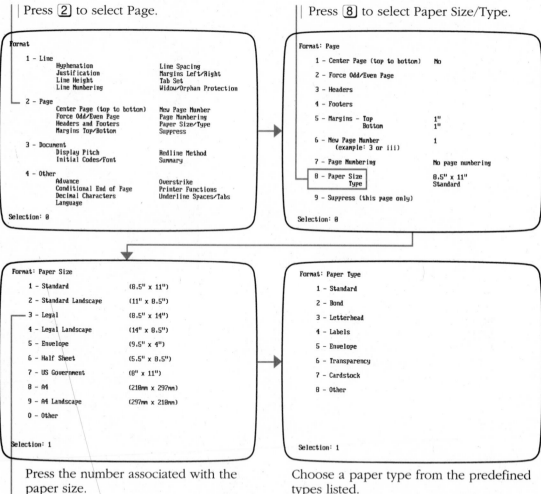

Press the number associated with the paper size.

For instance, press 3 to select Legal.

Choose a paper type from the predefined types listed.

Press F7 to return to your document.

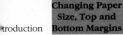

Changing Paper Size, Top and Bottom Margins | Centering Pages, Using Advance | Designing Headers and Footers | Numbering Pages | Controlling Page Breaks | Using Redline and Strikeout | Using Special Characters and Typing Equations | Creating and Using Styles

troduction

Changing Top and Bottom Margins

The top margin is the distance between the top edge of the paper and the first line of text. The bottom margin is calculated from the bottom edge of the paper to the last line of text.

Move the cursor to the position in your document where you want to set margins— usually at the beginning of the document.

Press ⇧Shift F8 to display the Format menu.

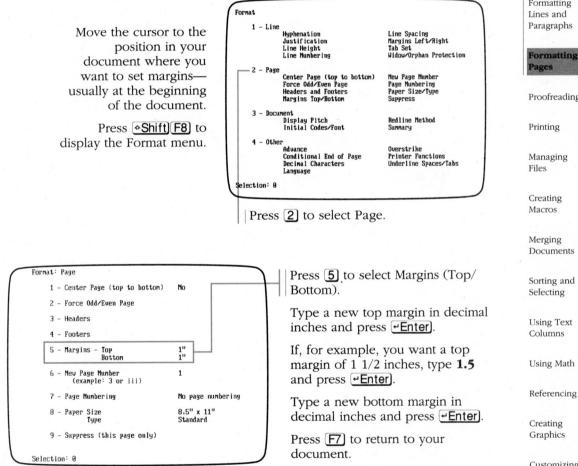

Press 2 to select Page.

Press 5 to select Margins (Top/ Bottom).

Type a new top margin in decimal inches and press ↵Enter.

If, for example, you want a top margin of 1 1/2 inches, type **1.5** and press ↵Enter.

Type a new bottom margin in decimal inches and press ↵Enter.

Press F7 to return to your document.

147

Centering Pages, Using Advance

Centering Pages Top to Bottom

When you center a page top to bottom, the setting applies to just one page—the page where you make the setting. You may, for example, want to center the title page of a sales report. The end of a centered page can be defined by either a soft page break or a hard page break. Ending the centered page with a hard page break ensures that the page never accidentally merges with the next page.

Before you insert the code to center a page, be sure that the cursor rests at the beginning of the page, before any other formatting codes and text. You can press Reveal Codes (Alt-F3, or F11) to verify the cursor position.

To center a page, you press Format (Shift-F8) to display the Format menu. From this menu, you select Page (2). Then you choose Center Page (1). WordPerfect inserts a [Center Pg] code. Finally, you press Exit (F7) to return to your document.

Although the page doesn't appear centered on-screen, it will be centered when you print your document. If you change your mind, delete the [Center Pg] code.

To adjust the centered text on the page, you can change the top and bottom margins by pressing Format (Shift-F8), selecting Page (2), and specifying new settings for Margins (Top/Bottom) (5).

Using Advance

You can use WordPerfect's Advance feature to insert in your document a code that instructs your printer to move left, right, up, or down before printing. You also can use Advance to tell your printer to start printing at a specific location on the page. (Some printers can't "advance" backward.) With some laser printers, you need to use Advance to position text over a line drawing.

To use Advance, you first position the cursor at the location where you want Advance to begin. Then you press Format (Shift-F8) to display the Format menu. Next, you select Other (4) to display the Format: Other menu. From this menu, you choose Advance (1).

You can advance up, down, right, left, or to a specified position. You type the number associated with your selection. Then you type the distance to advance and press Enter. The distance you enter for Advance Up, Down, Right, or Left is relative to the current cursor position. If you choose Position, the distance you enter specifies an absolute position on the page from the edge of the paper. The final step is to press Exit (F7) to return to your document.

When WordPerfect encounters an Advance code, the status line changes to reflect the new print position, but the cursor does not move. To return the print head to its original position, you must enter a separate code to advance in the opposite direction.

Centering Pages, Using Advance

Centering Pages Top to Bottom

You may want to center a page top to bottom. You may, for example, want to center the title page of a sales report.

Position the cursor at the top left margin of the page, before any other formatting codes. You can press [Alt][F3], or [F11] (Reveal Codes) to verify the cursor position.

Press [⇧Shift][F8] to display the Format menu.

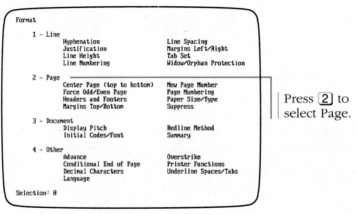

Press [2] to select Page.

Press [1] for Center Page.

Press [F7] to return to your document.

Although the text does not appear centered on-screen, it will be centered when you print the page.

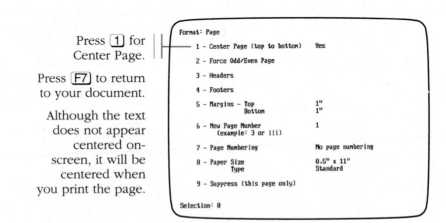

Using Advance

Use the Advance feature to instruct your printer to move left, right, up, or down before printing or to tell your printer to start printing at a specific location on the page.

Position the cursor at the location where you want Advance to begin.

Press ⟨⇧Shift⟩⟨F8⟩ to display the Format menu.

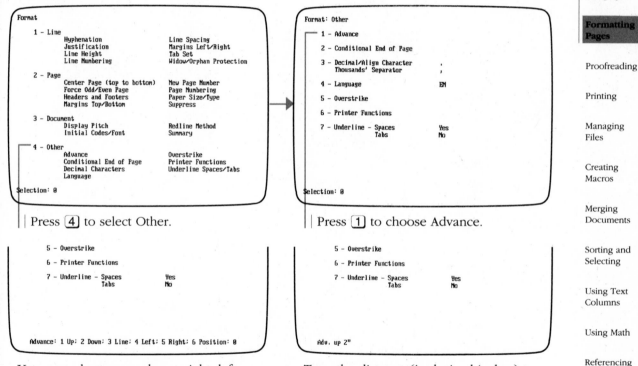

Press ⟨4⟩ to select Other.

Press ⟨1⟩ to choose Advance.

You can advance up, down, right, left, or to a specified position.

Type the number associated with your selection.

Type the distance (in decimal inches) to advance and press ⟨⏎Enter⟩.

The distance you enter for Advance Up or Advance Down is relative to the current cursor position. If you choose Position, the distance you enter specifies an absolute position on the page.

Press ⟨F7⟩ to return to your document.

Designing Headers and Footers

A *header* is information (text, numbers, or graphics) that prints automatically at the top margin of each page. A *footer* is information that prints automatically at the bottom margin of each page. Typical header and footer information may include chapter titles and page numbers, or revision numbers and dates.

You cannot see headers or footers on-screen. You can use either View Document (Shift-F7, 6) or Reveal Codes (Alt-F3, or F11) to view header and footer text.

Creating a Header or Footer

To create a header or footer, you first press Format (Shift-F8) to display the Format menu. Then you select Page (2) to display the Format: Page menu. Next, you can choose either Headers (3) or Footers (4).

You can create two headers (A and B) and two footers (A and B). From the menu that appears, you select the header or footer you want to create. From the next menu that appears, you select one of the following specifications:

- Select Every Page (2) if you want the header (or footer) to appear on every page.
- Select Odd Pages (3) if you want the header (or footer) to appear on odd pages only.
- Select Even Pages (4) if you want the header (or footer) to appear on even pages only.

You type the header (or footer) text, using any of WordPerfect's formatting features. Finally, you press Exit (F7) twice to return to your document.

WordPerfect automatically skips one line between the header or footer and the first (for headers) or last (for footers) line of text. If you want to insert more blank lines between the header (or footer) and the text, include blank lines when you define the header or footer.

Editing a Header or Footer

You can make changes to a header or footer from anywhere in a document. For instance, you can change the text or the appearance of the text in your footer.

To edit a header or footer, you first press Format (Shift-F8) to display the Format menu. Then you select Page (2) to display the Format: Page menu. From this menu, you select either Headers (3) or Footers (4). Next, you select either Header A (or Footer A) or Header B (or Footer B). Then you select Edit (5). An editing screen with the header or footer text appears. You edit the header or footer. Finally, you press Exit (F7) twice to return to your document.

Including Automatic Page Numbering

In addition to including and formatting text, you can add automatic page numbering by including ^B (Ctrl-B) in the header or footer. For example, you can specify the footer to read *Page 1* and be numbered consecutively.

To include automatic page numbering in headers and footers, you first type any text that will precede the page number, such as *Page*. Then you press Ctrl-B. Finally, you press Exit (F7) to return to your document.

Designing Headers and Footers

Creating a Header or Footer

Print header or footer information automatically at the top or bottom margin, respectively, of the page.

Press ⸢⇧Shift⸣ ⸢F8⸣ to display the Format menu.

Press ⸢2⸣ to select Page.

Press ⸢3⸣ to select Headers, or ⸢4⸣ to select Footers.

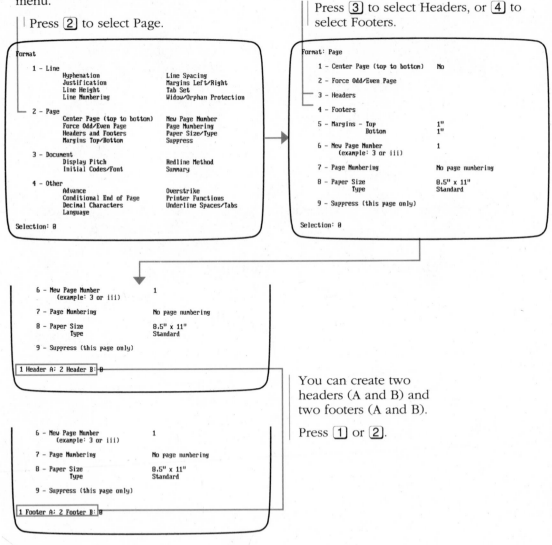

```
Format

   1 - Line
        Hyphenation                    Line Spacing
        Justification                  Margins Left/Right
        Line Height                    Tab Set
        Line Numbering                 Widow/Orphan Protection

   2 - Page
        Center Page (top to bottom)    New Page Number
        Force Odd/Even Page            Page Numbering
        Headers and Footers            Paper Size/Type
        Margins Top/Bottom             Suppress

   3 - Document
        Display Pitch                  Redline Method
        Initial Codes/Font             Summary

   4 - Other
        Advance                        Overstrike
        Conditional End of Page        Printer Functions
        Decimal Characters             Underline Spaces/Tabs
        Language

Selection: 0
```

```
Format: Page

   1 - Center Page (top to bottom)    No

   2 - Force Odd/Even Page

   3 - Headers

   4 - Footers

   5 - Margins - Top                  1"
                 Bottom               1"

   6 - New Page Number                1
         (example: 3 or iii)

   7 - Page Numbering                 No page numbering

   8 - Paper Size                     8.5" x 11"
            Type                      Standard

   9 - Suppress (this page only)

Selection: 0
```

```
   6 - New Page Number                1
         (example: 3 or iii)

   7 - Page Numbering                 No page numbering

   8 - Paper Size                     8.5" x 11"
            Type                      Standard

   9 - Suppress (this page only)

1 Header A; 2 Header B: 0
```

```
   6 - New Page Number                1
         (example: 3 or iii)

   7 - Page Numbering                 No page numbering

   8 - Paper Size                     8.5" x 11"
            Type                      Standard

   9 - Suppress (this page only)

1 Footer A; 2 Footer B: 0
```

You can create two headers (A and B) and two footers (A and B).

Press ⸢1⸣ or ⸢2⸣.

Press [2] if you want the header (or footer) to appear on every page.

Or

Press [3] if you want the header (or footer) to appear on odd pages only.

Or

Press [4] if you want the header (or footer) to appear on even pages only.

Type the header (or footer) text using any of WordPerfect's formatting features.

Press [F7] twice to return to your document.

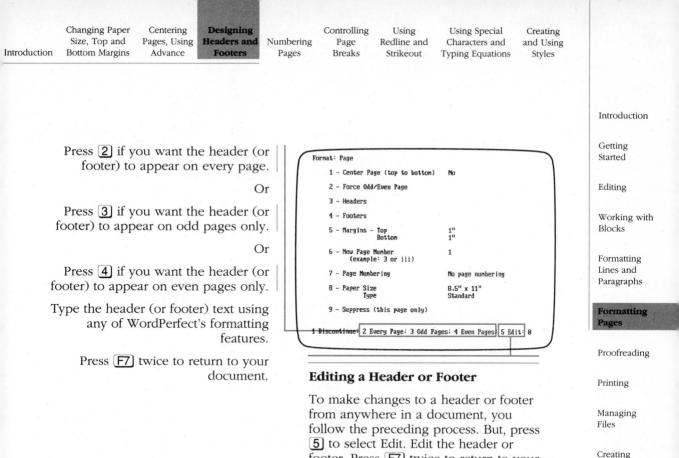

Editing a Header or Footer

To make changes to a header or footer from anywhere in a document, you follow the preceding process. But, press [5] to select Edit. Edit the header or footer. Press [F7] twice to return to your document.

Including Automatic Page Numbering

Add automatic page numbering by including ^B (Ctrl-B) in a header or footer.

Type any text that will precede the page number. For example, type **Page** and press the space bar once.

Press [Ctrl][B].

Press [F7] to return to your document.

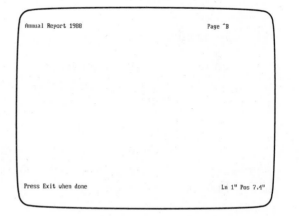

Numbering Pages

Numbering pages automatically, not as part of a header or footer, is easy as telling WordPerfect how and where you want the numbers to appear on the page. Numbering begins with whatever number you select. Be sure to place the cursor at the beginning of your document if you want page numbering to begin on the first page.

Selecting a Page Number Position

You can select among a variety of page number positions. You can position the number at the top or bottom of the page—at the left, right, or center. Or, you can number only alternate pages—the left side of even pages or the right side of odd pages.

To select a page number position, you first press Format (Shift-F8) to display the Format menu. Then you select Page (2) to display the Format: Page menu. Next, you select Page Numbering (7) to display the Format: Page Numbering menu. You type the number that corresponds to the position where you want page numbers to appear. Finally, you press Exit (F7) to return to your document.

Page numbers can be centered or aligned with the left or right margin. WordPerfect positions page numbers at the top or bottom margin and leaves a space between the page number and the body text equivalent to the line height of the page number font plus one line.

Page numbers don't appear on-screen, although the status line indicates the current page number. You can see the page numbers on-screen by pressing Print (Shift-F7) and choosing View Document (6).

If you turn on page numbering and later decide that you don't want page numbers, you must delete the page numbering code. To delete the page numbering code, you first move to the position where you invoked the page numbering function. Then you press Reveal Codes (Alt-F3, or F11). In the Reveal Codes screen, you delete the [Pg Numbering:] code.

Changing the Starting Page Number

You can change page numbering at any point in your document; the change takes effect from that point forward. Keep in mind that you can use Arabic numerals (1, 2, 3) or Roman numerals (i, ii, iii). If you want to use Roman numerals, you must use the following procedure to change the starting page number, even if you plan to start with Roman numeral i.

To change the starting page number, you first move the cursor to the top of the page where you want to start numbering. Then you press Format (Shift-F8) to display the Format menu. Next, you select Page (2) to display the Format: Page menu. Then you select New Page Number (6). You type the new page number (1 for Arabic or i for Roman) and press Enter. Finally, you press Exit (F7) to return to your document.

Suppressing Page Numbering

You can turn off page numbering for the entire document or for a single page of the document. To turn off page numbering for the entire document, you first press Format (Shift-F8) to display the Format menu. Then you select Page (2) to display the Format: Page menu. Next, you select Page Numbering (7). Then you choose No Page Numbers (9). Finally, you press Exit (F7) to return to your document.

You can suppress page numbering for a single page so that no number appears for that page but numbering continues on the following pages. For instance, you may not want the title page of a report to have a page number. To suppress page numbering for a single page, you first move to the top of the page on which you want numbering suppressed. Then you press Format (Shift-F8) to display the Format menu. Next, you select Page (2) to display the Format: Page menu. From this menu, you select Suppress (this page only) (9), choose Suppress Page Numbering (4), and press Y. Finally, you press Exit (F7) to return to your document.

Numbering Pages

To number pages, tell WordPerfect how and where you want the numbers to appear on the page.

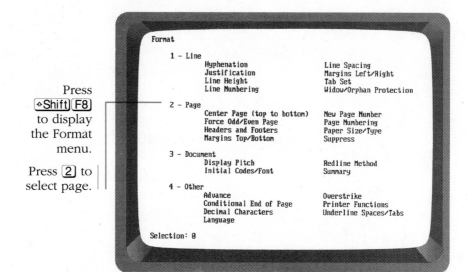

Press
⬆Shift F8
to display
the Format
menu.

Press 2 to
select page.

```
Format

    1 - Line
            Hyphenation                    Line Spacing
            Justification                  Margins Left/Right
            Line Height                    Tab Set
            Line Numbering                 Widow/Orphan Protection

    2 - Page
            Center Page (top to bottom)    New Page Number
            Force Odd/Even Page            Page Numbering
            Headers and Footers            Paper Size/Type
            Margins Top/Bottom             Suppress

    3 - Document
            Display Pitch                  Redline Method
            Initial Codes/Font             Summary

    4 - Other
            Advance                        Overstrike
            Conditional End of Page        Printer Functions
            Decimal Characters             Underline Spaces/Tabs
            Language

Selection: 0
```

```
Format: Page

    1 - Center Page (top to bottom)    No

    2 - Force Odd/Even Page

    3 - Headers

    4 - Footers                        FA Every page

    5 - Margins - Top                  1"
                  Bottom               1"

    6 - New Page Number                1
          (example: 3 or iii)

    7 - Page Numbering                 No page numbering

    8 - Paper Size                     8.5" x 11"
               Type                    Standard

    9 - Suppress (this page only)

Selection: 0
```

```
Format: Page Numbering

     Every Page              Alternating Pages

    1   2   3          4                      4

                       Even                 Odd

    5   6   7          8                      8


  9 - No Page Numbers


Selection: 0
```

To select a page number position, press ⑦ for Page Numbering, and type the number that corresponds to the position where you want page numbers to appear.

To turn off page numbering, press ⑦ for Page Numbering. Then press ⑨ for No Page Numbers.

```
Format: Suppress (this page only)

   1 - Suppress All Page Numbering, Headers and Footers
   2 - Suppress Headers and Footers
   3 - Print Page Number at Bottom Center   No
   4 - Suppress Page Numbering              No
   5 - Suppress Header A                    No
   6 - Suppress Header B                    No
   7 - Suppress Footer A                    No
   8 - Suppress Footer B                    No


Selection: 0
```

To change the starting page number, press ⑥ for New Page Number. Then type the new page number and press ⏎Enter.

To suppress page numbering, press ⑨ for Suppress (this page only). Then press ④ for Suppress Page Numbering, and press Ⓨ.

Controlling Page Breaks

WordPerfect offers a number of options to control where one page ends and the next begins. The options include WordPerfect's automatic page breaks, hard page breaks, the Block Protect command, the Conditional End of Page function, and the Widow/Orphan Protection feature.

Using Automatic Page Breaks

WordPerfect's automatic page breaks are based on an 8 1/2-by-11-inch page with 1-inch top and bottom margins. WordPerfect inserts a dashed line in your document on-screen wherever an automatic page break occurs. This *soft page break* produces a hidden [SPg] code. When you add or delete text from a page, soft page breaks are recalculated automatically.

Inserting Hard Page Breaks

To force a page break at a certain spot—for example, at the beginning of a new section in a report—you enter a *hard page break*. The page always ends at that point. On-screen a hard page break appears as a line of equal signs.

To insert a hard page break, you first move the cursor to the point where you want the page break to occur. Then you press Ctrl-Enter to insert a [HPg] code. To delete a hard page break, you press Reveal Codes (Alt-F3, or F11). Then you delete the [HPg] code. Finally, you press Reveal Codes (Alt-F3, or F11) again.

Using the Block Protect Command

With Block Protect, you define the text you want to protect as a block. If you later add or subtract lines from the block, WordPerfect keeps the block on the same page.

To use the Block Protect command, you first press Block (Alt-F4, or F12) and highlight the text you want to protect. (Be sure not to highlight the final return at the end of a paragraph.) Then you press

Format (Shift-F8). In response to the prompt, you press Y to protect the block.

Using the Conditional End of Page Function

The Conditional End of Page function is similar to Block Protect, but instead of blocking the text, you specify the number of lines to keep together. The Conditional End of Page function groups a given number of lines so that they don't break between two pages. Use this function, for example, when you want to be sure that a heading in a document is followed by at least three lines of text.

To use the Conditional End of Page command, you first count the lines that must remain together on the same page. Then you move the cursor to the line above the lines you want to keep together. Next, you press Format (Shift-F8) to display the Format menu. Then you select Other (4) to display the Format: Other menu. You choose Conditional End of Page (2). At the prompt for the number of lines to keep together, you enter the number of lines you counted and press Enter. Finally, you press Exit (F7) to return to your document.

Using the Widow/Orphan Protection Feature

WordPerfect can automatically prevent single lines from being "stranded" at the top or at the bottom of a page. The first line of a paragraph left at the bottom of a page is called a *widow*; the last line of a paragraph left at the top of a page is called an *orphan*.

To turn on the Widow/Orphan Protection feature, you first position the cursor at the top of the document (or wherever you want the protection to begin). Then you press Format (Shift-F8) to display the Format menu. Next, you select Line (1) to display the Format: Line menu. From this menu, you select Widow/Orphan Protection (9) and press Y to turn on the feature. Finally, you press Exit (F7) to return to your document. To turn off the feature, repeat this procedure, but press N instead of Y.

Controlling Page Breaks

You can use a number of WordPerfect features to control where one page ends and the next begins.

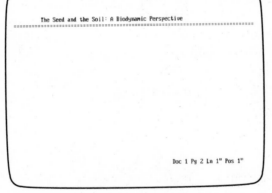

Using Automatic Page Breaks

WordPerfect automatically inserts a page break at the end of the page. This *soft page break* appears as a dashed line on-screen and produces a hidden [SPg] code.

Inserting Hard Page Breaks

Force a page break at a certain spot by entering a *hard page break*. The page always ends at that point. On-screen a hard page break appears as a line of equal signs and produces a hidden [HPg] code.

To insert a hard page break, move the cursor to where you want the page break to occur and press Ctrl ↵Enter.

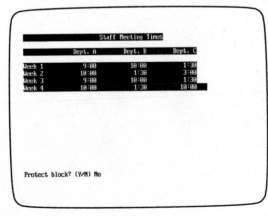

Using the Block Protect Command

Use the Block Protect command to define the text you want to protect as a block.

Press Alt F4 or F12 to turn on Block, and highlight the text you want to protect.

When you define the block, move the cursor to the end of the block but don't include the final return at the end of a paragraph.

Press ⇧Shift F8, the Format key.

Press Y to protect the block.

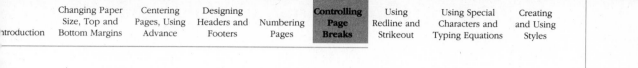

Changing Paper Size, Top and Bottom Margins | Centering Pages, Using Advance | Designing Headers and Footers | Numbering Pages | **Controlling Page Breaks** | Using Redline and Strikeout | Using Special Characters and Typing Equations | Creating and Using Styles

Introduction

Using the Conditional End of Page Function

The Conditional End of Page function groups a given number of lines so that they don't break between two pages.

Count the lines that must remain together on the same page.

Move the cursor to the line above the lines you want to keep together.

Press ⬆Shift F8 to display the Format menu.

Select 4 to select Other.

```
Format: Other

    1 - Advance

    2 - Conditional End of Page

    3 - Decimal/Align Character          .
        Thousands' Separator             ,

    4 - Language                         EN

    5 - Overstrike

    6 - Printer Functions

    7 - Underline - Spaces               Yes
                    Tabs                 No




Number of Lines to Keep Together:
```

Press 2 for Conditional End of Page.

Type the number of lines you counted and press ⏎Enter.

Press F7 to return to your document.

Using the Widow/Orphan Protection Feature

WordPerfect can automatically prevent single lines from being "stranded" at the bottom (as *widows*) or at the top (as *orphans*) of a page.

Position the cursor at the top of the document (or wherever you want the protection to begin).

```
Format: Line

    1 - Hyphenation                      Off

    2 - Hyphenation Zone - Left          10%
                           Right         4%

    3 - Justification                    Yes

    4 - Line Height                      Auto

    5 - Line Numbering                   No

    6 - Line Spacing                     1

    7 - Margins - Left                   1"
                  Right                  1"

    8 - Tab Set                          0", every 0.5"

    9 - Widow/Orphan Protection          No


Selection: 0
```

Press ⬆Shift F8 to display the Format menu.

Press 1 to select Line.

Press 9 to select Widow/Orphan Protection.

Press Y to turn on Widow/Orphan Protection.

Press F7 to return to your document.

Using Redline and Strikeout

Redline and strikeout are tools for marking the suggested editing changes in a manuscript. Redlining is a method of indicating particular segments of text where passages have been edited, added to, or deleted from a document. When several people work on a document, redlining is a useful way to let everyone know what changes are proposed. While redlining is generally used to identify text that has been modified, WordPerfect's strikeout feature is used to identify text the editor believes should be deleted.

In WordPerfect you can choose how redlining appears on the printed page. With many printers, redline appears as a mark in the margin next to the redlined text. With other printers, redlined text appears shaded or highlighted. If you have a color printer, redlined text prints red. Strikeout appears as characters superimposed over other characters.

Selecting the Redlining Method

To specify the way that redline should appear on the printed page, you first press Format (Shift-F8) to display the Format menu. Then you select Display (3) to display the Format: Document menu. From this menu, you select Redline Method (4). At this point, you designate one of the following redline methods:

- Select Printer Dependent (1) to mark redlined text according to your printer's definition of redlining.
- Select Left (2) to print a character in the margin to the left of the redlined text.
- Select Alternating (3) to print a redlined character in the outside margins of alternating pages.

After you designate the redline method, you press Exit (F7) to return to your document.

Marking Text with Redline or Strikeout

The procedures for marking text with redline and strikeout are the same, up until the last step. In both procedures, you begin by using Block (Alt-F4, or F12) to highlight the block you want to mark. Then you press Font (Ctrl-F8) to display the Font menu. From this menu, you select Appearance (2). The last step is to choose Redline (8) or Strikeout (9).

Removing Redline and Strikeout Markings

After your text is finalized, you finish editing your document by removing the redline and strikeout markings. When you remove the markings, only the markings for redline are removed, not the text itself. When you remove the strikeout markings, however, you delete the actual text marked for strikeout, not just the strikeout symbols. You can remove all redline and strikeout markings with one procedure.

To remove all redline and strikeout markings, you press Mark Text (Alt-F5). From the Mark Text menu, you choose Generate (6), and then you select Remove Redline Markings and Strikeout Text from Document (1). In response to the prompt confirming deletion, you press Y.

Using Redline and Strikeout

Selecting the Redlining Method

You can specify the way that redline should appear on the printed page.

Press ⟨⇧Shift⟩⟨F8⟩ to display the Format menu.

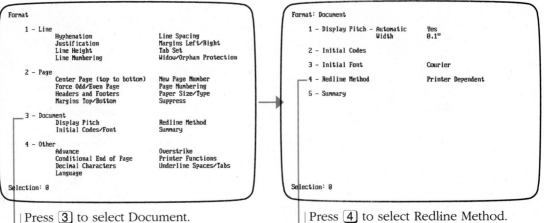

Press **3** to select Document.

Press **4** to select Redline Method.

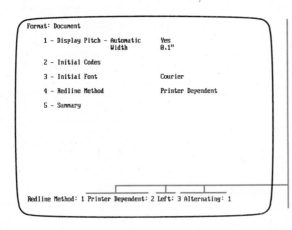

Press **1** to select Printer Dependent, which marks redline text according to your printer's definition of redlining.

Or

Press **2** to select Left, which prints a character in the margin to the left of the redlined text.

Or

Press **3** to select Alternating, which prints a redline character in the outside margins of alternating pages.

Press **F7** to return to your document.

Marking Text with Redline or Strikeout

The procedures for marking text with redline and strikeout are the same, up until the last step.

Press [Alt][4] or [F12] to turn on Block.

Highlight the block you want to redline.

Press [Ctrl]-[F8], the Font key.

Press [2] to select Appearance.

Press [8] to select Redline, or [9] to select Strikeout.

Removing Redline and Strikeout Markings

To finish editing your document, you need to remove the redline and strikeout markings. When you remove the markings, only the markings for redline are removed, not the text itself. When you remove the strikeout markings, however, you delete the actual text marked for strikeout, in addition to the strikeout symbols.

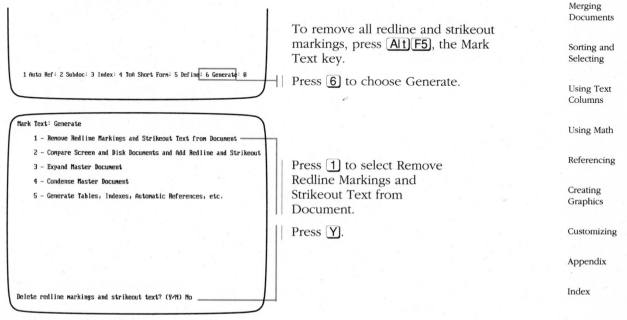

To remove all redline and strikeout markings, press [Alt][F5], the Mark Text key.

Press [6] to choose Generate.

Press [1] to select Remove Redline Markings and Strikeout Text from Document.

Press [Y].

167

Using Special Characters and Typing Equations

In your documents, you may need to create special characters or type equations. WordPerfect has features that allow you to create special characters and use super- and subscripts, half-line spacing, and space fill for equations.

Creating Special Characters

In most documents, only one character appears in a space. For special characters, you may want two characters to print in the same space, such as è or ç. You can use WordPerfect's Compose and Overstrike features to create special characters.

Using Compose

You can use Compose to insert one of WordPerfect's special characters or to combine two characters. (See the WordPerfect manual for a list of character sets.)

To create special characters with Compose, you first press Ctrl-2 (or Ctrl-V to display a prompt). At this point, you can use either of two methods. For the first method, you type the number of the character set, a comma, and then the number of the character; then you press Enter. For example, to create the German double-S character, you type **1,23** and press Enter.

Use the second method if the character is a combination of two characters. You type the first character, and then you type the second character. For example, for ç, type *c* and then a comma (,).

Using Overstrike

To create special characters with Overstrike—for example, to overstrike an O with a backslash, you first move the cursor to the point where you want to create an overstrike character. Then you press Format (Shift-F8) to display the Format menu. Next, you select Other (4), Overstrike (5), and Create (1). Then you type each character (or attribute) you want to appear in that character position and press Enter. You press Exit (F7) to return to your document.

As you type, you can see the characters and codes. When you return to your document, however, only the last character you've entered is visible.

All the characters you enter are printed in the same character position. To review the codes and characters, you use Reveal Codes (Alt-F3, or F11).

To edit a character created with Overstrike, you first move the cursor to the point where you want to edit an overstrike character. Then you press Format (Shift-F8) to display the Format menu. Next, you select Other (4), Overstrike (5), and Edit (2). Then you type the new overstrike characters and press Enter. You press Exit (F7) to return to your document.

Using Special Characters and Typing Equations

Using Superscripts and Subscripts

Superscript and subscript are font attributes located on the Font: Size menu. A *superscript* is a number or letter written immediately above, or above and to the right or left of, another character (for example, $E=mc^2$). A *subscript* is a distinguishing symbol written immediately below, or below and to the right or left of, another character (for example, H_2SO_4).

To create a subscript or superscript character, you first press Font (Ctrl-F8). Then you select Size (1). Next, you select either Superscript (1) or Subscript (2). You type the super- or subscripted characters. When you want to return to the normal font, you press the right-arrow key to move the cursor one character to the right, past the hidden attribute-off code.

The shifted characters look normal on-screen but are printed above or below the normal character baseline. The exact spacing depends on your printer's capabilities, and some printers may not be capable of printing superscripts or subscripts. The characters also are printed in small type, if your printer is capable of it.

If the text to be super- or subscripted is already typed, you define it as a Block (Alt-F4, or F12), press the Font key (Ctrl-F8), select Size (1), and then choose the appropriate appearance.

Typing Equations

To simplify the process of entering complex formulas, you can use half-line spacing and space fill. With half-line spacing, you can enter each level of super- and subscripts on a separate line, creating several levels. Space fill creates a blank area for you to type your equation.

To create an area for entering equations, you first position the cursor at the left margin of the first line where the equation will appear. Then you press Format (Shift-F8) to display the Format menu. Next, you select Line (1) and choose Line Spacing (6). You type **.5** for half-line spacing and press Enter. If Justification (on the Format: Line menu) is set to Yes, you select Justification (3) and type N to turn it off. Finally, you press Exit (F7) to return to your document.

At the document screen, you count the number of lines in the equation. Count normal lines, superscripts, and subscripts, as separate lines. Then you hold down the space bar to create a line of blank spaces; be sure to press Enter at the end of each line. Create as many lines as you need. When you type the equation, you press Ins to activate Typeover mode. In this mode, the blank spaces make moving the cursor in the equation area easier. You use the arrow keys to move the cursor to the line where you want to begin. Finally, you type the equation.

Using Special Characters and Typing Equations

Creating Special Characters

Use WordPerfect's Compose and Overstrike features to create special characters.

Using Compose

Use Compose to insert one of WordPerfect's special characters or to combine two characters.

Press [Ctrl][2] (or [Ctrl][V] to display a prompt).

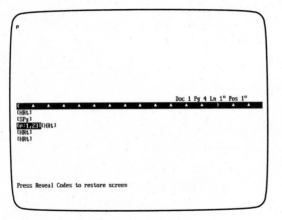

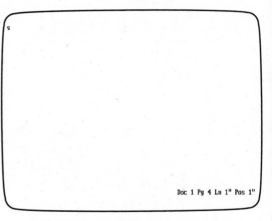

To insert one of WordPerfect's special characters, type the number of the character set, a comma, and then the number of the character; then press [↵Enter]. For example, type **1,23** and press [↵Enter] for the German double-S character.

To combine two characters, type the first character, and then type the second character. For example, for ç, type *c* and then a comma (,).

172

Using Overstrike

Use Overstrike to create special characters by combining more than one character in a single space.

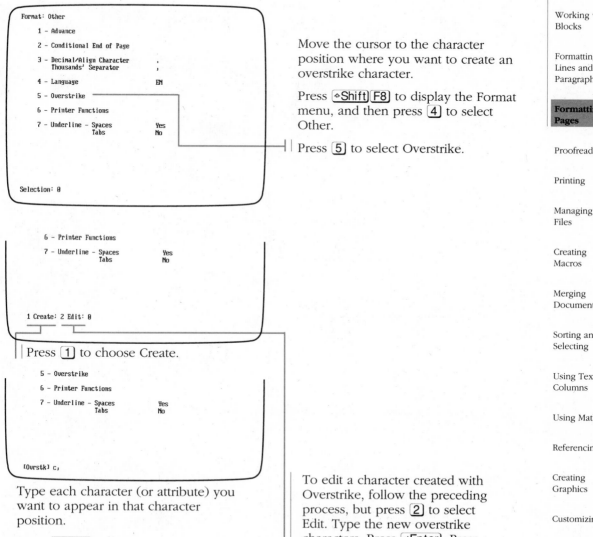

Move the cursor to the character position where you want to create an overstrike character.

Press ⬆Shift F8 to display the Format menu, and then press 4 to select Other.

Press 5 to select Overstrike.

Press 1 to choose Create.

Type each character (or attribute) you want to appear in that character position.

Press ⏎Enter.

Press F7 to return to your document.

To edit a character created with Overstrike, follow the preceding process, but press 2 to select Edit. Type the new overstrike characters. Press ⏎Enter. Press F7 to return to your document.

Using Special Characters and Typing Equations

Using Superscripts and Subscripts

Use superscripts to position numbers or letters immediately above, or above and to the right or left of, another character. Use subscripts to position numbers or letters immediately below, or below and to the right or left of, another character.

Press [Ctrl][F8], the Font key.

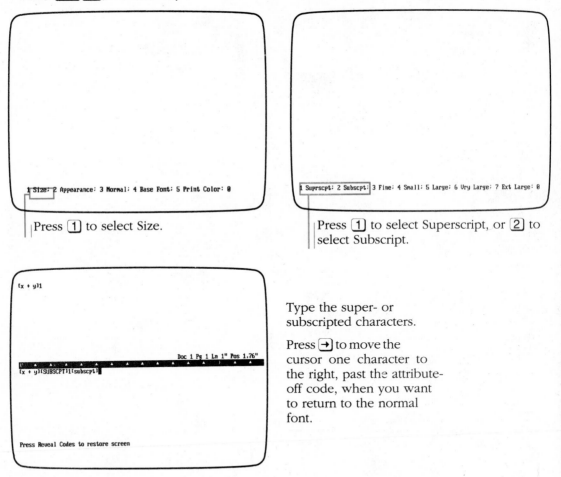

1 Size; 2 Appearance; 3 Normal; 4 Base Font; 5 Print Color; 0

Press [1] to select Size.

1 Suprscpt; 2 Subscpt; 3 Fine; 4 Small; 5 Large; 6 Vry Large; 7 Ext Large; 0

Press [1] to select Superscript, or [2] to select Subscript.

```
[x + y]1




                                          Doc 1 Pg 1 Ln 1" Pos 1.76"
[x + y]1[SUBSCPT]1[subscpt]




Press Reveal Codes to restore screen
```

Type the super- or subscripted characters.

Press [→] to move the cursor one character to the right, past the attribute-off code, when you want to return to the normal font.

Typing Equations

To simplify the process of entering complex formulas, use half-line spacing and space fill to create an area for entering equations.

To create an area for entering equations, position the cursor at the left margin of the first line where the equation will appear on the page.

Press ⬆Shift F8 to display the Format menu and press 1 to select Line.

```
Format: Line

    1 - Hyphenation                  Off

    2 - Hyphenation Zone - Left      10%
                          Right      4%

    3 - Justification                No

    4 - Line Height                  Auto

    5 - Line Numbering               No

    6 - Line Spacing                 0.5

    7 - Margins - Left               1"
                  Right              1"

    8 - Tab Set                      0", every 0.5"

    9 - Widow/Orphan Protection      No


Selection: 0
```

Press 6 to select Line Spacing.

Type .5 for half-line spacing.

Press ⏎Enter.

If Justification (on the Format: Line menu) is set to Yes, press 3 and press N to turn it off.

Press F7 to return to your document.

Count the number of lines in the equation. Count subscripts, superscripts, and normal lines as separate lines.

Hold down the space bar to create a line of blank spaces. Press ⏎Enter at the end of the line.

Create as many lines as you need.

Press Ins to activate Typeover mode.

Use the arrow keys to move the cursor to the line where you want to begin the equation.

Type the equation.

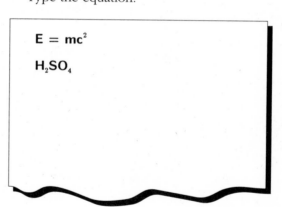

$$E = mc^2$$

$$H_2SO_4$$

Creating and Using Styles

You can use Style (Alt-F8) as a powerful tool to control the format of one document or a group of documents. A style is a group of WordPerfect codes (you can include text also) you turn on and off to control the format of your document. Styles save time by reducing the number of formatting keystrokes. For example, a style may contain all the codes needed to format a chapter heading, a long quotation, a bibliography entry, or margin and tab settings. Style definitions are saved with the current document, or you can save style definitions to a style library file so that you can use them on other documents.

WordPerfect's styles fall into two categories: *open* and *paired*. Open styles remain in effect until you override the style codes, either by using another style or by inserting other formatting codes manually. Use open styles for formatting that affects an entire document. For instance, use open styles to set margins, tabs, line spacing, hyphenation, and so forth. If you want the style to affect the entire document, move the cursor to the beginning of the document before turning on the style.

Paired styles are turned on and off. For instance, you can create a paired style called Heading that makes the text bold and italic. When you use this style, you insert [Style On: Heading] and [Style Off: Heading] codes around the text to be formatted. Use paired styles for titles, section headings, tables—any text element that has a beginning and an end.

Creating a Style

To create a style, you first press Style (Alt-F8). From the menu that appears, you select Create (3) to display the Styles: Edit menu. From this menu, you select Name (1), type a name for the style, and press Enter. The name you enter appears in Reveal Codes when you use this style; therefore, use a name that is easy to remember and tells what the style does. Next, you select Type (2). From the menu that appears, you can choose either Paired (1) to create a paired style or Open (2) to create an open style.

Next, you select Description (3), type a description of the style, and press Enter. Descriptions can be up to 54 characters long. Include the date so that you can keep track of style revisions.

You next select Codes (4). If you are creating an open style, a screen that resembles the Reveal Codes screen appears. If you are creating a paired style, a screen with a comment box appears. The comment box represents the text you will type (and format) when you use this style.

If you are creating an open style, you insert the formatting codes and text you want to include in the style just as if you were editing a normal WordPerfect document. Or, if you are creating a paired style, you enter the beginning format codes (and any text), press the down-arrow key to move past the comment box, and then enter the ending format codes.

Creating and Using Styles

If you are creating an open style, you press Exit (F7) three times to return to your document. The style creation process for an open style is now complete.

If you are creating a paired style, you continue by pressing Exit (F7) once, and then selecting Enter (5). Your next selection determines the effect that pressing Enter has on your style:

- Select HRt (1) if you want the Enter key to function normally (insert hard returns). Use this style to format passages of text containing hard returns.
- Select Off (2) if you want to turn off the style when you press Enter. Use this style for short sections of text, such as headings or titles.
- Select Off/On (3) if you want to turn off and then immediately turn on a style. Use this style to format several paragraphs (for instance, hanging paragraphs) in the same style.

To complete the creation process for a paired style, you press Exit (F7) twice to return to your document.

Using a Style

To use a style, you first move the cursor to where you want the style to begin. You press Style (Alt-F8) to display the Styles menu. Then you use the cursor keys to highlight the style you want to use. You select On (1) or press Enter to turn on the style. Finally, you type your text.

If you are using a paired style and defined Enter as Off, the style is turned off when you press Enter. If you are using a paired style and defined Enter as HRt or On/Off, you turn off the style by pressing Style (Alt-F8) and then Off (2).

To use a paired style with existing text, you first press Block (Alt-F4, or F12) and highlight the text. Then you press Style (Alt-F8) to display the Styles menu. You use the cursor keys to highlight the style you want to use. Then you select On (1) or press Enter to turn on the style.

Editing a Style Definition

To edit a style definition, you first press Style (Alt-F8) to display the Styles menu. Then you use the cursor keys to highlight the style you want to edit. Next, you select Edit (4) to display the Styles: Edit menu. You select any option and make changes. Finally, you press Exit (F7) twice to return to your document. All occurrences of the style in your document automatically reflect the edits.

Creating and Using Styles

Use styles to control the format of one document or a group of documents.

Creating a Style

Create either an *open* style or a *paired* style. Use open styles for formatting that affects an entire document. Use paired styles for titles, section headings, tables—any text element that has a beginning and an end.

Press [Alt][F8], the Style key.

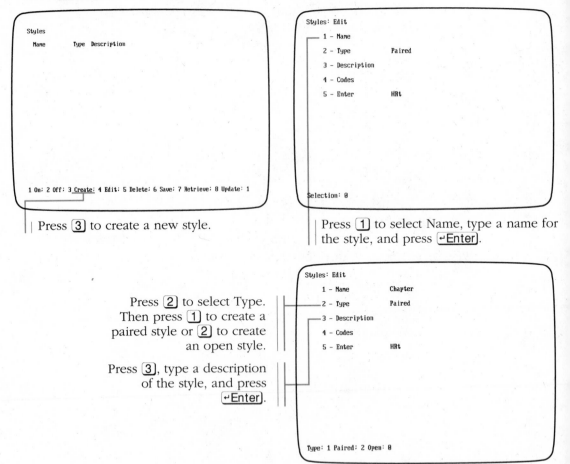

Press [3] to create a new style.

Press [1] to select Name, type a name for the style, and press [↵Enter].

Press [2] to select Type. Then press [1] to create a paired style or [2] to create an open style.

Press [3], type a description of the style, and press [↵Enter].

Creating an Open Style

Press ④ to select Codes.

A screen that resembles the Reveal Codes screen appears.

Insert the formatting codes and text you want to include in the style just as if you were editing a normal WordPerfect document.

Creating a Paired Style

Press ④ to select Codes.

A screen with a comment box appears. The comment box represents the text you will type (and format) when you use this style.

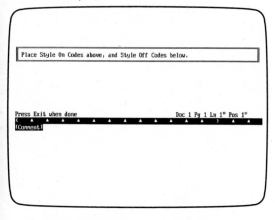

Enter the beginning format codes (and any text), press → to move past the comment box, and then enter the ending format codes.

Press F7.

Press ⑤ to select Enter.

Your next selection determines the effect that pressing Enter has on your style.

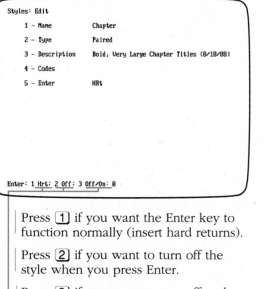

Press ① if you want the Enter key to function normally (insert hard returns).

Press ② if you want to turn off the style when you press Enter.

Press ③ if you want to turn off and then immediately turn on a style.

Creating and Using Styles

Using a Style

With existing text, press [Alt][F4] or [F12] and highlight the text. Or, for text you are about to type, move the cursor to where you want the style to begin.

Press [Alt][F8] to display the Styles menu.

```
Styles

Name        Type  Description

Chapter     Paired Bold, Very Large Chapter Titles (8/18/88)

1 On; 2 Off; 3 Create; 4 Edit; 5 Delete; 6 Save; 7 Retrieve; 8 Update: 1
```

Use the cursor keys to highlight the style you want to use.

Press [1] or [⏎Enter] to turn on the style.

Type your text (if you are not using styles with existing text).

Turning Off a Style

If you are using a paired style and defined Enter as Off, the style is turned off when you press [⏎Enter].

If you are using a paired style and defined Enter as HRt or On/Off, turn off the style by pressing [Alt][F8] and then pressing [2].

Editing a Style

Press [Alt] [F8] to display the Styles menu.

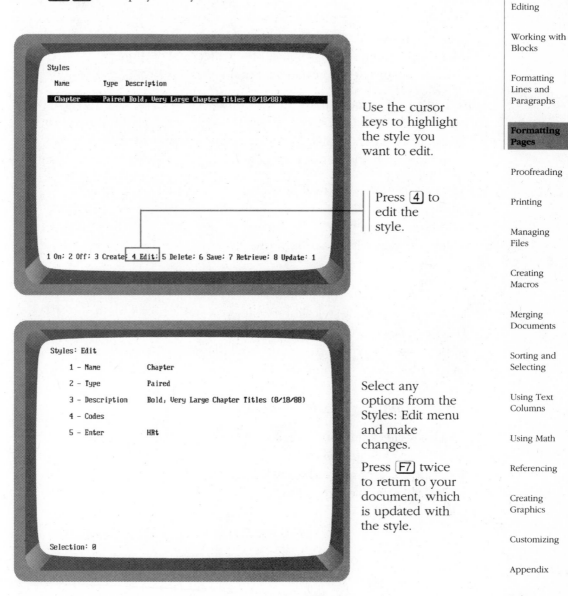

Use the cursor keys to highlight the style you want to edit.

Press [4] to edit the style.

Select any options from the Styles: Edit menu and make changes.

Press [F7] twice to return to your document, which is updated with the style.

Creating and Using Styles

Using Style Libraries

When you save your document, the style definitions are saved with your document regardless of whether you used them or not. Whenever you edit this document, the styles are available for use. You also can save style definitions to a special file called a style library; then you can use these styles on other documents.

To use styles in more than one document, you must save the style to a style library. A style library file is a WordPerfect document that consists solely of style definitions. You can make as many style libraries as you want, and each style library can contain as many styles as you want.

You can use any of WordPerfect's style libraries (with the .STY extension), found on the Conversion disk, or you can create your own style library. Moreover, you can set up one style library as your default; when you press Style (Alt-F8), this style list appears.

Specifying a Default Style Library File

To specify a default style library file, you first press Setup (Shift-F1). Then you select Location of Auxiliary Files (7). Next, you select Style Library File (6), type a file name (including a drive and directory), and press Enter. Finally, you press Exit (F7) to return to your document.

Saving Definitions to a Style Library

To save style definitions to a style library, you first press Style (Alt-F8) to display the Styles menu. Then you select Save (6). At the prompt, you type a file name and press Enter. To help keep track of your files, use .STY as the file extension. Finally, you press Exit (F7) to return to your document.

Retrieving a Style Library File

To retrieve a style library file, you first press Style (Alt-F8) to display the Styles menu. Then you select Retrieve (7) to retrieve the style. Next, you type a file name and press Enter.

If you have defined styles in your current document, you may be prompted:

```
Styles already exist. Replace? (Y/N) No
```

You can press Y to overwrite the style definitions with duplicate names in your document with the new style definitions. Or, you can press N to read in only the style definitions with different names from those in your document. Finally, you press Exit (F7) to return to your document.

Updating Documents with a Style

If you change a style definition in your style library and want to update the documents to which you've applied this style, you can use Update to reformat your documents with the modified style.

To update a document with a style, you first retrieve the document. Then you press Style (Alt-F8) and select Update (8). Finally, you press Exit (F7) and save your document.

Creating and Using Styles

Using Style Libraries

Save style definitions to a style library. Then you can use these styles on other documents.

Specifying a Default Style Library File

Set up one style library as your default. When you press [Alt][F8], this style list appears.

Press [⇧Shift][F1], the Setup key.

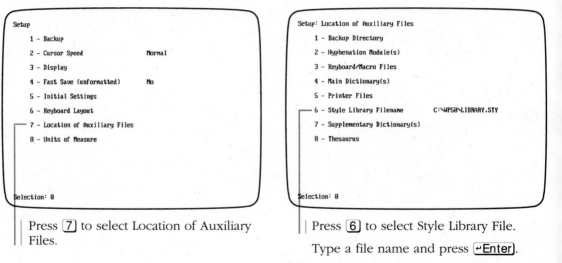

Setup

```
Setup

     1 - Backup
     2 - Cursor Speed                Normal
     3 - Display
     4 - Fast Save (unformatted)     No
     5 - Initial Settings
     6 - Keyboard Layout
     7 - Location of Auxiliary Files
     8 - Units of Measure




Selection: 0
```

Press [7] to select Location of Auxiliary Files.

```
Setup: Location of Auxiliary Files

     1 - Backup Directory
     2 - Hyphenation Module(s)
     3 - Keyboard/Macro Files
     4 - Main Dictionary(s)
     5 - Printer Files
     6 - Style Library Filename      C:\WP50\LIBRARY.STY
     7 - Supplementary Dictionary(s)
     8 - Thesaurus




Selection: 0
```

Press [6] to select Style Library File.

Type a file name and press [⏎Enter].

Press [F7] to return to your document.

Press Alt F8 to display the Styles menu.

```
Styles

  Name        Type  Description

  Bibliogrphy Paired·Bibliography
  Chapter     Paired Bold, Very Large Chapter Titles (8/18/88)
  Head        Paired bold and underline head
  Heading     Paired Chapter Heading
  Right Par   Paired Right-Aligned Paragraph Numbers
  Subheading  Paired Subheading




  1 On; 2 Off; 3 Create; 4 Edit; 5 Delete; 6 Save; 7 Retrieve; 8 Update: 1
```

Saving Definitions to a Style Library

You can save definitions to use with other documents.

Press 6 to save the style.

Type a file name and press ↵Enter.

Press F7 to return to your document.

Retrieving a Style Library File

When you want to use a style library, you retrieve the file.

Press 7 to retrieve the style.

Type a file name and press ↵Enter.

Press Y to overwrite the style definitions with duplicate names in your document with the new style definitions or press N to read in only the style definitions with different names from those in your document.

Press F7 to return to your document.

Updating Documents with a Style

If you change a style definition in your style library and want to update the documents to which you've applied this style, use Update to reformat your document with the modified style.

Press 8 to select Update.

Press F7.

Save your document.

6 *Proofreading*

WordPerfect makes two powerful tools available to you every time you begin your editing tasks—Search and Replace. If you've ever experienced the frustration of searching, sentence-by-sentence, for a mistake you know you've made, you will welcome these time-savers. In addition to these capabilities, you can use the Speller and Thesaurus to check and fine-tune your work.

Caution: Don't rely on WordPerfect to correct all your errors. WordPerfect finds only words that are misspelled, not words that are used incorrectly. Always give your manuscripts a thorough manual check.

Key Terms

String	A set of characters, including characters, codes, and spaces, that WordPerfect uses in Search and Replace operations.
Wild-card characters	Characters that can represent any single character (?) or any number of characters (*). Wild-card characters can be used to broaden or narrow an area of inquiry. For example, you can use wild-card characters with the Word Search feature and with the Speller.

Synonym	A word with the same or similar meaning as another word. You can use WordPerfect's Thesaurus feature to find synonyms.
Antonym	A word with opposite or nearly opposite meaning as another word. WordPerfect's Thesaurus feature lists both synonyms and antonyms.
Headword	The word you look up using the Thesaurus. This word has a body of similar words attached to it.

▲

Tasks Covered in This Chapter

In this chapter, you learn to perform the following tasks:

- Use the Search feature to search for a string—a single character, word, phrase, sentence, code, or combination of these
- Use the Replace feature to replace a string with another string
- Use the Word Search feature to search through and identify one or more disk files (without retrieving the files) for a given word or phrase
- Check the spelling of a word, a page, a block of text, or an entire document
- Find synonyms and antonyms with the Thesaurus feature

Using Search

The Search feature enables you to search for a single character, word, phrase, sentence, or code in either a forward or reverse direction from the location of your cursor. The group of characters, words, or codes you want to locate is called a string.

Suppose, for example, that you want to find where a particular topic, word, or phrase appears in a long document. Searching the document manually is time-consuming. But with WordPerfect's Search feature, you can find character strings, even codes, easily.

Launching a Search

To use search, you press Forward Search (F2) to search from the cursor position forward to the end of the document. You press Backward Search (Shift-F2) to search from the cursor to the beginning of the document.

If you select Forward Search, the following prompt appears at the lower left corner of the screen:

→Srch:

If you select Backward Search, the following prompt appears:

←Srch:

At the prompt, you type the text string or codes you want to find. You can type as many as 60 characters in your text string. Then you press Forward Search (F2) or Esc to begin the search. At this point, pressing Forward Search (F2) works for both Forward and Backward Search. When WordPerfect finds the first occurrence of the search target, the search stops. You then can edit and move around in the document.

If you want to continue the search, you press Forward Search (F2). You don't need to retype your text string or code because WordPerfect remembers your last search request. Press Forward Search (F2) or Esc again to find the next occurrence of the text string or code.

If WordPerfect can't find the search text, a * Not Found * message is displayed.

To return the cursor to its location before the search, you press GoTo (Ctrl-Home) twice.

Guidelines for Defining a Search String

To use Search effectively, you need to know how WordPerfect interprets a string. Here are some of the rules WordPerfect follows:

- If you type a string in lowercase, WordPerfect looks for *either* upper- or lowercase characters. For example, if you ask the program to find *search*, WordPerfect stops at *search*, *Search* and *SEARCH*. But if you ask the program to find *Search*, it stops at *Search* and *SEARCH*.
- Be careful how you enter a search string. If you enter the string **the**, for example, WordPerfect matches your string to every occurrence of the word *the* as well as to words that contain the string, such as *anesthesia*. To locate only the word *the*, enter a space before and after the word: *<space>***the***<space>*.
- If you think that the string you're looking for might be in a header, footer, footnote, endnote, graphic box caption, or text box, you must perform an *extended search*. An

Using Search

extended search is the same as a regular search except that you must press Home and then Forward Search (F2) for an extended forward search, and Home and then Backward Search (Shift-F2) for an extended backward search.

- If you need to find a hidden code, such as a margin setting, use the normal search procedure, but when the Srch: prompt appears, press the function key that creates the hidden code. When the search finds the hidden code, press Reveal Codes (Alt-F3, or F11) to view the code and perform any editing.

- When searching for paired codes, you can insert an ending code at the search (or replace) prompt by pressing the corresponding function key twice—for example, you can press Bold (F6) once to insert a [BOLD] code or twice to insert a [bold] code. To remove the [BOLD] code, use the cursor keys to move to the code, and then press the Del key to leave only the [bold] code in the search string.

- If you are searching for text that includes an element that changes from one occurrence to the next—for example, (1), (2), (3)—or if you are uncertain about the correct spelling of a word, use the matching character ^X (press Ctrl-V and then Ctrl-X). This *wild-card* character matches any single character within a character string. Enter (**^X**) at the →Srch: prompt, and the cursor stops at *(1)*, *(2)*, *(3)*, *(4)*, and so on. When you are uncertain about the spelling, enter **c^Xt**, for example, at the →Srch: prompt; the cursor stops at *cat, CAT, Cat, cot, cattle, cutting,* and so on. Be as specific about your character string as you can.

- To find a word at the end of a paragraph, type the word at the Srch: prompt, along with any following punctuation, and then press Enter to insert a hard return code ([HRt]). For example, type **Einstein**, press the period key (.), and press Enter. The search finds only occurrences of *Einstein* that are followed by a period and a hard return.

- At the Srch: prompt, you can change the direction of the search with the up- or down-arrow key. You enter the search string, press the up- or down-arrow key, and then press Forward Search (F2) or Esc to begin the search.

- You can use the Setup menu (Shift-F1) to set the program to beep when * Not Found * appears. For more information about the beep option, see Chapter 16, "Customizing."

- A common mistake is to press Enter instead of Forward Search (F2) or Esc to start the search. Pressing Enter inserts a [HRt] code in the search string, which may not be what you intended.

Using Search

Use the Search feature to search for a string—a single character, word, phrase, sentence, or code. For instance, you might use Search to find where you discuss a particular topic in a long document.

```
                        Writing Guideline
==================================================================

Brainstorming

When you have trouble determining a sharp focus for a document--
when you are uncertain what you want to say--consider trying a
semistructured writing exercise known as "brainstorming."

When you brainstorm a writing assignment on-screen, you record your
ideas in list form as they occur to you. When you brainstorm, you
don't worry about typos, spelling, or style. You turn off the
inclination to hone each sentence before you move on to the next
one. You can handle those matters later. Your goal is, rather, to
generate as many ideas as possible about the topic, the purpose,
or the audience.

Keeping an Idea File

An idea file is an extension of a brainstorming file. You can save
an idea file and retrieve it when you want to add more ideas later.

-> Srch:
```

```
                        Writing Guideline
==================================================================

Brainstorming

When you have trouble determining a sharp focus for a document--
when you are uncertain what you want to say--consider trying a
semistructured writing exercise known as "brainstorming."

When you brainstorm a writing assignment on-screen, you record your
ideas in list form as they occur to you. When you brainstorm, you
don't worry about typos, spelling, or style. You turn off the
inclination to hone each sentence before you move on to the next
one. You can handle those matters later. Your goal is, rather, to
generate as many ideas as possible about the topic, the purpose,
or the audience.

Keeping an Idea File

An idea file is an extension of a brainstorming file. You can save
an idea file and retrieve it when you want to add more ideas later.

-> Srch: prewriting
```

Press F2 to search from the cursor position forward to the end of the document.

Or

Press ⚹Shift F2 to search from the cursor to the beginning of the document.

Type the text string or code you want to find.

You can type as many as 60 characters in your text string.

Press F2 or Esc to begin the search.

When the program finds the first occurrence, it stops. You can edit and move around in the document.

```
don't worry about typos, spelling, or style. You turn off the
inclination to hone each sentence before you move on to the next
one. You can handle those matters later. Your goal is, rather, to
generate as many ideas as possible about the topic, the purpose,
or the audience.

Keeping an Idea File

An idea file is an extension of a brainstorming file. You can save
an idea file and retrieve it when you want to add more ideas later.

Using a Prewriting_Template

Prewriting is everything you do up to the actual step of writing
that first draft. It is very much a part of the planning stage.

A prewriting template is a set of prompts that force you to answer
some basic questions before you begin your document. As you plan
the document, you may find it helpful to use a prewriting template
to refine your thinking about a particular writing task. You can
ask the basic reporter's questions of "Who?" "What?" "Where?" "Why"
and "When?"

                                        Doc 1 Pg 2 Ln 4.33" Pos 2.8"
```

If you want to continue the search, press F2.

WordPerfect remembers your last search.

```
don't worry about typos, spelling, or style. You turn off the
inclination to hone each sentence before you move on to the next
one. You can handle those matters later. Your goal is, rather, to
generate as many ideas as possible about the topic, the purpose,
or the audience.

Keeping an Idea File

An idea file is an extension of a brainstorming file. You can save
an idea file and retrieve it when you want to add more ideas later.

Using a Prewriting Template

Prewriting is everything you do up to the actual step of writing
that first draft. It is very much a part of the planning stage.

A prewriting template is a set of prompts that force you to answer
some basic questions before you begin your document. As you plan
the document, you may find it helpful to use a prewriting template
to refine your thinking about a particular writing task. You can
ask the basic reporter's questions of "Who?" "What?" "Where?" "Why"
and "When?"

-> Srch: prewriting
```

Press F2 again.

```
one. You can handle those matters later. Your goal is, rather, to
generate as many ideas as possible about the topic, the purpose,
or the audience.

Keeping an Idea File

An idea file is an extension of a brainstorming file. You can save
an idea file and retrieve it when you want to add more ideas later.

Using a Prewriting Template

Prewriting_is everything you do up to the actual step of writing
that first draft. It is very much a part of the planning stage.

A prewriting template is a set of prompts that force you to answer
some basic questions before you begin your document. As you plan
the document, you may find it helpful to use a prewriting template
to refine your thinking about a particular writing task. You can
ask the basic reporter's questions of "Who?" "What?" "Where?" "Why"
and "When?"

                                          Doc 1 Pg 2 Ln 4.66" Pos 2"
```

WordPerfect finds the next occurrence of the string.

If WordPerfect can't find the search text, a * Not Found * message is displayed.

To return the cursor to its location before the search, press Ctrl Home twice.

Using Replace

WordPerfect's Replace feature automatically finds every occurrence of a string or code and replaces it with another string or code. You also can use Replace to remove a string or code completely. For instance, if you complete a long sales report and then need to remove all boldface type, you can use Replace to find all occurrences of the code and replace them with nothing.

Replacing a String

To replace a string, you first press Replace (Alt-F2). WordPerfect displays the following prompt:

```
w/Confirm? (Y/N) No
```

You can press Y if you want to approve each replacement separately. Or, you can press N or Enter if you want all occurrences replaced without confirming them.

At the →Srch: prompt, you type your search string. Then you press Forward Search (F2) or Esc. At the Replace with: prompt, you type the replacement string and press Enter. If you want the search string deleted and not replaced with anything, you don't enter anything in response to this prompt. Finally, you press Forward Search (F2) or Esc to start the search.

If you press N at the w/Confirm? (Y/N) No prompt, WordPerfect replaces all occurrences automatically. If you press Y at the prompt, the cursor stops at each occurrence of the search string and

Introduction

Using
Search

**Using
Replace**

Using Word
Search

Using the
Speller

Using the
Thesaurus

WordPerfect prompts: `Confirm? (Y/N) No`. You can press Y to replace the string or N if you don't want to replace the string. If you want to cancel the Search and Replace operation, you press Cancel (F1). Otherwise, WordPerfect continues searching the document. When all the occurrences have been found, the cursor stops.

To return the cursor to its location before the Replace operation, you press GoTo (Ctrl-Home) twice.

Replacing Hidden Codes

To replace hidden codes, you first press Replace (Alt-F2). In response to the prompt, you press Y if you want to confirm each replacement, or you press N if you want all occurrences replaced automatically.

When the →Srch: prompt appears, you press the function key you use to initiate the desired command—for example, to search for the boldface codes, press Bold (F6). If the function key command leads to a submenu, WordPerfect displays a list of menu items for entry into the search string. You press the number or letter of the menu item that represents the hidden command you want to replace. WordPerfect enters the appropriate code in the search string.

At the `Replace with:` prompt, you type the replacement string and press Enter. Or, to delete the hidden code and not replace it with anything, you don't enter anything in response to this prompt. To begin the Search and Replace operation, you press Forward Search (F2) or Esc.

Using Replace

Guidelines for Using Replace

To use Replace effectively, you need to keep in mind the following basic guidelines:

- WordPerfect doesn't allow you to search for codes with specific settings, such as [Margin Set:1,65], but you can find all occurrences of the command code [Margin Set].
- To limit a Replace operation to a specific section of your document, first define the text with Block (Alt-F4, or F12), and then proceed with the Search and Replace operation.
- Use Replace to enter a string of text that occurs frequently in a document. For example, enter a backslash (\) wherever you want *methyl ethyl chloride* to appear. When you finish typing, replace the backslash with the chemical term.
- WordPerfect's Replace function doesn't replace text in headers, footers, footnotes, endnotes, or graphics or text captions. To replace a string of characters in these locations, you must use *extended replace*. The procedure for extended replace is the same as for Replace, except the command for extended replace is Home and then Replace (Alt-F2).

WordPerfect won't accept all hidden codes in the Replace string. The following table shows the codes you cannot replace.

Code	*Function*
[Center Pg]	Center Page Top to Bottom
[Cntr]	Center Text
[Col On]	Beginning of Text Column
[Col Off]	End of Text Column
[ ]	Hard Space
[Just]	Justification On/Off
[←Mar Rel]	Margin Release
[Math On]	Beginning of Math
[Math Off]	End of Math
!	Formula Calculation
t	Subtotal Entry
^C, ^D, ^E, and so on	Merge Codes
–	Soft Hyphen (Ctrl-Hyphen)
[-]	Hyphen
/	Hyphenation Cancel
[Tab]	Tab
[Align]	Tab Align
[W/O]	Widow/Orphan
+	Calculate Subtotal
T	Total Entry
=	Calculate Total
*	Calculate Grand Total
[VRY LARGE][vry large]	Attribute Codes

Using Replace

Use Replace (Alt-F2) to replace a text string or hidden code. For instance, if you realize you misspelled a word throughout your text, you can use Replace to replace it with the correct spelling.

Replacing a Text String

Press [Alt][F2], the Replace key.

```
Pre-writing is everything you do up to the actual step of writing
that first draft. It is very much a part of the planning stage.

A pre-writing template is a set of prompts that force you to answer
some basic questions before you begin your document. As you plan
the document, you may find it helpful to use a pre-writing template
to refine your thinking about a particular writing task. You can
ask the basic reporter's questions of "Who?" "What?" "Where?" "Why"
and "When?"


w/Confirm? (Y/N) No
```

Press [Y] if you want to approve each replacement separately or [N] if you want all occurences replaced without confirming them.

```
Pre-writing is everything you do up to the actual step of writing
that first draft. It is very much a part of the planning stage.

A pre-writing template is a set of prompts that force you to answer
some basic questions before you begin your document. As you plan
the document, you may find it helpful to use a pre-writing template
to refine your thinking about a particular writing task. You can
ask the basic reporter's questions of "Who?" "What?" "Where?" "Why"
and "When?"


-> Srch: pref-)writing
```

Type your search string.

Press [F2] or [Esc].

```
Pre-writing is everything you do up to the actual step of writing
that first draft. It is very much a part of the planning stage.

A pre-writing template is a set of prompts that force you to answer
some basic questions before you begin your document. As you plan
the document, you may find it helpful to use a pre-writing template
to refine your writing about a particular writing task. You can
ask the basic reporter's questions of "Who?" "What?" "Where?" "Why"
and "When?"


Replace with: prewriting
```

If you want the string replaced, type the replacement string. Or, if you want the search string deleted and not replaced with anything, don't type anything.

Press [F2] or [Esc].

```
don't worry about typos, spelling, or style. You turn off the
inclination to hone each sentence before you move on to the next
one. You can handle those matters later. Your goal is, rather, to
generate as many ideas as possible about the topic, the purpose,
or the audience.

Keeping an Idea File

An idea file is an extension of a brainstorming file. You can save
an idea file and retrieve it when you want to add more ideas later.

Using a Pre-writing Template

Pre-writing is everything you do up to the actual step of writing
that first draft. It is very much a part of the planning stage.

A pre-writing template is a set of prompts that force you to answer
some basic questions before you begin your document. As you plan
the document, you may find it helpful to use a pre-writing template
to refine your thinking about a particular writing task. You can
ask the basic reporter's questions of "Who?" "What?" "Where?" "Why"
and "When?"


Confirm? (Y/N) No                    Doc 1 Pg 2 Ln 4.33" Pos 1.9"
```

If you pressed [N] at the w/Confirm? (Y/N) No prompt, the program automatically makes the replacements.

If you pressed [Y] at the prompt, the cursor stops at each occurrence of the search string. Press [Y] to replace or [N] not to replace. If you press [Y], WordPerfect makes the replacement and searches for the next occurrence of the string.

If you want to cancel the Search and Replace operation, press [F1] (Cancel).

Replacing a Hidden Code

Press Alt F2, the Replace key.

Press Y if you want to confirm each replacement or N if you want all occurrences replaced automatically.

```
                        Writing Guideline
==================================================================

Brainstorming

When you have trouble determining a sharp focus for a document--
when you are uncertain what you want to say--consider trying a
semistructured writing exercise known as "brainstorming."

When you brainstorm a writing assignment on-screen, you record your
ideas in list form as they occur to you. When you brainstorm, you
don't worry about typos, spelling, or style. You turn off the
inclination to hone each sentence before you move on to the next
one. You can handle those matters later. Your goal is, rather, to
generate as many ideas as possible about the topic, the purpose,
or the audience.

Keeping an Idea File

An idea file is an extension of a brainstorming file. You can save
an idea file and retrieve it when you want to add more ideas later.

-> Srch: [BOLD]
```

Press the function key you use to initiate the desired command—for example, to search for the boldface codes, press F6, the Bold key.

If the function key command leads to a submenu, WordPerfect displays a list of menu items for entry into the search string. Press the number or letter of the menu item that represents the hidden command you want to replace. WordPerfect enters the appropriate code in the search string.

```
                        Writing Guideline
==================================================================

Brainstorming

When you have trouble determining a sharp focus for a document--
when you are uncertain what you want to say--consider trying a
semistructured writing exercise known as "brainstorming."

When you brainstorm a writing assignment on-screen, you record your
ideas in list form as they occur to you. When you brainstorm, you
don't worry about typos, spelling, or style. You turn off the
inclination to hone each sentence before you move on to the next
one. You can handle those matters later. Your goal is, rather, to
generate as many ideas as possible about the topic, the purpose,
or the audience.

Keeping an Idea File

An idea file is an extension of a brainstorming file. You can save
an idea file and retrieve it when you want to add more ideas later.

Replace with:
```

Type the replacement string and press ↵Enter. Or, to delete the hidden code and not replace it with anything, don't type anything.

Press F2 to begin the Replace operation.

Using Word Search

WordPerfect offers several useful ways to locate specific text. One of the most powerful is Word Search from the List Files (F5) menu. Word Search searches through disk files for a given word or phrase on the first page of the document, anywhere within the document, or in a document summary.

Defining Word Search Conditions

Defining the search conditions is an important step in using the Word Search feature. The basic procedure is first to mark the files you want to search. Then you can choose to search only document summaries, only the first page of a document, or the entire document.

To define Word Search conditions, you first press List Files (F5) to display the List Files screen. At the Dir prompt, you can press Enter to see the named directory, or you can enter a new directory name.

If you want to search all files, you don't need to mark them. If you want to search selected files, you mark the files you want to include in the search by moving the cursor to the file name and pressing the asterisk (*) key. Generally, you should try to limit a word search to only those files that meet special conditions.

At the List Files screen, you select Word Search (9). WordPerfect displays the Search menu. At this point, you have a number of options:

- Select Doc Summary (1) to search only the document summaries of the marked files.
- Select First Page (2) to search only the first page of the marked files.
- Select Entire Doc (3) to search the entire text of each file you've marked.

You are prompted to enter a word pattern; you type a single word or a word pattern and press Enter to start the search.

When the search is completed, the names of files in which the word pattern is located are marked with an asterisk in the List Files screen. If no files contain the word pattern, a * Not Found * message is displayed, and no files on the List Files screen are marked with asterisks.

To move the cursor forward and backward from one marked file to another, you use Tab and Shift-Tab, respectively. To view a marked file, you move the cursor to the file name, and then select Look (6). WordPerfect displays the text of the document.

To return to the List Files menu from the Word Search menu and keep the same files marked after using Look, you press Exit (F7). You press Exit (F7) again to leave List Files. If you retrieve a file and want to return to the List Files screen with the same files still marked, you press List Files (F5) twice.

Using Wild Cards in Searches

When you conduct a word search and WordPerfect prompts you to enter a word pattern, you can use special wild-card characters. A question mark (?) represents a single character, and an asterisk (*) represents any number of characters up to a hard return. The following are some examples of allowable word patterns:

Using Word Search

Pattern entered	WordPerfect finds
duck	Files that contain the word *duck*
d?ck	Files that contain *duck, deck, Dick*, or *dock*
d*k	Files containing *duck, damask*, and *Derek*
ducks can	Files that contain such phrases as *ducks can waddle* and *ducks cannot stand on their heads*
ducks*can	Files that contain such text as *Ducks have adapted to many environments. They can*

Upper- and lowercase letters are treated the same. In this respect, Word Search differs from WordPerfect's Search functions (F2 and Shift-F2), which match capitalized letters in a search string. If you enter **Duck**, Search will not stop at *duck*, but Word Search will mark files that contain either *duck* or *Duck*.

Specifying Other Conditions

You can use the Conditions (4) option for even more flexible search options. To use this option, you select Conditions (4) from the Word Search menu. Here is a description of the Word Search options:

- Perform Search on (1). This option displays the number of files you have marked with an asterisk in List Files for inclusion in the search. After a search is executed, the number reflects the number of files that match the search conditions. Choosing this option with search conditions selected starts the search.

- Undo Last Search (2). This option resets the number of files included in the search to its previous level. For example, if a search of all 50 files in a subdirectory or disk results in 10 marked files, `Perform Search on` will reset to 10. If you want to change the search conditions and search all 50 files again, choose this option.

- Reset Search Conditions (3). Choose this option to return all search conditions to WordPerfect's default values.

- File Date (4). Use this option to search files created within a specified range of dates. You can enter dates in single-digit form: for example, 9/2/88 is the same as 09/02/88. You also can leave part of the date blank: for example, to search all files created in October, 1988, enter **10//88.**

- First Page (5). Choose this option to search only the first page of each document. Then enter a word pattern at the prompt. WordPerfect searches the first page or the first 4,000 characters of the document, whichever comes first.

- Entire Document (6). Use this option to search for the specified word pattern throughout the entire document.

- Document Summary (7). Choose this option, and then enter one or more word patterns next to the document summary data lines you want to search: Creation Date, Descriptive Name, Subject/Account, Author, Typist, and Comments. The word pattern you enter in the Document Summary line will be the object of the search throughout the entire document summary. Word patterns entered on the other lines are searched for only in those specific lines.

Using Word Search

Use the Word Search feature to search through one or more disk files (without retrieving the files) for a given word or phrase.

Press [F5] to display the List Files screen.

```
Dir C:\WP50\*.*                    (Type = to change default Dir)
```

Press [↵Enter] to view the files in the named directory, or type a new directory name and press [↵Enter].

```
08/16/88  15:09              Directory C:\WP50\*.*
Document size:        0  Free: 9312256  Used:     9895      Marked: 5

. <CURRENT>    <DIR>             .. <PARENT>   <DIR>
LEARN     .    <DIR>  05/16/88 11:32    SHELL    .    <DIR>  08/12/88 16:53
22F       .WPM     57 05/24/88 15:34    8514A    .WPD   3466 04/27/88 14:24
AIRPLANE.WPG     8484 04/27/88 14:24    ALTC     .WPM     78 04/29/88 09:00
ALTF     .WPM     65 06/01/88 16:43     ALTL     .WPM     98 05/24/88 15:32
ALTM     .WPM     72 04/29/88 09:00     ALTO     .WPM     95 06/01/88 16:40
ALTRNAT  .WPK    919 04/27/88 11:00     ALTS     .WPM    158 06/01/88 13:34
ALTU     .WPM     72 06/01/88 13:30     AMD      .WPG   1970 04/27/88 14:24
ANNOUNCE.WPG     5300 04/27/88 14:24    APPLAUSE.WPG   1522 04/27/88 14:24
ARROW1   .WPG    366 04/27/88 14:24     ARROW2   .WPG    738 04/27/88 14:24
ARTICLE .TXT     808 08/05/88 14:16     ARTICLE2.TXT    958 08/05/88 14:16
AWARD    .WPG   1746 04/27/88 14:24     BADNEWS .WPG   3750 04/27/88 14:24
BOOK     .WPG   1000 04/27/88 14:24     BORDER   .WPG  13510 04/27/88 14:24
BRAINSTR.        444 08/08/88 13:36     CALENDAR.WPM     85 05/23/88 11:28
CHAP1    .      1090* 08/04/88 09:11    CHAP1    .DOC   1549 08/12/88 09:06
CHAP2    .      1638* 08/12/88 15:48    CHAP2A   .      1070 08/15/88 10:25
CHAP2B   .       642 08/15/88 10:26     CHAP3    .      2462* 08/12/88 15:50
CHAP4    .      1049* 08/09/88 16:31    CHAP4    .DOC    250 08/12/88 15:54
CHAP5    .      2056* 08/16/88 15:06    CHECK    .WPG   1074 04/27/88 14:24

1 Retrieve; 2 Delete; 3 Move/Rename; 4 Print; 5 Text In;
6 Look; 7 Other Directory; 8 Copy; 9 Word Search; N Name Search: 6
```

Mark the files you want to include in the search by moving the cursor to the file name and pressing the asterisk (*) key. If you want to search all files, you do not need to mark the files.

Press [9] to choose Word Search.

206

```
08/16/88  15:09          Directory C:\WP50\*.*
Document size:      0   Free: 9312256   Used:    9895      Marked: 5

.  <CURRENT>    <DIR>                   ..  <PARENT>   <DIR>
LEARN   .       <DIR>  05/16/88 11:32   SHELL   .     <DIR>   08/12/88 16:53
22F     .WPM       57  05/24/88 15:34   8514A   .WPD   3466   04/27/88 14:24
AIRPLANE.WPG     8484  04/27/88 14:24   ALTC    .WPM     78   04/29/88 09:00
ALTF    .WPM       65  06/01/88 16:43   ALTL    .WPM     98   05/24/88 15:32
ALTM    .WPM       72  04/29/88 09:00   ALTO    .WPM     95   06/01/88 16:40
ALTRMAT .WPK      919  04/27/88 11:00   ALTS    .WPM    158   06/01/88 13:34
ALTV    .WPM       72  06/01/88 13:30   AMD     .WPG   1978   04/27/88 14:24
ANNOUNCE.WPG     5388  04/27/88 14:24   APPLAUSE.WPG   1522   04/27/88 14:24
ARROW1  .WPG      366  04/27/88 14:24   ARROW2  .WPG    738   04/27/88 14:24
ARTICLE .TXT      808  08/05/88 14:16   ARTICLE2.TXT    958   08/05/88 14:16
AWARD   .WPG     1746  04/27/88 14:24   BADNEWS .WPG   3750   04/27/88 14:24
BOOK    .WPG     1800  04/27/88 14:24   BORDER  .WPG  13518   04/27/88 14:24
BRAINSTR.         444  08/08/88 13:36   CALENDAR.WPM     85   05/23/88 11:28
CHAP1   .        1890* 08/04/88 09:11   CHAP1   .DOC   1549   08/12/88 09:06
CHAP2   .        1638* 08/12/88 15:40   CHAP2A  .      1070   08/15/88 10:25
CHAP2B  .         642  08/15/88 10:26   CHAP3   .      2462*  08/12/88 15:50
CHAP4   .        1849* 08/09/88 16:31   CHAP4   .DOC    250   08/12/88 15:54
CHAP6   .        2056* 08/16/88 15:06   CHECK   .WPG   1074   04/27/88 14:24

Search: 1 Doc Summary; 2 First Page; 3 Entire Doc; 4 Conditions: 0
```

To search only the document summaries of the marked files, press 1 to choose Doc Summary.

To search only the first page of the marked files, press 2 to choose First Page.

To search the entire text of each file you've marked, press 3 to choose Entire Doc.

```
08/16/88  15:09          Directory C:\WP50\*.*
Document size:      0   Free: 9312256   Used:    9895      Marked: 5

.  <CURRENT>    <DIR>                   ..  <PARENT>   <DIR>
LEARN   .       <DIR>  05/16/88 11:32   SHELL   .     <DIR>   08/12/88 16:53
22F     .WPM       57  05/24/88 15:34   8514A   .WPD   3466   04/27/88 14:24
AIRPLANE.WPG     8484  04/27/88 14:24   ALTC    .WPM     78   04/29/88 09:00
ALTF    .WPM       65  06/01/88 16:43   ALTL    .WPM     98   05/24/88 15:32
ALTM    .WPM       72  04/29/88 09:00   ALTO    .WPM     95   06/01/88 16:40
ALTRMAT .WPK      919  04/27/88 11:00   ALTS    .WPM    158   06/01/88 13:34
ALTV    .WPM       72  06/01/88 13:30   AMD     .WPG   1978   04/27/88 14:24
ANNOUNCE.WPG     5388  04/27/88 14:24   APPLAUSE.WPG   1522   04/27/88 14:24
ARROW1  .WPG      366  04/27/88 14:24   ARROW2  .WPG    738   04/27/88 14:24
ARTICLE .TXT      808  08/05/88 14:16   ARTICLE2.TXT    958   08/05/88 14:16
AWARD   .WPG     1746  04/27/88 14:24   BADNEWS .WPG   3750   04/27/88 14:24
BOOK    .WPG     1800  04/27/88 14:24   BORDER  .WPG  13518   04/27/88 14:24
BRAINSTR.         444  08/08/88 13:36   CALENDAR.WPM     85   05/23/88 11:28
CHAP1   .        1890* 08/04/88 09:11   CHAP1   .DOC   1549   08/12/88 09:06
CHAP2   .        1638* 08/12/88 15:40   CHAP2A  .      1070   08/15/88 10:25
CHAP2B  .         642  08/15/88 10:26   CHAP3   .      2462*  08/12/88 15:50
CHAP4   .        1849* 08/09/88 16:31   CHAP4   .DOC    250   08/12/88 15:54
CHAP6   .        2056* 08/16/88 15:06   CHECK   .WPG   1074   04/27/88 14:24

Word pattern: brainstorming
```

Type a single word or a word pattern.

Press ◄Enter to start the search.

```
08/16/88  15:10          Directory C:\WP50\*.*
Document size:      0   Free: 9312256   Used:    6367      Marked: 3

.  <CURRENT>    <DIR>                   ..  <PARENT>   <DIR>
LEARN   .       <DIR>  05/16/88 11:32   SHELL   .     <DIR>   08/12/88 16:53
22F     .WPM       57  05/24/88 15:34   8514A   .WPD   3466   04/27/88 14:24
AIRPLANE.WPG     8484  04/27/88 14:24   ALTC    .WPM     78   04/29/88 09:00
ALTF    .WPM       65  06/01/88 16:43   ALTL    .WPM     98   05/24/88 15:32
ALTM    .WPM       72  04/29/88 09:00   ALTO    .WPM     95   06/01/88 16:40
ALTRMAT .WPK      919  04/27/88 11:00   ALTS    .WPM    158   06/01/88 13:34
ALTV    .WPM       72  06/01/88 13:30   AMD     .WPG   1978   04/27/88 14:24
ANNOUNCE.WPG     5388  04/27/88 14:24   APPLAUSE.WPG   1522   04/27/88 14:24
ARROW1  .WPG      366  04/27/88 14:24   ARROW2  .WPG    738   04/27/88 14:24
ARTICLE .TXT      808  08/05/88 14:16   ARTICLE2.TXT    958   08/05/88 14:16
AWARD   .WPG     1746  04/27/88 14:24   BADNEWS .WPG   3750   04/27/88 14:24
BOOK    .WPG     1800  04/27/88 14:24   BORDER  .WPG  13518   04/27/88 14:24
BRAINSTR.         444  08/08/88 13:36   CALENDAR.WPM     85   05/23/88 11:28
CHAP1   .        1890  08/04/88 09:11   CHAP1   .DOC   1549   08/12/88 09:06
CHAP2   .        1638  08/12/88 15:40   CHAP2A  .      1070   08/15/88 10:25
CHAP2B  .         642  08/15/88 10:26   CHAP3   .      2462*  08/12/88 15:50
CHAP4   .        1849* 08/09/88 16:31   CHAP4   .DOC    250   08/12/88 15:54
CHAP6   .        2056* 08/16/88 15:06 ▼ CHECK   .WPG   1074   04/27/88 14:24

1 Retrieve; 2 Delete; 3 Move/Rename; 4 Print; 5 Text In;
6 Look; 7 Other Directory; 8 Copy; 9 Word Search; N Name Search: 6
```

When the search is completed, the names of files in which the word pattern is located are marked with an asterisk.

If no files contain the word pattern, a * Not Found * message is displayed, and no files are marked with asterisks.

Using the Speller

WordPerfect's Speller contains a dictionary with more than 115,000 words. You can use the Speller to search for spelling mistakes and common typing errors such as transposed, missing, extra, or wrong letters—even typing errors such as double words (*the the*). You also can use the Speller when you know what a word sounds like but you're unsure of its spelling. WordPerfect's Speller will check a single word, a page, a block of text, or an entire document.

The Speller compares each word in your document with the words in its dictionary. This dictionary contains a file that lists common words (words most frequently used) and main words (words generally found in dictionaries). WordPerfect checks every word against its list of common words, and if the program doesn't find the word there, it looks in its dictionary of main words. If you have created a supplemental dictionary, the program looks there as well. Words found in any of the dictionaries are considered correct.

If you are using an IBM Personal System/2, the Speller and Thesaurus files are stored on one 3 1/2-inch Speller/Thesaurus disk. If you have an IBM PC XT™, IBM® PC AT, or compatible, the Speller/Thesaurus files are stored on two 5 1/4-inch disks.

The main dictionary file, WP{WP}EN.LEX, contains the main and common word lists. When you run the Speller for the first time and add words to the dictionary, a supplemental dictionary file, WP{WP}EN.SUP, is created. You can use the Speller Utility, SPELLER.EXE, to make changes to the main dictionary.

If the WordPerfect program is loaded on a hard disk, the Speller files are immediately available. For the Speller function to work correctly, you must specify on the Location of Auxiliary Files screen that the files are in the WP.EXE subdirectory (see the Appendix for details).

Before you use the Speller on a dual floppy disk system, you remove the data disk from drive B and insert your copy of the Speller disk. (Do not remove the WordPerfect Program disk from drive A.) When you are finished checking spelling, you put your data disk back into drive B and save your document.

Checking a Word, Page, or Document

You can check a word, page, or entire document. To check a word or page, you first position the cursor anywhere in the word or page. When you check an entire document, the position of the cursor doesn't matter. Next, you press Spell (Ctrl-F2) to display the Spell menu.

You press the number or letter that identifies your menu selection. Choose from these options:

- Select Word (1) to check the word on which the cursor rests. If WordPerfect finds the word, the cursor moves to the next word, and the Spell menu remains displayed. You can continue checking word-by-word or select another option from the Spell menu. If the word isn't found, WordPerfect offers alternative spellings.

Using the Speller

- Select Page (2) to check every word on the page. After the page is checked, the Spell menu remains displayed. Continue checking words or select another option.
- Select Document (3) to check every word in your document.
- Select New Sup. Dictionary (4), type the name of the supplemental dictionary you want to use, and press Enter. Generally, you create supplemental dictionaries to contain words pertaining to specialized or technical areas, such as medicine, law, or science.
- Select Look Up (5) to check a word you aren't sure how to spell. In response to the `Word or word pattern` prompt, type your "rough guess" of the word's spelling. WordPerfect offers a list of words that fit the pattern.
- Select Count (6) to count the number of words in your document. Note that after a spell check, the number of words is displayed automatically.

When the Speller finds a word not in its dictionary, the Speller stops, highlights the word, generally provides a list of alternative spellings, and displays the Not Found menu.

Selecting from the Alternatives List

When the Speller checks a word and displays the Not Found menu, you have a number of options for correcting the highlighted word.

To select a word from the alternatives list, you first look for the correct spelling among the list of alternatives. If you do not see the correct spelling and WordPerfect prompts you to Press Enter for More Words, do so. When the correct spelling appears, type the letter next to the alternative you want to select. After you correct the word, the Speller continues checking the rest of your document.

Checking a Block

To check a block, you first press Block (Alt-F4, or F12) and define the block you want to check. Then you press Spell (Ctrl-F2). When you check a block, you skip the Spell menu because you've already told WordPerfect how much of your document you plan to check. Otherwise, the Speller operates as usual.

Using the Speller

Checking a Word, Page, or Document

If you plan to check just a word or a page, place the cursor anywhere in the word or page. If you plan to check the entire document, the position of the cursor does not matter.

Press Ctrl F2, the Spell key.

```
                        Writing Guideline
===============================================================================

Brainstorming

When you have troubel determining a sharp focus for a document--
when you are uncertain what you want to to say--consider trying a
semistructured writing exercise known as "brainstorming."

When you brainstorm a writing assignment on-screen, you record your
ideas in list form as they occur to you. When you brainstorm, you
don't worry about typos, spelling, or style. You turn off the
inclination to hone each sentence before you move on to the next
one. You can handle those matters later. Your goal is, rather, to
generate as many ideas as possible about the topic, the purpose,
or the audience.

Keeping an Idea File

An idea file is an extension of a brainstorming file. You can save
an idea file and retrieve it when you want to add more ideas later.

Check: 1 Word; 2 Page; 3 Document; 4 New Sup. Dictionary; 5 Look Up; 6 Count: 0
```

Press 1 for Word; WordPerfect checks its dictionaries for the word.

Press 2 for Page; WordPerfect looks up every word on the page.

Press 3 for Document; WordPerfect looks up every word in your document.

Press 4 for New Sup. Dictionary, type the name of the supplemental dictionary, and press ↵Enter.

Press 5 for Look Up. In response to the Word or Word Pattern prompt, type your "rough guess" of the word's spelling, and press ↵Enter. WordPerfect offers a list of words that fit the pattern.

Press 6 for Count; WordPerfect counts the number of words.

When the Speller finds a word not in its dictionary, the
Speller stops, highlights the word, provides a list of
alternative spellings, and displays the Not Found menu.
You have a number of options for correcting the
highlighted word.

Selecting from the Alternatives List

Find the correct spelling among the list
of alternatives.

```
┌────────────────────────────────────────────────┐
│                Writing Guideline                │
│=================================================│
│ Brainstorming                                   │
│                                                 │
│ When  yuo  have troubel determining a sharp focus for a document--│
│ when you are uncertain what you want to say--consider trying a   │
│ semistructured writing exercise known as "brainstorming."       │
│                                                 │
│ When you brainstorm a writing assignment on-screen, you record your│
│ ideas in list form as they occur to you. When you brainstorm, you│
│=================================================│
│ A. yo          B. you         C. a             │
│ D. aa          E. aaa         F. au            │
│ G. away        H. awe         I. aweigh        │
│ J. aye         K. e           L. eve           │
│ M. eye         N. i           O. ia            │
│ P. ie          Q. ii          R. iii           │
│ S. iou         T. iowa        U. ivo           │
│ V. o           W. oui         X. ov            │
│ Press Enter for more words                     │
│ Not Found: 1 Skip Once; 2 Skip; 3 Add Word; 4 Edit; 5 Look Up; 0│
└────────────────────────────────────────────────┘
```

```
┌────────────────────────────────────────────────┐
│                Writing Guideline                │
│=================================================│
│ Brainstorming                                   │
│                                                 │
│ When you have trouble determining a sharp focus for a document--│
│ when you are uncertain what you want to say--consider trying a   │
│ semistructured writing exercise known as "brainstorming."       │
│                                                 │
│ When you brainstorm a writing assignment on-screen, you record your│
│ ideas in list form as they occur to you. When you brainstorm, you│
│=================================================│
│ A. trouble     B. treble      C. triable       │
│ D. tribal                                      │
│                                                 │
│                                                 │
│                                                 │
│                                                 │
│                                                 │
│ Not Found: 1 Skip Once; 2 Skip; 3 Add Word; 4 Edit; 5 Look Up; 0│
└────────────────────────────────────────────────┘
```

If you do not see the correct
spelling and WordPerfect prompts
you to Press Enter for More
Words, do so.

Type the letter next to the
alternative spelling you want to
select.

After you correct the word, the Speller
continues checking the rest of your
document.

Checking a Block

When you spell-check a block, you skip the Spell menu, because you've
already told WordPerfect how much of your document you plan to check.

Press Alt F4 or F12 and define the block you want to check.

Press Ctrl F2.

The Speller continues as usual.

Using the Speller

Selecting Other Speller Options

Many correctly spelled words do not appear in WordPerfect's dictionary. Even with more than 115,000 words, some must be omitted. If the correct spelling is not displayed, you can choose from the options on the Not Found menu:

- Select Skip Once (1) to have the Speller ignore the word once, but stop at every occurrence of the word thereafter. Skip Once permits you to verify your spelling of the word—a good idea if the word is a difficult technical term.

- Select Skip (2) to skip all occurrences of what you know to be a correctly spelled word.

- Select Add Word (3) to add a word you use frequently to your supplemental dictionary. WordPerfect stores the word in memory and ignores all future occurrences. At the end of the check, all words added are saved to the current supplemental dictionary.

- Select Edit (4) when the correct alternative is not offered and when you know that the spelling is incorrect. You must make the corrections yourself. When you select Edit, the cursor moves to the word. Make the corrections using the right- and left-arrow keys. You can move only in the line that contains the word to be corrected. Press Exit (F7) to continue the spell check.

- Select Look Up (5) to look up a word. WordPerfect prompts you to enter a word or word pattern. You type your "rough guess" and press Enter. WordPerfect then displays all the possible matches. You can choose one of these alternative words. If you don't find the correct spelling, you can press Cancel (F1) twice; then select Edit (4) and enter the correction manually.

Finding Double Words

In addition to identifying misspelled words, the Speller notes double words, such as "the the." When the Speller encounters a double word, the program doesn't offer alternatives. Instead, it displays a different Not Found menu. You can choose from these options:

- Select Skip (1 or 2) if the double word is legitimate.
- Select Delete 2nd (3) if you accidentally typed two words instead of one. The second word is deleted.
- Select Edit (4) and make the appropriate corrections if one of the words is a typographical error.
- Select Disable Double Word Checking (5) if your document contains many legitimate double words and you are certain of your proofreading skill.

Using the Speller

Selecting Other Speller Options

Many correctly spelled words do not appear in WordPerfect's dictionary. Even with more than 115,000 words, some must be omitted. If the correct spelling does not appear, you can choose from the options on the Not Found menu.

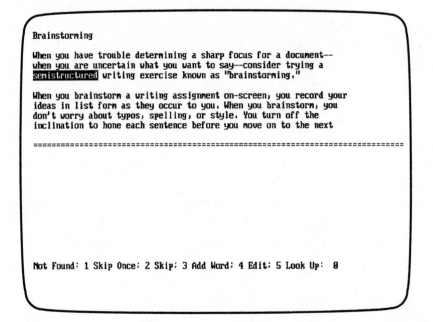

Press **1** to skip the word once, but stop at every occurrence of the word thereafter.

Press **2** to skip the word throughout the document.

Press **3** to add the word to the dictionary.

Press **4** for Edit, and the cursor moves to the word. Make the corrections using the **→** and **←** keys. You can move only in the line containing the word to be corrected. Press **F7**. The Speller rechecks the word you've corrected. If the corrected version is not in the dictionary, the Speller stops.

Press **5** for Look Up to look up a word you type.

```
Brainstorming

When you have trouble determining a sharp focus for a document--
when you are uncertain what you want to say--consider trying a
semistructured writing exercise known as "brainstorming."

When you brainstorm a writing assignment on-screen, you record your
ideas in list form as they occur to you. When you brainstorm, you
don't worry about typos, spelling, or style. You turn off the
inclination to hone each sentence before you move on to the next
one. You can handle those matters later. Your goal is, rather, to
generate as many ideas as possible about the topic, the purpose,
or the audience.

Keeping an Idea File

An idea file is an extension of a brainstorming file. You can save
an idea file and retrieve it when you want to add more ideas later.

Using a Prewriting Template

Prewriting is everything you do up to the actual step of writing

Word or word pattern: typogra*
```

Looking Up a Word

Press ⑤ for Look Up.

Type the word or word pattern and press ⏎Enter.

```
Brainstorming

When you have trouble determining a sharp focus for a document--
when you are uncertain what you want to say--consider trying a
semistructured writing exercise known as "brainstorming."

When you brainstorm a writing assignment on-screen, you record your
ideas in list form as they occur to you. When you brainstorm, you
don't worry about typos, spelling, or style. You turn off the
inclination to hone each sentence before you move on to the next

=============================================================

A. typographer        B. typographers        C. typographic
D. typographical      E. typographically     F. typographies
G. typography




Word or word pattern:
```

When the alternative words are displayed, you can choose one of those words to replace the not found word by pressing the letter associated with the word.

```
semistructured writing exercise known as "brainstorming."

When you brainstorm a writing assignment on-screen, you register
your ideas in list form as they occur to you. When you brainstorm,
you don't worry about typos, spelling, or style. You turn off the
inclination to to hone each sentence before you move on to the next
one. You can handle those matters later. Your goal is, rather, to
generate as many ideas as possible about the topic, the purpose,
or the audience.

Keeping an Idea File






Double Word: 1 2 Skip; 3 Delete 2nd; 4 Edit; 5 Disable Double Word Checking
```

Finding Double Words

In addition to finding misspellings, the program also stops on double words and displays a different Not Found menu.

Press ① or ② if the double word is legitimate.

Press ③ to delete the second word.

Press ④ to edit the word.

Press ⑤ to disable double word checking.

Using the Thesaurus

The Thesaurus is similar to the Speller, except that the Thesaurus lists alternative word choices instead of alternative spellings. The Thesaurus displays synonyms—words with the same or similar meanings—and *antonyms*—words with opposite or nearly opposite meanings for the selected word. The Thesaurus only lists these words; you must decide which one best fits your meaning.

Displaying Synonyms and Antonyms

If you are using a hard disk system, be sure that you have specified the location of the Thesaurus disk files on the Location of Auxiliary Files screen. If you are using a floppy disk system, you must remove the data disk from drive B and insert the Thesaurus disk. The WordPerfect Program disk must remain in drive A. You then start the Thesaurus. When you finish using the Thesaurus, you must remove the Thesaurus disk, replace it with your data disk, and save your document.

To use the Thesaurus, you place the cursor anywhere in the word you want to look up and press Thesaurus (Alt-F1). The word is highlighted, and the screen is split, with the document text in the top half and the Thesaurus menu and word list in columns in the bottom half.

The word you look up is called the *headword* because it has a body of similar words attached to it. The headword appears at the top of the column. Synonyms and antonyms for your headword are also noted. Words are divided into numbered groups and parts of speech. The column of letters to the left of the words is called the Reference menu. Remember that words marked with a bullet also are headwords; you can look up any of these words.

If your menu is empty and Word: appears at the bottom of your screen, either the cursor was not placed within the word boundary or the Thesaurus cannot find the word you want to look up. In either case, type the word you want to look up at the Word: prompt and press Enter.

Using the Thesaurus Menu

With the Thesaurus menu displayed, you can select among the
following options:

- Select Replace Word (1) to replace the highlighted word.
  At the prompt, type the letter from the Reference menu
  that corresponds to the replacement word. Use the right-
  or left-arrow key to move the letter choices to other
  columns. The Thesaurus menu disappears, and the
  program inserts the word you selected into the text.
- Select View Doc (2) if you are unsure of a word's exact
  meaning in the context of your writing. The cursor moves
  back to the document, and you can use the cursor keys to
  move around and view the surrounding text. Press Exit
  (F7) to return to the Thesaurus menu.
- Select Look Up Word (3) to look up other words that
  come to mind. At the `Word:` prompt, type the word you
  want to look up. If the word is a headword, the Thesaurus
  displays the word with all its subgroups of synonyms and
  antonyms. If the word is not a headword, WordPerfect
  either looks up another similar word or displays the
  message * Word Not Found *.
- Select Clear Column (4) to clear a column and make room
  for additional word columns.

Selecting More Words

If you don't see a word that is exactly right or you want to try other
words, you can expand the word list. You can display more
alternatives for any headword—a word with a bullet next to it. Choose
the headword that is close to the meaning of word for which you are
looking and press the letter next to that word. A new word list appears
in the column to the right of the previous headword.

Using the Thesaurus

Use the Thesaurus to find synonyms—words with the same or similar meanings—and antonyms—words with opposite or nearly opposite meanings.

Displaying Synonyms and Antonyms

Place the cursor anywhere in the word you want to look up.

Press ⎡Alt⎤⎡F1⎤ to start the Thesaurus feature.

Headword Part of speech Numbered subgroup

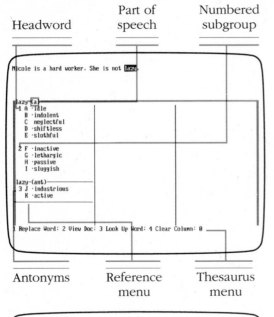

If your menu is empty and Word: *appears at the bottom of your screen, either the cursor was not placed within the word boundary or the Thesaurus cannot find the word you want to look up. In either case, type the word you want to look up at the* Word: *prompt and press* ⎡⏎Enter⎤.

Antonyms Reference menu Thesaurus menu

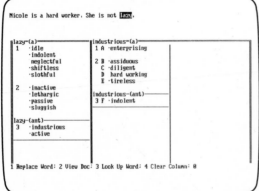

Selecting More Words

If you don't see a word that is exactly right or you want to try other words, you can expand the word list. You can display more alternatives for any headword—a word with a bullet next to it.

Press the letter associated with the word.

Using the Thesaurus Menu

With the Thesaurus menu displayed, you can select among the following options:

Press ① for Replace Word.

Type the letter that corresponds to the replacement word. Use → or ← to move the letter choices to other columns.

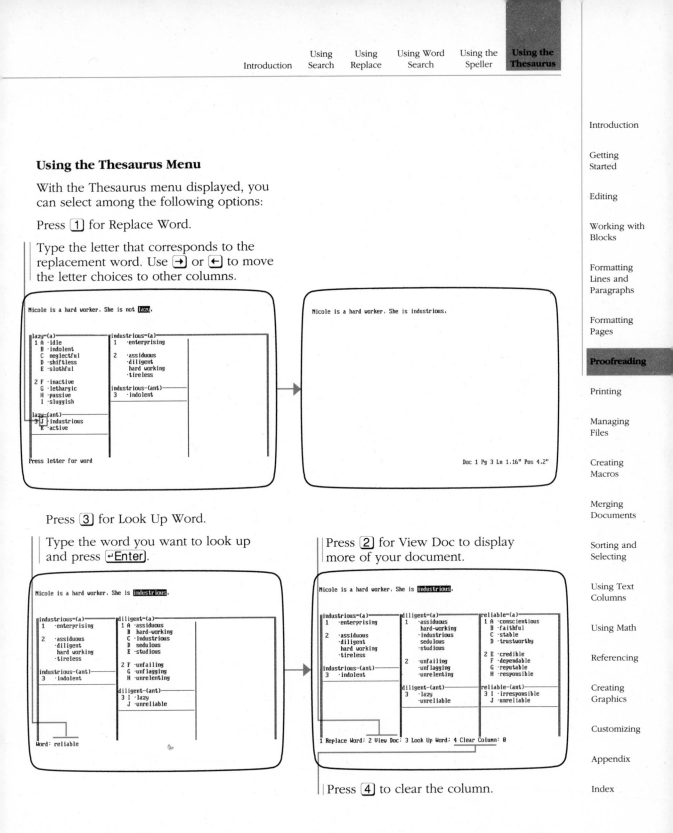

Press ③ for Look Up Word.

Type the word you want to look up and press ↵Enter.

Press ② for View Doc to display more of your document.

Press ④ to clear the column.

221

7 ▷ Printing

You can install many printers at a time and select from among them for particular print jobs. This chapter shows you not only how to select your printer, but also how to designate the many printing specifications, such as binding width, number of copies, and print quality.

You can print all or part of the document that currently appears on-screen directly from the screen, or you can print all or part of a document you have previously stored to disk. WordPerfect can keep track of multiple print jobs and print them in the order you specify. If you suddenly have a rush job, you can interrupt the printing and bump the job to first place in the printing queue.

WordPerfect also lets you use some printers as a typewriter, sending characters or lines of text directly to the printer as you type. This feature is useful for tasks such as addressing envelopes or filling in forms. Before you print, you can use WordPerfect's View Document feature to preview how the printed document will look and to avoid wasting time and paper.

Key Terms

Print queue   An internal list of jobs to be printed.

Typeface   A character style of given relative dimensions and line thicknesses.

Binding width   The extra space added to the inside edge of each page when a document is printed on both sides. Setting a binding width shifts odd-numbered pages to the right and even-numbered pages to the left by the specified amount.

Tasks Covered in This Chapter

In this chapter, you learn how to perform the following tasks:

- Define printers and select the one you want for the current printing job
- Print from the screen
- Print from disk
- Control multiple printing jobs
- Use your printer as a typewriter
- Preview a document before printing
- Designate specifications for your particular print job

223

Selecting a Printer

WordPerfect and the printer must be linked properly. If they are not, they cannot communicate; and if they cannot communicate, the printer will not print your documents. After following the instructions presented here, if your printer doesn't work, ask your dealer to help you determine the problem—perhaps a faulty connection (a wrong cable or incorrect hardware switch setting, for example).

Literally hundreds of printers are supported by WordPerfect. To make sure that you achieve the results you expect, you must tell WordPerfect which printer make and model you are using. You use the Select Printer feature to do this. The Select Printer feature is actually a combination of two features—*defining* a printer or printers in which you tell WordPerfect the kind of equipment you have, and *selecting* one of those defined printers for your current needs. You may install and have available for selection (from the Select Printer menu) any number of printer definitions at one time.

Defining a Printer

To define your printer, you first press Print (Shift-F7). Then you choose Select Printer (S). Next, you choose Additional Printers (2). If you didn't copy the printer disks to your hard disk or if you are using a floppy disk system, the Select Printer: Additional Printers screen is displayed with a message that says `Printer files not found`.

If you are using a hard disk, you must insert the 5 1/4-inch Printer 1 master disk or the 3 1/2-inch Printer 1/Printer 2 master disk into drive A. If you are using a dual floppy disk system, you insert into drive B the 5 1/4-inch Printer 1—Working disk or the 3 1/2-inch Printer 1/ Printer 2—Working disk.

Next, you select Other Disk (2). WordPerfect prompts: `Directory for printer files:`. If you are using a hard disk system, you type **a:**. If you are using a dual floppy system, you type **b:**. A list of the available printer devices on this printer disk is displayed.

If the name of your printer does not appear on the list of additional printers, you insert another Printer disk and select Other Disk (2) to view a second list of printers until you find the printer you want.

When the name does appear, you move the cursor to the name of the printer you want to add, and then choose Select (1). You can press Enter to accept the displayed name, or you can type a name of your own and press Enter. Then you should read the information on the Printer Helps and Hints Screen.

Next, you press Exit (F7) to move to the Select Printer: Edit menu. You can press Enter to accept the current settings, or you can enter the information required, such as assigning a proper printer port or initial font.

WordPerfect returns to the Select Printer screen, which has been updated and now lists the printer you have just defined. You have completed defining your printer. Next, you need to *select* this printer to tell WordPerfect you intend to print on that printer.

Selecting a Defined Printer

On the Select Printer screen, you move the highlight bar to your printer. Then you press Enter or choose Select (1) to select the defined printer.

You are returned to the main Printer menu, which has been updated and now shows the printer you defined as the active one. Any print operation will use this printer until you select a different one. You press Enter to return to your document.

Selecting a Printer

Before you can print, you need to define your printers, that is, tell WordPerfect what makes and models of printers you have. Then you need to select from those defined printers the printer you will be using to print your documents.

Press ⟨⇧Shift⟩ ⟨F7⟩, the Print key.

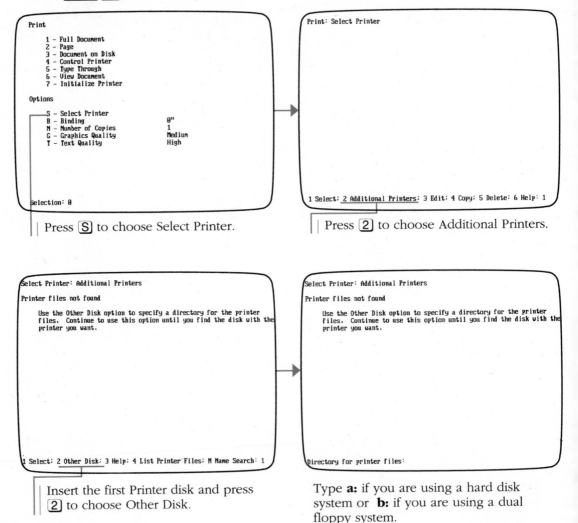

Press Ⓢ to choose Select Printer.

Press ② to choose Additional Printers.

Insert the first Printer disk and press ② to choose Other Disk.

Type **a:** if you are using a hard disk system or **b:** if you are using a dual floppy system.

If the name of your printer does not appear on the list of additional printers, insert another Printer disk and press ②︎ to view a second list of printers until you find the printer you want.

Move the cursor to the name of the printer you want to add and press ①︎ to select it.

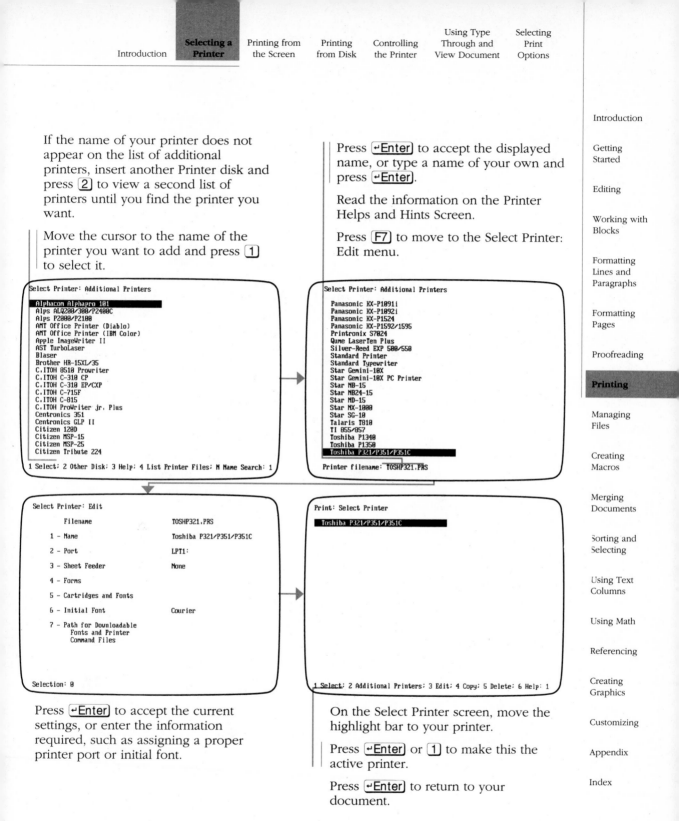

Press ⏎Enter to accept the displayed name, or type a name of your own and press ⏎Enter.

Read the information on the Printer Helps and Hints Screen.

Press F7 to move to the Select Printer: Edit menu.

Press ⏎Enter to accept the current settings, or enter the information required, such as assigning a proper printer port or initial font.

On the Select Printer screen, move the highlight bar to your printer.

Press ⏎Enter or ①︎ to make this the active printer.

Press ⏎Enter to return to your document.

Printing from the Screen

Printing a document from the screen is quicker than printing a document from disk—especially if your document is short. From the screen, you can print the entire document, a single page, or a block of text.

Printing an Entire Document

To print the entire document from the screen, you first display the document and place the cursor anywhere in it. Then you press Print (Shift-F7) to display the Print menu. From this menu, you choose Full Document (1).

Printing a Single Page

To print a single page from the displayed document, you place the cursor anywhere in the page you want to print. Then you press Print (Shift-F7) and select Page (2). If the page you've selected doesn't appear near the beginning of the document, you may notice a short pause before the page prints. WordPerfect scans the document for the last format settings (margins, tabs, and so on) before printing the page.

Printing a Block

Sometimes you may want to print only a single sentence, a paragraph, a page and a half, or five pages from a larger document. You can use WordPerfect's Block feature to specify what text you want to print.

Introduction   Selecting a   **Printing from**   Printing   Controlling   Using Type   Selecting
Printer   **the Screen**   from Disk   the Printer   Through and   Print
View Document   Options

To print a block of text from the screen, you first move the cursor to the first character of the block of text you plan to print. Then you press Block (Alt-F4, or F12). With the `Block on` message flashing, you move the cursor just beyond the last character of the block you plan to print. Then you press Print (Shift-F7). In response to the `Print block? (Y/N)` prompt, you press Y to print.

Adding a Print Job to the Queue

You can continue working on the document (or another document) while you print. If you finish working on a second document before the first document has finished printing, you can print the second file just as you did the first. WordPerfect adds the print job to the queue.

Making a Screen Print

When you need a quick printout of whatever appears on-screen (a hard copy of a WordPerfect Help screen, for instance), you can press Print Screen (on an Enhanced Keyboard) or Shift-PrtSc (on a PC keyboard). The hard copy won't show formatting codes, but it will include the information that appears on the status line.

Printing from the Screen

With a document displayed on-screen, you can print
the entire document, a single page, or a block of text.

The first step is to display the document on-screen.

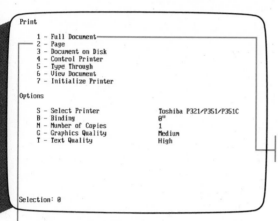

Printing an Entire Document

Place the cursor anywhere in the document.

Press ⇧Shift F7 to display the Print menu.

Press 1 to choose the Full Document option.

Printing a Single Page

Place the cursor anywhere in the page you want to print.

Press ⇧Shift F7 to display the Print menu.

Press 2 to select Page.

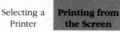

Printing a Block

Move the cursor to the first character of the block of text you plan to print.

Press Alt F4 or F12.

Move the cursor to the character space immediately following the last character of the block of text you plan to print.

Press ⇧Shift F7.

Press Y to print.

When you need a quick printout of whatever appears on-screen (a hard copy of a WordPerfect Help screen, for instance), press Print Screen (on an Enhanced Keyboard) or Shift-PrtSc (on a PC keyboard). The hard copy won't show formatting codes, but it will include the information that appears on the status line.

231

Printing from Disk

With WordPerfect, you can print a document from disk without displaying it on-screen. You can print from either the Print menu or the List Files menu. With both methods, you can specify which pages to print.

Printing from the Print Menu

When you print from the Print menu, you must know the complete file name before starting the operation. You cannot use List Files to look up the file after you've pressed Print (Shift-F7).

To use the Print menu to print a document from disk, you first press Print (Shift-F7). Then you select Document on Disk (3), type the file name, and press Enter. (If the document is stored in a different directory than the current directory, you must type the drive, path name, and directory name.)

If you want to print the entire document, you press Enter. If you want to print only particular pages, you type the pages you want to print and then press Enter. WordPerfect reads the file from disk, creates a print job, and adds the document to the print queue.

You type the page numbers according to the following specifications:

Specification	Pages Selected for Printing
5	Page 5 only
2,25	Pages 2 and 25 only
3–	Pages 3 through the end of the document
1–10	Pages 1 through 10
–3	Pages from the beginning of the document through Page 3

Introduction   Selecting a   Printing from   **Printing**   Controlling   Using Type   Selecting
Printer   the Screen   **from Disk**   the Printer   Through and   Print
View Document   Options

Printing from List Files

In addition to printing from the Print menu, you can print from the List Files screen. Printing from the List Files screen has two advantages: you don't need to remember the name of the file you want to print, and you can mark any number of files to print. The files are printed in the order they appear on the List Files screen.

To use the List Files screen to print a document from disk, you first press List Files (F5). Then, if the file resides in the current drive and directory, you press Enter. Or, if the file is in a different directory, you type the drive, path, and directory name, and then press Enter.

Next, you use the cursor keys to highlight the name of the file you want to print. Or, you select Name Search (N) and begin typing the file name; when the file you want is highlighted, you press Enter. Then you select Print (4). In response to the Pages: (All) message, you can press Enter to print the entire document, or you can type the pages you want to print and press Enter.

Marking Files To Print

From the List Files screen, you can mark several files to print. You mark each file, in turn, by using the cursor keys to highlight the name of the file you want to print and then pressing the asterisk (*) key. After you mark the files, you select Print (4). To confirm printing, you press Y. WordPerfect adds the files to the print queue and prints them in the order in which you marked them. If no files on the List Files screen are marked for printing and you want to mark *all the files* for printing, you press Home and then the asterisk (*) key.

Printing a Disk Directory

For a neatly formatted printout of a disk directory, you first press List Files (F5), and then press Enter. Finally, you press Print (Shift-F7).

Printing from Disk

Print a document from disk using either the
Print menu or List Files.

Printing from the Print Menu

Press ⟨⇧Shift⟩⟨F7⟩ to display the Print menu.

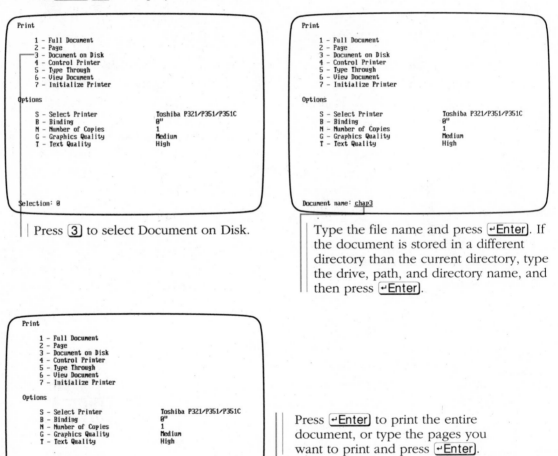

```
Print

    1 - Full Document
    2 - Page
    3 - Document on Disk
    4 - Control Printer
    5 - Type Through
    6 - View Document
    7 - Initialize Printer

Options

    S - Select Printer        Toshiba P321/P351/P351C
    B - Binding               0"
    N - Number of Copies      1
    G - Graphics Quality      Medium
    T - Text Quality          High




Selection: 0
```

Press ③ to select Document on Disk.

```
Print

    1 - Full Document
    2 - Page
    3 - Document on Disk
    4 - Control Printer
    5 - Type Through
    6 - View Document
    7 - Initialize Printer

Options

    S - Select Printer        Toshiba P321/P351/P351C
    B - Binding               0"
    N - Number of Copies      1
    G - Graphics Quality      Medium
    T - Text Quality          High




Document name: chap3
```

Type the file name and press ⟨↵Enter⟩. If
the document is stored in a different
directory than the current directory, type
the drive, path, and directory name, and
then press ⟨↵Enter⟩.

```
Print

    1 - Full Document
    2 - Page
    3 - Document on Disk
    4 - Control Printer
    5 - Type Through
    6 - View Document
    7 - Initialize Printer

Options

    S - Select Printer        Toshiba P321/P351/P351C
    B - Binding               0"
    N - Number of Copies      1
    G - Graphics Quality      Medium
    T - Text Quality          High




Page(s): (All)
```

Press ⟨↵Enter⟩ to print the entire
document, or type the pages you
want to print and press ⟨↵Enter⟩.

Printing from List Files

Press (F5) for List Files.

If the file resides in the current drive and directory, press (↵Enter). If the file is in a different directory, type the drive, path, and directory name, and then press (↵Enter).

Use the cursor keys to highlight the name of the file you want to print.

Press (4) to select Print.

Press (↵Enter) to print the entire document, or type the pages you want to print and press (↵Enter).

Marking Files To Print

From the List Files screen, use the cursor keys to highlight the name of the file you want to print.

Press (*) (asterisk) to mark each file you want to print. Press (Home) and then (*) to mark all files.

After you've marked each file, press (4) to select Print.

Press (Y).

Printing a Disk Directory

Press (F5) to display the List Files screen.

Press (↵Enter).

Press (⇧Shift)(F7) to begin printing.

Controlling the Printer

WordPerfect's Control Printer feature is a powerful tool for managing your printing activities. You can, with Control Printer, cancel print jobs, move a print job to the top of the list, display a list of jobs waiting to be printed, and suspend and then resume printing. You perform all these operations from the Printer Control screen.

To access the Printer Control screen, you first press Print (Shift-F7). Then you choose Control Printer (4). The Control Printer screen is divided into three sections: Current Job, Job List, and Control Printer menu. The Current Job section gives you information about the job that is currently printing. The Job List section displays information about the next three print jobs. And the Control Printer menu gives you the options you need to manage your printing activities.

Canceling a Print Job

With the Control Printer screen displayed, you choose Cancel Job(s) (1) to cancel individual print jobs or all print jobs while they are printing. WordPerfect displays a message that tells you the number of the job currently printing. You can press Enter to cancel the current job, or you can type the number of the job you want to cancel. Or, you can cancel all jobs by pressing the asterisk (*) key and then pressing Y to confirm the cancellation.

Rushing a Print Job

Choosing Rush Job (2) from the Control Printer menu lets you print a job in a hurry. You can use this option either to interrupt the current print job so that you can print another job in the queue or to print the rush job after the current job is printed.

After you choose Rush Job (2), WordPerfect prompts you to specify which job to rush. You type the number of the print job you want to move up. Then you either press Y to interrupt the current printing job, or you press N or Enter to print the job after the current job is finished printing.

If you elect to interrupt the job currently printing, the interrupted print job automatically resumes printing after the rush job is done. If necessary, WordPerfect prompts you to change forms for the rush job and prompts you again to reinsert the original form for the interrupted job.

Displaying a List of Jobs

The Control Printer screen can display only three of the jobs in the queue. To display additional jobs in the print queue, you can choose the Display Jobs (3) option from the Control Printer menu.

Suspending Printing

If your printer has jammed or needs a new ribbon, you may need to suspend and then resume printing. In this case, you choose the Stop (5) option from the Control Printer menu. Then you can correct the problem.

Before you resume printing, you must position the print head at the top of the next page. Then you press G to restart the printer. Printing resumes on page one if your document consists of only one page or if you stopped printing on page one. Otherwise, WordPerfect prompts you to enter the page number where you want printing to resume. You type the page number (if prompted) and press Enter.

Controlling the Printer

Use WordPerfect's Control Printer feature to manage
your printing activities.

Press ⎣◆Shift⎦ ⎣F7⎦ to display the Print menu.

```
Print
     1 - Full Document
     2 - Page
     3 - Document on Disk
     4 - Control Printer
     5 - Type Through
     6 - View Document
     7 - Initialize Printer

Options

     S - Select Printer          Toshiba P321/P351/P351C
     B - Binding                 0"
     N - Number of Copies        1
     G - Graphics Quality        Medium
     T - Text Quality            High




Selection: 0
```

Choose ⎣4⎦ to select
Control Printer.

The Control Printer screen is divided into three sections.

The Current Job section
gives you information
about the job that is
currently printing.

```
Print: Control Printer

Current Job

Job Number: 2                        Page Number:  1
Status:     Printing                 Current Copy: 1 of 1
Message:    None
Paper:      None
Location:   None
Action:     None


Job List

Job  Document          Destination      Print Options
 2   C:\WP50\CHAP2     LPT 1
 3   C:\WP50\CHAP3     LPT 1

Additional Jobs Not Shown: 2


1 Cancel Job(s); 2 Rush Job; 3 Display Jobs; 4 Go (start printer); 5 Stop: 0
```

The Job List section
displays information
about the next three
print jobs.

The Control Printer menu gives you the
options you need to manage your
printing activities.

Canceling a Print Job

Press 1 to choose Cancel Job(s).

Press ↵Enter to cancel the current job in the queue.

Or

Type the number of the job you want to cancel.

Or

Press * (asterisk) to cancel all the jobs in the queue and press Y to confirm the cancellation.

Rushing a Print Job

Press 2 to select Rush Job.

Type the number of the print job you want to move up.

Press Y if you want to interrupt the current printing job, or press N or ↵Enter to print the job after the current job is finished printing.

Displaying a List of Jobs

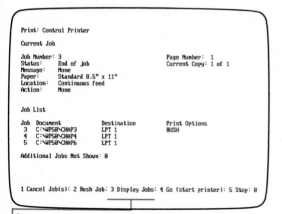

```
Print: Control Printer

Current Job

Job Number: 3                         Page Number:  1
Status:      End of Job               Current Copy: 1 of 1
Message:     None
Paper:       Standard 8.5" x 11"
Location:    Continuous feed
Action:      None


Job List

Job  Document          Destination      Print Options
3    C:\WP50\CHAP3     LPT 1            RUSH
4    C:\WP50\CHAP4     LPT 1
5    C:\WP50\CHAP6     LPT 1

Additional Jobs Not Shown: 0


1 Cancel Job(s); 2 Rush Job; 3 Display Jobs; 4 Go (start printer); 5 Stop: 0
```

Press 3 for Display Jobs to display additional jobs in the queue.

Suspending Printing

```
Print: Control Printer

Current Job

Job Number: 4                         Page Number:  1
Status:      Stopped                  Current Copy: 1 of 1
Message:     None
Paper:       Standard 8.5" x 11"
Location:    Continuous feed
Action:      Reset printer (press RESET or turn printer OFF and ON)
             Press "G" to restart, "C" to cancel

Job List

Job  Document          Destination      Print Options
4    C:\WP50\CHAP4     LPT 1
5    C:\WP50\CHAP6     LPT 1

Additional Jobs Not Shown: 0


Restart on page: 1
```

Press 5 to select Stop.

Make the desired corrections and position the print head at the top of the next page.

Press G to restart the printer.

Using Type Through and View Document

Two more options on the Print menu are Type Through and View Document. Use Type Through to send text directly to the printer. Use View Document to preview your document before you print it.

Using Type Through

With WordPerfect, you can use some printers as a typewriter. The Type Through feature is useful when you need to write a brief note or address an envelope. WordPerfect can send each character to the printer immediately after you type it or wait until you press Enter to send the line.

To use Type Through, you first press Print (Shift-F7) to display the Print menu. Then you select Type Through (5). Next, you select the Line (1) option or the Character (2) option.

If WordPerfect doesn't support Type Through for the currently selected printer, the program displays the following message:

```
Feature not available on this printer
```

The Line Option

You select the Line (1) option to send the line to the printer when you press Enter. After you choose the option, you type the text. Until you press Enter, you can use the Backspace and Del keys to edit the line.

The top line of the screen shows the previous line of text, which you cannot edit. To copy the top line to the bottom (current editing) line, you press Move (Ctrl-F4). When you are finished typing and editing, you press Enter to send the line to the printer. Then you press Exit (F7) twice to return to the editing screen.

Introduction

Selecting a
Printer

Printing from
the Screen

Printing
from Disk

Controlling
the Printer

**Using Type
Through and
View Document**

Selecting
Print
Options

The Character Option

You select the Character (2) option to send characters to the printer as you type. After you choose this option from the menu, you type the text. WordPerfect sends each character to the printer as you press the key. If you choose this option, you cannot correct any typing mistakes. You press Exit (F7) twice to return to the editing screen.

Viewing a Document

Use the View Document feature to preview your document before printing it. You save costly printer paper and time by first previewing your document, making changes if needed, and then printing the document when you're certain that it's perfect. Document pages appear on-screen as they will appear when printed on paper, including graphics (if your system can display graphics), footnotes, page numbers, line numbers, headers, footers, and justification.

To view a document, you first display the document you want to preview in either the Doc 1 or Doc 2 window. Then you position the cursor anywhere on the page you want to view. Next, you press Print (Shift-F7) and select View Document (6). At this point, you have a number of options:

- Select 100% (1) to view the document at its actual size.
- Select 200% (2) to view the document at twice its actual size.
- Select Full Page (3) to view the entire page.
- Select Facing Pages (4) to view the current page and its facing page (odd-numbered pages are displayed on the right side of the screen, even-numbered pages on the left).

You can press PgUp, PgDn, or GoTo (Ctrl-Home) to view other pages of the document. Note that you cannot edit this preview version of your document. When you have finished previewing the document, you press Exit (F7) to return to your regular document screen.

Using Type Through and View Document

Using Type Through

Use Type Through to send text directly to the printer either after you type each line or as you type each character.

Press ⬆Shift F7 to display the Print menu.

Press 5 to select Type Through.

```
Print

        1 - Full Document
        2 - Page
        3 - Document on Disk
        4 - Control Printer
        5 - Type Through
        6 - View Document
        7 - Initialize Printer

Options

        S - Select Printer           Toshiba P321/P351/P351C
        B - Binding                  0"
        N - Number of Copies         1
        G - Graphics Quality         Medium
        T - Text Quality             High




    Type Through by: 1 Line; 2 Character: 0
```

Press 1 to send the line to the printer when you press Enter.

Type the text. You use the Backspace and Del keys to edit the line.

Press ⏎Enter to send the line to the printer.

Press 2 to send characters to the printer as you type. If you make a typing mistake, you cannot correct it.

Type the text.

WordPerfect sends each character to the printer as you press the key.

Viewing a Document

Use the View Document feature to preview your document before printing it.

Display the document and press
⇧Shift F7 to display the Print menu.
Then press 6 to select View Document.

Press 1 to view the document at its actual size.

Press 3 to view the entire page.

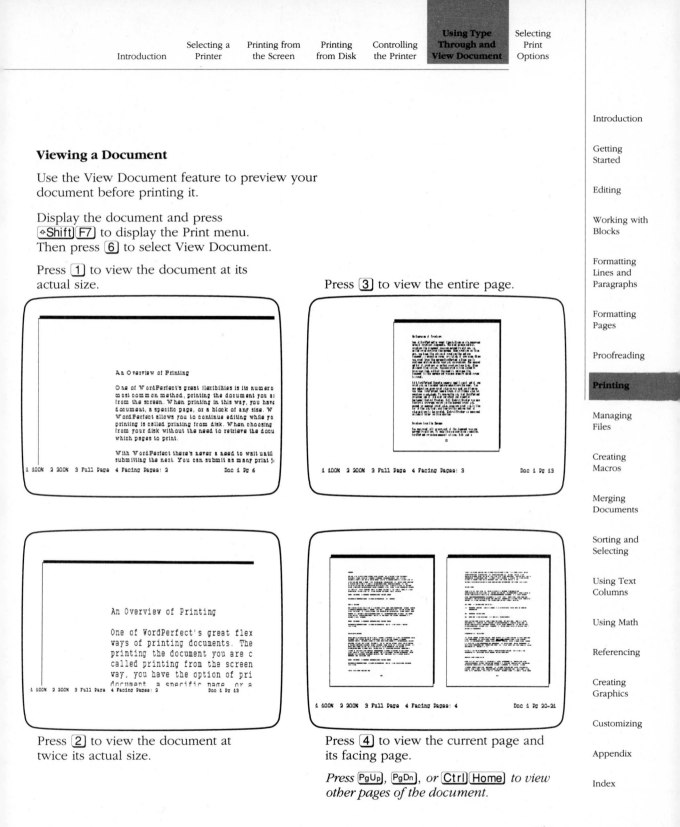

Press 2 to view the document at twice its actual size.

Press 4 to view the current page and its facing page.

Press PgUp, PgDn, or Ctrl Home to view other pages of the document.

243

Selecting Print Options

From the options listed at the bottom of the Print menu, you can select the following: the binding width, number of copies, and graphics and text quality. You use these options to set the printing specifications for particular print jobs.

Binding Width

The binding width is the extra space added at the inside edge of each page when the document is printed on both sides. Setting a binding width shifts odd-numbered pages to the right and even-numbered pages to the left by the specified amount. The binding option provides an extra margin along the inside edge of the paper to allow for binding or three-hole drilling the final copy.

To set the binding width, you first press Print (Shift-F7) to display the Print menu. Then you select Binding (B). Finally, you type the amount of extra space you want added to the normal inside margin of each page, and then press Enter. The binding width stays in effect until you change it again.

Number of Copies

If you need more than one copy of a print job, you can change the number of copies setting on the Print menu.

To specify the number of copies to print, you first press Print (Shift-F7). Then you select Number of Copies (N). You next type the number of copies you want to print and press Enter.

Until you change the Number of Copies back to 1, the number of copies you specified on the Print menu will be printed for all print jobs.

Introduction   Selecting a   Printing from   Printing   Controlling   Using Type   **Selecting**
Printer   the Screen   from Disk   the Printer   Through and   **Print**
View Document   **Options**

Print Quality

The Graphics Quality option controls the degree of resolution (sharpness) your printer uses to print graphics images. Text Quality is identical to Graphics Quality except that Text Quality controls text only.

To change print quality, you first press Print (Shift-F7) to display the Print menu. You then select Graphics Quality (G) and choose a desired setting from the Graphics Quality menu. Next, you select Text Quality (T). From the Text Quality menu, you select the desired print quality for text.

For both Graphics and Text, you can select the following print qualities:

- Select Do Not Print (1) if you don't want the graphics (or text) to print. If your printer can't print text and graphics in a single print run, select this option for Graphics Quality and print the text only. Then reload the paper, select this option for Text Quality, and print the graphics only.
- Select Draft (2) for a quick draft.
- Select Medium (3) for medium resolution.
- Select High (4) for high resolution. The higher the print resolution you select, the slower any pages containing graphics images will print.

Selecting Print Options

From the options listed at the bottom of the Print menu, you can select the binding width, number of copies, and print quality. Use these options to set the printing specifications for particular print jobs.

```
Print

     1 - Full Document
     2 - Page
     3 - Document on Disk
     4 - Control Printer
     5 - Type Through
     6 - View Document
     7 - Initialize Printer

Options

     S - Select Printer        Toshiba P321/P351/P351C
     B - Binding               1"
     N - Number of Copies      1
     G - Graphics Quality      Medium
     T - Text Quality          High




Selection: 0
```

Binding Width

The binding width is the extra space added at the inside edge of each page when the document is printed on both sides.

Press ⬆Shift F7 to display the Print menu.

Press B to select Binding.

Type the amount of extra space you want added to the normal inside margin of each page, and then press ⏎Enter.

```
Print

     1 - Full Document
     2 - Page
     3 - Document on Disk
     4 - Control Printer
     5 - Type Through
     6 - View Document
     7 - Initialize Printer

Options

     S - Select Printer        Toshiba P321/P351/P351C
     B - Binding               0"
     N - Number of Copies      2
     G - Graphics Quality      Medium
     T - Text Quality          High




Selection: n
```

Number of Copies

If you need more than one copy of a print job, change the number of copies setting on the Print menu.

Press ⬆Shift F7 to display the Print menu.

Press N for Number of Copies.

Type the number of copies you want to print.

Print Quality

The Graphics Quality option controls the degree of resolution (sharpness) your printer uses to print graphics images. Text Quality is identical to Graphics Quality except that Text Quality controls text only.

Press ⬆Shift F7 to display the Print menu.

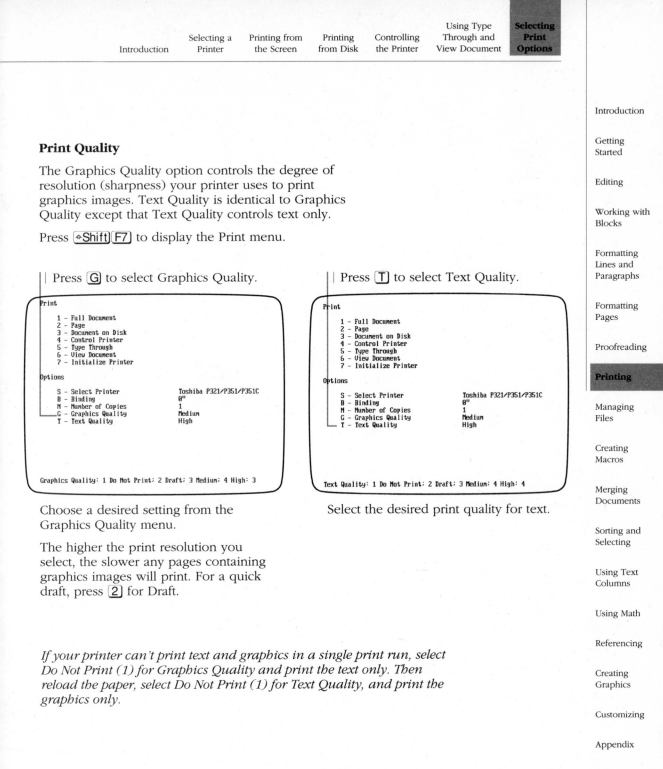

| Press G to select Graphics Quality.

Choose a desired setting from the Graphics Quality menu.

The higher the print resolution you select, the slower any pages containing graphics images will print. For a quick draft, press 2 for Draft.

| Press T to select Text Quality.

Select the desired print quality for text.

If your printer can't print text and graphics in a single print run, select Do Not Print (1) for Graphics Quality and print the text only. Then reload the paper, select Do Not Print (1) for Text Quality, and print the graphics only.

8 *Managing Files*

In this chapter, you learn how WordPerfect can help you deal with
DOS and manage your computer system. With WordPerfect's List Files
feature, you can manipulate files and directories to a much greater
degree than most word processing programs allow.

Key Terms

This chapter introduces the following key terms:

DOS	An acronym for disk operating system. DOS is a collection of programs that gives you control of your computer's resources. DOS controls the use of disk drives for storing and retrieving programs and data.
Directory	A disk area in which information about files is stored. Displayed on-screen, a directory is a list of files.
File specification	The drive and path name you enter for a file listing.

Tasks Covered in This Chapter

In this chapter, you learn to perform the following tasks:

- Use all parts of the List Files screen: the heading, the file listing, and the menu
- Use List Files to help you with common DOS and WordPerfect operations, such as deleting, moving, copying, and renaming files; making, changing, and deleting directories; and retrieving and printing documents

- Perform List Files operations on multiple files with a feature called *marking*
- Create document summaries

Using the List Files Screen

With List Files, you can accomplish—from within WordPerfect—much of the file and directory management you ordinarily perform from DOS. To get to the List Files screen, you press List Files (F5). WordPerfect displays a message in the lower left corner: `Dir`, followed by a file specification for all files in the current directory, such as

```
Dir C:\WP50\*.*
```

This message says that WordPerfect is ready to give you a file listing of all files in the current directory. If this is the directory you want, you simply press Enter. If it is not the directory you want, you can change the specification. If you type a new file specification, the original one disappears and is replaced by the new one you type. You also can edit the file specification, just as you edit regular text—using keys such as Del and Backspace. You change the file specification to what you want; then you press Enter.

After you type the file specification and press Enter, the List Files screen appears. The three areas on this screen are the *heading*, the *file listing*, and the *menu*.

The Heading

At the top of the List Files screen, you see the two-line heading, which contains useful information. Listed at the top left and going across to the right are the date, the time (given as 24-hour time), and the directory being listed. On the second line, starting again at the left, are the size of the document currently being edited, the amount of free space left on the disk, the amount of disk space taken up by files in the current directory, and the number of files shown in the listing.

The File Listing

The second section of the List Files screen is a two-column file listing in alphabetical order across the screen. (Files whose names start with numbers are listed first.) This listing shows the complete file name, file size, and date and time the file was created or last modified. You can print this listing, along with most of the information in the heading, by pressing Print (Shift-F7).

Notice that the top line of the file listing contains the following:

```
.   <CURRENT>  <DIR>      ..   <PARENT>  <DIR>
```

<DIR> indicates that the items are directories. Other directories in the listing are similarly labeled. The entry labeled <CURRENT> refers to the currently listed directory. The other entry, labeled <PARENT>, refers to the parent directory of the listed directory.

A highlight bar also appears on the top left name. You can move this bar with the cursor keys to highlight any name in the listing.

The List Files Menu

The List Files menu appears at the bottom of the screen. You can select from 10 command choices on the menu. Each choice acts on the highlighted file or directory.

After you make a menu selection, WordPerfect often asks for confirmation. For example, if you select Delete (2) to delete the file EXAMPLE.WP, WordPerfect displays the following prompt:

```
Delete C:\WP50\EXAMPLE.WP? (Y/N) No
```

Although WordPerfect displays the No response, you can answer either Y (to delete the file) or N (to cancel the command).

Using the List Files Screen

From within WordPerfect, you can use List Files to accomplish much of the file and directory management you ordinarily perform from DOS.

Press F5, the List Files key.

To list all files in this directory, press ↵Enter.

Or

To list files in a different directory, edit the name or type a new name, and then press ↵Enter.

Dir C:\WP50*.*   (Type = to change default Dir)

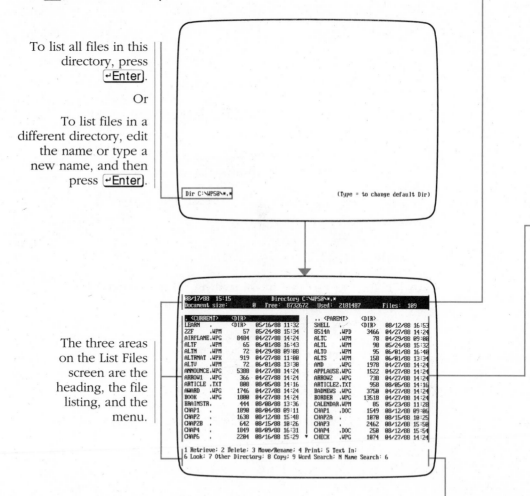

The three areas on the List Files screen are the heading, the file listing, and the menu.

```
08/17/88  15:15              Directory C:\WP50\*.*
Document size:        0   Free:  8732672   Used:  2181487        Files:  109

. <CURRENT>    <DIR>                        .. <PARENT>    <DIR>
LEARN     .       <DIR>   05/16/88 11:32    SHELL     .        <DIR>    08/12/88 16:53
22F       .WPM      57   05/24/88 15:34    8514A     .WPD      3466    04/27/88 14:24
AIRPLANE  .WPG    8484   04/27/88 14:24    ALTC      .WPM        78    04/29/88 09:00
ALTF      .WPM      65   06/01/88 16:43    ALTL      .WPM        98    05/24/88 15:32
ALTN      .WPM      72   04/29/88 09:00    ALTO      .WPM        95    06/01/88 16:40
ALTRMAT   .WPK     919   04/27/88 11:00    ALTS      .WPM       158    06/01/88 13:34
ALTU      .WPM      72   06/01/88 13:30    AND       .WPG      1978    04/27/88 14:24
ANNOUNCE  .WPG    5388   04/27/88 14:24    APPLAUSE  .WPG      1522    04/27/88 14:24
ARROW1    .WPG     366   04/27/88 14:24    ARROW2    .WPG       738    04/27/88 14:24
ARTICLE   .TXT     800   08/05/88 14:16    ARTICLE2  .TXT       958    08/05/88 14:16
AWARD     .WPG    1746   04/27/88 14:24    BADNEWS   .WPG      3750    04/27/88 14:24
BOOK      .WPG    1800   04/27/88 14:24    BORDER    .WPG     13518    04/27/88 14:24
BRAINSTR  .       444   08/08/88 13:36    CALENDAR  .WPM        85    05/23/88 11:20
CHAP1     .      1890   08/04/88 09:11    CHAP1     .DOC      1549    08/12/88 09:06
CHAP2     .      1638   08/12/88 15:48    CHAP2A    .        1070    08/15/88 10:25
CHAP2B    .       642   08/15/88 10:26    CHAP3     .        2462    08/12/88 15:50
CHAP4     .      1849   08/09/88 16:31    CHAP4     .DOC       250    08/12/88 15:54
CHAP6     .      2284   08/16/88 15:29 ▼  CHECK     .WPG      1074    04/27/88 14:24

1 Retrieve; 2 Delete; 3 Move/Rename; 4 Print; 5 Text In;
6 Look; 7 Other Directory; 8 Copy; 9 Word Search; N Name Search: 6
```

The Heading

The first line of the two-line heading displays the date, the time (given as 24-hour time), and the directory being listed. The second line shows the size of the document currently being edited, the amount of free space left on the disk, the amount of disk space taken up by files in the current file listing, and the number of files shown in the listing.

The File Listing

The two-column file listing displays file names and directories alphabetically across the screen. (Files whose names start with numbers are listed first.) The listing shows the complete file name, file size, and date and time the file was created or last modified.

Note the top line. <DIR> indicates that items are directories. Other directories in the listing are similarly labeled. The entry labeled <CURRENT> refers to the currently listed directory. The other entry, labeled <PARENT>, refers to the parent directory of the listed directory.

A highlight bar appears on the top left name. You can use the cursor keys to move this bar to highlight any name in the listing.

The List Files Menu

From the List Files menu, you can select from 10 command choices. Make a selection by pressing either the number or the highlighted letter next to the option. Each choice acts on the highlighted file or directory.

Using the List Files Menu

You can use the options on the List Files menu to manage your files without leaving WordPerfect and going to DOS. The first step you perform for any operation is to highlight the name of the file or directory on which you want to operate. You can use the cursor keys to move to the entry, or you can use Name Search.

Name Search

With the Name Search (N) option on the List Files menu, you can move the highlight bar to a file name as you type the name. You first press N, and then you type the first letter of the file name (for example, BUSINESS.LTR) for which you want to search. If you type **B**, for instance, the highlight bar jumps to the first file name starting with that letter. If you type **U** as the second letter of the name, the highlight bar jumps to the first file name that starts with these *two* letters. If you still don't find the file, you type the third letter—for example, you type **S**, and the highlight bar jumps to the first file name starting with these *three* letters.

If you make a mistake or change your mind, you can press Backspace, and the highlight bar jumps to the previous position. When the file name you want is highlighted, you turn off Name Search by pressing either Cancel (F1), Enter, or one of the arrow keys. Then you can perform any of the List Files operations described in this chapter.

Retrieve

The Retrieve (1) option on the List Files menu, discussed in detail in Chapter 2, works like Retrieve (Shift-F10) from the editing screen: it brings a file into WordPerfect for editing. Like Retrieve (Shift-F10), this command inserts the newly retrieved file at the cursor position.

Introduction

Using the List
Files Screen

**Using the List
Files Menu**

Using Document
Summaries

If you already have a file on-screen, Retrieve (1) inserts the file into the document on-screen at the cursor position. To prevent you from accidentally combining files, WordPerfect prompts `Retrieve into current document? (Y/N)` whenever you pick this option with a file already on-screen. You answer Y if you want to combine the new file with the file already on-screen. Or, you answer N if you don't want to combine the files.

WordPerfect tries to protect you from retrieving improper files. It does not retrieve program files, nor does it retrieve any temporary or permanent WordPerfect system files.

Delete

The Delete (2) option on the List Files menu deletes either files or directories. If the highlight bar is on a file, that file is deleted. If the bar is on a directory, the directory is deleted *as long as the directory does not contain any files.* If the directory contains files, WordPerfect displays an error message. Whether you are deleting files or directories, WordPerfect prompts `Delete C:\WP50\CHAP12? (Y/N) No`. You can press Y to confirm the deletion, or you can press N to cancel the deletion.

Move/Rename

To move or rename a file, you first highlight the name of the file you want to move. Then you press Move/Rename (3). If you are moving the file, you type the directory or drive where you want to move the file and press Enter. *Moving* a file means transferring it to a different directory or disk drive. If you are renaming the file, you type the new name (the displayed name disappears) and press Enter. You can't rename a file with the name of an existing file.

Using the List Files Menu

Copy

The Copy (8) option on the List Files menu copies the file just as the DOS COPY command does. To copy a file, you highlight the name of the file you want to copy and select Copy (8). WordPerfect displays the message `Copy this file to:`. You can copy the file to another disk or directory by typing the drive or directory, or you can make a copy of the file in the current directory by entering a new file name.

Print

The Print (4) option on the List Files menu prints the highlighted file on the currently selected printer. Unlike many programs, WordPerfect can print while you continue to edit another document. You even can tell WordPerfect to print more than one file. For a detailed discussion of the Print option, see Chapter 7, "Printing."

Text In

The Text In (5) option on the List Files menu retrieves a *text* file (sometimes called an ASCII file), not a WordPerfect format file. This command is the same as retrieving a DOS text file into the editing screen with Text In/Out (Ctrl-F5) and the Dos Text (1) option.

Look

The Look (6) option on the List Files menu displays the highlighted file without retrieving it to the editing screen. Note that Look (6) is the default menu choice. You don't have to select Look (6) to display a file (although you can if you want); you can just press Enter. Use Look to examine files quickly. You may, for example, forget which file you need to edit.

The file name and size are displayed at the top of the screen. You can move the cursor through the file with the usual WordPerfect cursor-movement commands. You cannot edit the file. The Look option also continuously displays or scrolls each succeeding line of the document if you press S. Pressing S again stops the scroll. You press Exit (F7) or Enter to leave Look.

You also can use Look to display other directories. With the highlight bar at the top left of the List Files screen, you press Enter once, edit the displayed file specification or type a new one, and press Enter again. This procedure does not change directories; it just lets you see a file listing of another directory.

You can use the Look command to inspect directories another way. You place the highlight bar on a directory entry (other than <CURRENT>) in the file listing. Then you press Enter. WordPerfect displays a `Dir` message followed by the file specification. You press Enter again, and WordPerfect displays the file listing of this highlighted directory. You can look at any directories in this new listing the same way. You can travel up or down the directory tree, examining each directory in turn. Remember, however, that you have not changed your current directory. You are simply listing files in other directories.

When a document is displayed with Look (6), you can use Forward Search (F2) and Backward Search (Shift-F2) to search for text. You can't, however, search for text in headers, footers, or footnotes.

Using the List Files Menu

Before you select an option from the List Files menu, display the List Files screen for the directory from which you want to manipulate files.

For all operations, you first move the highlight bar to the file on which you want to operate.

Name Search

```
08/17/88 15:24         Directory C:\WP50\*.*
Document size:     0  Free:  8730624  Used:  2181792      Files:  110

. <CURRENT>   <DIR>                      .. <PARENT>   <DIR>
LEARN    .    <DIR>  05/16/88 11:32      SHELL    .    <DIR>  08/12/88 16:53
ZZF      .WPM    57  05/24/88 15:34      8514A    .WPD   3466  04/27/88 14:24
AIRPLANE.WPG   8484  04/27/88 14:24      ALTC     .WPM     78  04/29/88 09:00
ALTF     .WPM    65  06/01/88 16:43      ALTL     .WPM     98  05/24/88 15:32
ALTN     .WPM    72  04/29/88 09:00      ALTO     .WPM     95  06/01/88 16:40
ALTMAT  .WPK   919  04/27/88 11:00      ALTS     .WPM    150  06/01/88 13:34
ALTU     .WPM    72  06/01/88 13:30      AND      .WPG   1970  04/27/88 14:24
ANNOUNCE.WPG   5388  04/27/88 14:24      APPLAUSE.WPG   1522  04/27/88 14:24
ARROW1   .WPG   366  04/27/88 14:24      ARROW2   .WPG    738  04/27/88 14:24
ARTICLE .TXT    888  08/05/88 14:16      ARTICLE2.TXT    958  08/05/88 14:16
AWARD   .WPG   1746  04/27/88 14:24      BADNEWS .WPG   3750  04/27/88 14:24
BOOK    .WPG   1888  04/27/88 14:24      BORDER   .WPG  13518  04/27/88 14:24
BRAINSTR.       444  08/08/88 13:36      BUSINESS.LTR    305  08/17/88 15:23
CALENDAR.WPM     85  05/23/88 11:28      CHAP1    .      1890  08/04/88 09:11
CHAP1   .DOC   1549  08/12/88 09:06      CHAP2    .      1638  08/12/88 15:48
CHAP2A  .      1870  08/15/88 10:25      CHAP2B   .       642  08/15/88 10:26
CHAP3   .      2462  08/12/88 15:58      CHAP4    .      1849  08/09/88 16:31
CHAP4   .DOC    250  08/12/88 15:54   ▼  CHAP6    .      2204  08/16/88 15:29

B                      (Name Search: Enter or arrows to Exit)
```

Press **N** for Name Search to move the highlight bar to a file name as you type the name.

Type the first letter of the file name for which you want to search. For example, if you want to find the file BUSINESS.LTR, type **B**.

```
08/17/88 15:24         Directory C:\WP50\*.*
Document size:     0  Free:  8730624  Used:  2181792      Files:  110

. <CURRENT>   <DIR>                      .. <PARENT>   <DIR>
LEARN    .    <DIR>  05/16/88 11:32      SHELL    .    <DIR>  08/12/88 16:53
ZZF      .WPM    57  05/24/88 15:34      8514A    .WPD   3466  04/27/88 14:24
AIRPLANE.WPG   8484  04/27/88 14:24      ALTC     .WPM     78  04/29/88 09:00
ALTF     .WPM    65  06/01/88 16:43      ALTL     .WPM     98  05/24/88 15:32
ALTN     .WPM    72  04/29/88 09:00      ALTO     .WPM     95  06/01/88 16:40
ALTMAT  .WPK   919  04/27/88 11:00      ALTS     .WPM    150  06/01/88 13:34
ALTU     .WPM    72  06/01/88 13:30      AND      .WPG   1970  04/27/88 14:24
ANNOUNCE.WPG   5388  04/27/88 14:24      APPLAUSE.WPG   1522  04/27/88 14:24
ARROW1   .WPG   366  04/27/88 14:24      ARROW2   .WPG    738  04/27/88 14:24
ARTICLE .TXT    888  08/05/88 14:16      ARTICLE2.TXT    958  08/05/88 14:16.
AWARD   .WPG   1746  04/27/88 14:24      BADNEWS .WPG   3750  04/27/88 14:24
BOOK    .WPG   1888  04/27/88 14:24      BORDER   .WPG  13518  04/27/88 14:24
BRAINSTR.       444  08/08/88 13:36      BUSINESS.LTR    305  08/17/88 15:23
CALENDAR.WPM     85  05/23/88 11:28      CHAP1    .      1890  08/04/88 09:11
CHAP1   .DOC   1549  08/12/88 09:06      CHAP2    .      1638  08/12/88 15:48
CHAP2A  .      1870  08/15/88 10:25      CHAP2B   .       642  08/15/88 10:26
CHAP3   .      2462  08/12/88 15:50      CHAP4    .      1849  08/09/88 16:31
CHAP4   .DOC    250  08/12/88 15:54   ▼  CHAP6    .      2204  08/16/88 15:29

BU                     (Name Search: Enter or arrows to Exit)
```

Type the second letter of the name. For example, type **U**. If you still don't find the file, type the third letter.

When the correct file is highlighted, press **⏎Enter**, **F1**, or an arrow key to end Name Search.

Retrieve

Press **1** for Retrieve to bring a file into WordPerfect for editing. See Chapter 2 for more details about retrieving files.

Delete

Press **2** for Delete to delete either files or directories.

Answer **Y**.

If the highlight bar is on a file, that file is deleted. If the bar is on a directory, the directory is deleted *as long as the directory does not contain any files.*

```
08/17/88 15:15         Directory C:\WP50\*.*
Document size:     0  Free:  8732672  Used:  2181487      Files:  109

. <CURRENT>   <DIR>                      .. <PARENT>   <DIR>
LEARN    .    <DIR>  05/16/88 11:32      SHELL    .    <DIR>  08/12/88 16:53
ZZF      .WPM    57  05/24/88 15:34      8514A    .WPD   3466  04/27/88 14:24
AIRPLANE.WPG   8484  04/27/88 14:24      ALTC     .WPM     78  04/29/88 09:00
ALTF     .WPM    65  06/01/88 16:43      ALTL     .WPM     98  05/24/88 15:32
ALTN     .WPM    72  04/29/88 09:00      ALTO     .WPM     95  06/01/88 16:40
ALTMAT  .WPK   919  04/27/88 11:00      ALTS     .WPM    150  06/01/88 13:34
ALTU     .WPM    72  06/01/88 13:30      AND      .WPG   1970  04/27/88 14:24
ANNOUNCE.WPG   5388  04/27/88 14:24      APPLAUSE.WPG   1522  04/27/88 14:24
ARROW1   .WPG   366  04/27/88 14:24      ARROW2   .WPG    738  04/27/88 14:24
ARTICLE .TXT    888  08/05/88 14:16      ARTICLE2.TXT    958  08/05/88 14:16
AWARD   .WPG   1746  04/27/88 14:24      BADNEWS .WPG   3750  04/27/88 14:24
BOOK    .WPG   1888  04/27/88 14:24      BORDER   .WPG  13518  04/27/88 14:24
BRAINSTR.       444  08/08/88 13:36      CALENDAR.WPM     85  05/23/88 11:28
CHAP1   .      1890  08/04/88 09:11      CHAP1    .DOC   1549  08/12/88 09:06
CHAP2A  .      1638  08/12/88 15:48      CHAP2A   .      1870  08/15/88 10:25
CHAP2B  .       642  08/15/88 10:26      CHAP3    .      2462  08/12/88 15:54
CHAP4   .      1849  08/09/88 16:31      CHAP4    .DOC    250  08/12/88 15:54
CHAP6   .      2204  08/16/88 15:29   ▼  CHECK    .WPG   1074  04/27/88 14:24

Delete C:\WP50\CHAP1? (Y/N) No
```

```
08/17/88  15:17            Directory C:\WP50\*.*
Document size:      0   Free:  8732672   Used:  2181487     Files:  109

.  <CURRENT>    <DIR>                     ..  <PARENT>   <DIR>
LEARN    .      <DIR>      05/16/88 11:32  SHELL    .      <DIR>      08/12/88 16:53
22F      .WPM       57     05/24/88 15:34  8514A    .WPD     3466     04/27/88 14:24
AIRPLANE .WPG     8484     04/27/88 14:24  ALTC     .WPM       78     04/29/88 09:00
ALTF     .WPM       65     06/01/88 16:43  ALTL     .WPM       98     05/24/88 15:32
ALTN     .WPM       72     04/29/88 09:00  ALTO     .WPM       95     06/01/88 16:40
ALTRNAT  .WPK      919     04/27/88 11:00  ALTS     .WPM      158     06/01/88 13:34
ALTU     .WPM       72     06/01/88 13:30  AND      .WPG     1978     04/27/88 14:24
ANNOUNCE .WPG     5388     04/27/88 14:24  APPLAUSE .WPG     1522     04/27/88 14:24
ARROW1   .WPG      366     04/27/88 14:24  ARROW2   .WPG      738     04/27/88 14:24
ARTICLE  .TXT      808     08/05/88 14:16  ARTICLE2 .TXT      958     08/05/88 14:16
AWARD    .WPG     1746     04/27/88 14:24  BADNEWS  .WPG     3750     04/27/88 14:24
BOOK     .WPG     1800     04/27/88 14:24  BORDER   .WPG    13510     04/27/88 14:24
BRAINSTR .       444     08/08/88 13:36  CALENDAR .WPM       85     05/23/88 11:28
CHAP1    .       1890     08/04/88 09:11  CHAP1    .DOC     1549     08/12/88 09:06
CHAP2    .       1638     08/12/88 15:48  CHAP2A   .        1070     08/15/88 10:25
CHAP2B   .        642     08/15/88 10:26  CHAP3    .        2462     08/12/88 15:50
CHAP4    .       1849     08/09/88 16:31  CHAP4    .DOC      250     08/12/88 15:54
CHAP6    .       2204     08/16/88 15:29  CHECK    .WPG     1074     04/27/88 14:24

New name: C:\WP50\CHAP1
```

Move/Rename

Press ③ for Move/Rename to move the file to a different directory or disk drive, or to rename the file.

To move the file, type the directory or drive where you want to move the file and press ⏎Enter.

To rename the file, type the new name and press ⏎Enter.

```
08/17/88  15:23            Directory C:\WP50\*.*
Document size:      0   Free:  8732672   Used:  2181487     Files:  109

.  <CURRENT>    <DIR>                     ..  <PARENT>   <DIR>
LEARN    .      <DIR>      05/16/88 11:32  SHELL    .      <DIR>      08/12/88 16:53
22F      .WPM       57     05/24/88 15:34  8514A    .WPD     3466     04/27/88 14:24
AIRPLANE .WPG     8484     04/27/88 14:24  ALTC     .WPM       78     04/29/88 09:00
ALTF     .WPM       65     06/01/88 16:43  ALTL     .WPM       98     05/24/88 15:32
ALTN     .WPM       72     04/29/88 09:00  ALTO     .WPM       95     06/01/88 16:40
ALTRNAT  .WPK      919     04/27/88 11:00  ALTS     .WPM      158     06/01/88 13:34
ALTU     .WPM       72     06/01/88 13:30  AND      .WPG     1978     04/27/88 14:24
ANNOUNCE .WPG     5388     04/27/88 14:24  APPLAUSE .WPG     1522     04/27/88 14:24
ARROW1   .WPG      366     04/27/88 14:24  ARROW2   .WPG      738     04/27/88 14:24
ARTICLE  .TXT      808     08/05/88 14:16  ARTICLE2 .TXT      958     08/05/88 14:16
AWARD    .WPG     1746     04/27/88 14:24  BADNEWS  .WPG     3750     04/27/88 14:24
BOOK     .WPG     1800     04/27/88 14:24  BORDER   .WPG    13510     04/27/88 14:24
BRAINSTR .       444     08/08/88 13:36  CALENDAR .WPM       85     05/23/88 11:28
CHAP1    .       1890     08/04/88 09:11  CHAP1    .DOC     1549     08/12/88 09:06
CHAP2    .       1638     08/12/88 15:48  CHAP2A   .        1070     08/15/88 10:25
CHAP2B   .        642     08/15/88 10:26  CHAP3    .        2462     08/12/88 15:50
CHAP4    .       1849     08/09/88 16:31  CHAP4    .DOC      250     08/12/88 15:54
CHAP6    .       2204     08/16/88 15:29  CHECK    .WPG     1074     04/27/88 14:24

Copy this file to:
```

Copy

Press ⑧ for Copy to make a duplicate of a file. You can copy the file to another disk or directory, or you can make a copy of the file in the current directory by entering a new file name instead of a drive or directory.

Type the new name and press ⏎Enter.

Using the List Files Menu

Print

Press ④ for Print to print the high-lighted file on the currently selected printer. Unlike many programs, WordPerfect can print while you continue to edit another document. You even can tell WordPerfect to print more than one file.

Text In

Press ⑤ for Text In to retrieve a *text* file (sometimes called an ASCII file), not a WordPerfect format file.

```
Filename C:\WP50\CHAP6                          File size:      2204


                         Writing Guideline
================================================================================
Brainstorming

When you have trouble determining a sharp focus for a document--
when you are uncertain what you want to say--consider trying a
semistructured writing exercise known as "brainstorming."

When you brainstorm a writing assignment on-screen, you register
your ideas in list form as they occur to you. When you brainstorm,
you don't worry about typos, spelling, or style. You turn off the
inclination to hone each sentence before you move on to the next
one. You can handle those matters later. Your goal is, rather, to
generate as many ideas as possible about the topic, the purpose,
or the audience.

Keeping an Idea File


Press Exit when done                    (Use Cursor Keys for more text)
```

Look

Press ⑥ for Look to display the highlighted file without retrieving it into WordPerfect. Although you cannot edit files displayed with Look, you can use this option to display files quickly.

Move the cursor through the file with the usual cursor-movement commands.

To scroll through the document, press ⑤. Press ⑤ again to stop scrolling.

Press ⑦ or ↵Enter to leave Look.

You can use either of two methods to display another directory. Note that displaying a directory in either way does not change to that directory.

Method 1

With the highlight bar at the top left of the List Files screen, press ⏎Enter.

Edit the displayed file specification or type a new one.

Press ⏎Enter.

Method 2

Use the cursor keys to move the highlight bar to a directory entry (other than <CURRENT>) in the file listing.

Press ⏎Enter.

Press ⏎Enter again.

Using the List Files Menu

Other Directory

Use the Other Directory (7) option on the List Files menu to change
the current directory. You first place the highlight bar on any directory
name other than <CURRENT>, and then select Other Directory (7).
WordPerfect displays in the lower left corner of the screen the message
New directory = followed by the name of the highlighted
directory.

You press Enter; WordPerfect displays the file specification for all the
files in the highlighted directory. Finally, you press Enter to change to
the new directory and display its listing. If you decide that you don't
want to change directories, you can press Cancel (F1) before pressing
Enter the second time.

You can edit both the New directory = and Dir messages. You
thereby can change directly to any directory on your hard disk.

You can create a new directory by selecting Other Directory (7) and
entering a unique name. For example, if you enter **book**, WordPerfect
prompts Create c:\book? (Y/N) No. You can answer Y to
create a new subdirectory called BOOK. Or, you can answer N if this
isn't what you want.

You also can use the List Files key (F5) to change or create directories
from the WordPerfect editing screen. You press List Files (F5), and
then you type an equal sign (=). WordPerfect responds the same way
as in the List Files screen.

Word Search

With the Word Search (9) option on the List Files menu, you can
search one or more files in the file listing for a word or phrase without

retrieving the files into WordPerfect. You can, for example, determine which documents are about a certain subject by searching for a word or phrase related to that subject. The Word Search feature is discussed in detail in Chapter 6, "Proofreading."

Marking Files

With a List Files feature called *marking*, you can indicate on which files you want to concentrate. To mark files, you first press List Files (5) and then Enter. Next, you move the highlight bar to the first file you want to mark. Then you press the asterisk key (*).

WordPerfect puts a bold asterisk next to the file-size column of the highlighted file name, then moves the highlight bar automatically to the next file name in the listing. You next move the highlight bar to each file you want to include and mark it with an asterisk.

You can use another method to specify files. To display only certain files in the List Files screen, you can use a wild-card file specification such as *.DOC or CH10.*. You type this pattern after pressing List Files (F5); then only those files fitting the pattern appear on the List Files screen for you to work on.

If you want to mark *all* the files in the listing, you press Home and then the asterisk key. To unmark all marked files, you press Home and the asterisk key again.

You can perform the following List Files operations on a number of marked files simultaneously: Delete (2); Move (3), but not Rename; Print (4), on the currently selected printer; Copy (8), to a different drive or directory; and Word Search (9).

Using the List Files Menu

Other Directory

Change the current directory or create a new one using either of two methods.

Method 1: From the List Files Screen

```
10/18/88 13:09         Directory C:\WP50\*.*
Document size:      0  Free: 9537536  Used: 2101911      Files: 110

. <CURRENT>  <DIR>                      .. <PARENT>  <DIR>
LEARN    .      <DIR> 05/16/88 11:32    SHELL    .     <DIR>  08/12/88 16:53
22F      .WPM      57 05/24/88 15:34    8514A    .WPD   3466  04/27/88 14:24
AIRPLANE.WPG     8404 04/27/88 14:24    ALTC     .WPM     78  04/29/88 09:00
ALTF     .WPG      65 06/01/88 16:43    ALTL     .WPM     90  05/24/88 15:32
ALTM     .WPM      72 04/29/88 09:00    ALTO     .WPM     95  06/01/88 16:40
ALTRMAT .WPK      919 04/27/88 11:00    ALTS     .WPM    150  06/01/88 13:34
ALTU     .WPM      72 06/01/88 13:30    AND      .WPG   1970  04/27/88 14:24
ANNOUNCE.WPG     5300 04/27/88 14:24    APPLAUSE.WPG   1522  04/27/88 14:24
ARROW1   .WPG     366 04/27/88 14:24    ARROW2   .WPG    738  04/27/88 14:24
ARTICLE .TXT      800 08/05/88 14:16    ARTICLE2.TXT    958  08/05/88 14:16
AWARD    .WPG    1746 04/27/88 14:24    BADNEWS .WPG   3750  04/27/88 14:24
BOOK     .WPG    1800 04/27/88 14:24    BORDER   .WPG  13510  04/27/88 14:24
BRAINSTR.LTR      444 08/08/88 13:36    BUSINESS.LTR    326  08/17/88 15:28
CALENDAR.WPM       85 05/23/88 11:28    CHAP1    .      1914  08/17/88 15:29
CHAP1    .DOC    1549 08/12/88 09:06    CHAP2    .      1694  08/18/88 09:36
CHAP2A   .       1070 08/15/88 10:25    CHAP2B   .       642  08/15/88 10:26
CHAP3    .       2462 08/12/88 15:50    CHAP4    .      1049  08/09/88 16:31
CHAP4    .DOC     250 08/12/88 15:54 ▼  CHAP6    .      2222  08/18/88 12:30

New directory = C:\WP50\LEARN
```

```
10/05/88 16:20         Directory C:\LEARN\*.*
Document size:      0  Free: 17000640  Used:   264426      Files: 69

. <CURRENT>  <DIR>                      .. <PARENT>  <DIR>
ADDRESS .TUT      826 04/27/88 18:14    ADDRESS .WKB     642  04/27/88 18:14
ADVANCED.TUT        3 04/27/88 18:14    ALTI     .WPM    132  04/27/88 18:14
BANNER   .TUT     631 04/27/88 18:14    BEGIN    .TUT     11  04/27/88 18:14
BRIEF    .WKB    6640 04/27/88 18:14    CHART    .WKB   4218  04/27/88 18:14
CLIENTS .WKB     1357 04/27/88 18:14    COMPASS .WKB   2924  04/27/88 18:14
CUSTOMER.WKB     1729 04/27/88 18:14    FUTURE   .WKB   3136  04/27/88 18:14
GRAPH    .WPG    1198 04/27/88 18:14    INCOME   .WKB   1823  04/27/88 18:14
INTRO    .TUT   29953 04/27/88 18:14    INTRO_1 .TUT   9615  04/27/88 18:14
INVOICE .WKB     1848 04/27/88 18:14    ITIMERY .WKB   2257  04/27/88 18:14
LEARN    .BAT     335 04/27/88 18:14    LABELB   .WKB    929  04/27/88 18:14
LESS1    .TUT    5859 04/27/88 18:14    LESS     .TUT     11  04/27/88 18:14
LESS3    .TUT    7866 04/27/88 18:14    LESS2    .TUT   9001  04/27/88 18:14
LESS5    .TUT   13505 04/27/88 18:14    LESS4    .TUT  10779  04/27/88 18:14
LETTER   .STY     799 04/27/88 18:14    LESS6    .TUT   7213  04/27/88 18:14
LETTER1  .TUT     956 04/27/88 18:14    LETTER   .TUT    772  04/27/88 18:14
LETTER_P.TUT      771 04/27/88 18:14    LETTER_F.TUT    833  04/27/88 18:14
MASTER   .WKB     808 04/27/88 18:14 ▼  MEMO     .TUT    530  04/27/88 18:14

1 Retrieve; 2 Delete; 3 Move/Rename; 4 Print; 5 Text In;
6 Look; 7 Other Directory; 8 Copy; 9 Word Search; N Name Search: 6
```

Use the cursor keys to move the highlight bar to any directory name other than <CURRENT>.

Press 7 to select Other Directory.

Press ←Enter.

Press ←Enter again.

Method 2: From the Editing Screen

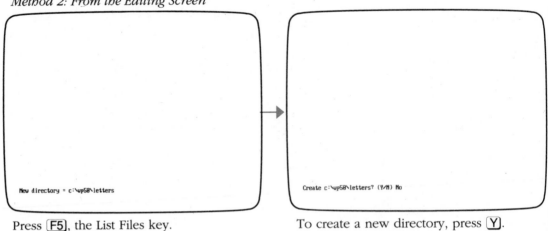

```
New directory = c:\wp50\letters
```

```
Create c:\wp50\letters? (Y/N) No
```

Press F5, the List Files key.

Press =.

Type the complete path information, for example, type **c:\wp50\letters**, and then press ←Enter or the space bar.

To create a new directory, press Y.

Word Search

Press 9 for Word Search to search one or more files in
the file listing for a word or phrase without retrieving
the files into WordPerfect. The Word Search feature is
discussed in detail in Chapter 6, "Proofreading."

```
08/17/88  15:26              Directory C:\WP50\*.*
Document size:        0  Free:  8730624  Used:     749     Marked: 2

.  <CURRENT>    <DIR>                      ..  <PARENT>    <DIR>
LEARN    .      <DIR>  05/16/88 11:32      SHELL    .      <DIR>  08/12/88 16:53
22F      .WPM       57 05/24/88 15:34      8514A    .WPD     3466 04/27/88 14:24
AIRPLANE.WPG      8484 04/27/88 14:24      ALTC     .WPM       78 04/29/88 09:00
ALTF     .WPM       65 06/01/88 16:43      ALTL     .WPM       98 05/24/88 15:32
ALTN     .WPM       72 04/29/88 09:00      ALTO     .WPM       95 06/01/88 16:40
ALTRNAT .WPK       919 04/27/88 11:00      ALTS     .WPM      158 06/01/88 13:34
ALTV     .WPM       72 06/01/88 13:30      AMD      .WPG     1978 04/27/88 14:24
ANNOUNCE.WPG      5300 04/27/88 14:24      APPLAUSE.WPG     1522 04/27/88 14:24
ARROW1   .WPG      366 04/27/88 14:24      ARROW2   .WPG      730 04/27/88 14:24
ARTICLE .TXT       808 08/05/88 14:16      ARTICLE2.TXT      958 08/05/88 14:16
AWARD    .WPG     1746 04/27/88 14:24      BADNEWS .WPG     3750 04/27/88 14:24
BOOK     .WPG     1800 04/27/88 14:24      BORDER   .WPG    13510 04/27/88 14:24
BRAINSTR.LTR       444*08/08/88 13:36      BUSINESS.LTR      305*08/17/88 15:23
CALENDAR.WPM        85 05/23/88 11:28      CHAP1    .        1890 08/04/88 09:11
CHAP1    .DOC     1549 08/12/88 09:06      CHAP2    .        1630 08/12/88 15:40
CHAP2A   .        1070 08/15/88 10:25      CHAP2B   .        642 08/15/88 10:26
CHAP3    .        2462 08/12/88 15:50      CHAP4    .        1049 08/09/88 16:31
CHAP4    .DOC      250 08/12/88 15:54      CHAP6    .        2204 08/16/88 15:29

1 Retrieve; 2 Delete; 3 Move/Rename; 4 Print; 5 Text In;
6 Look; 7 Other Directory; 8 Copy; 9 Word Search; N Name Search: 6
```

Marking Files

On the List Files screen, mark
particular files and then perform
certain List Files operations on only
those files.

Move the highlight bar to each file
you want to mark and press *.

```
08/17/88  15:26              Directory C:\WP50\*.DOC
Document size:        0  Free:  8730624  Used:    1799     Marked: 2

.  <CURRENT>    <DIR>                      ..  <PARENT>    <DIR>
CHAP1    .DOC     1549*08/12/88 09:06      CHAP4    .DOC      250*08/12/88 15:54

1 Retrieve; 2 Delete; 3 Move/Rename; 4 Print; 5 Text In;
6 Look; 7 Other Directory; 8 Copy; 9 Word Search; N Name Search: 6
```

To list a subgroup of files and then mark
them all, press F5, the List Files key.

Type a pattern that fits all the files you
want to list. In the pattern, use a wild-card
file specification, such as *.DOC, to specify
the files.

Press ↵Enter to list the specified files.

Press Home and then * to mark all the
files.

Note: To unmark all the files, press Home
and then * again.

Using Document Summaries

With WordPerfect, you can place a document summary box at the beginning of your file before you save the document to disk. Use this feature to display the file name, the date the document was created, the author's name, the typist's name, and any other informative comments that may help you identify the document and its contents. You can view document summaries on-screen, but they are not printed with documents.

Entering Document Summary Information

You can create and edit a document summary from anywhere in your document. To create a document summary, you first display your document, and then you press Format (Shift-F8) to display the Format menu. From this menu, you select Document (3) to display the Format: Document menu. From this menu, you choose Summary (5). A screen for creating the summary is displayed.

If you have previously saved the file, WordPerfect automatically enters your file name and the date the file was created. If you have not saved the file, a (Not named yet) message appears, and the file name is added when you save the document.

Next, you need to select each of the options, in turn, and enter the requested information. You can enter a description of the document, the subject, the name of the author, the name of the typist, and any comments. Each entry (except for the comments) can be up to 40 characters long; comments can be as many as 780 characters long. After each entry, you press Enter. To save your work and return to your document, you press Exit (F7).

Displaying a Document Summary

To look at a document summary, you press List Files (F5) and display the directory that contains the file you want to view. Then you move the highlight bar to that document and select Look (6). The document is displayed with the document summary shown first.

Notice that the first 400 characters of your document are placed automatically in the Comments section. Comments you added while creating the document summary also are displayed. If you want to see the rest of the document, you can press PgDn or the down-arrow key.

Creating a Document Summary Prompt

To remind you to create a document summary, you can create a document summary prompt. When you create a prompt, WordPerfect reminds you to create a document summary whenever you save or exit a file. You first press Setup (Shift-F1) to display the Setup menu. From this menu, you select Initial Settings (5). Then you select Document Summary (3), select Create on Save/Exit (1), and press Y. Finally, you press Exit (F7) to return to your document.

Using Document Summaries

Place a document summary box at the top of your file before you save the document to disk.

```
Format: Document

    1 - Display Pitch - Automatic      Yes
                        Width          0.1"

    2 - Initial Codes

    3 - Initial Font                   Courier

    4 - Redline Method                 Printer Dependent

    5 - Summary ───────────────────────────────────────




Selection: 0
```

Entering Document Summary Information

From anywhere in your document, press ⌐Shift⌐ ⌐F8⌐ to display the Format menu and then press ⌐3⌐ to select Document

Press ⌐5⌐ to choose Summary.

```
Document Summary

        System Filename          C:\WP50\CHAP1

        Date of Creation         August 17, 1988

    1 - Descriptive Filename

    2 - Subject/Account

    3 - Author

    4 - Typist

    5 - Comments
    ┌──────────────────────────────────────────────┐
    │                                              │
    │                                              │
    │                                              │
    └──────────────────────────────────────────────┘

Press Exit when done
```

If you have previously saved that file, WordPerfect automatically enters your file name and the date the file was created. If you have not saved the file, a (Not named yet) message appears, and the file name is added when you save the document.

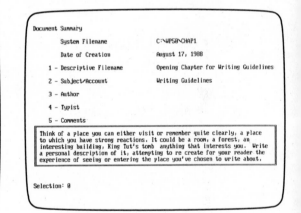

Press ⌐1⌐, type a description of the document, and press ⌐Enter⌐.

Press ⌐2⌐, type the subject, and press ⌐Enter⌐.

Press ⌐3⌐, type the name of the author, and press ⌐Enter⌐.

Press ⌐4⌐, type the name of the typist, and press ⌐Enter⌐.

Press ⌐5⌐, type any comments, and press ⌐Enter⌐.

Press ⌐F7⌐ to save your work and return to your document.

Displaying a Document Summary

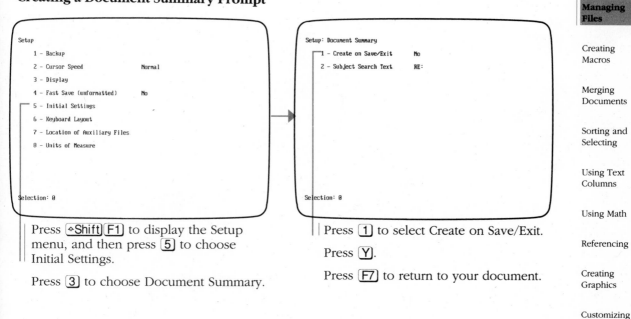

Display the List Files screen and
highlight the file you want to
view.

Press **6** to select Look.

Press **PgDn** or **↓** to see the rest
of the documents.

Creating a Document Summary Prompt

Press **⇧Shift F1** to display the Setup
menu, and then press **5** to choose
Initial Settings.

Press **3** to choose Document Summary.

Press **1** to select Create on Save/Exit.

Press **Y**.

Press **F7** to return to your document.

9 *Creating Macros*

If you perform any task repeatedly, even one as simple as deleting a line, you can do it more quickly with a macro. Macros can automate simple tasks, such as typing *Sincerely yours* and your name. Macros also can perform complex operations that include both text and WordPerfect commands. After you create a macro, you press only one or two keystrokes to do almost instantly what would otherwise require many keystrokes.

Key Terms

Macro
A series of prerecorded keystrokes assigned to a single key or key combination. Macros greatly relieve the tedium of repetitive typing.

Permanent macro
A macro you name and store on disk. You can use a permanent macro in any session of WordPerfect by issuing a special command that refers to the macro's name.

Temporary macro
A macro that works as you have defined it until you create another temporary macro. Each temporary macro you create replaces the previous one.

Tasks Covered in This Chapter

In this chapter, you learn to perform the following tasks:

- Create two types of macros: permanent and temporary
- Run macros
- Stop macros
- Replace macros

Permanent Macros

You can create two kinds of permanent macros: Alt-*letter* macros and descriptive macros. Alt-*letter* macros have names that consist of the Alt key plus a letter from A to Z—for example, Alt-K or Alt-X. Descriptive macros have names of one to eight characters—for example, TABS or MARGIN5.

The macros that are simplest to create and use are the Alt-*letter* macros. Therefore, choose Alt-*letter* names for the macros you will use most often. Be sure to use macro names that will remind you of what your macros do; for example, you might use the name Alt-C for a macro that centers text.

Permanent macros are saved to disk in a file with the macro name you've specified and the extension .WPM—for example, ALTA.WPM or LTRHEAD.WPM. You don't have to provide the .WPM extension for either type of macro.

Creating Permanent Macros

When you create a macro, you enter into your current document the keystrokes and commands you want the macro to "play back" when you run the macro. When you create a macro to change your tab settings, for example, you also change your tab settings at the cursor position in your current document. So that these macro keystrokes and commands do not interfere with any of your permanent files, you should save any document you are working on and clear your screen before you practice with macros. If you need some text for the macro to work on, you can type a few lines.

To create a permanent macro, you first press Macro Define (Ctrl-F10). The screen displays the prompt `Define macro:`. You type the name of the macro. For an Alt-*letter* macro, you press the Alt key and a letter from A to Z. For a descriptive macro, you type one to eight characters (letters or numbers) and press Enter.

The screen displays the prompt `Description:`. You type a short description of what the macro does and press Enter. You can use any description, up to 39 characters, that will help remind you of the macro's commands.

`Macro Def` blinks at the bottom of the screen. This blinking message reminds you that the program is recording your keystrokes.

You next type the keystrokes you want to record for this macro. You type them in the exact order you want them played back when you run the macro. When you finish recording all the keystrokes for the macro, you press Macro Define (Ctrl-F10) again.

Running Permanent Macros

When you run (play back) a permanent macro, the steps vary depending on whether you are running an Alt-*letter* macro or a descriptive macro.

To run an Alt-*letter* macro you have created, you press the Alt-*letter* combination. If you have created an Alt-C macro to center a line of text, for example, you invoke the macro by holding down the Alt key while pressing the letter C.

To run a descriptive macro you have created, you press Macro (Alt-F10), type the name of the macro (one to eight characters), and then press Enter.

Notice that the command to *run* a descriptive macro—Macro (Alt-F10)—is different from the one you use to *create* a macro—Macro Define (Ctrl-F10). If you press Macro Define (Ctrl-F10) by mistake, you can press Cancel (F1).

Permanent Macros

You can create two kinds of permanent macros: Alt-*letter* macros and descriptive macros. The types of permanent macros differ in the way you name and run them.

Creating Permanent Macros

Suppose that you want to create a macro that inserts your return address; you want to position each line of the address flush with the right margin.

Press Ctrl F10, the Macro Define key.

```
Define macro: ad
```

```
Description: Return address, flush right
```

Type the name of the macro. For an Alt-*letter* macro, press Alt and a letter from A to Z. For a descriptive macro, type one to eight characters (letters or numbers) and press Enter.

For the return address macro, type **ad** and press Enter.

Type a short description (up to 39 characters) of what the macro does, and then press Enter.

For the example, type **Return address, flush right** and press Enter.

Type the keystrokes you want to record for this macro. Type them in the exact order you want them played back when you run the macro.

For the return address macro, press Alt F6, the Flush Right key.

Type **1010 Rose Avenue** (or the first line of your actual address) and press Enter.

Press Alt F6, the Flush Right key.

Type **Gabe, CA 90505** (or your actual city, state, and ZIP code).

Press Enter to position the cursor one line below the return address.

Press Ctrl F10 to end macro recording.

```
                                        1010 Rose Avenue
                                        Gabe, CA 90505




Macro Def                               Doc 1 Pg 1 Ln 1.33" Pos 1"
```

Running Permanent Macros

When you run (play back) a permanent macro, the steps vary depending on whether you are running an Alt-*letter* macro or a descriptive macro.

Running Alt-Letter Macros

Press the Alt-*letter* combination you assigned to the macro.

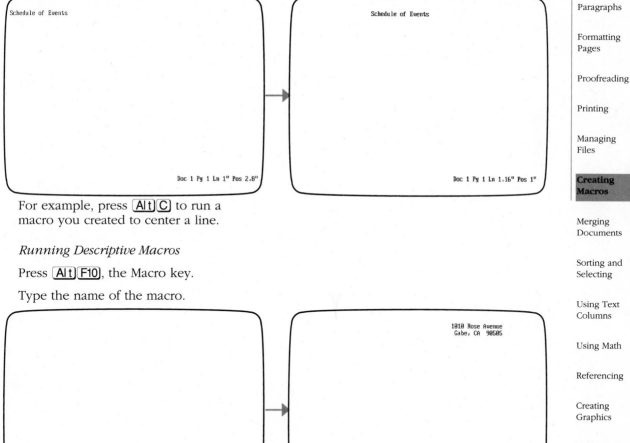

For example, press Alt C to run a macro you created to center a line.

Running Descriptive Macros

Press Alt F10, the Macro key.

Type the name of the macro.

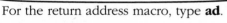

For the return address macro, type **ad**.

Press ↵Enter.

Temporary Macros

A temporary macro works only until you create another one. You can have only one temporary macro at a time because each temporary macro you create replaces the previous one. A temporary macro can be useful, for instance, when you have a long or complicated name or title you must type repeatedly in a particular document.

A temporary macro is preserved from one session to another. If you create a temporary macro that types your name, for example, and then you exit WordPerfect before creating another temporary macro, you still can use that temporary macro the next time you use WordPerfect.

Creating Temporary Macros

You create temporary macros just like you create descriptive macros, but instead of entering one to eight characters and pressing Enter, you just press Enter.

Introduction

Permanent
Macros

**Temporary
Macros**

Stopping Macros,
Replacing Macros

To create a temporary macro, you first press Macro Define (Ctrl-F10).
When the screen displays the prompt Define macro:, you don't
enter a name. Instead, you press Enter. WordPerfect automatically
assigns your temporary macro the name WP{WP}.WPM.

Notice that you are not prompted for a description when you create a
temporary macro. The screen displays the blinking message Macro
Def. You then type the keystrokes you want to record in the
temporary macro. To stop recording keystrokes, you press Macro
Define (Ctrl-F10) again.

Running Temporary Macros

Running your temporary macro is simple. You press Macro (Alt-F10),
and then press Enter.

If you run your temporary macro and it doesn't do what you expected,
try creating another temporary macro. The new temporary macro will
replace the preceding one.

Temporary Macros

A temporary macro works only until you create another one. You can have only one temporary macro at a time because each temporary macro you create replaces the previous one.

Creating Temporary Macros

Suppose that you want to create a temporary macro that types the title of an article— *"Selma Stanislavsky and Modern Russian Theater."*—that appears a number of times in your document.

Press Ctrl F10, the Macro Define key.

Type the keystrokes you want to record in the temporary macro.

```
"Selma Stanislavsky and Modern Russian Theater."




Macro Def                          Doc 1 Pg 1 Ln 1" Pos 5.8"
```

```
Define macro:
```

Press ↵Enter.

For the title example, type **"Selma Stanislavsky and Modern Russian Theater."**

Press Ctrl F10 again to stop recording keystrokes for the temporary macro.

Running Temporary Macros

When you want to run your temporary macro—for instance, the macro that inserts the article title, you first position your cursor where you want the macro to begin.

Press $\boxed{\text{Alt}}\,\boxed{\text{F10}}$, the Macro key.

```
    Three interesting articles to read are "Elizabeth Deter's
Theory of Creative Writing," "Mary Anne Ericson's Approach to
Spiritual Conseling," and




Macro:
```

Press $\boxed{\text{↵Enter}}$.

```
    Three interesting articles to read are "Elizabeth Deter's
Theory of Creative Writing," "Mary Anne Ericson's Approach to
Spiritual Conseling," and "Selma Stanislavsky and Modern Russian
Theater,"




                                          Doc 1 Pg 1 Ln 1.5" Pos 1.9"
```

Stopping Macros, Replacing Macros

Stopping Macros

You use the Cancel key (F1) in many situations to "back out" of a process you started. You can use this key also to back out of a definition you are creating for a macro or to stop a macro in progress.

Backing Out of a Macro Definition

Before you name a macro, you can back out of a macro definition. If you start to create a macro using Macro Define (Ctrl-F10) and have not yet named it, pressing Cancel (F1) cancels the macro definition and returns you to your document.

After you name a macro, you cannot cancel it, but you can end macro definition by pressing Macro Define (Ctrl-F10). Although the macro still is created with the name you assigned it, you then can delete, rename, replace, or edit the macro.

Stopping a Macro in Progress

You can stop a macro while it is running by pressing Cancel (F1). For example, if the macro is not doing what you expected, you can press Cancel (F1).

After you cancel a macro, press Reveal Codes (Alt-F3, or F11) to check your document for any unwanted codes. An incomplete macro can create codes in your document that you don't want.

Replacing Macros

Imperfect macros, fortunately, are replaced easily. You may want to replace a macro you created for any of several reasons:

- You get an error message when you run the macro.
- The macro finishes but does not do what you want.
- You change your mind about exactly what you want the macro to do.

You can change what a permanent macro does in either of two ways:

- Replace the macro.
- Edit the macro.

Often the simpler procedure is to replace a short macro rather than to edit it. Editing macros is a subject beyond the scope of this book.

To replace a macro with another one of the same name, you first press Macro Define (Ctrl-F10). Then you enter the same name as the previous version of the macro. The program asks whether you want to Replace (1) or Edit (2) the named macro. You choose Replace (1).

Then you enter a description of the macro, type the keystrokes you want the macro to record, and press Macro Define (Ctrl-F10) to end the macro definition. Notice that the procedure is exactly like creating a macro for the first time, but you are prompted to replace or edit the macro.

Stopping Macros, Replacing Macros

Stopping Macros

Press F1 to back out of a definition you are creating for a macro
or to stop a macro in progress.

Backing Out of a Macro Definition

Before you name a macro, back out of
a macro definition by pressing F1.

After you name a macro, you cannot
cancel it. To end macro definition, press
Ctrl F10, the Macro Define key.

Stopping a Macro in Progress

To stop a macro while it is running,
press F1.

Replacing Macros

The easiest way to revise a simple macro that is unsuccessful or
that doesn't do what you want it to do is to replace it. Suppose,
for example, that you want to replace your AD macro with a
macro that inserts both your return address and the current date.

Press Ctrl F10, the Macro Define key.

Type the same name as the previous version of the macro and
press ↵Enter.

For example, type **ad** and press ↵Enter.

Define macro: ad

AD.WPM is Already Defined. 1 Replace; 2 Edit: 0

Press 1 to select Replace.

Introduction

Permanent
Macros

Temporary
Macros

**Stopping Macros,
Replacing Macros**

Description: <u>Return address and date, flush right</u>

Type a description of the macro and press ⏎Enter. For example, type **Return address and date, flush right** and press ⏎Enter.

Type the keystrokes you want the macro to record. For the example, press Alt F6, the Flush Right key.

Type **1010 Rose Avenue** (or the first line of your actual address) and press ⏎Enter.

Press Alt F6.

Type **Gabe, CA 90505** (or your actual city, state, and ZIP code) and press ⏎Enter.

Press Alt F6.

Press ⇧Shift F5, the Date/Outline key.

Press 3 to select Date Format.

Regardless of the date format already shown, type **3 1, 4** and press ⏎Enter.

Press 1 to select Date Text.

Press ⏎Enter twice to include two blank lines after your return address.

```
                                    1010 Rose Avenue
                                    Gabe, CA 90505
                                    August 19, 1988








 Macro Def                    Doc 1 Pg 1 Ln 1.66" Pos 1"
```

Press Ctrl F10 to end macro recording.

10 *Merging Documents*

The Merge feature, frequently referred to as mail merge, is one of WordPerfect's most versatile tools for increasing office productivity. You use Merge anytime you need to insert variable data into a fixed format. For example, you can use Merge to create personalized form letters from an address list, produce phone lists, print labels, piece together complicated reports, or fill in forms.

Key Terms

Merge To assemble a document by inserting variable data into a fixed format.

Primary file A skeleton document into which pieces of data are merged.

Secondary merge file A file that contains the data (or variable information) that is merged into the primary file. Information in the secondary file is organized like information on filing cards.

Fields The units of information that make up a record. Each field should contain the same type of information: for example, a person's name; a street address; a city, state, and ZIP code.

Record A collection of fields with related information in a file: a line of data, a paragraph, or a name and address in a secondary merge file.

Tasks Covered in This Chapter

In this chapter, you learn to perform the following tasks:

- Create primary and secondary merge files
- Merge from the keyboard
- Merge two files to the screen or to the printer

Understanding the Basics

A Merge operation requires a primary file, often in combination with a secondary merge file. A secondary merge file contains records, which in turn are comprised of fields.

A primary file is a skeleton document into which pieces of data are merged. The primary file contains two items: fixed text and merge codes. You plant merge codes where you want to insert variable items into fixed text. When a merge is completed, the codes are replaced with entries from the keyboard or from a secondary merge file. The document is completed with a minimum of effort.

The most typical and timesaving merge requires a secondary merge file that contains related variable data, such as an address list. The address list includes names, streets, cities, states, and ZIP codes. The program inserts these items into the primary file by matching the codes in the primary and secondary merge files.

Information in the secondary merge file is organized like information on filing cards. The information on one filing card (or one secondary merge file entry) is known as a *record*. Each record is divided into *fields*. Using the address list as an example, all the information related to one person is a record; the separate items, such as name, street, and ZIP code, are fields.

Understanding Merge Codes

Fields, records, and other items are controlled by merge codes. You must place these codes in the right places and in the right order for a merge to be successful. The following table lists all the merge codes and briefly explains the purpose of each one. The use of these codes is illustrated throughout the chapter.

Code	Function
^C	Halts a merge temporarily to display a message or to allow an entry from the keyboard
^D	Inserts the current date into the merge document
^E	Marks the end of a secondary merge file record
^F*n*^	Indicates a field name or number in a primary file
^G	Activates a macro
^N	Looks for the next record in order to continue the merge in progress (for a primary file)
	References a field by name (for a secondary merge file)
^O	Displays a menu, prompt, message, or instruction
^P	Activates a primary file
^Q	Quits (terminates) a merge
^R	Marks the end of a field in a secondary merge file
^S	Activates a secondary merge file
^T	Sends the merged text to the printer
^U	Updates (rewrites or views) the screen displaying the merge in progress
^V	Transfers merge codes to a document created by a merge

Understanding the Basics

A Merge operation requires a primary file, often in combination with a secondary merge file. A secondary merge file contains records, which in turn are comprised of fields.

Secondary Merge File

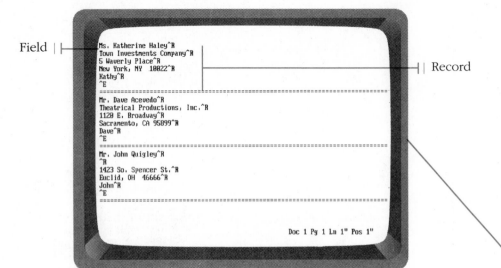

Field

```
Ms. Katherine Haley^R
Town Investments Company^R
5 Waverly Place^R
New York, NY  10022^R
Kathy^R
^E
===================================================
Mr. Dave Acevedo^R
Theatrical Productions, Inc,^R
1128 E, Broadway^R
Sacramento, CA 95899^R
Dave^R
^E
===================================================
Mr, John Quigley^R
^R
1423 So, Spencer St,^R
Euclid, OH  46666^R
John^R
^E
===================================================
```

Record

Doc 1 Pg 1 Ln 1" Pos 1"

Primary File

```
^D

^F1^
^F2?^
^F3^
^F4^

Dear ^F5^:

Simpson Travel and Tours wants to help with all of your travel
plans, Whether you are going across the state, across the country,
or around the world, give me a call, I'll guarantee you the best
fares and the most convenient connections,

Enclosed is a brochure that describes some of this season's best
travel bargains, Call me for additional details on prices and
schedules,

Sincerely,

Sally Oceans
Travel Agent
```

C:\WP50\CHAP18   Doc 1 Pg 1 Ln 4.66" Pos 1"

June 16, 1989

Ms. Katherine Haley
Town Investments Company
5 Waverly Place
New York, NY 10022

Dear Kathy:

Simpson Travel and Tours wants to help with all of your travel
plans. Whether you are going across the state, across the country,
or around the world, give me a call. I'll guarantee you the best
fares and the most convenient connections.

Enclosed is a brochure that describes some of this season's best
travel bargains. Call me for additional details on prices and
schedules.

Sincerely,

Sally Oceans
Travel Agent

These letters resulted
from merging the
secondary merge file
and the primary file
on the preceding
page.

June 16, 1989

Mr. Dave Acevedo
Theatrical Productions, Inc.
1120 E. Broadway
Sacramento, CA 95899

Dear Dave:

Simpson Travel and Tours wants to help with all of your travel
plans. Whether you are going across the state, across the country,
or around the world, give me a call. I'll guarantee you the best
fares and the most convenient connections.

Enclosed is a brochure that describes some of this season's best
travel bargains. Call me for additional details on prices and
schedules.

Sincerely,

Sally Oceans
Travel Agent

June 16, 1989

Mr. John T. Quigley
1423 So. Spencer St.
Euclid, OH 46666

Dear John:

Simpson Travel and Tours wants to help with all of your travel
plans. Whether you are going across the state, across the country,
or around the world, give me a call. I'll guarantee you the best
fares and the most convenient connections.

Enclosed is a brochure that describes some of this season's best
travel bargains. Call me for additional details on prices and
schedules.

Sincerely,

Sally Oceans
Travel Agent

Merging from the Keyboard

The simplest form of merge is the keyboard merge. This kind of merge uses a special merge code that makes merge-printing pause so that you can enter information from the keyboard. Keyboard merges are useful for filling in preprinted forms, addressing memos, and entering frequently updated information in a form letter.

Preparing the Primary File for a Keyboard Merge

For a keyboard merge, you need only a primary file with text and a few merge codes. Suppose, for example, that you regularly send a memo announcing the time, date, and subject of a monthly meeting. Your primary file can contain the regular text of a letter and the merge codes that hold the places for the variable information.

Two kinds of merge codes are useful in the primary file for the memo:

- Use ^C to indicate where an entry from the keyboard is placed.
- Use ^D to indicate where the current date is displayed.

To prepare the primary file for the keyboard merge, you begin typing the memo. At the place where you want the current date entered, you enter the date merge code. You first press Merge Codes (Shift-F9), and then you press D. On-screen, WordPerfect enters ^D. You must use the Merge Code menu to enter merge codes. You cannot use the caret key (^) on the keyboard because WordPerfect does not recognize the caret as part of a merge code.

At the places where you want the merge to pause and wait for input from the keyboard, you enter ^C merge codes. To enter a ^C code, you press Merge Codes (Shift-F9), and then you press C. On-screen, WordPerfect enters ^C.

Running a Keyboard Merge

To merge-print the memo, you first press Merge/Sort (Ctrl-F9). Then you select Merge (1). You type the name of the primary file and press Enter. Because you are not using a secondary merge file for this merge, you do not enter a name; you simply press Enter again.

The primary file appears on-screen. When the merging process reaches the ^D code, WordPerfect replaces the code with the current date automatically. If you have a battery-backed clock/calendar or you have entered the correct date at the beginning of each session, the display shows the correct date; otherwise, an incorrect date may appear.

The cursor rests at the location of the first ^C code, which is no longer displayed. You enter the first segment of variable text. When you finish entering the text, you press Merge R (F9) to continue the merge. (Note: Do not press Enter unless you want to enter a hard return.) The cursor moves to the next ^C code so that you can type the text for that code.

When a merge is in progress, WordPerfect displays the message * Merging * on the status line. When you enter the last item and press Merge R (F9) another time, the message disappears. The merge is now complete. You then can save and print the document.

Merging from the Keyboard

A keyboard merge uses a special merge code that makes merge-printing pause so that you can enter information from the keyboard.

For a keyboard merge, you need only a primary file with text and a few merge codes. Suppose, for example, that you regularly send a memo announcing the time, date, and subject of a monthly meeting.

^D indicates where the current date is displayed.

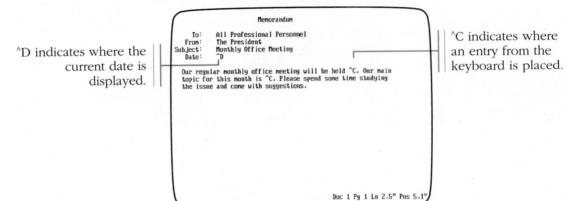

^C indicates where an entry from the keyboard is placed.

Preparing the Primary File for a Keyboard Merge

Your primary file contains the regular text of the memo and the merge codes that hold the places for the variable information.

Begin typing the memo.

To enter the date merge code (^D), position the cursor at the spot where you want the current date entered, press ⬥Shift F9, and then press D.

To enter the merge codes that pause for keyboard input (^C), position the cursor at each spot where you want the merge to pause, press ⬥Shift F9, and then press C.

Finish typing the memo and save it with the name MEMO.PMF.

Running a Keyboard Merge

When you run the keyboard merge, WordPerfect pauses and waits for keyboard input whenever the program reaches a ^C code. The ^D code is replaced with the current date automatically.

1 Merge; 2 Sort; 3 Sort Order: 0

Press **Ctrl F9**, the Merge/Sort key.

Press **1** to select Merge.

Primary file: memo.pmf

Type the name of the primary file and press **Enter**. For the example, type **memo.pmf** and press **Enter**.

Because you are not using a secondary file for this merge, press **Enter** again.

```
                    Memorandum
     To:      All Professional Personnel
     From:    The President
     Subject: Monthly Office Meeting
     Date:    August 19, 1988

     Our regular monthly office meeting will be held .  Our main
     topic for this month is ^C. Please spend some time studying
     the issue and come with suggestions.


 * Merging *                    Doc 1 Pg 1 Ln 2.16" Pos 6.3"
```

```
                    Memorandum
     To:      All Professional Personnel
     From:    The President
     Subject: Monthly Office Meeting
     Date:    August 18, 1988

     Our regular monthly office meeting will be held 3:00 P.M.,
     Thursday, August 25.  Our main topic for this month is the
     company's sagging profit.  Please spend some time studying the
     issue and come with suggestions.
```

Enter the first segment of variable text. For the example, type **3:00 P.M., Thursday, August 25**

Press **F9** to continue the merge.

The cursor goes to the position of the next ^C code so that you can type the text for this code.

Enter the next segment of variable text. For the example, type **the company's sagging profit**

Press **F9**.

Save and print the memo.

293

Merging Text Files

A text file merge combines two existing files—a primary and a secondary merge file. Before you can execute such a merge, you must create these files. Create the secondary merge file first so that you know the field layout before you build the primary file.

Creating a Secondary Merge File

A secondary merge file consists of records, which have a number of fields. The structure must be uniform; otherwise, the merge won't work properly. Every data record must have the same number of fields, and the fields must be in the same order in all records. For example, if the first name is in field 1, but one record has the last name in field 1, WordPerfect prints a last name where the first name should be.

When you create a secondary merge file, you include certain codes to indicate where each record ends and where each field ends. You use ^R to indicate the end of a field and to enter a hard return code. To enter ^R, you press Merge R (F9). You use ^E to indicate the end of a record and to enter a hard page code. To enter ^E, you press Merge Codes (Shift-F9) and press E.

If your records contain any blank fields, such as a field that doesn't have an entry for the company name, you must acknowledge the presence of those fields. You do this by pressing Merge R (F9) to insert a ^R code in the blank field.

When you finish entering data into your secondary merge file, you save the file with a name that indicates the file's purpose. For example, you might call your address file ADDRESS.SMF; the SMF extension can remind you that the file is a secondary merge file.

Creating a Primary File

A primary file contains fixed text and certain merge codes. The codes tell WordPerfect to insert certain items from the secondary merge file where the codes are implanted.

The most commonly used code is the field number code, $^\wedge$F$n^\wedge$. The n indicates the field number of each record in the secondary merge file. For example, when you specify $^\wedge$F3$^\wedge$, you instruct WordPerfect to enter at that particular location the information found in field number 3. To enter $^\wedge$F$n^\wedge$, you press Merge Codes (Shift-F9), press F, enter a field number, and press Enter.

If your records contain any fields that are blank and are followed by hard returns, the empty fields will be printed as blank lines. To prevent the blank lines from appearing, you add a question mark after the field number. For example, you might change the code for the $^\wedge$F2$^\wedge$ field to $^\wedge$F2?$^\wedge$ in your primary file.

Make sure that you enter the field numbers correctly. Each field number must match the appropriate field in the secondary merge file; otherwise, an incorrect item will be merged.

When you finish creating the primary file, save the file with a name that indicates the file's purpose. For example, you might call the file TRAVEL.PMF; the PMF serves as a useful reminder that this is a primary file.

Merging Text Files

A text file merge combines two existing files—a primary and a secondary merge file.

Creating a Secondary Merge File

A secondary merge file consists of records (ending with ^E), which have a number of fields (ending with ^R).

Use ^R to indicate the end of a field and to enter a hard return code.

```
Ms. Katherine Haley^R
Town Investments Company^R
5 Waverly Place^R
New York, NY  10022^R
Kathy^R
^E
===================================================================
Mr. Dave Acevedo^R
Theatrical Productions, Inc.^R
1120 E. Broadway^R
Sacramento, CA 95899^R
Dave^R
^E
===================================================================
Mr. John Quigley^R
^R
1423 So. Spencer St.^R
Euclid, OH  46666^R
John^R
^E
===================================================================
                              Doc 1 Pg 3 Ln 1.83" Pos 1"
```

Use ^E to indicate the end of a record and to enter a hard page code.

When a field is blank, you must acknowledge the blank field's presence. For instance, Mr. Quigley's record contains no company name. You must insert a ^R code in the blank field.

296

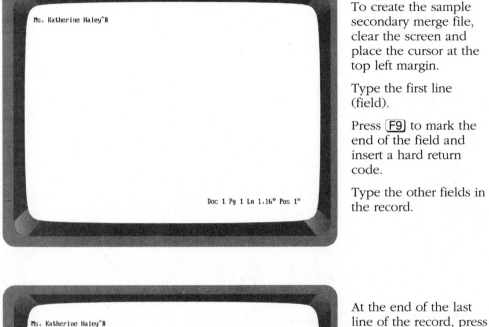

```
Ms. Katherine Haley^R
```
Doc 1 Pg 1 Ln 1.16" Pos 1"

```
Ms. Katherine Haley^R
Town Investments Company^R
5 Waverly Place^R
New York, NY 10022^R
Kathy^R
^E
============================================================================
```
Doc 1 Pg 2 Ln 1" Pos 1"

To create the sample secondary merge file, clear the screen and place the cursor at the top left margin.

Type the first line (field).

Press **F9** to mark the end of the field and insert a hard return code.

Type the other fields in the record.

At the end of the last line of the record, press **⇧Shift** **F9**.

Press **E** to mark the end of the record and insert a hard page code.

Enter the next record.

When you finish entering data, save the file under a name that indicates its purpose—for example, ADDRESS.SMF.

297

Merging Text Files

Creating a Primary File

A primary file contains fixed text and merge codes.

Use ^F*n*^ codes to tell WordPerfect to insert certain items from the secondary merge file where the codes are entered.

Use ^F*n*?^ codes to prevent blank lines from appearing where empty fields exist in the secondary merge file.

```
^D

^F1^
^F2?^
^F3^
^F4^

Dear ^F5^:

Simpson Travel and Tours wants to help with all of your travel
plans. Whether you are going across the state, across the country,
or around the world, give me a call. I'll guarantee you the best
fares and the most convenient connections.

Enclosed is a brochure that describes some of this season's best
travel bargains. Call me for additional details on prices and
schedules.

Sincerely,

Sally Oceans
Travel Agent

C:\WP50\CHAP10                              Doc 1 Pg 1 Ln 4.5" Pos 2.2"
```

To create the sample primary file, begin typing the sample letter shown in the figure.

At the line where you want the addressee's name entered, press [⇧Shift][F9].

```
^D


















^C: ^D: ^E: ^F: ^G: ^N: ^O: ^P: ^Q: ^S: ^T: ^U: ^V:
```

Press [F].

```
^D


















Field:
```

Press the number of the current field ([1], in the example), and then press [↵Enter].

WordPerfect inserts a ^F1^ code in your document at the cursor.

To enter the ^F2?^ code, position the cursor where you want to enter the code, press [⇧Shift][F9], press [F], press [2], press [?], and then press [↵Enter].

To enter each of the ^F3^, ^F4^, and ^F5^ codes, position the cursor where you want to enter the code, press [⇧Shift][F9], press [F], press the appropriate number, and then press [↵Enter].

When you finish typing the letter, save the file under a name that indicates its purpose—for example, TRAVEL.PMF.

Merging Text Files

Merging the Primary and Secondary Merge Files

After you create the primary and secondary merge files, you are ready to start the merge. If you have a small secondary merge file, you can merge the files to the screen. If you have a large secondary merge file, you can merge directly to the printer.

Merging to the Screen

If you have a small secondary merge file, you can merge the files to the screen and check each one before you print. Merging to the screen is a good way to check for errors in the merge.

To merge the text files to the screen, you first press Merge/Sort (Ctrl-F9) to display the Merge/Sort menu. From this menu, you select Merge (1). When WordPerfect prompts you for the name of your primary file, you type the name and press Enter. When WordPerfect prompts you for the name of your secondary merge file, you type the name and press Enter.

When the merge is completed, the screen displays the last completed letter in the merge operation. If you move the cursor to the beginning of the document, you find the first completed letter. Notice that all the necessary items are filled in, and each letter is separated from the others with a hard page code. The letters are ready to print; each letter will print on a separate page.

Merging Directly to the Printer

When you are creating a large number of form letters, all the merged letters may not fit in memory. WordPerfect therefore won't be able to complete the merge and display the letters on-screen. To solve this problem—or simply to save time by eliminating the step of displaying the letters on-screen—you can send the results of a merge operation directly to the printer.

Before you can merge to the printer, you need to enter the merge codes ^T^N^P^P at the end of the primary file. To enter each merge code, you position the cursor at the spot where you want the code entered, press Merge Codes (Shift-F9), and then press the letter of the code.

The ^T code instructs WordPerfect to send any text merged up to this point to the printer. The ^N code retrieves the next record in the secondary merge file. The ^P code is for the primary file. If you want to use another primary file, you enter its name between the two ^P codes, as in ^Pfile2.pf^P. If the same primary file is to be used again and again, you enter nothing between the two codes.

After you add the ending merge codes, you save the letter, turn on your printer, and merge the text files with the same procedure you used to merge to the screen. WordPerfect then prints your letters.

If your computer freezes while the screen displays the * Merging * message, don't panic—you probably forgot to turn on your printer. If you turn on the printer, the document starts to print, and the screen returns to normal.

Merging to the printer is an excellent way to automate your office. If you have a fast printer, you can print many personalized letters with minimum effort.

Merging Text Files

Merging the Primary and Secondary Merge Files

After you create the primary and secondary merge files, you are
ready to start the merge. You can merge the files to the screen (if
you have a small secondary merge file) or directly to the printer (if
you have a large secondary merge file).

Merging to the Screen

Press Ctrl F9, the Merge/Sort key.

```
1 Merge: 2 Sort: 3 Sort Order: 0
```

Press 1 to select Merge.

```
Primary file: travel.pmf
```

Type the name of the primary
file (**travel.pmf**, for example)
and press ↵Enter.

```
Secondary file: address.smf
```

Type the name of the secondary
merge file (**address.smf**, for
example) and press ↵Enter.

```
June 16, 1989

Mr. John Quigley
1423 So. Spencer St.
Euclid, OH 46666

Dear John:

Simpson Travel and Tours wants to help with all of your travel
plans. Whether you are going across the state, across the country,
or around the world, give me a call. I'll guarantee you the best
fares and the most convenient connections.

Enclosed is a brochure that describes some of this season's best
travel bargains. Call me for additional details on prices and
schedules.

Sincerely,

Sally Oceans
Travel Agent


C:\WP50\CHAP10                    Doc 1 Pg 1 Ln 2" Pos 1.9"
```

The merge is now complete. The screen
displays the last completed letter. If you
move the cursor to the beginning of the
document, you find the first completed
letter.

All the necessary items are filled in, and
each letter is separated from the others
with a hard page code. The letters are
ready to print; each letter will print on a
separate page.

Merging Directly to the Printer

Before you merge to the printer, plant the merge codes ^T^N^P^P at the end of the primary file. To enter each merge code, position the cursor at the spot where you want the code entered, press ⇧Shift F9, and then press the letter of the code.

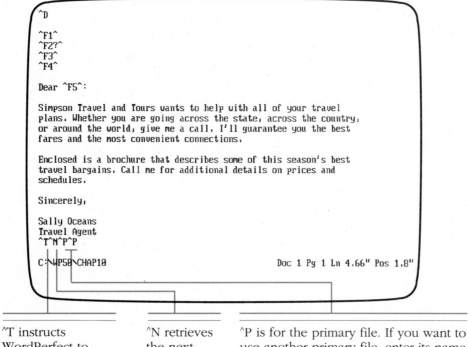

^T instructs WordPerfect to send to the printer any text merged up to this point.

^N retrieves the next record in the secondary merge file.

^P is for the primary file. If you want to use another primary file, enter its name between the two ^P codes, as in ^Pfile2.pmf^P. If the same primary file is to be used again and again, enter nothing between the two codes.

After you add the ending merge codes, save the letter, turn on your printer, and merge the text files with the same procedure you used to merge to the screen.

WordPerfect prints your letters.

11 *Sorting and Selecting*

Although WordPerfect's Sort feature cannot compete with specialized database management programs in all areas, it has enough power and versatility to handle many record-keeping tasks. When Sort is combined with other WordPerfect features—such as Search, Replace, Merge, Math, and Macros—it becomes a useful management tool.

Examples of two simple applications of the Sort command are sorting lines to create alphabetical phone lists or rosters and sorting mailing lists by ZIP code to conform with postal service rules for large mailings. WordPerfect can work with three kinds of records: a line, a paragraph, or a secondary merge file.

Key Terms

Keys   The characters or numbers in a specific file location that
                  WordPerfect uses to sort and select.

Location   The elements that describe the location of a key
identifiers   word, such as the record, field, line, and word.

Record   A collection of related information in a file: a line of
                  data, a paragraph, or a name and address in a
                  secondary merge file.

Fields   The components that make up a record. Each field
                  should contain the same type of information: for
                  example, a person's first name, the name of a city, or a
                  ZIP code.

Input file   The file you intend to sort.

Output file   The sorted (or selected) file, which you can display on-
                  screen or save to disk.

Tasks Covered in This Chapter

In this chapter, you learn to perform the following tasks:

- Use the options on the Sort screen
- Sort by line, paragraph, and secondary merge file
- Select particular data

Understanding the Sort Screen

You can sort files displayed on-screen or files stored on disk, and you can return the sorted results to the screen or to a new file on disk. Sort works with three kinds of data: line, paragraph, or a secondary merge file. You must use a different type of sort for each kind of database. Use line sort when records are lines (a name or an item, for example); use paragraph sort when records are paragraphs (as in a standard legal clause or a glossary, perhaps); use merge sort when records are in a secondary merge file (a list of names and addresses, for instance).

Before you perform a sort, you must be sure that your data file is set up properly. A line record must end with a hard or soft return, and records should be formatted with one tab per field. A paragraph record must end with two hard returns.

Displaying the Sort Screen

To display the Sort screen, you first press Merge/Sort (Ctrl-F9). When WordPerfect displays the Merge/Sort menu, you select Sort (2). At the prompt for input file, you press Enter if you want to sort the file already displayed on-screen, or you type the input file name if you want to sort a file stored on disk. At the prompt for the output file, you press Enter if you want the sorted results to replace the screen display, or you type the output file name if you want the sorted results saved to disk in a new file. The Sort screen is then displayed.

The Sort screen is divided into five parts:

- The heading displays the current Sort type. The default is Sort by Line.
- The second part of the screen displays nine keys, each of which has three fields where you can enter criteria for the sort.
- The third part is the Select field, where you enter the formulas to select (extract) certain records from your database.
- The fourth part indicates the Action, Order, and Type (which coincides with the heading) of the sort.
- The last part is the Sort and Select menu.

The Sort and Select menu offers seven options:

Option	*Action*
Perform Action (1)	Instructs WordPerfect to begin sorting or selecting.
View (2)	Moves the cursor from the Sort screen into the document to be sorted. Use this option to change the tab settings on the menu to those in the document. You can move the cursor to view the data, but you cannot edit it. Press Exit (F7) to return to the Sort screen.
Keys (3)	Moves the cursor into the key definition area so that you can define and change the keys (criteria) for the Sort operation. When you select this option, the bottom of the screen displays the Keys menu from which you can select an alphanumeric or a numeric sort.
Select (4)	Moves the cursor into the Select area so that you can enter a description (a formula) of the information you want to select. This formula directs WordPerfect to select certain records.
Action (5)	Is activated only when you choose Select (4). You can choose Select and Sort (1) to both select and sort the data, or you can choose Select Only (2) to just select the data.
Order (6)	Offers you a choice of Ascending (A-Z) or Descending (Z-A) order.
Type (7)	Offers you a choice of sorting by line, paragraph, or secondary merge file.

Understanding the Sort Screen

Displaying the Sort Screen

If you want to sort a file while it's displayed on-screen, retrieve the file to the screen.

Press Ctrl F9, the Merge/Sort key.

```
Peggy O'Brien        890 Geyser Peak      Bodega Bay, CA    95301
John Bartleet        213 Oak Pass         Bodega Bay, CA    95301
Jim Daniels          1910 Vine Trail      Santa Rosa, CA    95401
Zigler Xavier        456 Redwood Way      Petaluma, CA      95408
Jude Matheson        515 Ross St.         Petaluma, CA      95408
Loretta Murphy       468 Mountain Ln.     Santa Rosa, CA    95401




1 Merge; 2 Sort; 3 Sort Order: 0
```

Press 2 to choose Sort.

```
Peggy O'Brien        890 Geyser Peak      Bodega Bay, CA    95301
John Bartleet        213 Oak Pass         Bodega Bay, CA    95301
Jim Daniels          1910 Vine Trail      Santa Rosa, CA    95401
Zigler Xavier        456 Redwood Way      Petaluma, CA      95408
Jude Matheson        515 Ross St.         Petaluma, CA      95408
Loretta Murphy       468 Mountain Ln.     Santa Rosa, CA    95401



Input file to sort: (Screen)
```

Press ↵Enter if you want to sort the file already displayed on-screen.

Or

Type the input file name if you want to sort a file stored on disk.

Press ↵Enter if you want the sorted results to replace the screen display.

Or

Type the output file name if you want the sorted results saved to disk in a new file.

```
Peggy O'Brien        890 Geyser Peak      Bodega Bay, CA    95301
John Bartleet        213 Oak Pass         Bodega Bay, CA    95301
Jim Daniels          1910 Vine Trail      Santa Rosa, CA    95401
Zigler Xavier        456 Redwood Way      Petaluma, CA      95408
Jude Matheson        515 Ross St.         Petaluma, CA      95408
Loretta Murphy       468 Mountain Ln.     Santa Rosa, CA    95401




Output file for sort: (Screen)
```

The Sort screen is displayed.

The heading displays the current Sort type. The default is Sort by Line.

Each of nine keys has three fields where you can enter the criteria for the sort.

```
   Peggy O'Brien        890 Geyser Peak    Bodega Bay, CA    95301
   John Bartleet        213 Oak Pass       Bodega Bay, CA    95301
   Jim Daniels          1910 Vine Trail    Santa Rosa, CA    95401
   Zigler Xavier        456 Redwood Way    Petaluma, CA      95408
   Jude Matheson        515 Ross St.       Petaluma, CA      95408
   Loretta Murphy       468 Mountain Ln.   Santa Rosa, CA    95401



                                            Doc 2 Pg 1 Ln 1" Pos 1"
   {   ▲   ▲   ▲   ▲   ▲   ▲   ▲   ▲   ▲   ▲   }   ▲   ▲
   ----------------------------- Sort by Line -----------------------------

   Key Typ Field Word    Key Typ Field Word    Key Typ Field Word
    1   a    1    1        2                     3
    4                      5                     6
    7                      8                     9
   Select

   Action                Order                Type
   Sort                  Ascending            Line sort

   1 Perform Action; 2 View; 3 Keys; 4 Select; 5 Action; 6 Order; 7 Type: 0
```

The Select field is where you enter the formulas to select (extract) certain records from your database.

The Sort and Select menu and its seven options allow you to specify the type of sort, the order, and the sort criteria. After you enter this information, you start the sort from this menu.

This part of the screen indicates the Action, Order, and Type (which coincides with the heading) of the sort.

Sorting Lines and Paragraphs

WordPerfect can sort the lines and paragraphs in any standard text file. This feature is useful when you want to sort office phone lists, personnel rosters, columns on charts, dated paragraphs, and so on.

Displaying the Sort Screen

To sort lines or paragraphs, you first retrieve the file to the screen, if you want, and then display the Sort screen. To display the Sort screen, you press Merge/Sort (Ctrl-F9), choose Sort (2), and then enter the input and output file names.

Choosing the Sort Type

You can choose to sort by lines or paragraphs. Sort lines when you plan to sort rosters and lists. Use paragraph sort when sorting notes or reports.

Sorting Lines

Notice the tab ruler above the legend `Sort by Line`. The tab settings shown on this tab ruler must be set one tab per field with no unused tabs between fields. If the tabs in the tab ruler do not reflect your one-tab-per-field setting, you select View (2). The cursor moves into your document. You move the cursor to the middle of a line of data. The tab ruler changes to reflect your tab settings. Press Exit (F7) to return to the Sort screen.

Next, you choose Type (7) and select Line (2). The title on the Sort screen displays `Sort by Line`, and the key location headings are `Field` and `Word`. You identify the location of key words by their Field and Word numbers in each line. Fields are separated by tabs, and words are separated by spaces.

Sorting Paragraphs

If you want to sort by paragraph, you select Paragraph (3). The title on the Sort screen displays `Sort by Paragraph`, and the key location headings are `Field`, `Line`, and `Word`. Identify the location of key words by their Field, Line, and Word in each paragraph. Paragraphs are separated by two or more hard returns.

Selecting the Sort Order

Select Order (6) to display the Order menu. From this menu, you choose either Ascending (1) for A-to-Z sort order or Descending (2) for Z-to-A sort order.

Specifying the Key Locations

Next, you choose Keys (3) to display the Keys menu. The cursor moves under the a in the `Typ` column so that you can enter the location of each sort key. You type **a** to specify an alphanumeric sort for Key1, or you type **n** to specify a numeric sort for Key1.

You enter the location of Key1. The default values in Key1 are preset at a 1 1. These values mean that the Sort type is alphanumeric and that the first word in the first field is to be used as the basis for sorting. You can enter negative values in each key. For example, if you want to use the third word from the end, enter –3 under the `Word` category.

If sorting by Key1 results in ties (equal values, such as the same names or numbers), you can sort on more than one field by using Key2, Key3, and so on. You press the right-arrow key to move to Key2, and then enter the values for this key.

Performing the Sort

After you enter information for the keys, you press Exit (F7). Then you choose Perform Action (1) to sort the file. If you specified that the output goes to the screen, the results appear on-screen. If you specified that the output goes to the file, the results are sent to the file.

Sorting Lines and Paragraphs

WordPerfect can sort the lines in any standard text file, as long as the file is formatted correctly. A line record must end with a hard or soft return, and records must be formatted with one tab per field with no unused tabs between fields. A paragraph record must end with two hard returns.

Displaying the Sort Screen

To sort lines or paragraphs, first retrieve the file to the screen, if you want, and then display the Sort screen. Press [Ctrl][F9], press [2], and enter the input and output file names.

Choosing the Sort Type

Press [7] to select Type.

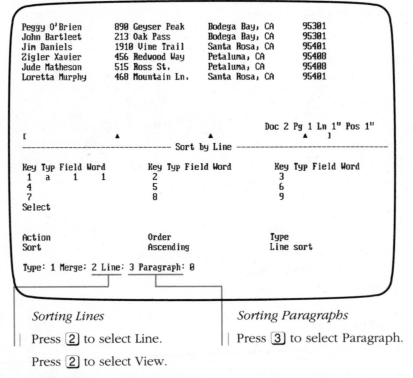

Sorting Lines

Press [2] to select Line.

Press [2] to select View.

Move the cursor to the middle of the line and press [F7] to change the tab settings on the Sort screen to those in the document.

Sorting Paragraphs

Press [3] to select Paragraph.

Selecting the Sort Order

Press 6 to choose Order.

```
Peggy O'Brien      898 Geyser Peak    Bodega Bay, CA    95301
John Bartleet      213 Oak Pass       Bodega Bay, CA    95301
Jim Daniels        1910 Vine Trail    Santa Rosa, CA    95401
Zigler Xavier      456 Redwood Way    Petaluma, CA      95408
Jude Matheson      515 Ross St.       Petaluma, CA      95408
Loretta Murphy     468 Mountain Ln.   Santa Rosa, CA    95401



                                          Doc 2 Pg 1 Ln 1" Pos 1"
[              ▲              ▲        ▲  ]
--------------------- Sort by Line ----------------------

Key Typ Field Word     Key Typ Field Word     Key Typ Field Word
 1  a   1    1          2                       3
 4                      5                       6
 7                      8                       9
Select

Action                 Order                  Type
Sort                   Ascending              Line sort

Order: 1 Ascending; 2 Descending: 0
```

Press 1 to choose
Ascending for A-to-Z
sort order.

Or

Press 2 to choose
Descending for Z-to-A
sort order.

Specifying the Key Locations

Press 3 to choose Keys.

```
Peggy O'Brien      898 Geyser Peak    Bodega Bay, CA    95301
John Bartleet      213 Oak Pass       Bodega Bay, CA    95301
Jim Daniels        1910 Vine Trail    Santa Rosa, CA    95401
Zigler Xavier      456 Redwood Way    Petaluma, CA      95408
Jude Matheson      515 Ross St.       Petaluma, CA      95408
Loretta Murphy     468 Mountain Ln.   Santa Rosa, CA    95401



                                          Doc 2 Pg 1 Ln 1" Pos 1"
[              ▲              ▲        ▲  ]
--------------------- Sort by Line ----------------------

Key Typ Field Word     Key Typ Field Word     Key Typ Field Word
 1  a   1    1          2                       3
 4                      5                       6
 7                      8                       9
Select

Action                 Order                  Type
Sort                   Ascending              Line sort

Type: a = Alphanumeric; n = Numeric; Use arrows; Press Exit when done
```

Type **a** to specify an
alphanumeric sort for Key1.

Or

Type **n** to specify a numeric sort
for Key1.

Enter the location of Key1.

If you want to sort on more than
one field, press the → key to
move to Key2 and enter the key
location. Move to and enter
information for other keys.

After entering the key locations,
press F7 to return to the main
Sort and Select menu.

Performing the Sort

Press 1 to choose Perform Action and
sort the file.

Sorting Lines and Paragraphs

Sorting Lines

Suppose that you want to sort the lines in the example by ZIP code. You also want to sort the last names within each ZIP code.

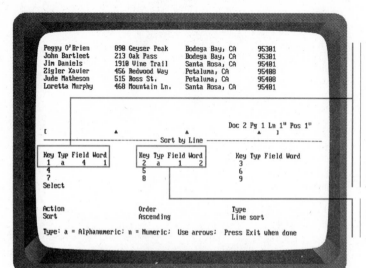

The ZIP code is specified by Key1 as the first word in field number 4. Notice that the Typ is a (alphanumeric) for all the keys, including ZIP codes, because ZIP codes that begin with a zero (such as 01772) won't sort properly if you choose the numeric type (Typ = n).

The last name is specified by Key2 as the second word in the first field.

The lines are sorted by ZIP code. Within each ZIP code, the last names are listed alphanumerically.

Sorting Paragraphs

Notice that each paragraph is a field. However, the first
three words in each paragraph are an index for each
quotation: speaker, main topic, subtopic. Suppose that
you want the paragraphs sorted by main topic and then
by subtopic.

The main topic is the
second word in the first
tab on the first line.

The subtopic is the third
word in the first tab on
the first line.

```
Galbraith Mind Changing -- Faced with the choice between changing
one's mind and proving that there is no need to do so, almost
everyone gets busy on the proof.

Phelps Mind Lazy -- At a certain age some people's minds close up:
they live on their intellectual fate.

Phaedrus Mind Amused -- The mind ought sometimes to be amused, that
it may the better return to thought, and to itself.

                                        Doc 2 Pg 1 Ln 1" Pos 1"
{  ▲  ▲  ▲  ▲  ▲  ▲  ▲  ▲  ▲  ▲  }  ▲  ▲
---------------------- Sort by Paragraph ----------------------
Key Typ Line Field Word  Key Typ Line Field Word  Key Typ Line Field Word
 1   a    1    1    2     2   a    1     1    3     3
 4                        5                        6
 7                        8                        9
Select

Action              Order                Type
Sort                Ascending            Paragraph sort

Type: a = Alphanumeric; n = Numeric;  Use arrows;  Press Exit when done
```

The paragraphs are sorted
alphanumerically by the
main topic (second word);
within the main topic,
they are sorted by the
subtopic (third word).

```
Phaedrus Mind Amused -- The mind ought sometimes to be amused, that
it may the better return to thought, and to itself.

Galbraith Mind Changing -- Faced with the choice between changing
one's mind and proving that there is no need to do so, almost
everyone gets busy on the proof.

Phelps Mind Lazy -- At a certain age some people's minds close up:
they live on their intellectual fate.




                                        Doc 1 Pg 1 Ln 1" Pos 1"
```

315

Sorting Secondary Merge Files

A secondary merge file is nothing more than a database with merge codes. WordPerfect can sort your secondary merge files so that the form letters, mailing lists, or labels you have previously typed will print in any order you choose.

Before you perform a sort, you must be sure that your data file is set up properly. A secondary merge file contains records, each of which contains fields. Each field must end with a ^R merge code, and each record must end with a ^E merge code.

Displaying the Sort Screen

To sort a secondary merge file, you first retrieve the file to the screen. Then you display the Sort screen by pressing Merge/Sort (Ctrl-F9), selecting Sort (2), and entering the names of the input and output files.

Choosing the Type of Sort

From the Sort and Select menu, you choose Type (7). Then you select Merge (1) to sort a secondary merge file. The screen heading becomes `Sort Secondary Merge File`, and the location headings for each key become `Field`, `Line`, and `Word`.

Selecting the Sort Order

Select Order (6) to display the Order menu. From this menu, you choose either Ascending (1) for A-to-Z sort order or Descending (2) for Z-to-A sort order.

Specifying the Key Locations

Next, you choose Keys (3) to display the Keys menu. The cursor moves under the a in the `Typ` column so that you can enter the location of each sort key. You type **a** to specify an alphanumeric sort for Key1, or you type **n** to specify a numeric sort for Key1.

Enter the location of Key1. The default values in Key1 are preset at a 1 1 1. These values mean that the Sort type is alphanumeric and that the first word on the first line in the first field is to be used as the basis for sorting.

If sorting by Key1 results in ties (equal values, such as the same names or numbers), you can sort on more than one field by using Key2, Key3, and so on. You press the right-arrow key to move to the entry area for Key2.

Performing the Sort

You press Exit (F7) to return to the Sort and Select menu. Then you select Perform Action (1) to start the Sort operation. WordPerfect sorts the file based on your sort criteria.

Converting a Database to a Secondary Merge File

Suppose that you have a database which is organized in lines (with each line ending with a hard return and each field separated by a tab), and you want to use the data in a merge operation. You can convert the line database to a secondary merge file with the following procedure.

Move the cursor to the beginning of the file (or block the needed portion) and press Replace (Alt-F2). Press N to indicate that you don't want to confirm. Press Enter and Esc to enter [HRt] (a hard return code) as the search string. Press Ctrl-E and Enter to enter ^E[HRt] as the replacement string. Press Esc to begin the operation. All lines now end with ^E.

Go back to the beginning of the file (or reblock the needed portion) and replace each [Tab] code (by pressing Tab) with ^R[HRt] (by pressing F9 and Enter).

Sorting Secondary Merge Files

WordPerfect can sort your secondary merge files so that the form letters, mailing lists, or labels you have previously typed will print in any order you choose.

Display the Sort Menu

To sort a secondary merge file, first retrieve the file to the screen, if you want, and then display the Sort screen. Press (Ctrl)(F9), press (2), and enter the input and output file names.

Selecting the Type and Order

Press (7) to select Type.

Press (1) to choose Merge.

Press (6) to choose Order.

Press (1) to choose Ascending for A-to-Z sort order.

Or

Press (2) to choose Descending for Z-to-A sort order.

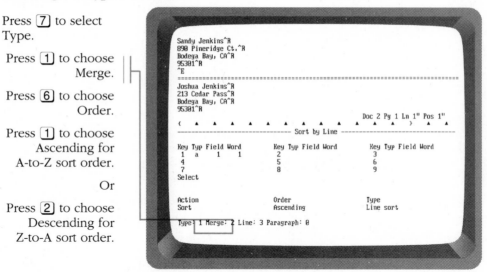

Choosing Key Locations

Press (3) to choose Keys.

Type **a** to specify an alphanumeric sort for Key1.

Or

Type **n** to specify a numeric sort for Key1.

Enter the location of Key1.

If you want to sort on more than one field, press the (→) key to move to Key2 and enter the key location. Move to and enter information for other keys.

318

Suppose that you want to sort the secondary merge file in the example by state. Within each state, you also want to sort entries by last name and then by first name.

```
 Sandy Jenkins^R
 890 Pineridge Ct.^R
 Bodega Bay, CA^R
 95301^R
 ^E
 ===========================================================
 Joshua Jenkins^R
 213 Cedar Pass^R
 Bodega Bay, CA^R
 95301^R
                                      Doc 2 Pg 1 Ln 1" Pos 1"
 <  ▲   ▲       ▲      ▲    ▲   ▲  ▲   }  ▲   ▲
 ------------------- Sort Secondary Merge File -------------------
 Key Typ Field Line Word  Key Typ Field Line Word  Key Typ Field Line Word
  1   a    3     1   -1     2   a    1     1   -1     3   a    1     1    1
  4                         5                         6
  7                         8                         9
 Select

 Action                   Order                  Type
 Sort                     Ascending              Merge sort

 Type: a = Alphanumeric; n = Numeric; Use arrows; Press Exit when done
```

Key1 is the state abbreviation (first word from the right in the third field).

Key2 is the last name (first word from the right in the first field).

Key3 is the first name (first word in the first field).

For all three keys, select alphanumeric sorting (a). ZIP codes must be sorted alphanumerically; otherwise, codes that begin with zero will not sort correctly.

```
 Joshua Jenkins^R
 213 Cedar Pass^R
 Bodega Bay, CA^R
 95301^R
 ^E
 ===========================================================
 Sandy Jenkins^R
 890 Pineridge Ct.^R
 Bodega Bay, CA^R
 95301^R
 ^E
 ===========================================================
 Pam Wagner^R
 309 South St.^R
 Bodega Bay, CA^R
 95301^R
 ^E
 ===========================================================



                                      Doc 1 Pg 1 Ln 1" Pos 1"
```

After entering the key locations, press F7 to return to the main Sort and Select menu.

Performing the Sort

Press 1 to choose Perform Action and sort the file.

Selecting Data

When you are working with a large database, you often need to select only particular data, and you need to be precise about your selection. Using the Select feature (included in WordPerfect's Sort menu), you can choose only those paragraphs, lines, or secondary merge records that contain a specific combination of data—for example, the names of customers who live in Texas. The steps in selecting are the same as those used in sorting, but you must include a statement that describes the records you want to select.

Displaying the Sort Screen

To define a selection, you first display the Sort screen by pressing Merge/Sort (Ctrl-F9), selecting Sort (2), and entering the names of the input and output files.

Choosing the Type and Order

You then select Type (7) and specify whether you are selecting records from a line, paragraph, or secondary merge file. You next select Order (6) and specify Ascending (1) or Descending (2).

Specifying the Key Locations

Then you select Keys (3). Even though you may not want to sort your data, you must use *Sort* keys to tell the program where to find the data you want.

You can type **a** to specify an alphanumeric sort for Key1, or you can type **n** to specify a numeric sort for Key1. Then you type the location for Key1.

Introduction

Understanding
the Sort Screen

Sorting Lines and
Paragraphs

Sorting Secondary
Merge Files

**Selecting
Data**

You can use the right-arrow key to move to the Key2 entry area and type the location for that key. Move to other Key entry areas and type their locations, if necessary.

Entering the Selection Criteria

To return to the Sort and Select menu, you press Exit (F7). Then you choose Select (4). WordPerfect moves the cursor under the word `Select` and displays a list of Select codes at the bottom of the screen.

Under `Select`, you enter a selection statement. For example, a simple statement might be the following:

```
Key1=petaluma
```

This selection statement tells WordPerfect to select only those records in which the city is *petaluma* or *Petaluma*. (WordPerfect's Sort and Select features do not differentiate between upper- and lowercase.)

You press Exit (F7) to return to the Sort and Select menu. Then you choose Action (5). From the displayed menu, you can choose Select and Sort (1) if you want to sort and select the records, or you can choose Select Only (2) if you want to select records without sorting them. WordPerfect returns you to the Sort and Select menu.

Performing the Sort

You choose Perform Action (1). The selected records are sent to the screen or to a disk file, as you requested.

Selecting Data

Use the Select feature to choose only those paragraphs, lines, or secondary merge records that contain a specific combination of data.

Selecting Sort Type and Order

To define a selection, first display the Sort screen by pressing Ctrl F9, pressing 2 for Sort, and entering the input and output file names.

Press 7 to select Type.

Type the number associated with the type of record you are sorting or selecting.

Press 6 for Order and press 1 for Ascending or 2 for Descending.

Specifying the Key Locations

Press 3 for Keys.

Type **a** or **n** to specify the sort type for Key1.

Type the location for Key1. Use the → key to move to the Key2 entry area. Type the location for Key2. Move to other Key entry areas and type their locations.

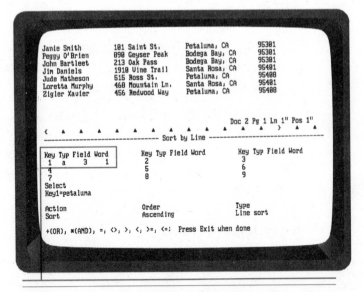

In this example, a Sort key has been entered as the specification for Key1: Typ = a (alphanumeric), Field = 3 (city and state field), and Word = 1 (city). This step tells WordPerfect where to look for the Select key.

Press [F7] to return to the Sort and Select menu.

```
 Janie Smith       101 Saint St.     Petaluma, CA    95301
 Peggy O'Brien     890 Geyser Peak   Bodega Bay, CA  95301
 John Bartleet     213 Oak Pass      Bodega Bay, CA  95301
 Jim Daniels       1910 Vine Trail   Santa Rosa, CA  95401
 Jude Matheson     515 Ross St.      Petaluma, CA    95408
 Loretta Murphy    468 Mountain Ln.  Santa Rosa, CA  95401
 Zigler Xavier     456 Redwood Way   Petaluma, CA    95408

                                     Doc 2 Pg 1 Ln 1" Pos 1"
 {  ▲  ▲  ▲  ▲  ▲  ▲  ▲  ▲  ▲  ▲  }  ▲  ▲
 ─────────────────── Sort by Line ──────────────────
 Key Typ Field Word    Key Typ Field Word   Key Typ Field Word
  1  a    3    1         2                     3
  4                      5                     6
  7                      8                     9
 Select
 Key1=petaluma

 Action                Order              Type
 Select and sort       Ascending          Line sort

 Action: 1 Select and Sort; 2 Select Only: 0
```

Press [1] to choose Select and Sort if you want to both sort and select records.

Or

Press [2] to choose Select Only if you want to select records without sorting them.

Selecting Criteria

Press [4] to choose Select.

Under Select, enter a selection statement such as **Key1=petaluma**. This selection statement tells WordPerfect to select only those records in which the city is *petaluma* or *Petaluma*.

Press [F7] to return to the Sort and Select menu.

Press [5] to choose Action.

```
 Zigler Xavier     456 Redwood Way   Petaluma, CA    95408
 Jude Matheson     515 Ross St.      Petaluma, CA    95408
 Janie Smith       101 Saint St.     Petaluma, CA    95301

                                     Doc 1 Pg 1 Ln 1" Pos 1"
```

Performing the Sort

Press [1] to choose Perform Action.

WordPerfect performs the desired action, sending the selected records either to the screen or to a disk file, as you requested.

323

12 *Using Text Columns*

WordPerfect offers you a powerful feature that lets you put your text in one of two types of columns: newspaper style or parallel. Text in newspaper-style columns wraps from the bottom of one column to the top of the next column and then wraps back to the first column on the left of the next page. Newspaper columns are read from top to bottom. Parallel columns are read from left to right; therefore, data is arranged across the page.

Newspaper-style columns are used for magazine articles, newsletters, lists, and indexes. Parallel columns are handy for inventory lists, personnel rosters, and duty schedules.

Tasks Covered in This Chapter

In this chapter, you learn to perform the following tasks:

- Define newspaper-style columns
- Define parallel columns
- Enter text into columns

325

Newspaper-Style

Newspaper-style columns are read from top to bottom. The text flows from the bottom of one column to the top of the next. You can define newspaper-style columns either before or after you type the text. Keep in mind that you can use the normal editing commands to modify text within a newspaper-style column.

Defining Columns before You Type

To define newspaper-style columns before you type the text, you first move the cursor to the position where you want the columns to begin. Then you press Math/Columns (Alt-F7) to display the Math/Columns menu. From this menu, you select Column Def (4) to display the Column Definition menu.

At the Column Definition menu, you do not need to select Type (1) because Newspaper is WordPerfect's default setting. You choose Number of Columns (2) from the menu, enter the number of columns you want on your page (up to 24), and press Enter.

You next select Distance Between Columns (3). WordPerfect automatically calculates the margin settings, with 0.5″ (one-half inch) between columns, but you can space your columns as close together or as far apart as you want. In most cases, you will accept the default margin settings. To accept the default settings, you press Enter.

If you plan to use columns of different widths, however, you must type the margin specifications. You can indicate the specifications in either of two ways: you can type the amount of space you want between your columns and press Enter; or you can choose Margins (4), and then enter the new settings for Left and Right column margins. You press Enter after each number.

You press Exit (F7) to return to the Math/Columns menu. From this menu, you select Column On/Off (3) to turn on the Column feature.

You then can begin typing. Typing with the Column feature turned on is the same as typing in a regular WordPerfect document. Text wraps within the column until you reach the bottom of the page, and then text wraps to the top of the next column.

To turn off the Column feature, you press Math/Columns (Alt-F7), and then you choose Column On/Off (3). After you've turned off the Column feature, any text you type is formatted in the normal way, and the column number disappears from the status line.

Creating Columns from Existing Text

To create newspaper-style columns from existing text, you first place the cursor at the beginning of the text you want to change to column format. If the text includes a centered heading, you place the cursor on the line below the heading, unless you plan to include the heading in the first column.

You then press Math/Columns (Alt-F7), define the columns according to the procedure described in the preceding text, and then press Exit (F7).

From the Math/Columns menu, you next select Column On/Off (3) to turn on the Column feature. Then you press the down-arrow key, and WordPerfect automatically reformats your text into columns.

Displaying a Single Column

Instead of displaying all the columns on-screen at once, you can display only one column at a time. To display one newspaper column at a time, you first press Setup (Shift-F1). Then you choose Display (3). Next, you select Side-by-side Columns Display (8), and you press N to tell WordPerfect to display only one column at a time on-screen. Finally, you press Exit (F7). To return to multiple-column display, you repeat the same procedure, but you press Y instead of N.

Newspaper-Style

Newspaper-style columns are read from top to bottom. The text flows from the bottom of one column to the top of the next. You can define newspaper-style columns either before or after you type the text.

Johannes Gutenberg, the fifteenth-century inventor of movable type, brought the written word to the public, and thus is responsible for publishing as it has been known for five hundred years. In the last quarter century, Gutenberg's metal type has been replaced by electronic typesetting-- faster, more flexible, but still very expensive, and still only part of the complex process or publishing. Today, personal computers bring a new generation of publishing to the individual. The technology is called "desktop publishing," and it represents a whole new approach to a very old art.

Desktop publishing starts with a personal computer. Your high-powered computer, along with the right software, gives you all the tools you need to design and publish a variety of printed materials at your own desk. Write a press release or create a simple letterhead with a word processing program like WordPerfect.

Defining Columns before You Type

Move the cursor to the position where you want columns to begin.

Press ⟨Alt⟩⟨F7⟩, the Math/Columns key.

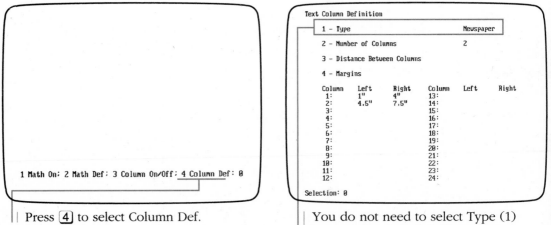

```
1 Math On; 2 Math Def; 3 Column On/Off; 4 Column Def; 0
```

Press ④ to select Column Def.

```
Text Column Definition

  1 - Type                        Newspaper

  2 - Number of Columns           2

  3 - Distance Between Columns

  4 - Margins

  Column   Left    Right   Column   Left    Right
    1:      1"      4"        13:
    2:      4.5"    7.5"      14:
    3:                        15:
    4:                        16:
    5:                        17:
    6:                        18:
    7:                        19:
    8:                        20:
    9:                        21:
   10:                        22:
   11:                        23:
   12:                        24:

Selection: 0
```

You do not need to select Type (1) because the default is Newspaper.

To change the default settings, press ②
to choose Number of Columns.

Enter the number of columns you want
on your page (up to 24), and then press
⏎Enter.

Press ③ for Distance Between Columns.

WordPerfect automatically calculates the
margin settings, with 0.5″ (one-half
inch) between columns, but you can
space your columns as close together or
as far apart as you want.

To accept the default margin settings,
press ⏎Enter.

Or

Type the amount of space you want
between your columns, and then press
⏎Enter.

```
Text Column Definition

  1 - Type                              Newspaper

  2 - Number of Columns                 3

  3 - Distance Between Columns          0.5"

  4 - Margins

   Column   Left    Right    Column   Left    Right
    1:      1"      2.83"     13:
    2:      3.33"   5.16"     14:
    3:      5.66"   7.5"      15:
    4:                        16:
    5:                        17:
    6:                        18:
    7:                        19:
    8:                        20:
    9:                        21:
   10:                        22:
   11:                        23:
   12:                        24:

Selection: 0
```

Or

To enter new settings manually, press ④
to choose Margins. Then enter the new
settings for Left and Right column
margins. Be sure to press ⏎Enter after
each number.

Press F7 to accept the settings.

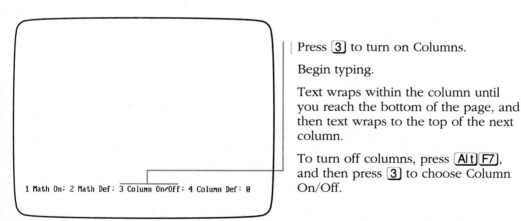

```
1 Math On; 2 Math Def; 3 Column On/Off; 4 Column Def: 0
```

Press ③ to turn on Columns.

Begin typing.

Text wraps within the column until
you reach the bottom of the page, and
then text wraps to the top of the next
column.

To turn off columns, press Alt F7,
and then press ③ to choose Column
On/Off.

Newspaper-Style

Creating Columns from Existing Text

Place the cursor at the beginning of the text you want to change to column format.

If the text includes a centered heading, place the cursor on the line below the heading, unless you plan to include the heading in the first column.

```
Johannes Gutenberg, the fifteenth-century inventor of movable type,
brought the written word to the public, and thus is responsible
for publishing as it has been known for five hundred years. In the
last quarter century, Gutenberg's metal type has been replaced by
electronic typesetting--faster, more flexible, but still very
expensive, and still only part of the complex process or
publishing. Today, personal computers bring a new generation of
publishing to the individual. The technology is called "desktop
publishing," and it represents a whole new approach to a very old
art.
===============================================================
Desktop publishing starts with a personal computer. Your high-
powered computer, along with the right software, gives you all the
tools you need to design and publish a variety of printed materials
at your own desk. Write a press release or create a simple
letterhead with a word processing program like WordPerfect.




                                        Doc 1 Pg 1 Ln 1" Pos 1"
```

Press **Alt F7**, the Math/Columns key.

```
Text Column Definition

    1 - Type                                Newspaper

    2 - Number of Columns                   2

    3 - Distance Between Columns            0.5"

    4 - Margins

    Column   Left     Right    Column   Left   Right
    1:       1"       4"       13:
    2:       4.5"     7.5"     14:
    3:                         15:
    4:                         16:
    5:                         17:
    6:                         18:
    7:                         19:
    8:                         20:
    9:                         21:
    10:                        22:
    11:                        23:
    12:                        24:

Selection: 0
```

Define your columns as described in the preceding material, and then press **F7**.

Press **3** to turn on Columns.

Press the **↓** key, and WordPerfect automatically reformats your text into columns.

```
Johannes Gutenberg, the          Desktop publishing starts with
fifteenth-century inventor of    a personal computer. Your high-
movable type, brought the        powered computer, along with
written word to the public, and  the right software, gives you
thus is responsible for pub-     all the tools you need to de-
lishing as it has been known     sign and publish a variety of
for five hundred years. In the   printed materials at your own
last quarter century,            desk. Write a press release or
Gutenberg's metal type has been  create a simple letterhead with
replaced by electronic type-     a word processing program like
setting--faster, more flexible,  WordPerfect.
but still very expensive, and
still only part of the complex
process or publishing. Today,
personal computers bring a new
generation of publishing to the
individual. The technology is
called "desktop publishing,"
and it represents a whole new
approach to a very old art.



                          Col 2 Doc 1 Pg 1 Ln 1.66" Pos 7.3"
```

Displaying a Single Column

Instead of displaying all the columns on-screen at once, you
can display only one column at a time.

Press ⬆Shift F1, the Setup key.

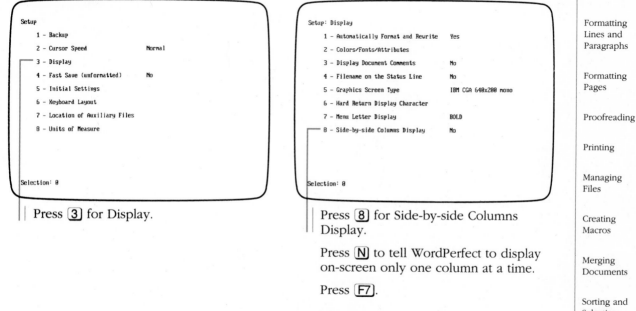

Press ③ for Display.

Press ⑧ for Side-by-side Columns
Display.

Press Ⓝ to tell WordPerfect to display
on-screen only one column at a time.

Press F7.

The columns are
separated by a hard
page break and appear
one per page. Note that
in column 2, the cursor
position still indicates
that you are on page 1.

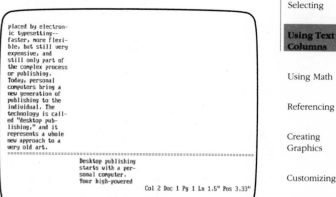

To return to multiple-column display,
repeat this procedure, but press Ⓨ
instead of Ⓝ.

331

Parallel

Parallel columns are read from left to right across the page. You might, for example, use parallel columns in a script in which names or brief instructions are typed in the first column and the words to be spoken are typed in the second column. You first define the columns you need, and then you enter the headings and text. Keep in mind that you can use the normal editing commands to modify text within a parallel column.

Before you begin to define and type text in parallel columns, you might want to enter a heading for the document. To do so, you press Center (Shift-F6), type the document's heading, and then press Enter twice to move down the page.

Defining Columns

To define parallel columns, you first press Math/Columns (Alt-F7). Then you choose Column Def (4). You next select Type (1).

At this point, you can choose either Parallel (2) or Parallel with Block Protect (3). The Parallel with Block Protect option prevents a horizontal block of columnar text from being split by a soft page break. If a column reaches the bottom margin and is too long to fit on the page, the entire block of columns is moved to the next page.

You next select Number of Columns (2), type the desired number of columns, and press Enter. You then select Distance Between Columns (3) and press Enter to accept the default (0.5"). If you want to specify a distance between columns that differs from the default, you enter a new specification and press Enter. You then choose Margins (4), type margin specifications, and press Enter.

To return to the Math/Columns menu, you press Exit (F7). Then you select Column On/Off (3) to turn on the Column feature.

Entering Column Headings

Above each of your parallel columns, you can enter a centered column heading. To do so, you first press Center (Shift-F6). Then you type the first column heading. You press Hard Page (Ctrl-Enter) to move to the next column. With the cursor in that column, you again press Center (Shift-F6) and type the column heading. You repeat this procedure until all the column headings have been entered. After you type the last column heading, you press Hard Page (Ctrl-Enter). WordPerfect inserts a blank line and positions the cursor at the first column location at the left of your page.

Entering Text

You type text into parallel columns by moving from column to column across the page. After typing the text in the first column, you press Hard Page (Ctrl-Enter) to move the cursor to the next column location. When you press Hard Page in the far right column, the cursor returns to the first column on the left. You can begin typing the next group of column entries. WordPerfect automatically inserts one blank line to separate the groups of text.

To create an empty column, you press Hard Page (Ctrl-Enter) twice.

Parallel

Parallel columns are read from left to right across the page. You first define the columns you need, and then you enter the headings and text.

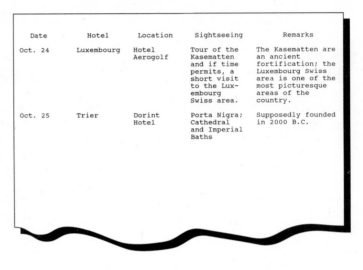

Date	Hotel	Location	Sightseeing	Remarks
Oct. 24	Luxembourg	Hotel Aerogolf	Tour of the Kasematten and if time permits, a short visit to the Luxembourg Swiss area.	The Kasematten are an ancient fortification; the Luxembourg Swiss area is one of the most picturesque areas of the country.
Oct. 25	Trier	Dorint Hotel	Porta Nigra; Cathedral and Imperial Baths	Supposedly founded in 2000 B.C.

Defining Columns

Press Alt F7, the Math/Columns key.

Press 4 to choose Column Def.

Press 1 to select Type.

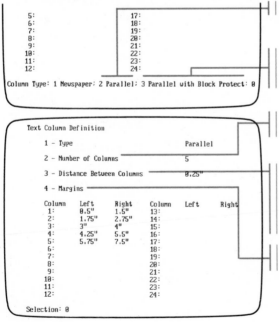

Press 2 to select Parallel.

Or

Press 3 to select Parallel with Block Protect so that blocks of columns are kept together on a page.

To change the default settings, press 2 to choose Number of Columns, type the desired number of columns, and press ↵Enter.

Press 3 for Distance Between Columns and press ↵Enter to accept the default (0.5″). Or, if you want to specify a distance between columns that differs from the default, type a new specification, and press ↵Enter.

Press 4 to choose Margins, type margin specifications, and press ↵Enter.

Press F7 to return to the Math/Columns menu.

Press 3 to turn on Columns.

334

Entering Column Headings

```
 Date    Location     Hotel   Sightseeing      Remarks








                                      Col 1 Doc 1 Pg 1 Ln 1.33" Pos 0.5"
```

Press ⬆Shift F6, the Center key, and type the column heading.

Press Ctrl ⏎Enter, the Hard Page command, to move to the next column.

Repeat this procedure until all the column headings have been entered. After you type the last column heading, press Ctrl ⏎Enter.

Entering Text

```
   Date       Location    Hotel   Sightseeing       Remarks
Oct. 24








                                      Col 2 Doc 1 Pg 1 Ln 1.33" Pos 1.75"
```

You type text into parallel columns by moving from column to column across the page.

With the cursor positioned at the left margin, type the text for the first column.

When you finish typing a column entry, press Ctrl ⏎Enter to move to the next column.

Repeat this procedure to enter text into the other columns.

When you finish typing text under the last column heading, press Ctrl ⏎Enter to insert a blank line and return the cursor to the left margin.

To create an empty column, press Ctrl ⏎Enter twice.

13 Using Math

WordPerfect's Math feature is designed to provide limited calculation capabilities for simple math operations, such as preparing an invoice or developing a sales report. WordPerfect can calculate subtotals, totals, and grand totals down columns of numbers. The program can add, subtract, multiply, and divide, as well as calculate averages. The most common and simplest math operations calculate and display the totals of numbers down a column. More complex operations calculate and display the results of computations involving numbers in different columns on the same line.

Key Terms

Math operators   Symbols that tell WordPerfect both the type of calculation you want to perform and where the result will be displayed.

Math definition   The instructions you enter on the Math Definition screen that define the column type and format for math columns.

Task Covered in This Chapter

In this chapter, you learn to perform the following tasks:

- Enter numbers down a column and calculate simple subtotals, totals, and grand totals
- Perform more complex math operations by defining the type and format of columns
- Write formulas that calculate numbers across a row of your document

Performing Simple Math Operations

Math operations that involve only totals down a column of numbers are the simplest to perform. For these operations, you set the tab stops for the columns, turn on the Math feature, enter the data and math operators, calculate the results, and turn off the Math feature.

Step 1: Set the tabs for your math columns.

To set tabs for math columns, you first position the cursor on the line following your column headings (if any). Then you press Format (Shift–F8) and select Line (1). Next, you choose Tab Set (8). You press 0 and then Enter to move the cursor to the 0 position. You next press Delete to End of Line (Ctrl-End) to remove all existing tab stops.

You move the cursor to the position where you want to place the first tab, and you press L for Left to set the tab stop for the first column. You then repeat this procedure for the remaining columns. Finally, you press Exit (F7) twice.

Be sure that your columns are wide enough to accommodate the largest numbers you will use. Also, keep in mind that the first math column begins at the first tab stop, not at the left margin. The left margin is reserved for labels, row headings, or other material that is not calculated.

Step 2: Turn on the Math feature.

To turn on Math, you press Math/Columns (Alt-F7) and select Math On (1). The Math indicator appears in the lower left of the screen to indicate that the cursor is in the math area.

Step 3: Enter numbers and math operators in the columns.

To enter numbers and math operators, you press Tab until the cursor rests in the correct column. The program displays the following prompt:

```
Align char = . Math
```

You enter the number and/or math operator you want to appear in that column. If you enter a number that contains a period, the number is aligned on the decimal point. You then press Tab to move to the next column and enter data. When you are ready to begin the next row of columns, you press Enter.

You can use four math operators to perform a simple math operation down a column of numbers. Use a + operator to subtotal the numbers in the column above the symbol. Use an = to total any subtotals from the column above it. Use an * (asterisk) to give a grand total of any totals listed above it. And use N in front of any negative number. When you enter an operator, only the operator is displayed. The math results are not shown until you calculate the results.

Step 4: Calculate the results.

To perform calculations, you first position the cursor anywhere in the math area. Then you press Math/Columns (Alt-F7). Finally, you choose Calculate (2). WordPerfect calculates the results and inserts them next to the math operators; the results are aligned on the tabs. Note that the math operators displayed on-screen do not appear in the printed document. If you make changes to the numbers or operators, you must recalculate.

Step 5: Turn off the Math feature.

When you are satisfied that your document is accurate and complete, you need to turn off the Math feature. To turn off Math, you first place the cursor after the math area. Then you press Math/Columns (Alt-F7) and select Math Off (1).

Performing Simple Math Operations

Math operations that involve only totals down a column of numbers are the simplest to perform.

Step 1: Set the tabs for your math columns.

Position the cursor on the line following your column headings (if any).

Press ⟨✦Shift⟩⟨F8⟩, the Format key.

Press ⟨1⟩ to select Line.

Press ⟨8⟩ to select Tab Set.

Press ⟨0⟩ and then ⟨⏎Enter⟩ to move the cursor to the 0 position.

Press ⟨Ctrl⟩⟨End⟩ to remove all existing tab stops.

Move the cursor to the position where you want to place the tab.

Press ⟨L⟩ for Left to set the tab stop of the first column.

Set tabs for each remaining column by positioning the cursor and pressing ⟨L⟩.

Press ⟨F7⟩ twice.

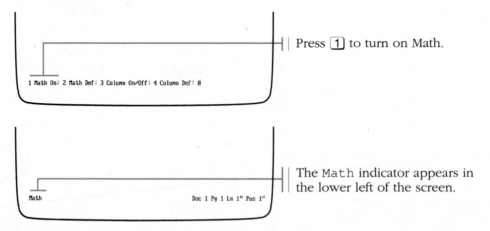

```
.................................L...........................................L.................
  |    ^    |    ^    |    ^    |    ^    |    ^    |    ^    |    ^    |    ^    |
  0"       1"        2"        3"        4"        5"        6"        7"
Delete EOL (clear tabs); Enter Number (set tab); Del (clear tab);
Left; Center; Right; Decimal; .= Dot Leader
```

Step 2: Turn on the Math feature.

Press ⟨Alt⟩⟨F7⟩, the Math/Columns key.

```
1 Math On; 2 Math Def; 3 Column On/Off; 4 Column Def; 0
```

Press ⟨1⟩ to turn on Math.

```
Math                                Doc 1 Pg 1 Ln 1" Pos 1"
```

The Math indicator appears in the lower left of the screen.

Step 3: Enter numbers and math operators in the columns.

Press [Tab⁚] until the cursor rests in the correct column.

Enter the number and/or math operator you want to appear in the column.

```
            Loaf and Mug Cafe
           Bank Reconciliation
              June 31, 1989

Balance per bank statement        $2,345.77
Add: Deposit in transit             644.26

                                       +

Less: Checks outstanding

    No. 2775 (Eden Foods)          355.00
    No. 2776 (Elmer's Bakery)       30.00
    No. 2777 (Oldenburg Farms)     125.00
    No. 2778 (S.M. Dairy)           25.00

                                       N

Adjusted balance                       =


Math                      Doc 1 Pg 1 Ln 4.16" Pos 1"
```

Enter any of the following math operators:

[+] for subtotals

[=] for totals

[*] for grand totals

[N] for negative numbers

Press [Tab⁚] to move to each of the remaining columns and enter data.

Press [↵Enter] to begin the next row of columns.

Step 4: Calculate the results.

With the cursor in the math area, press [Alt][F7], the Math/Columns key.

Press [2] to select Calculate.

WordPerfect calculates the results and inserts them next to the math operators.

```
1 Math Off; 2 Calculate; 3 Column On/Off; 4 Column Def; 0
```

```
            Loaf and Mug Cafe
           Bank Reconciliation
              June 31, 1989

Balance per bank statement        $2,345.77
Add: Deposit in transit             644.26
                                  2,990.03+

Less: Checks outstanding

No. 2775 (Eden Foods)             355.00
No. 2776 (Elmer's Bakery)          30.00
No. 2777 (Oldenburg Farms)        125.00
No. 2778 (S.M. Dairy)              25.00
                                 N535.00+

Adjusted balance                 2,455.03=


Math                      Doc 1 Pg 1 Ln 3.83" Pos 1"
```

Step 5: Turn off the Math feature.

Place the cursor after the math area.

Press [Alt][F7], the Math/Columns key.

Press [1] to turn off Math.

Performing More Complex Math Operations

More complex math operations in WordPerfect require you to use the Math Definition screen to "define" each column. Math columns that are defined require more planning than simple math columns. On the Math Definition screen, you must identify each column as numeric, total, text, or calculation. When you build complex math columns, you use the same procedure you used to build simple math columns, but you add the step of defining your columns after you set your tab stops.

When you define the column type and format, you specify what calculations you want performed and how you want the results displayed. The instructions you provide are called the *math definition*.

You can define four types of columns in your math definition:

- *Numeric* is the default column setting because it is the most common type of column used in math functions. This type of column calculates and displays the subtotals, totals, or grand totals below the other numbers in the column.
- *Total* columns set apart a total derived from the numbers in the column immediately to the left.
- *Text* columns are used for entering captions. Although you can enter either numbers or text in text columns, anything entered in text columns cannot be used in calculations.
- *Calculation* columns display the results of calculations performed with math formulas. You can use a calculation column to calculate numbers that are displayed *across* the page.

To set your math definition, you first position the cursor after any heading in the math area. Then you press Math/Columns (Alt-F7) to display the Math/Columns menu. From that menu, you select Math Def (2) to display the Math Definition screen.

The Math Definition screen is divided into three parts. The top part allows you to specify certain characteristics of the columns. WordPerfect uses the letters A through X to identify the 24 possible math columns. Notice, near the top of the screen, that all the columns are preset to Numeric (2).

Keep in mind that WordPerfect references columns in left-to-right order. The left margin is not a math column; numbers in it cannot be added, but it can be used for text and noncalculated numbers. Therefore, the first tab stop, not the left margin, is column A; the second tab stop is column B; and so on.

In the middle part of the Math Definition screen, you can specify calculation formulas for as many as four columns. The bottom part of the screen explains the codes used to indicate the type of column. You can't insert information or changes on the bottom part of the screen.

If you want to use the default settings (numeric columns, negative numbers displayed in parentheses, and two digits to the right of the decimal point), you do not need to define your math columns. You simply press Exit (F7) to complete your math definition.

If you are making setting changes, however, you need to perform some additional steps. You first use the arrow keys to move the cursor under the column letter. Then you press the number for the Type of Column. You next press (or – to specify how negative math results should be displayed. Finally, you type the number of the decimal digits for each column. Decimals are rounded to the degree of accuracy you specify. When you finish defining type and formats for each column, you press Exit (F7).

Performing More Complex Math Operations

You can define four types of math columns: numeric, total, text, and calculation.

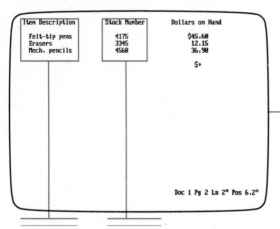

Column A and column B are descriptions that do not involve math; therefore, they should be defined as text columns.

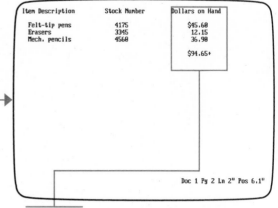

Column C is a numeric column that can be used in calculations. The text in the heading of column C does not affect the calculations.

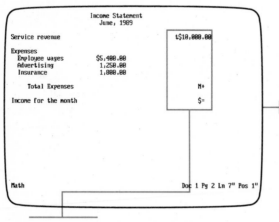

A total column is convenient for offsetting totals from the numbers added in the column immediately to the left.

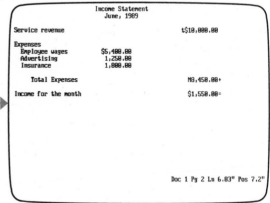

344

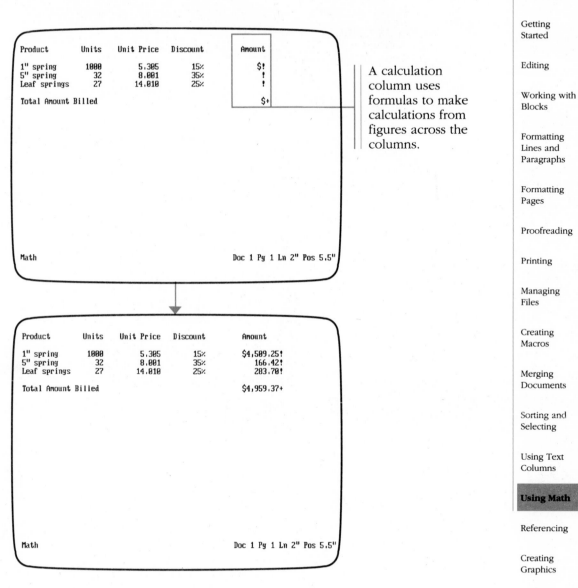

A calculation column uses formulas to make calculations from figures across the columns.

Performing More Complex Math Operations

In more complex math operations, you need to "define" the column type and format for the math columns.

Position the cursor after any heading in the math area.

Press ⌐Alt⌐F7⌐, the Math/Columns key.

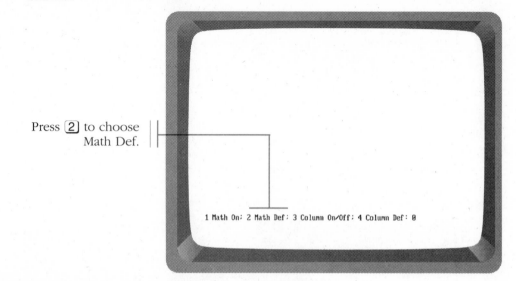

Press ⌐2⌐ to choose Math Def.

    1 Math On; 2 Math Def; 3 Column On/Off; 4 Column Def; 0

Math Definition	Use arrow keys to position cursor
Columns	A B C D E F G H I J K L M N O P Q R S T U V W X
Type	2 2 2 2 2 2 2 2 2 2 2 2 2 2 2 2 2 2 2 2 2 2 2 2
Negative Numbers	((
Number of Digits to the Right (0-4)	2 2 2 2 2 2 2 2 2 2 2 2 2 2 2 2 2 2 2 2 2 2 2 2

```
Calculation   1
  Formulas    2
              3
              4

Type of Column:
  0 = Calculation   1 = Text   2 = Numeric   3 = Total

Negative Numbers
  ( = Parentheses (50.00)        - = Minus Sign  -50.00


Press Exit when done
```

On the top part of the Math Definition screen, you specify certain characteristics of the columns. WordPerfect uses the letters A through X to identify the 24 possible math columns. Column A refers to the first tab stop, not the left margin.

The middle part of the screen lets you specify calculation formulas for as many as four columns.

The bottom part of the screen explains the codes used in the first part. You can't insert information or make changes on this part of the screen.

Press F7 if you want to use the default settings: numeric columns, negative numbers displayed in parentheses, and two digits to the right of the decimal point.

Or

If you are making setting changes, complete the following procedure:

Use the arrow keys to move the cursor under the column letter.

Press the Type of Column number.

Press (or - to specify how negative math results should be displayed.

Type the number of decimal digits for each column. (Decimals will be rounded to the degree of accuracy you specify.)

Press F7 when you've finished defining type and formats for each column.

```
Math Definition        Use arrow keys to position cursor

Columns                A B C D E F G H I J K L M N O P Q R S T U V W X

Type                   2 2 2 3 2 2 2 2 2 2 2 2 2 2 2 2 2 2 2 2 2 2 2 2

Negative Numbers       - - - - ( ( ( ( ( ( ( ( ( ( ( ( ( ( ( ( ( ( ( (

Number of Digits to    2 2 2 2 2 2 2 2 2 2 2 2 2 2 2 2 2 2 2 2 2 2 2 2
  the Right (0-4)

Calculation    1
  Formulas     2
               3
               4

Type of Column:
    0 = Calculation    1 = Text    2 = Numeric    3 = Total

Negative Numbers
    ( = Parentheses (50.00)        - = Minus Sign  -50.00


Press Exit when done
```

Using Calculation Columns

Calculation columns use formulas to calculate numbers across a row of a WordPerfect document. When you enter 0 for the column type on the Math Definition screen, WordPerfect automatically moves the cursor to the middle of the screen so that you can enter a formula for the calculation column. You can enter formulas in as many as 4 of WordPerfect's possible 24 math columns.

To build calculation columns, you first display the Math Definition screen by positioning the cursor in the math area, pressing Math/Columns (Alt-F7), and selecting Math Def (2).

Then you move the cursor in the Type row until the cursor rests under the appropriate column letter, and you press 0. The cursor jumps to the first available Calculation Formulas line. You type the formula. Then you press Enter to leave the formula line and return to the top part of the Math Definition screen.

Formulas are composed of numbers, column identifiers, and math operators. If you include a column letter, such as A, the formula uses the number in column A in the calculations. When you type a calculation formula, don't include any spaces. Also, don't press Enter until you have completed entering the formula.

Some sample formulas follow:

Formula	Result
3*3–2	7
3*A+B	17 (if column A=4 and column B=5)

A calculation formula can include numbers in other columns (either to the left or right of the calculation column) in the same row of your document. A formula also can include the number appearing in the calculation column on the preceding line of your document and any numbers you type into the formula.

Also, a formula can include the following four standard arithmetic operators:

+ Add

– Subtract

* Multiply

/ Divide

You must enter certain special math operators by themselves on the formula line:

+ Adds the numbers in the numeric columns

+/ Averages the numbers in the numeric columns

= Adds the numbers in the total columns

=/ Averages the numbers in the total columns

A formula is calculated from left to right. If you want a math term to calculate before other items, enclose that term in parentheses. Unlike algebra, however, you cannot use nested parentheses, as in (3+(3*A))–B. If you want to include a fraction, place it in parentheses or use its decimal equivalent—(1/3) or .33.

If you move to a formula line that has already been entered and press Enter without making a change, the program erases the entire formula.

When you enter a formula that is too long for WordPerfect to accept, the following error message is displayed:

```
Formula exceeds maximum storage available!
```

You must shorten your formula until WordPerfect will accept it.

In your document, WordPerfect inserts a ! when you tab over to a column that is defined as a calculation column.

Using Calculation Columns

Use calculation columns to calculate numbers across a row in your document.

To build calculation columns, you first display the Math Definition screen by positioning the cursor in the math area, pressing `Alt` `F7`, and pressing `2` for Math Def.

Move the cursor in the Type row until it rests under the appropriate column letter.

Press `0`.

Type the formula.
Press `↵Enter`.

Introduction

Getting Started

Editing

Working with Blocks

Formatting Lines and Paragraphs

Formatting Pages

Proofreading

Printing

Managing Files

Creating Macros

Merging Documents

Sorting and Selecting

Using Text Columns

Using Math

Referencing

Creating Graphics

Customizing

Appendix

Index

Press F7 to return to the Math/Columns menu.

Press 1 to turn on Math.

Type your columns.

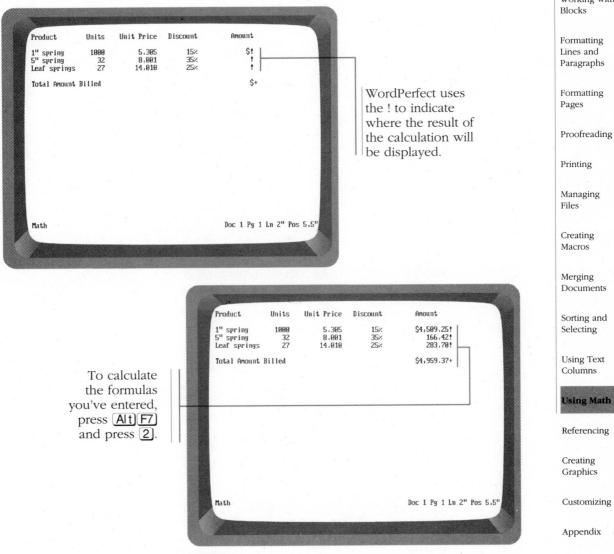

WordPerfect uses the ! to indicate where the result of the calculation will be displayed.

To calculate the formulas you've entered, press Alt F7 and press 2.

14 Referencing

When you create a formal document, you often need to develop the manuscript through a number of drafts. Moreover, the document may need to include elements beyond the main text, such as footnotes and a table of contents. WordPerfect has a number of referencing tools to help you both develop the main manuscript and create the related elements.

As you develop a manuscript, you will find WordPerfect's Outline, Paragraph Numbering, and Line Numbering features valuable for getting your project organized, and you will find those features convenient when conferring with others about particular passages. In addition, the Document Comment feature is handy for making notes to yourself about items that need further research or development. As your manuscript evolves through a number of stages, you may want to use WordPerfect's date and time code to enter the current date on each draft.

You can use WordPerfect's Footnote and Endnote feature to help you easily keep track of and enter reference information. WordPerfect also helps you create other related elements for your manuscript—tables of contents, indexes, and other document references.

Key Terms

Document comments   Notes and reminders you can type into a WordPerfect file. The comments appear on-screen but are not printed.

Master document   A document, such as a dissertation, compiled from a number of subdocuments, such as a title page, table of contents, and list of tables.

Tasks Covered in This Chapter

In this chapter, you learn to perform the following tasks:

- Create footnotes and endnotes
- Use a code to insert the current date and time in a document
- Create and edit outlines and numbered paragraphs
- Number lines automatically
- Insert document comments

In addition, you are introduced to some of WordPerfect's more advanced referencing features. Although the specifics of using these features are beyond the scope of this book, you will learn how to access the referencing tools for creating a list, an index, a table of contents, and a table of authorities. You also are introduced to WordPerfect's features for creating automatic references, creating a master document, and comparing documents.

Creating Footnotes and Endnotes

Footnotes and endnotes provide a simple, standard way of referencing sources as well as offering the reader additional parenthetical information. Footnotes appear at the bottom or *foot* of the page; endnotes are grouped at the end of your document. (Some authors group endnotes at the end of each chapter or section.) Both types of notes are marked in the text either by a number or by a character you specify.

Typing a Footnote or Endnote

To create a footnote or an endnote, you first move the cursor to the position where you want to insert a note number. Then you press Footnote (Ctrl-F7) to display the Footnote/Endnote menu. At this point, you choose either Footnote (1) or Endnote (2). Then you select Create (1).

An editing screen appears with the cursor to the immediate right of the current footnote or endnote number. As you enter text, you can use all the normal editing and function keys. You also can spell-check the note. After you type the text, you press Exit (F7) to return to your document.

WordPerfect inserts a code that includes the first 50 characters of the note. You can view the code and partial text with Reveal Codes (Alt-F3, or F11). To see how the notes will appear when printed, you can use View Document (Shift-F7, 6).

Editing a Footnote or Endnote

To edit a note, you press Footnote (Ctrl-F7), select Footnote (1) or Endnote (2), and choose Edit (2).

WordPerfect prompts `Footnote number?` (or `Endnote number?`) followed by the number of the note that immediately follows the cursor. You press Enter if the number is correct, or you type the number of the footnote or endnote you want to edit and press Enter. You then edit the text. To return to your document, you press Exit (F7).

Deleting a Footnote or Endnote

Because the entire note (number and text) is in one code, you can delete the note in the same way you delete any other WordPerfect code. To delete a note, you move the cursor under the note number you want to delete and press Del. You then press Y to confirm the deletion. Or, you can press Reveal Codes (Alt-F3, or F11), place the cursor over the note code, and press Del. WordPerfect automatically renumbers the other notes.

Creating Footnotes and Endnotes

Positioning and Generating Endnotes

Unlike footnotes, which are printed at the bottom of the page on which you create them, endnotes are placed together at the end of the document. If you want to place endnotes in a different position, you can enter an endnote placement code. When WordPerfect encounters this code, the program collects all the endnotes between the code and the beginning of the document (or a previous endnote placement code).

To position endnotes in a place other than the end of the document, you move the cursor to the place where you want to compile endnotes. Then you press Footnote (Ctrl-F7) and select Endnote Placement (3). At the prompt, you press Y or Enter to restart numbering with 1; or, if you want the endnotes to continue with the same numbering, you press N.

You next need to generate the endnotes. You press Mark Text (Alt-F5), choose Generate (6), and select Generate Tables, Indexes, Automatic References, etc. (5). At the prompt, you press Y. To print endnotes on a separate page, press Ctrl-Enter to insert a Hard Page code before the Endnote Placement code.

Selecting a Format for Footnotes and Endnotes

If you don't like the format WordPerfect has chosen for footnotes and endnotes, you can change the numbering style, placement, and format. You press Footnote (Ctrl-F7) and choose either Footnote (1) or Endnote (2). You next select Options (4) to display the Options menu. You select the options you want to change and enter the needed information. Then you press Exit (F7).

Creating Footnotes and Endnotes

Use footnotes and endnotes to reference sources or to offer readers additional parenthetical information. Footnotes appear at the bottom or foot of the page; endnotes are grouped at the end of the document (or at the end of each section).

Typing a Footnote or Endnote

Move the cursor to the position where you want to insert a note number.

Press Ctrl F7, the Footnote key.

```
In Charles Dicken's story of Nicholas Nickleby, one of the villains
is Mr. Wackford Squeers:

    Mr. Squeers's appearance was not prepossessing. He had
    but one eye, and the popular prejudice runs in favour of
    two.... The blank side of his face was much wrinkled and
    puckered up, which gave him a very sinister appearance,
    especially when he smiled, at which times his expression
    bordered closely on the villainous.... He wore,..a suit
    of scholastic black, but his coat sleeves being a great
    deal too long, and his trousers a great deal too short,
    he appeared ill at ease in his clothes, and as if here
    were in a perpetual state of astonishment at finding
    himself so respectable.




1 Footnote: 2 Endnote: 3 Endnote Placement: 0
```

```
In Charles Dicken's story of Nicholas Nickleby, one of the villains
is Mr. Wackford Squeers:

    Mr. Squeers's appearance was not prepossessing. He had
    but one eye, and the popular prejudice runs in favour of
    two.... The blank side of his face was much wrinkled and
    puckered up, which gave him a very sinister appearance,
    especially when he smiled, at which times his expression
    bordered closely on the villainous.... He wore,..a suit
    of scholastic black, but his coat sleeves being a great
    deal too long, and his trousers a great deal too short,
    he appeared ill at ease in his clothes, and as if here
    were in a perpetual state of astonishment at finding
    himself so respectable.




Footnote: 1 Create: 2 Edit: 3 New Number: 4 Options: 0
```

| Press 1 to select Footnote.

Or

| Press 2 to select Endnote.

| Press 1 to select Create.

The menu for Endnotes is the same, but the first word is Endnote.

```
    1Charles Dickens, The Life and Adventures of Nicholas Nickleby
(Philadelphia: University of Pennsylvania Press, 1982), vol. 1, p.
24.








Press Exit when done                          Doc 1 Pg 1 Ln 4" Pos 1.3"
```

Type the text.

Press F7 to return to your document.

Introduction

**Creating
Footnotes and
Endnotes**

Using a
Date and
Time Code

Outlining and
Numbering
Paragraphs

Numbering
Lines

Using
Document
Comments

Using Other
Referencing
Features

Editing a Footnote or Endnote

Follow the same steps to create a
footnote or endnote.

Press [2] to select Edit.

Footnote number? 2

Press [↵Enter] if the number is correct.

Or

Type the number of the footnote (or
endnote) you want to edit and press
[↵Enter].

Edit the text.

Press [F7] to return to your document.

Deleting a Footnote or Endnote

Move the cursor under the footnote
or endnote you want to delete.

Press [Del].

Delete [Footnote:1]? (Y/N) No

Press [Y] to confirm the deletion.

WordPerfect renumbers the other
notes in your document automatically.

Selecting a Format for Footnotes and Endnotes

If you want to use footnotes or endnotes, but don't like the format
WordPerfect has chosen for them, you can change the numbering
style, placement, and format.

```
Footnote Options

    1 - Spacing Within Footnotes         1
             Between Footnotes           0.16"

    2 - Amount of Note to Keep Together  0.5"

    3 - Style for Number in Text         [SUPRSCPT][Note Num][suprscpt]

    4 - Style for Number in Note                  [SUPRSCPT][Note Num][suprscp

    5 - Footnote Numbering Method        Numbers

    6 - Start Footnote Numbers each Page No

    7 - Line Separating Text and Footnotes  2-inch Line

    8 - Print Continued Message          No

    9 - Footnotes at Bottom of Page      Yes


Selection: 0
```

Follow the steps to create a footnote or
endnote.

Press [4] to display the Options menu.

The options for footnotes and endnotes are
the same, but the last four options are not
available for endnotes.

Select the options you want to change and
enter the necessary information.

Press [F7] to return to your document.

Creating Footnotes and Endnotes

Positioning and Generating Endnotes

WordPerfect places endnotes together at the end of the document.
If you want to place endnotes in a different position, you must
enter an Endnote Placement code. You first enter the code to mark
the position of the endnotes, and then you generate the notes.

Positioning Endnotes

Move the cursor to the place where
you want to compile endnotes.

Press (Ctrl)(F7), the Footnote key.

```
                                              David Macaulay, in his book Cathedral, uses the fictional cathedral
                                              of Chutreaux" to detail the painstaking, collaborative effort that
                                              went into the making of a 13th-century Gothic cathedral. After the
                                              architect or master builder created the original design, he
                                              assembled a team of the best craftsmen he could find:

                                                   The craftsmen were the master quarryman, the master stone
                                                   cutter, the master sculptor, the master mortar maker, the
                                                   master mason, the master carpenter, the master
                                                   blacksmith, the master roofer, and the master glass
                                                   maker.1




1 Footnote; 2 Endnote; 3 Endnote Placement: 0     Restart endnote numbering? (Y/N) Yes
```

Press **3** to choose Endnote Placement.

To restart numbering with 1, press (Y)
or (↵Enter).

Or

Press (N) if you want the endnotes to
continue with the same numbering.

```
David Macaulay, in his book Cathedral, uses the fictional cathedral
of Chutreaux" to detail the painstaking, collaborative effort that
went into the making of a 13th-century Gothic cathedral. After the
architect or master builder created the original design, he
assembled a team of the best craftsmen he could find:

     The craftsmen were the master quarryman, the master stone
     cutter, the master sculptor, the master mortar maker, the
     master mason, the master carpenter, the master
     blacksmith, the master roofer, and the master glass
     maker.1
================================================================

 Endnote Placement
 It is not known how much space endnotes will occupy here.
 Generate to determine.

================================================================

                        Doc 1 Pg 3 Ln 1" Pos 1"
```

Generating Endnotes

Press 〔Alt〕〔F5〕, the Mark Text key.

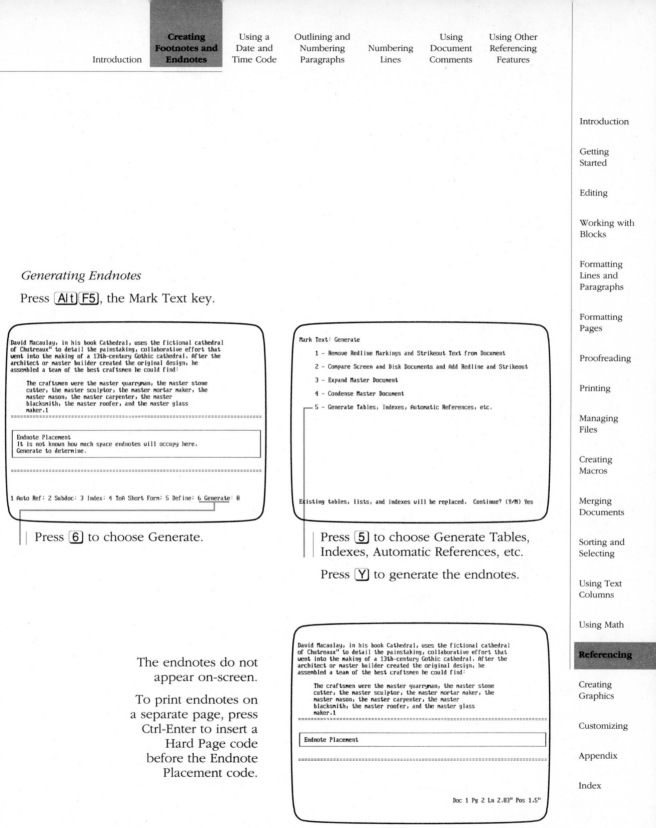

Press 〔6〕 to choose Generate.

Press 〔5〕 to choose Generate Tables, Indexes, Automatic References, etc.

Press 〔Y〕 to generate the endnotes.

The endnotes do not appear on-screen.

To print endnotes on a separate page, press Ctrl-Enter to insert a Hard Page code before the Endnote Placement code.

Using a Date and Time Code

WordPerfect can check your computer's clock and insert the current date and time in a document. The program also can insert a code that updates the date and time automatically every time you retrieve the document.

Note: WordPerfect cannot insert the correct date and time unless your computer's clock is set correctly. Check the instruction manual for your computer to learn how to reset the clock.

Inserting a Date and Time Code

To insert a date and time code, you first move the cursor to the position where you want to insert the code. Then you press Date/ Outline (Shift-F5) to display the Date/Outline menu.

From this menu, you can select Date Text (1) to insert the current date, the current time, or both the date and time in your document. WordPerfect immediately types the current date—for example, July 18, 1990. If you have set the Date/Time format to include the time, the current time is also included—for example, July 18, 1990 — 10:32 am. This date and time information is not updated the next time you retrieve or print the document.

If you select Date Code (2) from the Date/Outline menu, WordPerfect inserts the current date (or time, or both the date and time) and a date code into your document. The date code updates the date information each time you retrieve or print the document.

Setting the Format for Date and Time

To set the format for the date and time, you first press Date/Outline (Shift-F5). Then you choose Date Format (3) to display the Date Format menu. You enter new options. Then you press Exit (F7) twice to return to your document.

The Date and Time options on the Date Format menu establish the format that WordPerfect uses to print the date and time. You can mix format numbers with any text you want to print; for example, your prompt can include the following:

Today's date is 3 1, 4, and the time is 8:90.

With this prompt, WordPerfect enters the following when you enter a Date/Time code:

```
Today's date is March 28, 1989, and the
time is 12:47 pm.
```

To print just the first three characters of month and day names, you type a percent sign before the appropriate code. For example, you can enter the following:

%3. 1, 4 (%6)

With this prompt, WordPerfect enters the following:

```
Mar. 28, 1989 (Tue)
```

Using a Date and Time Code

You can insert the current date and time in a document, or you can insert the date and time and a code that updates the date information every time you retrieve the document.

Note: WordPerfect inserts the date and time according to your computer's clock.

Inserting a Date and Time Code

Move the cursor to the position where you want to insert the Date/Time code.

Press ⇧Shift F5, the Date/Outline key.

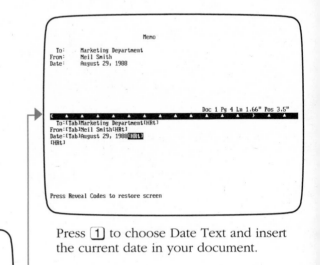

Press 1 to choose Date Text and insert the current date in your document.

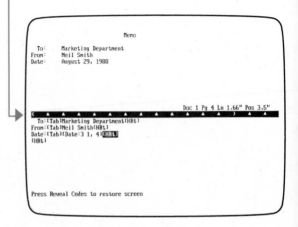

Press 2 to choose Date Code and insert the date and time and a code that updates the date every time you retrieve or print the document.

Setting the Format for Date and Time

Press ⇧Shift F5, the Date/Outline key.

Press 3 to choose Date Format.

Enter new options.

Press F7 twice to return to your document.

```
Date Format

    Character    Meaning
        1        Day of the Month
        2        Month (number)
        3        Month (word)
        4        Year (all four digits)
        5        Year (last two digits)
        6        Day of the Week (word)
        7        Hour (24-hour clock)
        8        Hour (12-hour clock)
        9        Minute
        0        am / pm
        %        Used before a number, will:
                     Pad numbers less than 10 with a leading zero
                     Output only 3 letters for the month or day of the week


    Examples:  3 1, 4       = December 25, 1984
               %6 %3 1, 4   = Tue Dec 25, 1984
               %2/%1/5 (6)  = 01/01/85 (Tuesday)
               8:90         = 10:55am


Date format: 3 1, 4
```

To print just the first three characters of month and day names, type a percent sign before the appropriate code.

Outlining and Numbering Paragraphs

With WordPerfect's Outline feature, you can create an outline and generate paragraph numbers automatically. If you prefer to enter paragraph numbers manually, you can use WordPerfect's Paragraph Numbering feature instead. Paragraph numbering is convenient when you have few numbers and a large amount of text.

Creating an Outline

If you want to title your outline, you first press Center (Shift-F6), type the title, and press Enter. Then, to create the outline, you move the cursor to the position where you want the outline to begin and press Date/Outline (Shift-F5). You next select Outline (4); the `Outline` indicator appears at the bottom left corner of the screen.

While `Outline` appears on-screen, the Enter and Tab keys perform special functions. Each time you press Enter, you create a new paragraph number. Within the line, each time you press Tab, you create a different level number.

You press Enter to insert the first paragraph number in the outline ("I." in Outline style). The default numbering style is Outline: uppercase Roman numerals for level one, uppercase letters for level two, Arabic numbers for level three, and so on.

You press Indent (F4) to establish the level number and position the cursor, and then you type the text for the first entry. Consecutive lines of text wrap underneath the indent. When you press Enter, WordPerfect moves the cursor to the next line and automatically enters the next number. If you want, you can press Enter again to insert a blank line and move the number down.

You press Tab to move in one level. The number follows and changes to the next level number ("A." in Outline style). You press Indent (F4), type the text for the entry, and press Enter.

You repeat these steps to complete your outline. If you press Tab too many times, you can move back one level by pressing Margin Release (Shift-Tab). To turn off the Outline feature, you press Date/Outline (Shift-F5) and choose Outline (4).

Editing an Outline

You can edit an outline by changing the text within the numbered paragraphs, changing the level numbers of paragraphs, deleting the paragraph numbers, adding paragraphs, deleting paragraphs, moving paragraphs, and adding unnumbered paragraphs. When you add, delete, or move numbered paragraphs, WordPerfect automatically renumbers the paragraphs for you. To redisplay the screen with the correct numbers, you move the cursor through the document, or you press Screen (Ctrl-F3) and press Enter.

Changing a Paragraph Number

To change a paragraph number, you place the cursor under the number you want to change. Then you either press Tab to move the line to the right and to change the number to a lower level, or you press Margin Release (Shift-Tab) to move the line to the left and to change the number to a higher level. Finally, you press the down-arrow key to renumber and redisplay the screen.

Deleting a Paragraph Number

To delete a paragraph number, you press Reveal Codes (Alt-F3, or F11) and move the cursor to the [Par Num] code that represents the number you want to delete. You then press Del. You press Reveal Codes (Alt-F3, or F11) to return to the normal editing screen.

Outlining and Numbering Paragraphs

Adding a Paragraph Number

To add a paragraph number, you turn on the Outline feature and press Enter to create a new heading number or letter. Then you press Tab to place the paragraph appropriately. You next press Indent (F4), type the text for the new paragraph (unless the text is already entered), and turn off the Outline feature.

Deleting a Numbered Paragraph

To delete a numbered paragraph, you position the cursor at the beginning of the section you want to delete. Then you press Block (Alt-F4, or F12) and highlight the section you want to delete. You press Del or Backspace, and then press Y to confirm the deletion of the block.

Moving a Numbered Paragraph

To move a numbered paragraph, you first delete the paragraph as described in the preceding text. You then move the cursor to where you want to place the paragraph and press Cancel (F1). Finally, you select Restore (1) to restore the paragraph in the new location.

Adding an Unnumbered paragraph

To add an unnumbered paragraph to your outline, you can turn off the Outline feature, type the paragraph, and then turn on the Outline feature again. Or, you can use a second method to enter an unnumbered paragraph. To add an unnumbered paragraph with the Outline feature on, you place the cursor where you want the paragraph to begin, press Enter and Tab to space the paragraph properly within the outline, and press Backspace to delete the paragraph number. Then you press Indent (F4) to line up the paragraph under the preceding levels, type the text, and press Enter. Finally, you press Backspace to delete the paragraph number.

Numbering Paragraphs

Paragraph numbering differs from outlining because you must insert numbers manually. Also, unlike the Outline feature, the Paragraph Numbering feature lets you choose the level number, regardless of the cursor position. You can edit numbered paragraphs using the same techniques you use to edit an outline. When you add or delete a paragraph number, WordPerfect automatically renumbers the remaining sections.

To number paragraphs, you position the cursor where you want to begin the paragraph. Then you press Date/Outline (Shift-F5) and choose Para Num (5). At the prompt, you can press Enter to have WordPerfect insert the number that corresponds to the level at the cursor position, or you can type the level number you want to assign and press Enter. Finally, you press Indent (F4) and type the paragraph.

Changing the Numbering Style

Outline levels are determined by tab stops and by the style of numbering selected. The default numbering style is Outline, but you can specify a different style for outlines and paragraph numbers.

To change the numbering style, you press Date/Outline (Shift-F5) and select Define (6) to display the Paragraph Number Definition menu. From this menu, you can choose from the selection of predefined numbering styles (options 2 through 5 on the menu). If you want to create your own style, you can choose User-defined (6); the cursor moves to the Current Definition line. Then you type a level number, press Enter to move to the next level, and press Exit (F7) when you have completed your numbering definition. After you specify your numbering style, you press Exit (F7) twice to return to your document.

Outlining and Numbering Paragraphs

Creating an Outline

Use WordPerfect's Outline feature to create an outline and generate paragraph numbers automatically.

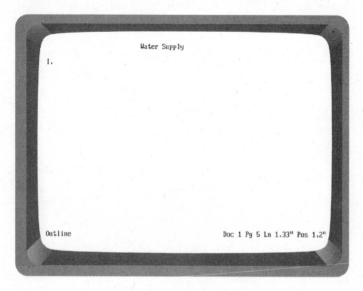

If you want to title your outline, press [⬆Shift][F6], type the title, and press [⏎Enter].

Move the cursor to the position where you want the outline to begin.

Press [⬆Shift][F5], the Date/Outline key.

Press [4] to turn on Outline.

Press [⏎Enter] to insert the first paragraph number in the outline.

Press [F4], the Indent key, to establish the level number and position the cursor.

Type the text for the first entry.

Press ↵Enter to move to the next line and automatically enter the next number. If you want to insert a blank line, press ↵Enter again to insert the line and move the number down.

Press Tab⇄ to move in one level and change the number to the next level number.

Press F4, type the text for the entry, and press ↵Enter.

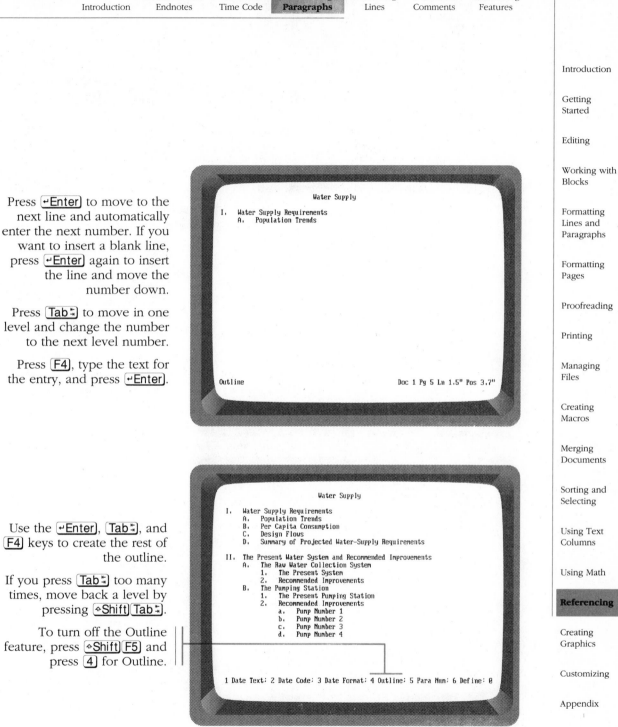

```
                          Water Supply

I.   Water Supply Requirements
     A.   Population Trends




Outline                              Doc 1 Pg 5 Ln 1.5" Pos 3.7"
```

Use the ↵Enter, Tab⇄, and F4 keys to create the rest of the outline.

If you press Tab⇄ too many times, move back a level by pressing ⇧Shift Tab⇄.

To turn off the Outline feature, press ⇧Shift F5 and press 4 for Outline.

```
                          Water Supply

I.   Water Supply Requirements
     A.   Population Trends
     B.   Per Capita Consumption
     C.   Design Flows
     D.   Summary of Projected Water-Supply Requirements
II.  The Present Water System and Recommended Improvements
     A.   The Raw Water Collection System
          1.   The Present System
          2.   Recommended Improvements
     B.   The Pumping Station
          1.   The Present Pumping Station
          2.   Recommended Improvements
               a.   Pump Number 1
               b.   Pump Number 2
               c.   Pump Number 3
               d.   Pump Number 4


1 Date Text; 2 Date Code; 3 Date Format; 4 Outline; 5 Para Num; 6 Define: 0
```

Outlining and Numbering Paragraphs

Numbering Paragraphs

If you have lengthy text and only a few numbers, use the Paragraph Numbering feature to number paragraphs manually. You choose the level number, regardless of the cursor position.

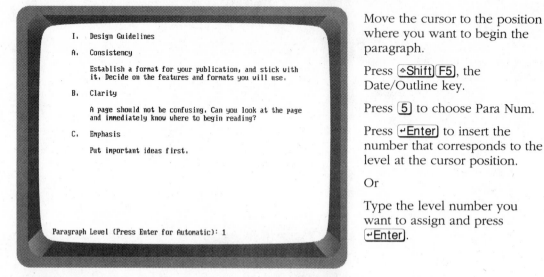

Move the cursor to the position where you want to begin the paragraph.

Press ⬆Shift F5, the Date/Outline key.

Press 5 to choose Para Num.

Press ↵Enter to insert the number that corresponds to the level at the cursor position.

Or

Type the level number you want to assign and press ↵Enter.

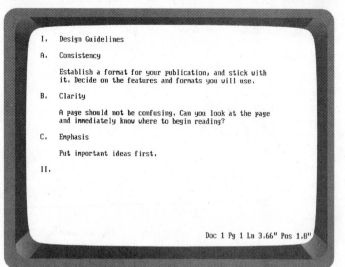

Press F4 and type the text.

Changing the Numbering Style

The default numbering style is Outline: uppercase Roman numerals for level one, uppercase letters for level two, Arabic numbers for level three, and so on. You can specify a different style for outline and paragraph numbers.

```
Paragraph Number Definition

  1 - Starting Paragraph Number          1
      (in legal style)

                                    Levels
                         1   2   3   4   5   6   7   8
  2 - Paragraph          1,  a,  i,  (1) (a) (i) 1)  a)
  3 - Outline            I,  A,  1,  a,  (1) (a) i)  a)
  4 - Legal (1.1.1)      1   .1  .1  .1  .1  .1  .1  .1
  5 - Bullets            •   o   -   ■   *   +   ·   x
  6 - User-defined

  Current Definition     I,  A,  1,  a,  (1) (a) i)  a)

      Number Style              Punctuation
      1 - Digits                #   - No punctuation
      A - Upper case letters    #,  - Trailing period
      a - Lower case letters    #)  - Trailing parenthesis
      I - Upper case roman      (#) - Enclosing parentheses
      i - Lower case roman      .#  - All levels separated by period
      Other character - Bullet      (e.g. 2.1.3.4)

  Selection: 0
```

Press [⇧Shift][F5], the Date/Outline key.

Press [6] to choose Define.

Choose from the selection of predefined numbering styles (options 2 through 5 on the menu).

Or press [6] to select User-defined; the cursor moves to the Current Definition line. Then type each level number, press [↵Enter] to move to the next level, and press [F7] when you complete your numbering definition.

Press [F7] twice to return to your document.

Outlining and Numbering Paragraphs

Editing an Outline

When you add, delete, or move numbered paragraphs, WordPerfect automatically renumbers the paragraphs for you.

To redisplay the screen with the correct numbers, use the ↓ to move the cursor through the document. Or, press Ctrl F3, the Screen key, and then press ↵Enter.

Changing a Paragraph Number

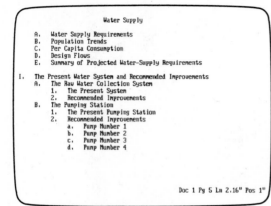

```
                    Water Supply

      A.   Water Supply Requirements
      B.   Population Trends
      C.   Per Capita Consumption
      D.   Design Flows
      E.   Summary of Projected Water-Supply Requirements

I.    The Present Water System and Recommended Improvements
      A.   The Raw Water Collection System
           1.   The Present System
           2.   Recommended Improvements
      B.   The Pumping Station
           1.   The Present Pumping Station
           2.   Recommended Improvements
                a.   Pump Number 1
                b.   Pump Number 2
                c.   Pump Number 3
                d.   Pump Number 4



                               Doc 1 Pg 5 Ln 2.16" Pos 1"
```

Place the cursor under the number you want to change.

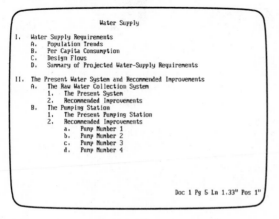

```
                    Water Supply

I.    Water Supply Requirements
      A.   Population Trends
      B.   Per Capita Consumption
      C.   Design Flows
      D.   Summary of Projected Water-Supply Requirements

II.   The Present Water System and Recommended Improvements
      A.   The Raw Water Collection System
           1.   The Present System
           2.   Recommended Improvements
      B.   The Pumping Station
           1.   The Present Pumping Station
           2.   Recommended Improvements
                a.   Pump Number 1
                b.   Pump Number 2
                c.   Pump Number 3
                d.   Pump Number 4


                               Doc 1 Pg 5 Ln 1.33" Pos 1"
```

Press Tab⇥ to move the line to the right and to change the number to a lower level.

Or

Press ⇧Shift Tab⇥ to move the line to the left and to change the number to a higher level.

Introduction

Creating
Footnotes and
Endnotes

Using a
Date and
Time Code

**Outlining and
Numbering
Paragraphs**

Numbering
Lines

Using
Document
Comments

Using Other
Referencing
Features

Deleting a Paragraph Number

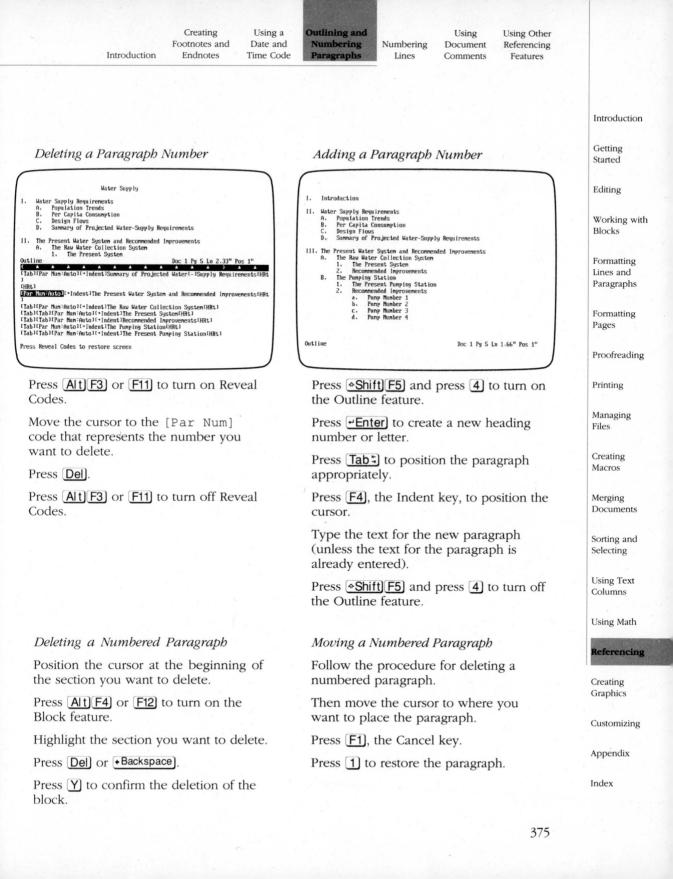

```
                    Water Supply

I.   Water Supply Requirements
     A.   Population Trends
     B.   Per Capita Consumption
     C.   Design Flows
     D.   Summary of Projected Water-Supply Requirements

II.  The Present Water System and Recommended Improvements
     A.   The Raw Water Collection System
          1.   The Present System
Outline                              Doc 1 Pg 5 Ln 2.33" Pos 1"
( ▲  ▲  ▲  ▲  ▲  ▲  ▲  ▲  ▲  ▲  ▲  ▲  )  ▲  ▲  ▲
[Tab][Par Num:Auto][→Indent]Summary of Projected Water[-]Supply Requirements[HRt
]
[HRt]
[Par Num:Auto][→Indent]The Present Water System and Recommended Improvements[HRt
]
[Tab][Par Num:Auto][→Indent]The Raw Water Collection System[HRt]
[Tab][Tab][Par Num:Auto][→Indent]The Present System[HRt]
[Tab][Tab][Par Num:Auto][→Indent]Recommended Improvements[HRt]
[Tab][Tab][Par Num:Auto][→Indent]The Present Pumping Station[HRt]

Press Reveal Codes to restore screen
```

Press [Alt][F3] or [F11] to turn on Reveal
Codes.

Move the cursor to the [Par Num]
code that represents the number you
want to delete.

Press [Del].

Press [Alt][F3] or [F11] to turn off Reveal
Codes.

Deleting a Numbered Paragraph

Position the cursor at the beginning of
the section you want to delete.

Press [Alt][F4] or [F12] to turn on the
Block feature.

Highlight the section you want to delete.

Press [Del] or [◆Backspace].

Press [Y] to confirm the deletion of the
block.

Adding a Paragraph Number

```
I.    Introduction

II.   Water Supply Requirements
      A.    Population Trends
      B.    Per Capita Consumption
      C.    Design Flows
      D.    Summary of Projected Water-Supply Requirements

III.  The Present Water System and Recommended Improvements
      A.    The Raw Water Collection System
            1.    The Present System
            2.    Recommended Improvements
      B.    The Pumping Station
            1.    The Present Pumping Station
            2.    Recommended Improvements
                  a.    Pump Number 1
                  b.    Pump Number 2
                  c.    Pump Number 3
                  d.    Pump Number 4

Outline                              Doc 1 Pg 5 Ln 1.66" Pos 1"
```

Press [◆Shift][F5] and press [4] to turn on
the Outline feature.

Press [◆Enter] to create a new heading
number or letter.

Press [Tab⇥] to position the paragraph
appropriately.

Press [F4], the Indent key, to position the
cursor.

Type the text for the new paragraph
(unless the text for the paragraph is
already entered).

Press [◆Shift][F5] and press [4] to turn off
the Outline feature.

Moving a Numbered Paragraph

Follow the procedure for deleting a
numbered paragraph.

Then move the cursor to where you
want to place the paragraph.

Press [F1], the Cancel key.

Press [1] to restore the paragraph.

Numbering Lines

In addition to numbering paragraphs, WordPerfect can number the lines in your document. With line numbering, you easily can refer to a particular clause in a legal document or to a specific passage in a manuscript. For instance, you can cite a passage by referring to page 11, line 26.

When you number lines in WordPerfect, the body text as well as the footnotes and endnotes are numbered; headers and footers are not numbered. Numbers are not displayed on-screen; they appear when you print the document or use View Document (Shift-F7, 6).

Turning On Automatic Line Numbering

To number lines automatically, you first move the cursor to the position where you want line numbering to begin (usually at the beginning of your document). Then you press Format (Shift-F8) to display the Format menu. You next select Line (1) to display the Format: Line menu. Then you select Line Numbering (5). You press Y to turn on line numbering and display the Format: Line Numbering menu.

If you want to accept the default line numbering settings, you press Enter. Otherwise, you select the option you want to change and enter the desired modification. You press Exit (F7) to return to the editing screen.

Selecting Line Numbering Options

When you turn on the Line Numbering feature, you can change how the lines are numbered with the following options:

- *Count Blank Lines:* To count blank lines, press Y; to exclude blank lines from line numbering, press N.

- *Number Every n Lines:* Use this option to specify how often you want line numbers printed. For instance, select this option, type **5**, and press Enter to print numbers for only every 5 lines (5, 10, 15, and so on).

- *Position of Number from Left Edge:* Line numbers are printed six-tenths of an inch from the left edge. To change this distance, select this option, type a measurement (from the left edge of the page), and press Enter.

- *Starting Number:* This option specifies the beginning number for line numbering. Use this option to continue numbers for a document containing text in another disk file or to restart line numbering in a file in which you previously used line numbering.

- *Restart Number on Each Page:* Press Y to restart line numbering on each page; press N to number lines consecutively throughout the document. Continuous numbering is helpful when pages are not numbered.

Turning Off Automatic Line Numbering

To turn off automatic line numbering, you press Format (Shift-F8), select Line (1), and choose Line Numbering (5). Then you press N. You press Exit (F7) to return to your document.

Numbering Lines

Use WordPerfect's automatic Line Numbering feature to number the lines in your document. Line numbers let you easily cite particular passages, such as page 11, line 26.

Turning On Automatic Line Numbering

Move the cursor to the position where you want line numbering to begin (usually at the beginning of your document).

Press ⬆Shift F8, the Format key.

```
Format

   1 - Line
          Hyphenation                  Line Spacing
          Justification                Margins Left/Right
          Line Height                  Tab Set
          Line Numbering               Widow/Orphan Protection

   2 - Page
          Center Page (top to bottom)  New Page Number
          Force Odd/Even Page          Page Numbering
          Headers and Footers          Paper Size/Type
          Margins Top/Bottom           Suppress

   3 - Document
          Display Pitch                Redline Method
          Initial Codes/Font           Summary

   4 - Other
          Advance                      Overstrike
          Conditional End of Page      Printer Functions
          Decimal Characters           Underline Spaces/Tabs
          Language

Selection: 0
```

Press 1 to select Line.

```
Format: Line

   1 - Hyphenation                          Off

   2 - Hyphenation Zone - Left              10%
                          Right             4%

   3 - Justification                        Yes

   4 - Line Height                          Auto

   5 - Line Numbering                       No

   6 - Line Spacing                         1

   7 - Margins - Left                       1"
                 Right                      1"

   8 - Tab Set                              0", every 0.5"

   9 - Widow/Orphan Protection              No

Selection: 0
```

Press 5 to select Line Numbering.

Press Y to turn on line numbering.

Press ⏎Enter to accept the default settings.

Or

Select the option you want to change and enter the desired modification.

Press F7 to return to the editing screen.

```
Format: Line Numbering

   1 - Count Blank Lines                      Yes

   2 - Number Every n Lines, where n is       1

   3 - Position of Number from Left Edge      0.6"

   4 - Starting Number                        1

   5 - Restart Numbering on Each Page         Yes

Selection: 0
```

Displaying Line Numbers

Line numbers do not appear on-screen. View the numbers in either of two ways: print the document or use View Document (press ⌜Shift⌟ ⌜F7⌟ and ⌜6⌟).

```
 1    Brainstorming
 2
 3    When you have trouble determining a sharp focus for a document--
 4    when you are uncertain what you want to say--consider trying a
 5    seminstructured writing exercise knwon as "brainstorming."
 6
 7    When you brainstorm a writing assignment on-screen, you register
 8    your ideas in list form as they occur to you. When you brainstorm,
 9    you don't worry about typos, spelling, or style. You turn off the
10    inclination to hone each sentence before you move on to the next
11    one. You can handle those matters later. Your goal is, rather, to
12    generate as many ideas as possible about the topic, the purpose,
13    or the audience.
14
15    Keeping an Idea File
16
17    An idea file is an extension of a brainstorming file. You can save
18    an idea file and retrieve it when you want to add more ideas later.
19
20    Using a Prewriting Template
21
22    Prewriting is everything you do up to the actual step of writing
23    that first draft. It is very much a part of the planning stage.
```

Turning Off Automatic Line Numbering

Press ⌜Shift⌟ ⌜F8⌟, the Format key.

Press ⌜1⌟ to select Line.

Press ⌜5⌟ to choose Line Numbering.

Press ⌜N⌟.

Press ⌜F7⌟ to return to your document.

Using Document Comments

You can insert notes and reminders called *comments* in your document. Document comments are useful for reminding you what you had in mind during a particular writing session. The comments are displayed only on-screen; they are not printed. If you want to print the comments, however, you can do so by first converting them to text.

Creating a Comment

To create a document comment, you first press Text In/Out (Ctrl-F5). Then you select Comment (5) to display the Comment menu. From this menu, you choose Create (1).

WordPerfect places the cursor in the Document Comment editing box. In the comment box, you type the text of your comment. You must keep your text within the lines of the box—approximately seven lines of text. You can use bold or underline to emphasize text within the box.

You press Exit (F7) to return to your document. The document comment appears on-screen in the middle of your text as a double-ruled box.

Editing a Comment

To edit a document comment, you first move the cursor to a position after the comment. Then you press Text In/Out (Ctrl-F5) and select Comment (5). From the Comment menu, you select Edit (2).

WordPerfect looks backward from the cursor, displays the first comment found, and places the cursor at the beginning of the comment text. You then can edit the comment. To return to your document, you press Exit (F7). If no comment is found, the error message *Not Found* appears at the bottom of the screen.

Converting Comments to Text

If you want to print document comments, you must convert them to text. To change a comment to text, you first move the cursor to a point after the comment you want to convert. Then you press Text In/Out (Ctrl-F5) and select Comment (5). Finally, you choose Convert to Text (3).

WordPerfect searches backward from the cursor and converts the first comment found.

Converting Text to Comments

To change text to a comment, you use Block (Alt-F4, or F12) to highlight the text you want to convert. Then you press Text In/Out (Ctrl-F5). When WordPerfect asks whether you want to create a comment, you press Y. WordPerfect places the marked text inside a comment box. Note that some formatting codes may be lost during this process.

Using Document Comments

Use document comments to insert notes and reminders within your document.

Creating a Comment

Press [Ctrl][F5], the Text In/Out key.

```
                    Writing Guideline
============================================================

Brainstorning

When you have trouble determining a sharp focus for a document--
when you are uncertain what you want to say--consider trying a
semistructured writing exercise known as "brainstorning."

When you brainstorm a writing assignment on-screen, you register
your ideas in list form as they occur to you. When you brainstorm,
you don't worry about typos, spelling, or style. You turn off the
inclination to to hone each sentence before you move on to the next
one. You can handle those matters later. Your goal is, rather, to
generate as many ideas as possible about the topic, the purpose,
or the audience.

Keeping an Idea File

An idea file is an extension of a brainstorning file. You can save
an idea file and retrieve it when you want to add more ideas later.

Using a Prewriting Template

1 DOS Text; 2 Password; 3 Save Generic; 4 Save WP 4.2; 5 Comment; 0
```

| Press [5] to choose Comment.

```
                    Writing Guideline
============================================================

Brainstorning

When you have trouble determining a sharp focus for a document--
when you are uncertain what you want to say--consider trying a
semistructured writing exercise known as "brainstorning."

When you brainstorm a writing assignment on-screen, you register
your ideas in list form as they occur to you. When you brainstorm,
you don't worry about typos, spelling, or style. You turn off the
inclination to to hone each sentence before you move on to the next
one. You can handle those matters later. Your goal is, rather, to
generate as many ideas as possible about the topic, the purpose,
or the audience.

Keeping an Idea File

An idea file is an extension of a brainstorning file. You can save
an idea file and retrieve it when you want to add more ideas later.

Using a Prewriting Template

Comment: 1 Create; 2 Edit; 3 Convert to Text; 0
```

| Press [1] to choose Create.

```
Document Comment

 ┌──────────────────────────────────────────────────────┐
 │ Include a list of topics that resulted from brainstorning. │
 │                                                        │
 │                                                        │
 │                                                        │
 └──────────────────────────────────────────────────────┘

Press Exit when done
```

Type the text of your comment.

Press [F7] to return to your document.

```
you don't worry about typos, spelling, or style. You turn off the
inclination to to hone each sentence before you move on to the next
one. You can handle those matters later. Your goal is, rather, to
generate as many ideas as possible about the topic, the purpose,
or the audience.

 ┌──────────────────────────────────────────────────────┐
 │ Include a list of topics that resulted from brainstorning. │
 └──────────────────────────────────────────────────────┘
Keeping an Idea File

An idea file is an extension of a brainstorning file. You can save
an idea file and retrieve it when you want to add more ideas later.

Using a Prewriting Template

Prewriting is everything you do up to the actual step of writing
that first draft. It is very much a part of the planning stage.

A prewriting template is a set of prompts that force you to answer
some basic questions before you begin your document. As you plan
the document, you may find it helpful to use a prewriting template
to refine your thinking about a particular writing task. You can
ask the basic reporter's questions of "Who?" "What?" "Where?" "Why"
                                        Doc 1 Pg 2 Ln 3.33" Pos 1"
```

Editing a Comment

Follow the steps to create a comment.

Press 2 to choose Edit.

WordPerfect looks backward from the cursor, displays the first comment found, and places the cursor at the beginning of the comment text.

Edit the comment.

Press F7 to return to your document.

Converting Comments to Text

If you want to print document comments, you first must convert them to text.

Move the cursor to a point after the comment you want to convert.

Follow the steps to create a comment.

Press 3 to choose Convert to Text.

WordPerfect searches backward from the cursor and converts the first comment found.

Converting Text to Comments

Use Alt F4 or F12 highlight the text as a block.

Press Ctrl F5, the Text In/Out key.

Press Y to convert the marked text to a comment.

WordPerfect places the marked text inside a comment box.

```
when you are uncertain what you want to say--consider trying a
semistructured writing exercise known as "brainstorming."

When you brainstorm a writing assignment on-screen, you register
your ideas in list form as they occur to you. When you brainstorm,
you don't worry about typos, spelling, or style. You turn off the
inclination to to hone each sentence before you move on to the next
one. You can handle those matters later. Your goal is, rather, to
generate as many ideas as possible about the topic, the purpose,
or the audience.

Keeping an Idea File

An idea file is an extension of a brainstorming file. You can save
an idea file and retrieve it when you want to add more ideas later.

Using a Prewriting Template

Prewriting is everything you do up to the actual step of writing
that first draft. It is very much a part of the planning stage.

A prewriting template is a set of prompts that force you to answer
some basic questions before you begin your document. As you plan
Create a comment? (Y/N) No
```

Using Other Referencing Features

When you create a professional document, especially a lengthy one, you often need to include supplementary reference material. For example, when you create a book, manual, or research report, you might include lists of figures and tables, a table of contents, and an index. When you create a legal document, you might need to include a table of legal citations. WordPerfect has built-in features to make the preparation of these materials easier. In addition, WordPerfect offers three other features that are handy when preparing reference materials: automatic referencing, master document, and document comparison.

Although the specifics of these reference features are beyond the scope of this book, this section introduces you to the kinds of reference documents you can create with WordPerfect. For detailed instructions on creating these materials, refer to Que's *Using WordPerfect 5*.

You use WordPerfect's Mark Text (Alt-F5) key to control the creation of reference materials. You use the options on this menu to identify those items you want to incorporate into a list, table of contents, index, or table of authorities. You also use this menu to specify the format and style of these special sections of your document and to generate the references where they need to be included.

Whether you are creating a list, table of contents, or index, you follow the same basic procedure. You first use Block (Alt-F4, or F12) to highlight the entry; then you press Mark Text (Alt-F5) to mark the text. You can mark text as you create your document, or you can go back later and to do so.

Next, you press Mark Text (Alt-F5) and select Define (5). From the Mark Text: Define menu, you select the item you want to define; from the definition menu, you choose the format and specify how you want the reference material to look on the page. Finally, you press Mark Text (Alt-F5), select Generate (6), and then select to generate the reference material at the appropriate place in the document.

Creating a Table of Contents

When you create a table of contents, you generally use text taken directly from the document—chapter headings, for example. A table of contents is included as part of a document's front matter.

Creating an Index

WordPerfect's indexing feature creates an alphabetized list of index headings and subheadings (called *entries*) for a document. You can choose to omit page numbers from the index or to have them displayed in one of several formats. You can include words and phrases you use often in a concordance file to save you the time of marking each entry individually. You can generate an index only at the end of a document.

Creating a Table of Authorities

The term *table of authorities* may be unfamiliar unless you work with legal briefs or scholarly manuscripts. A table of authorities is a list of court cases, rules of court, statutes, agency opinions, and miscellaneous authorities mentioned in a document. Each type of authority usually is assigned its own section in the table. Within each section, the citations are listed alphabetically, with page references.

A table of authorities can contain up to 16 sections. You enter the first reference (or *full form*) of the authority in a special editing screen. Then, if you have subsequent references to the same citation, you give these a unique *short form* identifier so that WordPerfect can collect these subsequent references and compile them in a table with their page references. You can mark authorities in footnotes, endnotes, and graphics boxes, as well as in the body text.

Using Other Referencing Features

Creating a List

If your document contains figures, illustrations, tables, maps, and other illustrations, you can list these resources in a reference table. Usually a list appears on a page by itself following the table of contents. You can create up to nine lists per document.

Using Automatic References

To guide your readers to related information in the document, you can use the Automatic Reference feature to reference page numbers, footnote numbers, section numbers, endnote numbers, and graphics box numbers. If you make changes, the references are renumbered automatically.

You create an automatic reference using two types of codes: a *reference code* marks the place you make the reference, and a *target code* marks the place to which you refer. For example, on page 10, if you refer to related information on page 20, you place the reference code on page 10 and the target code on page 20.

Creating a Master Document

You can use WordPerfect's Master Document feature to manage large projects with the following cycle:

- Maintain and store sections of a long document as individual files called *subdocuments*

- Build a skeleton or *master document* that includes references to each subdocument
- Temporarily *expand* the master document to link all the individual files (to generate a table of contents, for example)
- Separate or *condense* the expanded document into its component parts (subdocuments)

A master document consists of two kinds of files: a master document file and subdocument files. The master document file is a regular WordPerfect file which contains codes that reference the subdocument files. In addition to the codes, the master document file can contain anything else you want to include (such as the table of contents). The subdocuments contain the text for each section of the total document. You can include as many subdocuments as you need. Each subdocument is created and saved as a regular WordPerfect document file.

Comparing Documents

If you have saved a copy of the document to disk under another name, WordPerfect can compare the new version of a document with an old version. Sections of the on-screen document that don't exist in the disk file are redlined. Text that exists in the disk file but not in the on-screen document is copied to the on-screen document and marked with strikeout.

Using Other Referencing Features

WordPerfect's Mark Text (Alt-F5) key is the starting point for creating the supplementary reference materials you often need when you are preparing a professional document.

Whether you are creating a list, table of contents, or index, you follow the same basic procedure. Shown here is the basic process for creating a table of contents.

Table of Contents

When you create a table of contents, you generally use text taken directly from the document—chapter headings, for example. A table of contents is included as part of a document's front matter.

Press ⟨Alt⟩⟨F4⟩ or ⟨F12⟩ and highlight the entry.

Press ⟨Alt⟩⟨F5⟩, the Mark Text key.

To mark an entry, press ⟨1⟩.

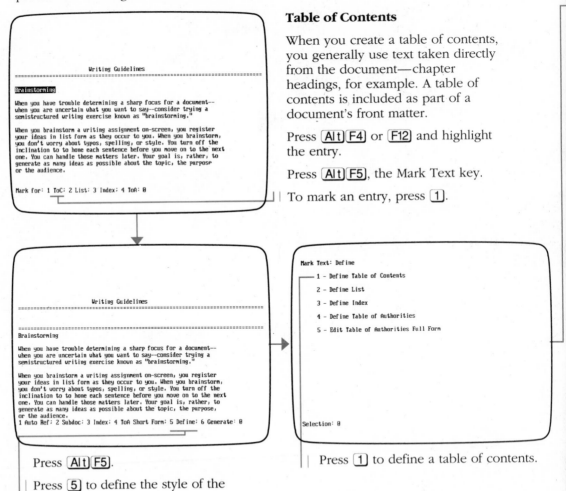

Press ⟨Alt⟩⟨F5⟩.

Press ⟨5⟩ to define the style of the reference list.

Press ⟨1⟩ to define a table of contents.

Introduction

Getting
Started

Editing

Working with
Blocks

Formatting
Lines and
Paragraphs

Formatting
Pages

Proofreading

Printing

Managing
Files

Creating
Macros

Merging
Documents

Sorting and
Selecting

Using Text
Columns

Using Math

Referencing

Creating
Graphics

Customizing

Appendix

Index

```
Table of Contents Definition

    1 - Number of Levels                    1

    2 - Display Last Level in               No
        Wrapped Format

    3 - Page Numbering - Level 1    Flush right with leader
                         Level 2
                         Level 3
                         Level 4
                         Level 5




Selection: 0
```

Define the numbering style for the table of contents.

```
Mark Text: Generate

    1 - Remove Redline Markings and Strikeout Text from Document

    2 - Compare Screen and Disk Documents and Add Redline and Strikeout

    3 - Expand Master Document

    4 - Condense Master Document

    5 - Generate Tables, Indexes, Automatic References, etc.




Selection: 0
```

Press **Alt F5**, the Mark Text Key.

Press **6**.

Press **5** to generate the reference list at the appropriate place in the document.

```
                    Writing Guidelines
==========================================================

                   Table of Contents

Brainstorming. . . . . . . . . . . . . . . . . . . . .  3

Keeping an Idea File . . . . . . . . . . . . . . . . .  7

Freewriting. . . . . . . . . . . . . . . . . . . . . .  9

Using a Prewriting Template. . . . . . . . . . . . . . 11

Planning Documents . . . . . . . . . . . . . . . . . . 13

==========================================================
Brainstorming

When you have trouble determining a sharp focus for a document--
when you are uncertain what you want to say--consider trying a
semistructured writing exercise known as "brainstorming."

When you brainstorm a writing assignment on-screen, you register
                          Doc 1 Pg 2 Ln 1.33" Pos 1"
```

Using Other Referencing Features

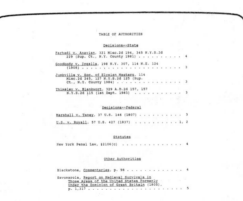

Index

WordPerfect's indexing feature creates an alphabetized list of index headings and subheadings (called *entries*) for a document. You can generate an index only at the end of a document.

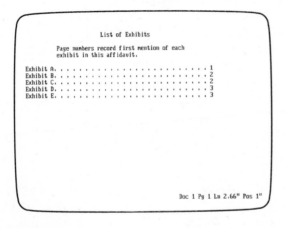

Table of Authorities

A table of authorities is a list of court cases, rules of court, statutes, agency opinions, and miscellaneous authorities mentioned in a document. Each type of authority is usually assigned its own section in the table. Within each section, the citations are listed alphabetically, with page references.

List

If your document contains figures, illustrations, tables, maps, and other illustrations, you can list these resources in a reference table. Usually a list appears on a page by itself following the table of contents. You can create up to nine lists per document.

Automatic References

Use WordPerfect's Automatic Reference feature to reference page numbers, footnote numbers, section numbers, endnote numbers, and graphics box numbers. If you make changes, the references are renumbered automatically.

```
Brainstorming

When you have trouble determining a sharp focus for a document--
when you are uncertain what you want to say--consider trying a
semistructured writing exercise known as "brainstorming."

When you brainstorm a writing assignment on-screen, you register
your ideas in list form as they occur to you. When you brainstorm,
you don't worry about typos, spelling, or style. You turn off the
inclination to to hone each sentence before you move on to the next
one. You can handle those matters later. Your goal is, rather, to
generate as many ideas as possible about the topic, the purpose,
or the audience. See the discussion of planning documents on
page 9.

Keeping an Idea File

An idea file is an extension of a brainstorming file. You can save
an idea file and retrieve it when you want to add more ideas later.

                                        Doc 1 Pg 3 Ln 3" Pos 1"
```

Master Document

A master document consists of a master document file and subdocument files.

The master document file contains codes that reference the subdocument files.

Each subdocument contains the text for a particular section of the total document.

```
Subdoc: TITLE

Subdoc: ABSTRACT
========================================
Subdoc: ACKNOWL
========================================
Subdoc: CHAP1

Subdoc: CHAP2
```

Document Comparison

Use WordPerfect to compare the new version of a document with an old version. Sections of the on-screen document that don't exist in the disk file are redlined. Text that exists in the disk file but not in the on-screen document is copied to the on-screen document and marked with strikeout.

```
In the old days, writers had to stop editing days before a
document was due and start combing through the main text to
prepare the document references. One of WordPerfect 5's handiest
features is that it speeds up that process. One of WordPerfect
5's handiest features is that it speeds up the process of
assembling document references. With a little foresight and
planning, you can work on a document right down to a few hours
before a deadline, confident that as your main text changes, the
document references will keep right up with it.

This chapter shows you how to create lists, tables of contents,
tables of authorities, and indexes. You also learn to use
automatic cross-referencing, which lets you change the structure
of your document and automatically maintain accurate references
to footnotes, pages and sections. which lets you change the
structure of your document and automatically maintain accurate
references to certain spots in a document. Finally, you learn to
use the Document Compare feature so that you can show someone
else what was omitted from, you learn to use the Document Compare
feature so that you can see what was omitted from, or added to, a
document, without having to mark all those changes yourself.
```

15 *Creating Graphics*

With WordPerfect's Graphics feature, you can enhance the appearance of your document with graphics boxes and lines. You can use four types of boxes: figure, table, text box, and user-defined box.

In the boxes, you can insert text; graphics from the Fonts/Graphics disk; or graphics, charts, and graphs created with external programs such as 1-2-3®. Or, you can create an empty box and enter text or graphics later. Graphics boxes can be placed in the body of a document as well as in headers, footers, and endnotes.

Although WordPerfect offers many advanced graphics capabilities, not all computers are equipped to match WordPerfect's power. If you have a graphics card, such as a Hercules or InColor card, then graphics appear correctly on the regular editing screen. If you don't have a graphics card, you will have to use the View Document feature to see lines, boxes, shades, and imported graphics.

Key Terms

Bit-mapped images   Images composed of dots.

Offset   A short distance established as a boundary to avoid the collision of two elements, such as a graphics image and a box.

Tasks Covered in This Chapter

In this chapter, you learn to perform the following tasks:

- Create figures, tables, text boxes, and user-defined boxes
- Select the options for each type of box—for example, the borders of the box, the caption style, and the spacing
- Import graphics into boxes
- Edit a graphics image, making it smaller or larger, rotating it, or inverting it
- Draw lines

393

Defining Graphics Boxes

Each box type has a default definition. The definition includes the border of the box, the inside and outside border space, the caption numbering method and style, the minimum offset, and the shading. You can use the default box styles, or you can define your own. Defining boxes gives you a consistent set of boxes to use in your documents. For instance, you can place clip art in figures, statistical data in tables, text in text boxes, and photographs (which you paste in later) in user-defined boxes.

To change the default box definition, you first press Graphics (Alt-F9). From the menu, you select a box type: figure, table, text box, or user-defined box. You then choose Options (4), select the options you want to change, and enter the necessary information. Finally, you press Exit (F7) to return to your document.

You can change any (or all) of the following box options:

- *Border Style:* To select a border for each side of the box, select this option, and then choose a border (none, single, double, dashed, dotted, thick, or extra thick).
- *Outside Border Space:* To change the space between the border of the box and the text, select this option, and then type a distance for each of the sides.
- *Inside Border Space:* To change the space between the border and the contents of the box, select this option, and then type a distance for each of the sides.
- *First Level Numbering Method:* To select the numbering for the caption, select this option, and then choose the first level numbering method (off, numbers, letters, or Roman numerals).

    WordPerfect automatically numbers your box (within the caption). This option, however, only defines the numbering style; you must add the caption when you create the box.

- *Second Level Numbering Method:* If you want two levels of numbering, select this option, and then choose the second level numbering method. If you choose letters or Roman numerals, they print in lowercase.

- *Caption Number Style:* To specify the text for numbering the caption, select this option, and then type the text you want for the caption; for example, type **Figure 1.2**. Press 1 to include first level numbering; press 2 to include second level numbering.

  You can include formatting codes within the caption style. Keep in mind that this option only defines the caption style; you must add the caption when you create the box.

- *Position of Caption:* To select where the caption appears, select this option. Then choose to place the caption above or below the box, outside or inside the border.

- *Minimum Offset from Paragraph:* To set the minimum paragraph offset, select this option, and then type the minimum offset.

  A paragraph-type box is offset from the top of a paragraph by the amount you specify. If the paragraph falls at the end of the page, the box may not fit. In this option, you specify how much the offset can be reduced to fit the box on the page.

- *Gray Shading (% of black):* To add a gray shade to the box, select this option, and then type a percentage from 1 to 100. Zero percent shading is white; 100 percent shading is black.

Defining Graphics Boxes

Each of the four box types has a default definition that includes the border of the box, the inside and outside border space, the caption numbering method and style, the minimum offset, and the shading.

Press Alt F9, the Graphics key.

Select a box type to display the default definition for that type of box.

1 Figure; 2 Table; 3 Text Box; 4 User-defined Box; 5 Line: 0

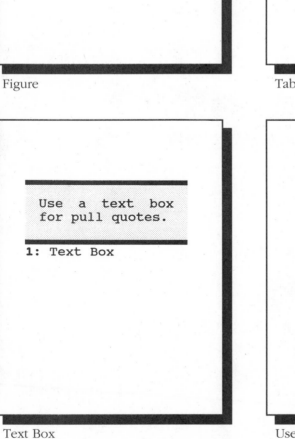

Figure 1: BOOK.WPG

Figure

Table I. Election Poll		
Street	Decided	Undecided
Rosslyn	53%	47%
Primrose	49%	51%
Kingsley	57%	43%
Norwaldo	62%	38%
Crestview	55%	45%

Table

Use a text box
for pull quotes.

1: Text Box

Text Box

1. THINKER.WPG

User-defined Box

Defining Graphics Boxes

You can change the default definition for any of the four box types.

Suppose that you want to change the definition for a figure.

Press Alt F9, the Graphics key.

Press 1 for Figure.

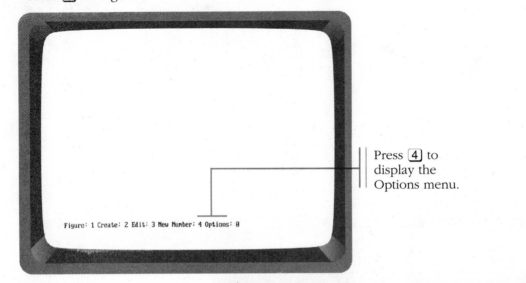

Figure: 1 Create; 2 Edit; 3 New Number; 4 Options: 0

Press 4 to display the Options menu.

Select the options you want to change (as described in the preceding text pages) and enter the necessary information.

Press F7 to return to your document.

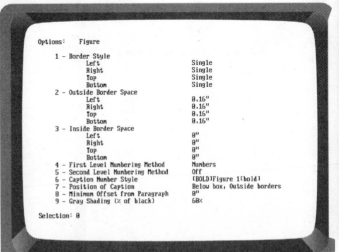

```
Options:    Figure

        1 - Border Style
              Left                                     Single
              Right                                    Single
              Top                                      Single
              Bottom                                   Single
        2 - Outside Border Space
              Left                                     0.16"
              Right                                    0.16"
              Top                                      0.16"
              Bottom                                   0.16"
        3 - Inside Border Space
              Left                                     0"
              Right                                    0"
              Top                                      0"
              Bottom                                   0"
        4 - First Level Numbering Method               Numbers
        5 - Second Level Numbering Method              Off
        6 - Caption Number Style                       [BOLD]Figure 1[bold]
        7 - Position of Caption                        Below box, Outside borders
        8 - Minimum Offset from Paragraph              0"
        9 - Gray Shading (% of black)                  60%

Selection: 0
```

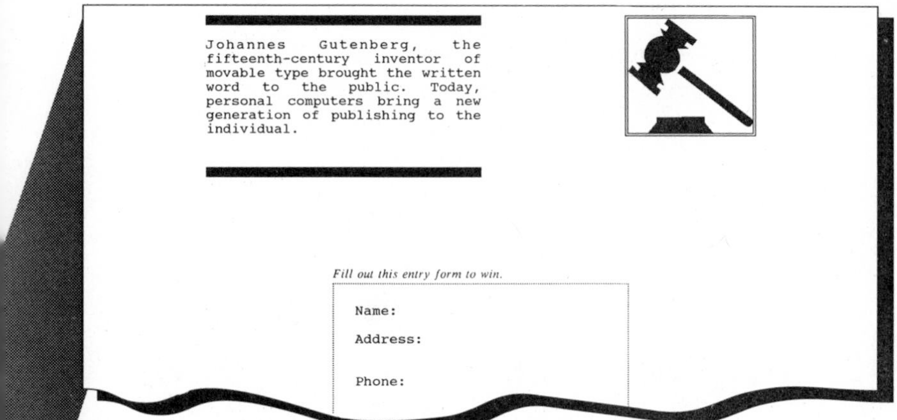

Johannes Gutenberg, the fifteenth-century inventor of movable type brought the written word to the public. Today, personal computers bring a new generation of publishing to the individual.

Fill out this entry form to win.

Name:

Address:

Phone:

Fig. 1-1. The PC.

Different border styles

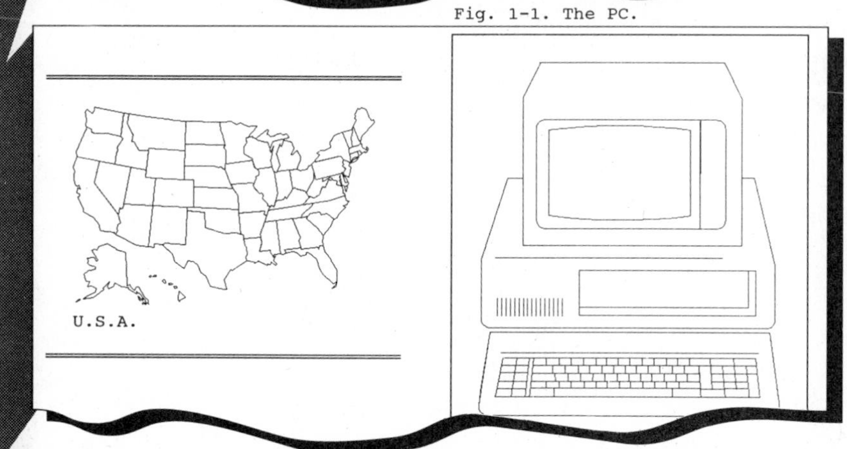

U.S.A.

Different caption placements

Above all, your publication should be clear and readable.

Above all, your publication should be clear and readable.

Above all, your publication should be clear and readable.

Various shades of gray

Creating Graphics Boxes

You can create a figure, table, text box, or user-defined box. When you create a box, you specify its contents, caption, type, placement on the page, and size. Only an outline appears on-screen. To view the document as it will appear when printed, you use View Document (Shift-F7, 6).

To create a graphics box, you first move the cursor to the position where you want the box to appear. Then you press Graphics (Alt-F9) and select a box type. You choose Create (1) to display the Definition menu. You select the options you want and enter the changes. Then you press Exit (F7) to return to your document.

You can create a box by specifying the following options:

- *Filename:* If you want to import a file (text file or graphics file, for instance), select this option, type the name of the file, and press Enter. WordPerfect inserts the file in the box. To create an empty box and enter the contents later, leave this option blank.
  WordPerfect's Fonts/Graphics disk contains clip-art files (with a .WPG extension) you can import. Check your WordPerfect manual to review the other types of file formats you can import to WordPerfect.

- *Caption:* Select this option to add a caption to the box. An editing screen appears with the default caption numbering and text (set when you defined the box). You can delete, change, or add text to the default. Captions conform to the width of the current box.

- *Type:* Select this option, and then choose one of three types of boxes: paragraph, page, or character. A paragraph-type box stays with the paragraph to which it is assigned. If the paragraph moves, the box moves. A page-type box is anchored to the page and stays in that position regardless of any editing changes. A character-type box is treated as a character and wraps with the line of text to which it is anchored.

- *Vertical Position:* Specify the vertical alignment of the box with this option. The type of box determines the placement options. For a paragraph-type box, enter the offset from the top of the paragraph. For a page-type box, choose one of five types of alignment: full page, top, center, bottom, or set position (enter an exact position). For a character-type box, choose to align the text with the top, center, or bottom of the box.

- *Horizontal Position:* Select this option to specify where your box is positioned horizontally. Again, the type of box determines the placement options. For a paragraph-type box, select to align the box with the left or the right margin, centered between the margins, or extended from margin to margin. For a page-type box, select to align the box with the margins or the columns (left, right, center, or from the left to the right margin or column), or use Set Position to enter an exact location. A character-type box is aligned only vertically.

- *Size:* Select the size of the box and enter the width, height, or both. If you enter only the width or height, WordPerfect calculates the other dimension.

- *Wrap Text Around Box:* Text automatically wraps around the box. If you want text to flow through the box, select this option and change the default from Yes to No.

- *Edit:* Select this option to insert text in the box. An editing screen appears, and you can type the text. When you import a graphics file, you use this option to edit the file.

Creating Graphics Boxes

When you create a figure, table, text box, or user-defined box, you specify its contents, caption, type, placement on the page, and size.

Suppose that you want to import the figure of a pencil from the WordPerfect Fonts/Graphics disk.

Move the cursor to the point in your document where you want the image to appear.

Press Alt F9, the Graphics key.

The options for all box types are the same; only the first word of the menu varies.

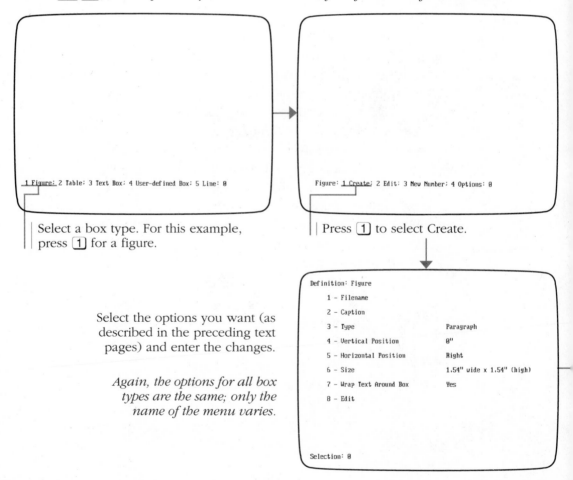

1 Figure; 2 Table; 3 Text Box; 4 User-defined Box; 5 Line: 0

Figure: 1 Create; 2 Edit; 3 New Number; 4 Options: 0

Select a box type. For this example, press 1 for a figure.

Press 1 to select Create.

Select the options you want (as described in the preceding text pages) and enter the changes.

Again, the options for all box types are the same; only the name of the menu varies.

Definition: Figure

1 – Filename	
2 – Caption	
3 – Type	Paragraph
4 – Vertical Position	0"
5 – Horizontal Position	Right
6 – Size	1.54" wide x 1.54" (high)
7 – Wrap Text Around Box	Yes
8 – Edit	

Selection: 0

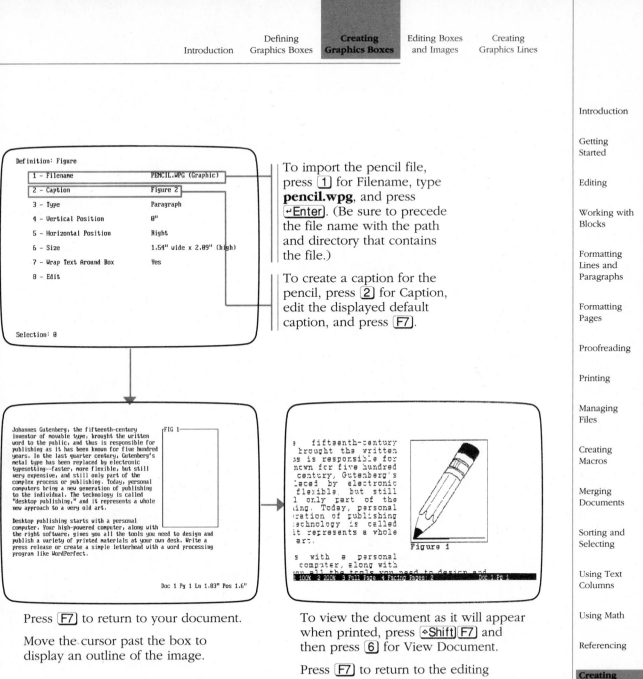

```
Definition: Figure

   1 - Filename                 PENCIL.WPG (Graphic)

   2 - Caption                  Figure 2

   3 - Type                     Paragraph

   4 - Vertical Position        0"

   5 - Horizontal Position      Right

   6 - Size                     1.54" wide x 2.09" (high)

   7 - Wrap Text Around Box     Yes

   8 - Edit



Selection: 0
```

To import the pencil file, press **1** for Filename, type **pencil.wpg**, and press **⏎Enter**. (Be sure to precede the file name with the path and directory that contains the file.)

To create a caption for the pencil, press **2** for Caption, edit the displayed default caption, and press **F7**.

```
Johannes Gutenberg, the fifteenth-century        ┌FIG 1┐
inventor of movable type, brought the written    │     │
word to the public, and thus is responsible for  │     │
publishing as it has been known for five hundred │     │
years. In the last quarter century, Gutenberg's  │     │
metal type has been replaced by electronic       │     │
typesetting--faster, more flexible, but still    │     │
very expensive, and still only part of the       │     │
complex process of publishing. Today, personal   │     │
computers bring a new generation of publishing   │     │
to the individual. The technology is called      │     │
"desktop publishing," and it represents a whole  │     │
new approach to a very old art.                   └─────┘

Desktop publishing starts with a personal
computer. Your high-powered computer, along with
the right software, gives you all the tools you need to design and
publish a variety of printed materials at your own desk. Write a
press release or create a simple letterhead with a word processing
program like WordPerfect.

                                    Doc 1 Pg 1 Ln 1.83" Pos 1.6"
```

Press **F7** to return to your document.

Move the cursor past the box to display an outline of the image.

```
 э  fifteenth-century
 brought the written
 ιs is responsible for
 ncwn for five hundred
 century, Gutenberg's
 laced by electronic
 flexible. but still
 l only part of the            [pencil image]
 ιing. Today, personal
 ration of publishing
 :echnology is called
 it represents a whole
 art.
                                  Figure 1
 s with a personal
 computer. along with
 ιu all the tools you need to design and
 1 100%  2 200%  3 Full Page  4 Facing Pages: 2        Doc 1 Pg 1
```

To view the document as it will appear when printed, press **⇧Shift F7** and then press **6** for View Document.

Press **F7** to return to the editing screen.

Editing Boxes and Images

You can edit both the box and the image within it. You can edit the box, for instance, by changing the numbering or type of box. If you import a graphics file into a box, you can edit the image by moving, scaling, rotating, mirroring, or inverting it.

Editing a Graphics Box

To edit a graphics box, you first press Graphics (Alt-F9) and select the type of box you want to edit. Then you choose Edit (2), type the number of the box, and press Enter. You next choose an option and make the desired changes. Finally, you press Exit (F7) to return to the editing screen.

You can renumber boxes, for example, to begin a new chapter (stored in its own disk file) with the proper numbering. To change a box number, you first move the cursor before the box you want to renumber. Then you press Graphics (Alt-F9) and select the type of box you want to number. You next choose New Number (3), type the new number, and press Enter. If you are using two-level numbering, you enter a new number for each level (for example, 3-e).

You can change the box type by pressing Graphics (Alt-F9), selecting the type of box you want to change, and selecting Edit (2). Then you type the number of the box you want to change and press Enter. Next, you select the new type of box you want and press Exit (F7). To display the change on-screen, move the cursor beyond the box.

Editing a Graphics Image

To edit an imported graphics image, you first press Graphics (Alt-F9) and choose the type of box you want to edit. Then you select Edit (2). You type the number of the figure, table, text box, or user-defined box, and then you press Enter. Next, you select Edit (8) from the Definition menu.

The graphic appears on-screen. The bottom of the screen shows the editing changes you can make; the top shows shortcuts to make those changes. With shortcuts, the image is changed by the amount shown in the bottom of the screen. Change this amount by pressing Ins until the amount you want appears: 1%, 5%, 10%, or 25%.

Moving an Image

You can use the cursor-arrow keys to move the image. Or, you can select Move (1), type the horizontal distance to move, and press Enter. Positive numbers move the image to the right; negative numbers, to the left. You type the vertical distance to move and press Enter. Positive numbers move the image up; negative numbers, down.

Scaling an Image

You can press PgUp to make the image larger or PgDn to make the image smaller. Or, you can select Scale (2) and enter horizontal and vertical scale factors, expressed in percentages. Positive numbers increase the size; negative numbers decrease the size.

Rotating and Mirroring an Image

You can press the minus sign (–) on the numeric keypad to rotate the image clockwise or press the plus sign (+) to rotate the image counterclockwise. Or, you can select Rotate (3) and enter the number of degrees to rotate the figure (positive numbers only). If you want to mirror the image, you press Y; if you don't, you press N.

Inverting an Image

To invert the image, you select Invert (4). WordPerfect redisplays the figure with each dot in its complementary color. For example, black-on-white becomes white-on-black. This feature works only on bit-mapped images.

Editing Boxes and Images

Editing a Graphics Box

You can edit a box by changing the box's definition, renumbering the boxes, or changing the type of box.

Changing the Definition of a Box

Press $\boxed{\text{Alt}}\boxed{\text{F9}}$, the Graphics key.

Choose the type of box you want to edit.

Press $\boxed{2}$ to select Edit.

Type the number of the box you want to edit and press $\boxed{\text{↵Enter}}$.

Choose an option and make the desired changes.

Press $\boxed{\text{F7}}$ to return to the editing screen.

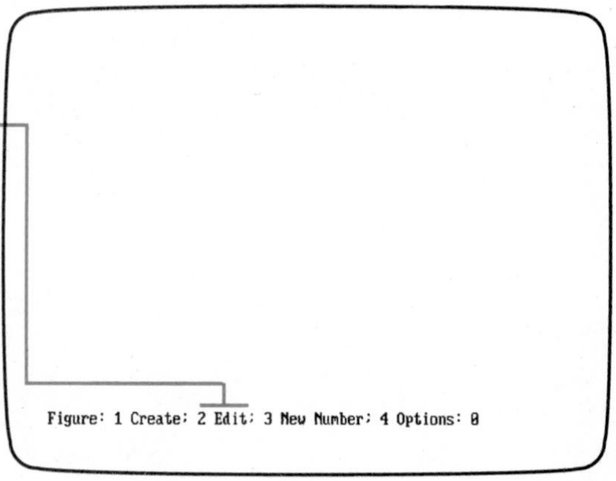

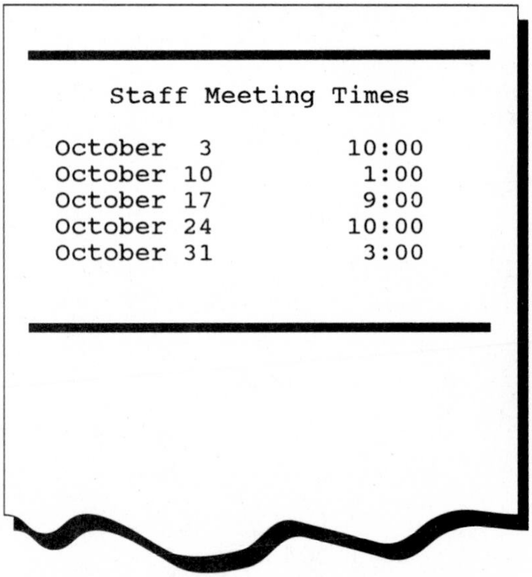

Figure: 1 Create: 2 Edit: 3 New Number: 4 Options: 0

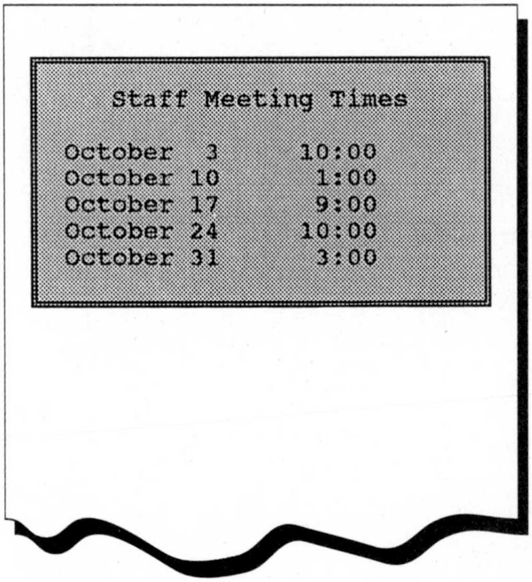

```
        Staff Meeting Times

October   3        10:00
October  10         1:00
October  17         9:00
October  24        10:00
October  31         3:00
```

```
        Staff Meeting Times

October   3        10:00
October  10         1:00
October  17         9:00
October  24        10:00
October  31         3:00
```

Changing a Box Number

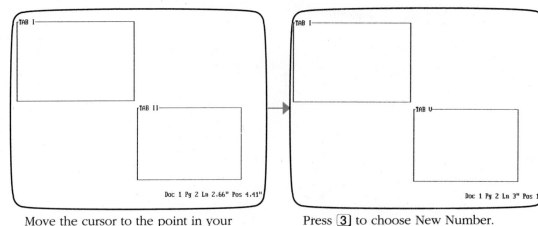

Move the cursor to the point in your document where you want to enter a new numbering code.

Press **Alt** **F9**, the Graphics key.

Select the type of the box you want to number.

Press **3** to choose New Number.

Type the new number and press **↵Enter**.

Changing the Type of Box

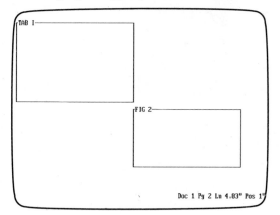

Press **Alt** **F9**, the Graphics key.

Select the type of box you want to change.

Press **2** to select Edit.

Type the number of the box you want to change and press **↵Enter**.

Select the new type of box you want.

Press **F7**.

To display the change on-screen, move the cursor beyond the box.

Editing Boxes and Images

Editing a Graphics Image

If you import a graphics file into a box, you can edit the image by
moving, scaling, rotating, mirroring, or inverting it.

Press [Alt][F9], the Graphics key.

Choose the type of box you want to edit.

Press [2] to select Edit.

Type the number of the box you want to change and press [⏎Enter].

Press [8] to select Edit.

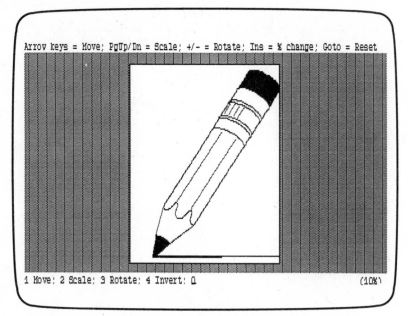

```
Arrow keys = Move; PgUp/Dn = Scale; +/- = Rotate; Ins = % change; Goto = Reset
```

```
1 Move; 2 Scale; 3 Rotate; 4 Invert: 0                          (10%)
```

The bottom of the screen shows the editing changes you
can make; the top of the screen shows shortcuts to make
those changes.

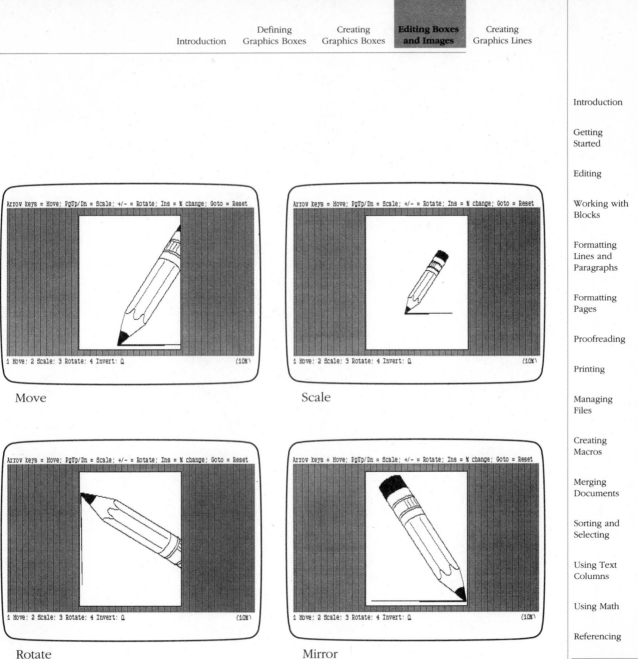

Move

Scale

Rotate

Mirror

Creating Graphics Lines

With WordPerfect, you can create vertical and horizontal lines on the printed page. The lines can be shaded or black.

To create graphics lines, you first position the cursor and press Graphics (Alt-F9). Then you select Line (5). Next, you choose Horizontal Line (1) or Vertical Line (2). WordPerfect displays the Horizontal Line menu or the Vertical Line menu, respectively. You choose an option and enter the appropriate information. Finally, you press Exit (F7) to return to the editing screen.

You can accept the defaults for the line, or you can select from the following options:

- *Horizontal Position:* For horizontal lines, this option lets you place the line against the left margin, against the right margin, centered between both margins, starting a specified distance from the left edge of the page, or extending from the left to the right margin.

  For vertical lines, you can position the line just outside the left or right margin or between a specified column and the column immediately to its right. Or, you can use Set Position to enter a specific position measured from the left edge of the page.

- *Vertical Position:* This option, available only for vertical lines, lets you place a line against the top or bottom margin, centered between the top and bottom margins, or at a specified distance from the top of the page.

You don't specify a vertical position for horizontal lines because they always align with the bottom of the current line of text.

- *Length of Line:* Specify the length of the line with this option. The default for horizontal lines is the distance between the current cursor position and the margin specified in the Horizontal Position option. For the default setting (Left & Right), WordPerfect automatically calculates the line length.

- *Width of Line:* Use this option to define the thickness of the line.

- *Gray Shading:* With this option, you can choose to print lines shaded between 0% (white) and 100% (black).

You cannot edit a graphics line. If the line does not appear as you want, you must delete it (by deleting the hidden code) and replace it with a new line. To see how a line will print, use View Document (Shift-F7, 6).

Keep in mind that text does not wrap around graphics lines. If you place a vertical or horizontal graphics line in the midst of text, it overprints the text.

Creating Graphics Lines

Create vertical and horizontal lines on the printed page. The lines can be shaded or black.

Position the cursor and press Alt F9, the Graphics key.

Press 5 to select Line.

Press 1 to select Horizontal Line.

```
Graphics: Horizontal Line

    1 - Horizontal Position          Left & Right

    2 - Length of Line

    3 - Width of Line                0.02"

    4 - Gray Shading (% of black)    100%













Selection: 3
```

Press 2 to select Vertical Line.

```
Graphics: Vertical Line

    1 - Horizontal Position          Column 1

    2 - Vertical Position            3"

    3 - Length of Line               7"

    4 - Width of Line                0.02"

    5 - Gray Shading (% of black)    100%










Selection: 4
```

Choose an option and enter the appropriate information.

Press F7 to return to the editing screen.

Horizontal line

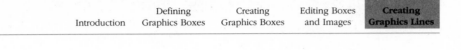

- the -
S E L F   P U B L I S H E R

PA Quarterly Journal   Fall, 1988

Desktop Publishing: New Technology For an Old Art

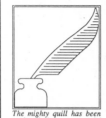

The mighty quill has been replaced by a powerful desktop computer

Johannes Gutenberg, the fifteenth-century inventor of movable type, brought the written word to the public, and thus is responsible for publishing as it has been known for five hundred years. In the last quarter century, Gutenberg's metal type has been replaced by electronic typesetting - faster, more flexible, but still very expensive, and still only part of the complex process of publishing. Today, personal computers bring a new generation of publishing to the individual.

Desktop publishing starts with a personal computer. It may be an IBM AT or compatible (such as a Compaq 286), or it may be a Macintosh SE. Your high-powered computer, along with the right software, gives you all the tools you need to design and publish a variety of printed materials at your own desk. Write a press release or create a simple letterhead with a word processing program like WordPerfect for IBM and compatible computers. Design a logo or business card with a graphics program like Adobe Illustrator or Aldus Freehand for the Macintosh. Create a newsletter and experiment with page layout with a page-design program like Aldus PageMaker for either IBM or Macintosh. Prepare graphs, illustrations, forms, applications, stationery, brochures, catalogs, reports, and much more - easily - with desktop publishing on a personal computer.

There are many software and hardware enhancements that can broaden your desktop publishing talents. Word processors give you powerful editing and document creation capabilities. Page-design software lets you shape your finished material into blocks or columns of text, and it lets you insert or outline illustrations. Graphics packages guide you in creating detailed illustrations or charts that you can add to a page you've already created. A scanner, video or optical, reproduces drawings of photos for you by electronically "reading" them with a camera or digitizer.

The laser printer, whether it's a Hewlett-Packard LaserJet or an Apple LaserWriter, is the printing department in your desktop publishing office. It prints near-typeset-quality text and graphics at a resolution of 300 dots per inch. Using laser printing technology, the laser printer produces finished pages that can be used as final copies or as originals for the mass reproduction on a printer's press.

Until now, publishing has belonged to the few: those with the knowledge, the money, and the time to engage in a complex process involving many players. The process begins with an idea. It continues with a writer, who originates the material to be published. An editor modifies it for accuracy and editorial slant; a designer gives the publication its shape; a typesetter sets the words; an illustrator enhances ideas with pictures; and a pasteup artist assembles the publication. A commercial printer completes the cycle. Each one of these skilled steps takes days or weeks, and must be precisely coordinated. Just managing that process can be a full-time job.

Johannes Gutenberg, the fifteenth-century inventor of movable type, brought the written word to the public. Today, personal computers bring a new generation of publishing to the individual.

But with desktop publishing, one individual can perform all of those complex functions and produce quality printed material - in much less time and at much less expense.

Welcome to desktop publishing!

The Self Publisher - A Quarterly Journal - Fall, 1988 - Page 1

Vertical line

16 *Customizing*

After you use WordPerfect for awhile, you may find that some of the program's default settings are not the best ones for your particular applications. For example, perhaps the default margin settings do not work with your letterhead, or perhaps you prefer your text to be ragged right instead of justified.

You can customize many aspects of the WordPerfect program to meet your needs. Among the options you can choose as permanent features of the program are timed automatic backups, a customized screen display, alternative keyboard assignments, and formatting specifications.

You can use the Setup menu at any time to customize the program. By changing the default settings within this menu, you can select the way many of WordPerfect's features work. The choices you make are permanent: they affect all documents every time you use WordPerfect, and the settings remain in effect until you use this menu again to change them.

Many settings can be overridden for a specific document. You can make setting changes that affect the current document only by using the options on the Format and Font menus.

Key Terms

Backups   Copies of your working file.

Cursor speed   In WordPerfect, the speed at which a character repeats when you hold down a key.

Units of measure   The segments (such as inches) of measurements used for margins, tabs, and other features.

Tasks Covered in This Chapter

In this chapter, you learn to perform the following tasks:

- Set automatic backups
- Increase the speed at which characters repeat
- Use the Fast Save option to save files quickly
- Change the screen display
- Customize the keyboard
- Use initial settings to set beeps, establish the repeat value, and change the date format
- Use initial codes to change many default format settings
- Specify to which directories certain files should be saved
- Change the unit of measure

Backups, Cursor Speed, and Fast Save

Setting Automatic Backups

WordPerfect's Setup menu offers two automatic backup features:
Timed Backup and Original Backup. Before you request automatic
backups, make sure that you have enough disk space for the original
and edited versions of the file, especially if you are using a dual floppy
disk system.

If you select the Timed Backup option, at specified intervals,
WordPerfect automatically saves the document displayed on-screen.
If you have documents in both windows (Doc 1 and Doc 2), only the
active document is backed up. WordPerfect creates backup files called
WP{WP}.BK1 (for Doc 1) and WP{WP}.BK2 (for Doc 2). These backup
files are only temporary. When you exit WordPerfect properly, the
temporary backup files are deleted. Therefore, you must save your
work manually even if you choose this option.

Timed Backup is useful in emergency situations. For example, if a
power failure occurs, you can retrieve the backup files from the disk
when you restart WordPerfect.

If you set the Original Backup option, WordPerfect saves both the
original file and the edited version. The original document is renamed
with the extension .BK!. For example, the original LETTER.JLS becomes
LETTER.BK!. Each time you edit and save the file, the .BK! file is
replaced with the last version. Note that with the Original Backup
feature turned on, WordPerfect assigns the same backup name to two
files if they share the same name but have different extensions. A
backup of either LETTER.JLS or LETTER.RMJ, for example, would
become LETTER.BK!.

To select an automatic backup option, you first press Setup (Shift-F1)
to access the Setup menu. Then you select Backup (1) to display the
Setup: Backup menu. From this menu, you choose either of the
backup options.

To select timed backups, you choose Timed Document Backup (1), press Y to turn on the feature, enter the interval (in minutes) you want between each backup, and press Enter. To make a backup copy of the last saved version, you select Original Document Backup (2) and press Y to turn on the feature. You can press Enter to return to the Setup menu, or you can press Exit (F7) to return to the document.

To retrieve a backup file, you first rename the file. Then you can press Retrieve (Shift-F10), or you can use the Retrieve option from the List Files menu.

Setting Cursor Speed

To change the rate of speed at which the cursor moves, you press Setup (Shift-F1) to access the Setup menu. Then you select Cursor Speed (2) and choose a rate in characters per second from the menu at the bottom of the screen. For example, you press 3 if you prefer a rate of 30 characters per second. To return the cursor speed to the normal value (10 characters per second), you select Normal (6). Press Exit (F7) to return to your document.

Using Fast Save

You can turn on Fast Save to save files quickly. Fast-saved files are not formatted, and you cannot print a fast-saved file from disk. Instead, you must retrieve the document to the screen and then print. Unless you have long files, turn off Fast Save so that files are saved and formatted.

To change the Fast Save selection, you press Setup (Shift-F1) to access the Setup menu. Then you select Fast Save (4). Finally, you press Y to turn on Fast Save or N to turn it off.

Backups, Cursor Speed, and Fast Save

Use WordPerfect's Setup menu at any time to customize the program.

Press ⇧Shift F1 to display the Setup menu.

Press F7 to leave the Setup menu and return to your document.

```
Setup

    1 - Backup

    2 - Cursor Speed              Normal

    3 - Display

    4 - Fast Save (unformatted)   No

    5 - Initial Settings

    6 - Keyboard Layout

    7 - Location of Auxiliary Files

    8 - Units of Measure



Selection: 0
```

Setting Automatic Backups

Choose either of WordPerfect's automatic backup options.

Press ☐1 to display the Backup menu.

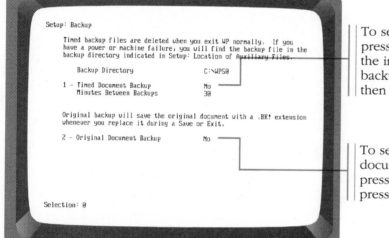

To select timed backups, press ☐1, press ☐Y, type the interval between backups (in minutes), and then press ↵Enter.

To select original document backups, press ☐2, and then press ☐Y.

Setting Cursor Speed

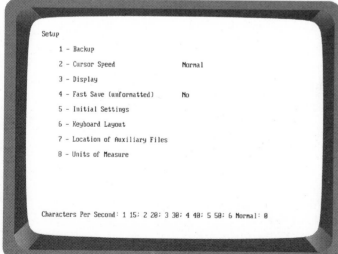

Increase the rate of speed at which the cursor moves.

Press ☐2 to choose Cursor Speed.

Press a number from 1 to 5 to choose the cursor speed. (To return the speed to 10 characters per second, press ☐6 for Normal.)

Using Fast Save

Use the Fast Save option to save files quickly; files are not formatted.

Press ☐4 to select Fast Save.

Press ☐Y to turn on Fast Save.

Screen Display

Adjusting the Screen Display

The Display option on the Setup menu controls many aspects of WordPerfect's screen display. For instance, you can change the color of normal text and various text attributes (if you have a color monitor), specify whether the current file name is displayed on the status line, and select how menus and columns are shown on-screen.

To customize the screen display, you press Setup (Shift-F1) to access the Setup menu. Then you select Display (3) to display the Setup: Display menu. From this menu, you select an item and enter the appropriate information. You press Exit (F7) to return to your document.

You can change the following options on the Display menu:

- *Automatically Format and Rewrite:* Select this option and press Y to format and rewrite the screen automatically when you change the length of a line or make other editing changes. Press N to reformat your document when you move the cursor past the current line. With Automatic Format and Rewrite turned off, you can rewrite the screen manually by pressing Screen (Ctrl-F3) twice, or by pressing Screen (Ctrl-F3) and then pressing 0, R, or Enter.
- *Colors/Fonts/Attributes:* The choices displayed when you select this option depend on your monitor and hardware. See your WordPerfect manual for a complete description of this feature.
- *Display Document Comments:* Select this option and press Y to display document comments on-screen. Press N to hide document comments.

- *Filename on the Status Line:* Select this option and press Y to display the drive, subdirectory, and name of the current document on the status line. Press N if you don't want this information displayed.

- *Graphics Screen Type:* WordPerfect automatically adjusts to your monitor and graphics card. If, for example, you have more than one monitor attached, you can use this option to switch the display type. Simply select this option, and then select a screen type from the list.

- *Hard Return Display Character:* WordPerfect displays hard returns with a space and inserts a [HRt] code that can be viewed with Reveal Codes (Alt-F3, or F11). If you want hard returns displayed with a character other than a space, select this option and type the character you want to use.

- *Menu Letter Display:* You select a menu choice by pressing a number or letter. Use this option to choose how the letter options (*mnemonics*) display. Then choose size and appearance attributes from the menu.

- *Side-by-side Columns Display:* To display newspaper-style columns side by side on-screen, select this option and press Y. To speed scrolling, screen rewriting, and editing, press N to make columns appear on separate pages. (Regardless of your choice here, columns are printed side by side.)

Screen Display

Adjusting the Screen Display

Use the Display option on the Setup menu to control many aspects of WordPerfect's screen display.

Press ⟨⇧Shift⟩⟨F1⟩ to display the Setup menu.

Press ⟨3⟩ to choose the Display option.

Choose an option (as described in the preceding text pages) and enter the desired information.

```
Setup: Display

    1 - Automatically Format and Rewrite    Yes

    2 - Colors/Fonts/Attributes

    3 - Display Document Comments           Yes

    4 - Filename on the Status Line         Yes

    5 - Graphics Screen Type                IBM CGA 640x200 mono

    6 - Hard Return Display Character

    7 - Menu Letter Display                 BOLD

    8 - Side-by-side Columns Display        No




Selection: 0
```

```
Brainstorming■

When you have trouble determining a sharp focus for a document--
when you are uncertain what you want to say--consider trying a
semistructured writing exercise known as "brainstorming."■

When you brainstorm a writing assignment on-screen, you register
your ideas in list form as they occur to you. When you brainstorm,
you don't worry about typos, spelling, or style. You turn off the
inclination to to hone each sentence before you move on to the next
one. You can handle those matters later. Your goal is, rather, to
generate as many ideas as possible about the topic, the purpose,
or the audience. See the discussion of planning documents on■
page 9.■
         ■

┌──────────────────────────────────────────────────────────────┐
│ Add list of topics that resulted from brainstorming.           │
└──────────────────────────────────────────────────────────────┘

    ■
Keeping an Idea File■
    ■
An idea file is an extension of a brainstorming file. You can save
an idea file and retrieve it when you want to add more ideas later.
C:\WP50\CHAP14.TOC                          Doc 1 Pg 3 Ln 4.16" Pos 1"
```

Hard return
display character

Document
comment

File name on
the status line

```
technology is call-
ed "desktop pub-
lishing," and it
represents a whole
new approach to a
very old art.■
=====================================================================
                   Desktop publishing
                   starts with a per-
                   sonal computer.
                   Your high-powered
                   computer, along
                   with the right
                   software, gives you
                   all the tools you
                   need to design and
                   publish a variety
                   of printed mater-
                   ials at your own
                   desk. Write a press
                   release or create a
                   simple letterhead
                   with a word pro-
                   cessing program
C:\WP50\CHAP12.NEW       Col 1 Doc 1 Pg 1 Ln 5.66" Pos 2.8"
```

Side-by-side
columns display

Keyboard Layout

WordPerfect assigns a specific key to each of the program's features. For instance, the F3 function key is assigned to the Help feature, and the Alt-F4 key combination is assigned to the Block feature. Several other useful keyboard definitions are supplied with the program. You can edit these definitions for your particular needs or create your own definitions.

Selecting a Keyboard Definition

To select a keyboard definition, you first press Setup (Shift-F1) to display the Setup menu. Then you select Keyboard Layout (6) to display the list of keyboard definitions.

The ALTRNAT keyboard definition moves the Help key (F3) to F1, moves Cancel (F1) to the Esc key, and moves the Esc key to F3. The ENHANCED keyboard definition assigns Home, Home, left arrow (go to the beginning of the line) to the Home key and moves Home to the number 5 key on the numeric keypad. Move Sentence (Ctrl-F4, 1) is assigned to Ctrl-up arrow and Ctrl-down arrow. The MACROS keyboard definition assigns useful macros to Alt- and Ctrl-key combinations.

Options on the Keyboard Layout screen let you select, delete, edit, or rename the highlighted key definition; create a new definition; or restore the keyboard to its original definition.

To select a new keyboard definition, you move the cursor to the definition you want and choose Select (1). The alternative definition remains in effect until you switch back to WordPerfect's default keyboard.

Returning to the Original Keyboard

To return to WordPerfect's original keyboard, you press Setup

(Shift-F1), select Keyboard Layout (6), and choose Original (6). Or, from the editing screen, press Ctrl-6.

Editing a Keyboard Definition

To edit a keyboard definition, you first press Setup (Shift-F1) and select Keyboard Layout (6). Then you move the cursor to the definition you want to edit and select Edit (5). WordPerfect displays the Keyboard Edit screen.

With the Edit options, you can change, delete, move, or create a key definition. You also can assign a WordPerfect macro to any key, or you can create a macro and assign it to a specific key.

To edit a key definition, you highlight the name of the definition and select Edit (1). WordPerfect displays the Key Edit screen. You select Description (1) and enter a brief description of the key. You choose Action (2) and assign a new definition to the key.

Some keys (such as the Cancel, Esc, and arrow keys) require you to press Ctrl-V before you can enter them as part of a definition. For example, you normally use the down-arrow key to move the cursor down one line in the Key Edit screen. If you want to enter the down-arrow key as part of a key definition, you must press Ctrl-V and then the down-arrow key to enter a {Down} code.

Creating a New Keyboard Definition

To create a new keyboard definition, you first press Setup (Shift-F1) and select Keyboard Layout (6). You select Create (4), type a name for your keyboard definition, and press Enter. WordPerfect displays the Keyboard Edit screen. You select Create (4), press the key you want to redefine, and begin editing the definition. Finally, you press Exit (F7) twice to return to the Keyboard Layout screen.

Keyboard Layout

WordPerfect assigns a specific key to each of the program's features. You can change these assignments to meet your needs.

Press (*Shift)(F1) to display the Setup menu.

Press (6) to select Keyboard Layout.

```
Setup: Keyboard Layout

  ┌─────────────┐
  │ ALTRNAT     │
  │ ENHANCED    │
  │ MACROS      │
  └─────────────┘




 1 Select; 2 Delete; 3 Rename; 4 Create; 5 Edit; 6 Original; N Name search: 1
```

Three keyboard definitions are supplied with WordPerfect.

Options on the Keyboard Layout screen let you select, delete, edit, or rename the highlighted key definition; create a new definition; or restore the keyboard to its original definition.

Selecting a Keyboard Definition

Move the cursor to the definition you want to select.

Press (1) to select the definition.

Returning to WordPerfect's Original Keyboard

Press (6) to restore the keyboard to its original definition.

Or

Press (Ctrl)(6) from the editing screen.

Editing a Keyboard Definition

Move the cursor to the definition you want to edit—ALTRNAT, in this example.

Press ⑤ to select Edit.

Highlight the name of a key definition.

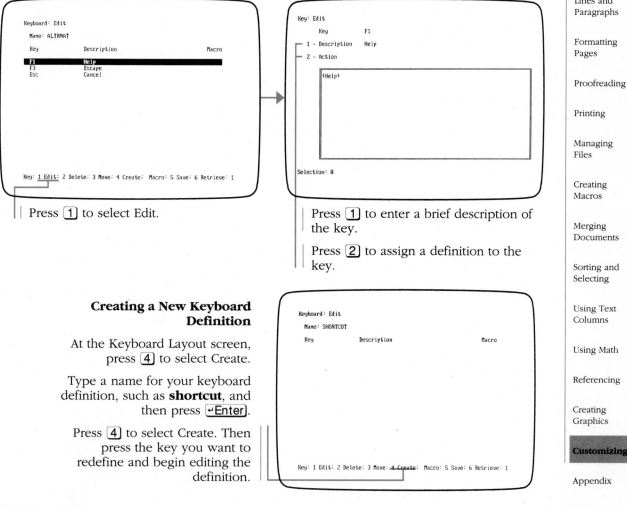

Press ① to select Edit.

Press ① to enter a brief description of the key.

Press ② to assign a definition to the key.

Creating a New Keyboard Definition

At the Keyboard Layout screen, press ④ to select Create.

Type a name for your keyboard definition, such as **shortcut**, and then press ⏎Enter.

Press ④ to select Create. Then press the key you want to redefine and begin editing the definition.

Initial Settings, File Location, Units of Measure

Selecting Initial Settings

With the Initial Settings menu in Setup, you can—for all your
documents—turn off beeps, change the date format, create a document
summary prompt, change many default format settings with initial
codes, set the repeat value, and determine the format for a table of
authorities.

To change initial settings, you first press Setup (Shift-F1) to display the
Setup menu. Then you choose Initial Settings (5), select an item from
the menu, and enter the information needed. Finally, you press Exit
(F7) to return to your document.

Use the Initial Settings menu to change the following options:

- *Beep Options:* Select this option and specify when
  WordPerfect beeps: on error, on hyphenation, on search
  failures.
- *Date Format:* Specify how the date and time appear with
  this option.
- *Document Summary:* This option governs whether a
  document summary is created automatically the first time
  you save or exit from a new document. Press Y to be
  prompted; press N if you don't want to be prompted. Use
  Subject Search Text to set the prompt you want displayed
  when searching document summaries with Word Search.
- *Initial Codes:* When you choose this option, WordPerfect
  displays an editing screen with Reveal Codes turned on.
  Choose formatting commands and change the default
  values you want; these codes become the default for all
  future documents.

For example, to turn off justification, press Format (Shift-F8), select
Line (1), choose Justification (3), and press N. Or, to change the
alignment character, press Format (Shift-F8), select Other (4), choose

Decimal/Align Character (3), type a new alignment character, and press Enter twice.

- *Repeat Value:* Reset the default value of the Repeat function with this option.
- *Table of Authorities:*. Specify the default format for tables of authorities with this option.

Specifying the Location of Auxiliary Files

With the Location of Auxiliary Files option, you can store different types of files in separate directories. To manage program and other special files, you can select separate subdirectories for the following files: backup, hyphenation, keyboard/macro, main dictionaries, printer, style library (enter a file name), supplementary dictionary, and thesaurus.

To specify a subdirectory for auxiliary files, you first press Setup (Shift-F1) to display the Setup menu. Then you select Location of Auxiliary Files (7). You next select the file type from the menu, type the drive and directory name, and press Enter. Finally, you press Exit (F7) to return to your document.

Selecting Units of Measure

Select the Units of Measure option to change the measurements used in screen displays and in the status line. WordPerfect's default measurement is inches; you can change this measurement to units (lines and columns), points, or centimeters. You can change both the way measurements appear on menus (and the type of measurement you enter) and the way measurements appear in the status line. Press Setup (Shift-F1) and choose Units of Measure (8). For more about changing the units of measure, see Chapter 4, "Formatting Lines and Paragraphs."

Initial Settings, File Location, Units of Measure

Selecting Initial Settings

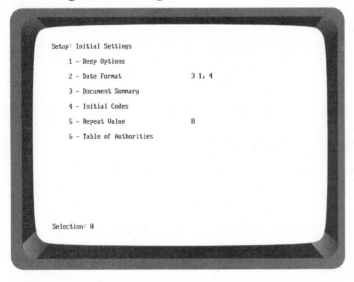

```
Setup: Initial Settings

    1 - Beep Options

    2 - Date Format              3 1, 4

    3 - Document Summary

    4 - Initial Codes

    5 - Repeat Value             8

    6 - Table of Authorities




Selection: 0
```

Use the Initial Settings menu to turn off beeps, change the date format, create a document summary prompt, change many default format settings with initial codes, set the repeat value, and determine the format for a table of authorities.

Press **⇧Shift** **F1** to display the Setup menu.

Press **5** to select the Initial Settings option.

Choose an item from the menu (as described in the preceding text pages) and enter the desired information.

Specifying the Location of Auxiliary Files

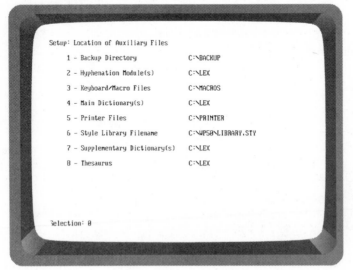

```
Setup: Location of Auxiliary Files

    1 - Backup Directory           C:\BACKUP

    2 - Hyphenation Module(s)      C:\LEX

    3 - Keyboard/Macro Files       C:\MACROS

    4 - Main Dictionary(s)         C:\LEX

    5 - Printer Files              C:\PRINTER

    6 - Style Library Filename     C:\WP50\LIBRARY.STY

    7 - Supplementary Dictionary(s) C:\LEX

    8 - Thesaurus                  C:\LEX




Selection: 0
```

Use the Location of Auxiliary Files option to store different types of files in separate directories.

Press **⇧Shift** **F1** to display the Setup menu.

Press **7** to select Location of Auxiliary Files.

Select the file type from the menu, type the drive and directory name, and press **⏎Enter**.

Selecting Units of Measure

Use the Units of Measure option to change the measurements used in screen displays and in the status line.

Press ⬆Shift F1 to display the Setup Menu.

Press 8 to select Units of Measure.

```
Setup: Units of Measure

       1 - Display and Entry of Numbers        "
               for Margins, Tabs, etc.

       2 - Status Line Display                 "


   Legend:

       " = inches
       i = inches
       c = centimeters
       p = points
       u = WordPerfect 4.2 Units (Lines/Columns)




   Selection: 0
```

Press 1 and enter the units you want for the screen display.

Press 2 and enter the units you want for the status line.

Initial Settings, File Location, Units of Measure

Setting Up a Standard Page

WordPerfect makes certain assumptions about the paper size, margin settings, justification, and many other formatting specifications. You can use the Initial Codes option on the Setup: Initial Settings menu to change these formatting defaults.

For instance, if you use paper that has a border on the left and bottom side, you can make the left and bottom margins larger by changing the default settings.

Press <kbd>⇪Shift</kbd> <kbd>F1</kbd> to display the Setup menu.

Press <kbd>5</kbd> to select the Initial Settings option.

Press <kbd>4</kbd> to choose Initial Codes.

If you have not made any permanent formatting changes, both halves of the screen are empty.

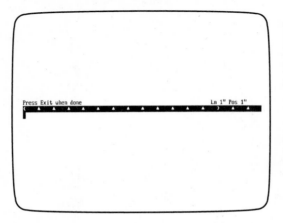

Enter the formatting codes you want to change.

For instance, press <kbd>⇪Shift</kbd> <kbd>F8</kbd>, the Format key.

To change the left margin, press <kbd>1</kbd> for Line, and then press <kbd>7</kbd> for Margins.

Type **1.5** for the left margin and press <kbd>↵Enter</kbd> twice.

Press <kbd>↵Enter</kbd> twice more to return to the Initial Codes screen.

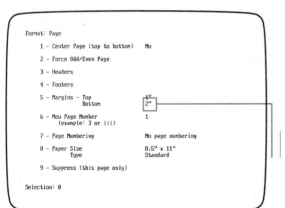

```
Format: Page

    1 - Center Page (top to bottom)    No

    2 - Force Odd/Even Page

    3 - Headers

    4 - Footers

    5 - Margins - Top                  1"
                  Bottom               2"

    6 - New Page Number                1
        (example: 3 or iii)

    7 - Page Numbering                 No page numbering

    8 - Paper Size                     8.5" x 11"
        Type                           Standard

    9 - Suppress (this page only)

Selection: 0
```

Press ⬆Shift F8, the Format key.

To change the bottom margin, press
2 for Page, and then press 5 for
Margins.

Press ⬇ to move the cursor to the
setting for the bottom margin.

Type **2** for bottom margin and press
⮐Enter twice.

Press ⮐Enter twice more to return to
the Initial Codes screen.

```
Press Exit when done                              Ln 1" Pos 1.5"
▲    (    ▲    ▲    ▲    ▲    ▲    ▲    ▲    ▲    )    ▲    ▲    ▲
[L/R Mar:1.5",1.5"][T/B Mar:1",2"]
```

These codes change the margin
settings permanently for all future
documents.

Press F7 twice to return to your
document.

Appendix

Installing WordPerfect

If WordPerfect is not already installed on your system, you must complete the installation procedure. Separate instructions are provided here for hard disk systems and dual floppy disk systems. After you complete the installation, turn to Chapter 1, "Getting Started," for instructions on how to start the program. (That chapter also tells you how to exit WordPerfect.) For instructions on how to select your printer(s), see Chapter 7, "Printing."

Hard Disk Systems

Step 1: Start your system.

1. Turn on your computer.

    If your system does not enter the date and time automatically, you must complete the steps that follow.
2. Type the current date and press Enter.
3. Type the current time and press Enter.

The DOS prompt C> appears on-screen.

Step 2: Copy the files from your master disks onto your hard disk.

You must copy the information stored on the WordPerfect master disks to subdirectories on your hard disk. You can use the INSTALL program on the Learning disk to create your subdirectories and copy your files.

Before you copy your master disks, put write-protect tabs over the square notch on the side of each 5 1/4-inch WordPerfect *master* disk to prevent you (or others) from accidentally writing information on these disks. To protect the 3 1/2-inch disks, use the point of a pencil and move the write-protect tab down to the open position.

To copy the WordPerfect files onto your hard disk, follow these steps:

1. If you have 5 1/4-inch disks, insert the disk labeled Learning into drive A.

   Or

   If you have 3 1/2-inch disks, insert the disk labeled Learning/Fonts/Graphics into drive A.

2. Type **a:** and press Enter.

3. Type **install** and press Enter.

4. Follow the prompts on-screen and insert the appropriate disks into drive A.

   You are prompted for the following disks: WordPerfect 1, WordPerfect 2, Fonts/Graphics, Speller, Thesaurus, PTR Program, and Learning. As you insert the disks and press a key, files are copied to subdirectories on your hard drive.

The INSTALL program does not copy the printer files to your hard drive. Because you use these files only when you install or change your printer, you do not need to copy them. Copying the files to your hard disk wastes disk space.

The INSTALL program creates two directories: C:\WP50 and C:\WP50\LEARN. WordPerfect 1, WordPerfect 2, Speller, Thesaurus, and Fonts/Graphics disk files are copied to the C:\WP50 directory; Learning disk files are copied to the C:WP50\LEARN directory. Also,

435

Installing WordPerfect

the program modifies your CONFIG.SYS file to include this line: FILES=20. The CONFIG.SYS file configures DOS for the number of files that can be opened at one time. You must specify at least 20 to run WordPerfect. (If you don't have a CONFIG.SYS file, the program creates one.)

You also might need to add a path command with your new directory to your AUTOEXEC.BAT file. See "WordPerfect and DOS" in the Appendix of the WordPerfect manual.

Step 3: Make backup copies of your master disks and store them in a safe separate location.

Even if you are installing WordPerfect on a hard disk system, you should make backup copies of the master disks. You need to copy each master disk onto a blank formatted disk. *Formatting* is the term used to describe the disk-preparation process. You cannot store information on a disk that has not been formatted.

To format a new disk, follow these steps:

1. Be sure that your computer is turned on and that the C> prompt is displayed.
2. Insert a blank disk into drive A.
3. At the C> prompt, type **format a:** and press Enter.
   Be sure that you specify drive A. Issuing a command to format drive C, the hard disk, erases all the information you have stored on your hard disk.
4. Press any key.
   The following message is displayed:

   ```
   Formatting...
   ```

The disk drive indicator light goes on. When formatting is complete, the display shows the number of bytes of available disk space. (One byte is equivalent to a single text character.) A screen message asks:

```
Format another (Y/N)?
```

5. Press Y and press Enter to format a backup disk for each of the WordPerfect master disks.

6. Press N at the `Format another (Y/N)?` message when you have enough formatted disks.

To make backup copies of the WordPerfect master disks, follow these steps:

1. Check to be sure that each master disk has a write-protect tab.

2. Put the disk to be copied into your floppy drive.

3. Type **a:** and press Enter to make drive A your current drive.

4. Type **diskcopy a: b:** and press Enter to copy all the files on the master disk in drive A to the new disk.

   This command is correct even if you don't have a drive B on your system.

5. Follow the instructions you see on-screen and change disks when prompted. You may have to swap disks more than once, depending on the size of your computer's memory.

6. Insert the next pair of disks and follow Steps 4 and 5 to make a backup disk for each of the master disks.

Installing WordPerfect

Be sure to label each backup disk with the name of the master disk. Store the master disks in a safe place, separate from your backup copies.

You are now ready to start WordPerfect. See Chapter 1, "Getting Started." To install your printer, see Chapter 7, "Printing."

Dual Floppy Disk Systems

Although WordPerfect works on a dual floppy disk system, you may find switching disks for different functions inconvenient. You also may not be able to use the program to its full capacity. For these reasons, you may want to consider buying a hard disk.

Step 1: Start your system.

1. Insert your DOS disk into drive A.
2. Turn on your computer.

   If your computer has a clock, the date and time are entered automatically. If not, complete the steps that follow.
3. Type the current date and press Enter.
4. Type the current time and press Enter.

The DOS prompt A> appears on-screen.

Step 2: Format your working disks.

Use working copies to eliminate the possibility of damaging the master program disks. If your working copy is damaged, making another copy of the master disk is simple. If, however, your master disks are damaged, you must purchase a replacement copy of the software.

You first must prepare your disks so that they can accept the information you want to store on them. *Formatting* is the term used to describe the disk-preparation process. Remember that you cannot store information on a disk that has not been formatted.

If your computer uses 5 1/4-inch disks, place the following labels on 13 blank disks before you begin the formatting procedure:

> WordPerfect 1 (sys)—Working
> WordPerfect 2—Working
> WordPerfect Help—Working
> Speller—Working
> Thesaurus—Working
> Conversion—Working
> Fonts/Graphics—Working
> Learning—Working
> PTR Program—Working
> Printer 1—Working
> Printer 2—Working
> Printer 3—Working
> Printer 4—Working

Note: You may need additional disks depending on the release date of your copy of WordPerfect.

Installing WordPerfect

If you have an IBM Personal System/2 computer, place the following labels on 8 blank 3 1/2-inch disks:

> WordPerfect 1/WordPerfect 2 (sys)—Working
>
> WordPerfect Help—Working
>
> Speller/Thesaurus—Working
>
> Conversion—Working
>
> Learning/Fonts/Graphics—Working
>
> Printer 1/Printer 2—Working
>
> Printer 3/PTR Program—Working
>
> Printer 4—Working

To format your working disks, follow these steps:

1. Insert your DOS disk into drive A.
2. Insert into drive B either the 5 1/4-inch disk labeled WordPerfect 1 (sys)—Working or the 3 1/2-inch disk labeled WordPerfect 1/WordPerfect 2 (sys)—Working. (Use the disks you just put labels on, not the distribution disks.)
3. Type **format b: /s** and press Enter.

   The /s is a *switch* that instructs DOS to place a copy of the operating system on the disk you are formatting in drive B. From now on, you can use this working disk to start your computer.
4. Press Enter when prompted.

   After your system has formatted the disk and the disk drive light goes out, the following message appears on-screen:

   ```
   Format another (Y/N)?
   ```

5. Press N, and then press Enter.

   This step tells your system that you do not want to format another disk with the /s format.

6. Remove the working disk from drive B.

7. Insert into drive B the disk labeled WordPerfect Help—Working.

8. Type **format b:** and press Enter twice to start formatting.

   After your system has completed the formatting process, the following message appears on-screen:

   ```
   Format another (Y/N)?
   ```

9. Press Y, and then press Enter.

10. Repeat Steps 6 through 9 to format the remaining labeled working disks. Note: If you use 5 1/4-inch disks, format the disk labeled WordPerfect 2—Working last.

    When you have formatted all your working disks, the following message appears on-screen:

    ```
    Format another (Y/N)?
    ```

11. Press N, and then press Enter.

12. If you have 5 1/4-inch disks, insert the DOS disk into drive A and the disk labeled WordPerfect 2—Working into drive B. Then type **copy a:command.com b:** and press Enter.

    Or

    If you have 3 1/2-inch disks, skip this step.

13. Remove both disks from the drives.

Format other disks to hold the documents you create later with WordPerfect.

441

Installing WordPerfect

Step 3: Copy the WordPerfect master disks.

After you format your working disks, you can copy the information stored on the WordPerfect master disks to these blank disks.

Before you copy your master disks, put write-protect tabs over the square notch on the side of each 5 1/4-inch WordPerfect *master* disk to prevent you (or others) from accidentally writing information onto those disks. To protect the 3 1/2-inch disks, use the point of a pencil and move the write-protect tab down to the open position. Note: WordPerfect will not run if you write-protect your working disks.

To copy the WordPerfect master disks, follow these steps:

1. Insert into drive A either the 5 1/4-inch WordPerfect 1 master disk or the 3 1/2-inch WordPerfect 1/WordPerfect 2 master disk.
2. Insert into drive B either your 5 1/4-inch WordPerfect 1 (sys)—Working disk or your 3 1/2-inch WordPerfect 1/ WordPerfect 2 (sys)—Working disk.
3. If you have 5 1/4-inch disks, type **copy a:wp.exe b:** and press Enter.
   Or
   If you have 3 1/2-inch disks, type **copy a:wp.* b:** and press Enter.
4. Type **copy a:*.?rs b:** and press Enter.
5. Remove the disk from drive B and insert the WordPerfect Help—Working disk into that drive.
6. Type **copy a:wphelp*.fil b:** and press Enter.
7. Remove the disks from drives A and B.

8. Insert into drive A either your 5 1/4-inch WordPerfect 2 master disk or your 3 1/2-inch Speller/Thesaurus master disk.

9. Insert into drive B either your 5 1/4-inch WordPerfect 2—Working disk or your 3 1/2-inch Speller/Thesaurus—Working disk.

10. Type **copy a:*.* b:** and press Enter.

11. To copy the remaining master disks to your formatted working disks, repeat Steps 8 through 10, pairing the appropriate master disk and the appropriate blank working disk each time you copy.

Users with floppy disk systems must create a CONFIG.SYS file on the system disk. To create a CONFIG.SYS file, follow these steps:

1. Insert into drive A the 5 1/4-inch disk labeled WordPerfect 1 (sys)—Working or the 3 1/2-inch disk labeled WordPerfect 1/WordPerfect 2 (sys)—Working.

2. Type **a:** and press Enter.

3. Type **copy a:config.sys+con a:config.sys** and press Enter.

4. Type **files=20** and press Enter.

5. Press F6 (to insert ^Z), and then press Enter.

Step 4: Store your master disks in a safe, separate location.

You are now ready to start WordPerfect. See Chapter 1, "Getting Started." To install your printer, see Chapter 7, "Printing."

Index

.BK! file extension, 416

C

calculation columns, 342, 345, 348-351

Cancel (F1) command, 32-33, 36, 71, 73, 75, 79, 94, 273, 280

canceling
  macro, 280, 282
  print job, 236, 239

Center (Shift-F6) command, 85, 87, 120-122, 332-336, 370

centering
  blocks, 84-85, 87
  pages, 148-152
  text, 120-124

Character option, 241

characters
  creating special, 168-176
  deleting, 56, 58
  hyphen, 128
  matching, 192-193
  wild-card, 192-193

clearing the screen, 41, 45

codes
  date/time, 362-365
  deletable soft return, 129
  displaying hidden, 60, 62
  field number (^Fn^), 295, 298
  hard page, 297
  hard return, 120, 122, 129
  hidden, 60, 62, 192, 197, 199, 201
  invisible soft return, 129
  merge, 286-287, 290-292, 297, 301
  paired, 192

Reveal (Alt-F3, F11), 60-64
  soft return, 129

Column Definition menu, 326

columns
  creating from existing text, 327, 330
  defining, 326-328, 332, 334
  displaying single, 327, 331
  headings, 334, 335
  newspaper-style, 326-331
  parallel, 332, 334
  widths, 326-329

commands
  see also macro commands
  Backward Search (Shift-F2), 190
  Block (Alt-F4, F12), 68, 71-79, 91, 102, 165, 167, 170, 229, 231, 381, 383-384
  Block Protect, 160-162
  Bold (F6), 85, 87, 100, 104
  Cancel (F1), 94, 273, 280
  Center (Shift-F6), 85, 87, 120-122, 332-333, 335, 336, 370
  Date/Outline (Shift-F5), 362-365, 366-367, 369-375
  DISKCOPY, 437
  Exit (F7), 40, 45, 95-99
  Flush Right (Alt-F6), 117, 119, 274
  Font (Ctrl-F8), 101-105, 165, 167, 170, 174
  Footnote (Ctrl-F7), 354-360
  Format (Shift-F8), 32, 94-97, 108, 111, 117-118, 121, 123-124, 126, 131, 133-137, 142-143, 146-154, 156-159, 161, 163-169, 171, 173, 175, 338, 340, 376-379, 428-433
  Forward Search (F2), 190, 196
  Graphics (Alt-F9), 394-413
  Hard Page (Ctrl-Enter), 333, 335

Introduction

Getting
Started

Editing

Working with
Blocks

Formatting
Lines and
Paragraphs

Formatting
Pages

Proofreading

Printing

Managing
Files

Creating
Macros

Merging
Documents

Sorting and
Selecting

Using Text
Columns

Using Math

Referencing

Creating
Graphics

Customizing

Appendix

Index

Index

D

E

Introduction

Getting
Started

Editing

Working with
Blocks

Formatting
Lines and
Paragraphs

Formatting
Pages

Proofreading

Printing

Managing
Files

Creating
Macros

Merging
Documents

Sorting and
Selecting

Using Text
Columns

Using Math

Referencing

Creating
Graphics

Customizing

Appendix

Index

Index

G

GoTo (Ctrl-Home) command, 28, 31, 70-73

Graphics (Alt-F9) command, 394-413

graphics, 2, 4
  boxes, 393-404
  card, 9
  creating lines, 410-413
  editing images, 404-405, 407-409

H

hanging paragraph, 113, 115

hard disk systems, 9, 12, 218, 434-438

Hard Page (Ctrl-Enter) command, 333, 335

hard page break, 138, 160, 162, 331

hard page code, 297, 300

hard return, 11

hard return code, 120, 122, 129

hardware required to run WordPerfect, 8-9

headers, 138, 152-155

headword, 189, 218-219

Help (F3) key, 8, 20-23

hidden codes
  deleting, 61, 63
  displaying, 60, 62
  replacing, 197, 201
  that cannot be replaced, 199
  to search for, 192

highlighted rectangle, 5

highlighting text, 70-74

hyphen character, 128

Hyphen key, 128

hyphenation
  settings, 124-127
  using, 124-133
  zones, 93, 130-133

hyphens, types of, 128-129

I

Indent (F4) command, 112-115, 366-369

indenting
  paragraphs, 113-115
  text, 112-116

index, creating, 385, 390

initial font, 92, 101

Initial Settings menu, 428-433

Input file, 305-306

Insert mode, 46, 52, 54-55

INSTALL program, 434-436

Introduction

Getting Started

Editing

Working with Blocks

Formatting Lines and Paragraphs

Formatting Pages

Proofreading

Printing

Managing Files

Creating Macros

Merging Documents

Sorting and Selecting

Using Text Columns

Using Math

Referencing

Creating Graphics

Customizing

Appendix

Index

Index

installing
    dual floppy systems, 438-443
    hard disk systems, 434-438
    using the INSTALL program, 434-436
invisible soft return code, 129

K

key locations, 320-322
    specifying, 311, 313, 316-319
keyboard, 14-19
    areas used, 15
    definition, 424-427
    layout, 424-427
    merge, 290-293
Keys menu, 311
keys
    alphanumeric, 15-17
    Backspace, 56, 58, 75, 108
    Cancel (F1), 32-33, 36, 71, 73, 75, 79
    cursor movement, 15, 30
    Delete, 56-58, 75, 108
    down-arrow, 330
    Escape, 57, 59
    function, 15-16, 19
    GoTo (Ctrl-Home), 70-73
    Help (F3), 20 22
    Hyphen, 128
    in sort, 305
    Num Lock, 17-18
    PgDn, 28, 31, 70, 72

PgUp, 28, 31, 70, 72
Print Screen, 229, 231
Repeat (Esc), 29
Tab, 112, 114

L

launching a search, 194-195
Left-Right Indent (Shift-F4) command,
    113-115
letter case, changing, 84
Line Numbering options, 377
Line option, 241
lines
    breaks, 129
    deleting, 57, 59
    height, 93, 134, 136
    inserting blank, 25, 27, 53
    numbering, 376-379
    record, 306
    sorting, 310, 312, 314
    spacing, 135, 137
List Files (F5) command, 202, 233, 235
List Files screen, 48-51, 202, 233, 235, 250
List Files menu, 254-265
lists, creating, 386, 390
Location, explained, 142
location identifiers, 305
Location of Auxiliary Files option, 429-
    430
lowercase letters, choosing, 84, 86

M

Macro (Alt-F10) command, 273, 275, 279

macro commands, 272-275, 277-281

Macro Define (Ctrl-F10), command, 272-274, 277-278, 280-281

macro definitions, backing out of, 280, 282

macros
Alt-letter, 272-275
backing out of, 280, 282
creating, 270-283
defined, 271
descriptive, 272-275
keyboard definition, 424
permanent, 271-275
replacing, 281-283
temporary, 271, 277-278

Margin Release (Shift-Tab) command, 113, 115, 367, 374

margins
changing, 94-100, 143, 147-148
default, 94
setting, 329

Mark Text (Alt-F5) command, 165, 167, 356, 361, 384, 388-389

Mark Text menu, 165, 167

master disks, copying, 442-443

master documents, 353, 386-387, 391

math columns
calculating, 339, 341
default settings, 343, 347

entering numbers in, 338-339, 341
selecting type, 343, 347, 350
setting tab stops for, 338, 340

math definition, 337, 342-343, 346-348, 350-351

math formulas, 348-351

math operators, 337-339, 341

Math/Columns (Alt-F7) command, 32, 326-330, 332, 334, 338-342, 346-348, 350-351

menu screens, 35

menus
backing out of, 33
Column Definition, 326
Date/Outline, 362-365
Definition, 400, 404
Display, 420-423
Font, 101, 103-104, 165, 167
Footnote/Endnote, 354-360
Format, 94, 117-118, 121, 123-124, 126, 131, 133-137, 142-143, 147-149, 152-154, 161, 163-169, 171, 173, 175, 376
Initial Settings, 428-433
keys, 311
List Files, 254-265
Mark Text, 165, 167
Math/Columns, 326
Move, 74-76, 81
Not Found, 216
Options, 357, 359
Page, 140
Paper/Size Type, 141
Paragraph Number Definition, 369
Print, 228-232, 234, 238-240, 242, 244-245

Index

Printer, 140
Reference, 218
Select Printer: Form Type, 141
selecting, 32, 34
Setup, 14, 95, 417, 420, 426
Sort and Select, 306, 309, 318
Spell, 209-210
Styles, 177, 179-180
Switch, 84
Thesaurus, 219, 221
Undelete, 75
Merge Codes (Shift-F9) command, 290-292, 294-295, 297, 299, 301, 303
Merge R (F9) command, 291, 293-294, 297
merge
codes, 286-287, 290-292, 297, 301
defined, 285
documents, 284-303
keyboard, 290-293
printing, 292
text files, 294-303
to printer, 300-301, 303
to screen, 300, 302
Merge/Sort (Ctrl-F9) command, 291, 293, 300, 302, 306, 308, 312, 320, 322
modes
Insert, 46, 52, 54-55
Typeover, 46, 53, 55, 171
Move (Ctrl-F4) command, 74-76, 81, 83, 88-90, 240
Move menu, 74-76, 81
move
blocks, 74-77
defined, 68

numbered paragraphs, 368
rectangles, 88-91
movement, cursor, 28-31

N

naming files, 39, 43
newspaper-style columns, 326-331
Not Found menu, 216
Num Lock key, 17-18
numbering
lines, 376-379
pages, 156-160
paragraphs, 368-369
numeric
columns, 342, 344
keys, 15
sort, 311

O

offset, 393
open style, 176-178, 181
Options menu, 357, 359
orientation, 142
original backup, 416-419

orphan, 139, 161, 163

outlines

    creating, 366-367, 370

    editing, 367, 374

output file, 305-306

overstrike, using with special characters, 169, 173

P

page breaks, 160-164, 331

Page menu, 140

page numbering

    changing, 157, 159

    code, 156, 159

    position, 156, 158-159

    suppressing, 157, 159

    with headers/footers, 153, 155

page offsets, 142

pages

    centering, 148-152

    deleting, 57, 59

    numbering, 156-160

paired

    codes, 192

    style, 176-178, 181

paper size, 140, 142, 146

Paper/Size Type menu, 141

Paragraph Number Definition menu, 369

paragraphs

    creating hanging, 113, 115

    indenting, 113-115

    numbering, 368-373, 375

    sorting, 310-312, 315

parallel columns, 332, 334

permanent macros, 271-275

PgDn key, 28, 31, 70, 72

PgUp key, 70, 72

position indicator, 15

positioning endnotes, 356, 360

power failure, starting WordPerfect after, 12

primary file, 285-286, 288-292, 295, 298-303

Print (Shift-F7) command, 38, 81-82, 141, 156, 224, 227-236, 238, 240-242, 244-245

Print menu, 103, 228, 231-232, 234, 238-240, 242, 244-245

Print Screen key, 229, 231

Printer Character option, 241

Printer Control screen, 236, 238

Printer Line option, 240

Printer menu, 140

printer

    defining, 224-226

    merging to, 300-301, 303

    selecting, 141, 225-227

printing

    blocks, 80-82, 228-231

    disk directory, 233-235

Index

Index

T

Introduction

Getting
Started

Editing

Working with
Blocks

Formatting
Lines and
Paragraphs

Formatting
Pages

Proofreading

Printing

Managing
Files

Creating
Macros

Merging
Documents

Sorting and
Selecting

Using Text
Columns

Using Math

Referencing

Creating
Graphics

Customizing

Appendix

Index

More Computer Knowledge from Que

Lotus Software Titles

1-2-3 QueCards...21.95
1-2-3 for Business, 2nd Edition................22.95
1-2-3 QuickStart...21.95
1-2-3 Quick Reference............................ 7.95
1-2-3 Release 2.2 Quick Reference........... 7.95
1-2-3 Release 2.2 QuickStart..................19.95
1-2-3 Release 3 Business Applications........39.95
1-2-3 Release 3 Quick Reference............ 7.95
1-2-3 Release 3 QuickStart......................19.95
1-2-3 Release 3 Workbook and Disk..........29.95
1-2-3 Tips, Tricks, and Traps, 2nd Edition......21.95
Upgrading to 1-2-3 Release 3 ....14.95
Using 1-2-3, Special Edition 24.95
Using 1-2-3 Release 2.2, Special Edition........24.95
Using 1-2-3 Release 3 ....24.95
Using 1-2-3 Workbook and Disk, 2nd Edition....29.95
Using Lotus Magellan...........................21.95
Using Symphony, 2nd Edition..................26.95

Database Titles

dBASE III Plus Applications Library............21.95
dBASE III Plus Handbook, 2nd Edition..........22.95
dBASE III Plus Tips, Tricks, and Traps........21.95
dBASE III Plus Workbook and Disk 29.95
dBASE IV Applications Library, 2nd Edition 39.95
dBASE IV Handbook, 3rd-Edition..............23.95
dBASE IV Programming Techniques............24.95
dBASE IV QueCards 21.95
dBASE IV Quick Reference.................... 7.95
dBASE IV QuickStart 19.95
dBASE IV Tips, Tricks, and Traps,
   2nd Edition 21.95
dBASE IV Workbook and Disk..................29.95
dBXL and Quicksilver Programming:
   Beyond dBASE 24.95
R:BASE User's Guide, 3rd Edition..............22.95
Using Clipper 24.95
Using DataEase..................................22.95
Using Reflex....................................19.95
Using Paradox 3 ....22.95

Applications Software Titles

AutoCAD Advanced Techniques 34.95
AutoCAD Quick Reference 7.95
CAD and Desktop Publishing Guide 24.95
Introduction to Business Software 14.95
PC Tools Quick Reference 7.95
Smart Tips, Tricks, and Traps 24.95
Using AutoCAD 29.95
Using Computers in Business.................24.95
Using DacEasy..................................21.95
Using Dollars and Sense: IBM Version,
   2nd Edition 19.95

Using Enable/OA...............................23.95
Using Excel: IBM Version 24.95
Using Generic CADD 24.95
Using Managing Your Money,
   2nd Edition 19.95
Using Q&A, 2nd Edition 21.95
Using Quattro 21.95
Using Quicken 19.95
Using Smart 22.95
Using SuperCalc5, 2nd Edition................22.95

Word Processing and Desktop Publishing Titles

DisplayWrite QuickStart 19.95
Microsoft Word 5 Quick Reference 7.95
Microsoft Word 5 Tips, Tricks, and Traps:
   IBM Version 19.95
Using DisplayWrite 4, 2nd Edition..............19.95
Using Harvard Graphics.........................24.95
Using Microsoft Word 5: IBM Version...........21.95
Using MultiMate Advantage, 2nd Edition 19.95
Using PageMaker: IBM Version,
   2nd Edition 24.95
Using PFS: First Choice.........................22.95
Using PFS: First Publisher 22.95
Using Professional Write 19.95
Using Sprint 21.95
Using Ventura Publisher, 2nd Edition 24.95
Using WordPerfect, 3rd Edition 21.95
Using WordPerfect 5.............................24.95
Using WordStar, 2nd Edition....................21.95
Ventura Publisher Techniques
   and Applications................................22.95
Ventura Publisher Tips, Tricks, and Traps.......24.95
WordPerfect Macro Library 21.95
WordPerfect Power Techniques 21.95
WordPerfect QueCards 21.95
WordPerfect Quick Reference 7.95
WordPerfect QuickStart 21.95
WordPerfect Tips, Tricks, and Traps,
   2nd Edition 21.95
WordPerfect 5 Workbook and Disk..............29.95

Macintosh and Apple II Titles

The Big Mac Book...............................27.95
Excel QuickStart 19.95
Excel Tips, Tricks, and Traps..................22.95
HyperCard QuickStart...........................21.95
Using AppleWorks, 2nd Edition 21.95
Using dBASE Mac................................19.95
Using Dollars and Sense........................19.95
Using Excel: Macintosh Verson 22.95
Using FullWrite Professional...................21.95
Using HyperCard: From Home
   to HyperTalk.................................24.95

Using Microsoft Word 4:
   Macintosh Version...........................21.95
Using Microsoft Works: Macintosh Version,
   2nd Edition 21.95
Using PageMaker: Macintosh Version 24.95
Using WordPerfect: Macintosh Version.........19.95

Hardware and Systems Titles

DOS QueCards 21.95
DOS Tips, Tricks, and Traps 22.95
DOS Workbook and Disk.........................29.95
Hard Disk Quick Reference.................... 7.95
IBM PS/2 Handbook 21.95
Managing Your Hard Disk, 2nd Edition 22.95
MS-DOS Quick Reference...................... 7.95
MS-DOS QuickStart 21.95
MS-DOS User's Guide, Special Edition 29.95
Networking Personal Computers, 3rd Edition 22.95
Understanding UNIX: A Conceptual Guide,
   2nd Edition 21.95
Upgrading and Repairing PCs 27.95
Using Microsoft Windows........................19.95
Using Novell NetWare 24.95
Using OS/2 ....23.95
Using PC DOS, 3rd Edition......................22.95

Programming and Technical Titles

Assembly Language Quick Reference 7.95
C Programmer's Toolkit 39.95
C Programming Guide, 3rd Edition 24.95
C Quick Reference 7.95
DOS and BIOS Functions Quick Reference 7.95
DOS Programmer's Reference, 2nd Edition 27.95
Power Graphics Programming 24.95
QuickBASIC Advanced Techniques.............21.95
QuickBASIC Programmer's Toolkit 39.95
QuickBASIC Quick Reference 7.95
SQL Programmer's Guide 29.95
Turbo C Programming 22.95
Turbo Pascal Advanced Techniques............22.95
Turbo Pascal Programmer's Toolkit............39.95
Turbo Pascal Quick Reference.................. 7.95
Using Assembly Language 24.95
Using QuickBASIC 4.............................19.95
Using Turbo Pascal..............................21.95

For more information, call

All prices subject to change without notice.
Prices and charges are for domestic orders
only. Non-U.S. prices might be higher.

Using WordPerfect 5
by Charles O. Stewart III, et al.

The #1 best-selling word processing book! Introduces Word-Perfect basics and helps readers learn to use macros, styles, and other advanced features. Also includes **Quick Start** tutorials, a tear-out command reference card, and an introduction to Word-Perfect 5 for 4.2 users.

Order #843
$24.95 USA
0-88022-351-0, 867 pp.

WordPerfect Tips, Tricks, and Traps, 2nd Edition
by Charles O. Stewart III, Daniel J. Rosenbaum, and Joel Shore

A series of helpful tips and techniques on style sheets, keyboard mapping, macro commands, integrated text and graphics, and laser printers.

Order #851
$21.95 USA
0-88022-358-8, 650 pp.

WordPerfect QueCards
Developed by Que Corporation

Housed in sturdy 3-ring binder, each 5″ x 8″ card shows how to perform a specific task. QueCards can be used with the built-in easel or removed and placed next to a computer keyboard.

Order #74
$21.95 USA
0-88022-273-5, 116 cards/232 pages

WordPerfect Quick Reference
Developed by Que Corporation

WordPerfect Quick Reference helps you quickly determine the proper WordPerfect 5 commands for important tasks, without wading through pages and pages of inapplicable information. This compact reference provides information on essential WordPerfect commands, common tasks and applications, and the uses of WordPerfect 5 function keys. This is the *perfect* instant reference for all WordPerfect 5 users!

Order #866
7.95 USA
0-88022-370-7, 148 pp.

Que Order Line: **1-800-428-5331**

All prices subject to change without notice. Prices and charges are for domestic orders only. Non-U.S. prices might be higher.

B